# From Ballot to Bench

# rom Ballot to Bench

**DICIAL ELECTIONS AND THE QUEST
R ACCOUNTABILITY**

by Philip L. Dubois

UNIVERSITY OF TEXAS PRESS, AUSTIN AND LONDON

Requests for permission to reproduce material from this work should be
sent to Permissions, University of Texas Press, Box 7819, Austin, Texas
78712.

Library of Congress Cataloging in Publication Data

Dubois, Philip L
    From ballot to bench.
    A revision of the author's thesis, University of Wisconsin,
1978, presented under title: Judicial elections in the States.
    Bibliography: p.
    Includes index.
    1. Judges—United States—States—Election.   2. Judges—
United States—States.   I. Title.
KF8785.D8   1980      347.73'14      80-12728
ISBN 0-292-72028-9

*For Lisa*

# Contents

# Tables

# Preface

UNLIKE the concern demonstrated for understanding the processes by which executives and legislators are elected, the study of judicial elections has interested few political scientists. It is not clear why this has been so. Certainly the lack of scholarly interest in judicial elections cannot be explained by the traditional view once expressed by United States Supreme Court Justice David Brewer that courts and judges "make no law, . . . make no policy . . . never enter[ing] into the domain of popular action." The central governmental role of state courts and the policy-making functions of state judges cannot be doubted today. Nor can the reason be that judicial elections are an insignificant part of the process by which judges are selected. Since the mid-1800s, elections have been the dominant method of judicial selection in the American states. And since then, even before, there has been a spirited and often highly rancorous debate among political leaders, within the legal profession, and in state legislatures and constitutional conventions over whether elections are an appropriate way to select judges.

Over the last several decades, hundreds of articles have filled the pages of legal journals with claims and counterclaims regarding the virtues and vices of judicial elections compared to the alternative methods of judicial selection. In particular, the so-called merit plan, or Missouri Plan, of selection has gained a widespread following among the most prominent segments of the legal profession. But most of the arguments mustered against judicial elections have been anecdotal, if not polemical, substantiated more often by mere assertion than by empirical evidence. Indeed, the case against judicial elections has almost been accepted as proven by virtue of the repetition of the criticisms leveled at them. Similarly, the benefits said to accompany the merit plan have been accepted largely without contradiction, not because of positive demonstrations of their validity but in the absence of research data to the contrary.

Despite the predominance of judicial elections and the wide-spread political and professional debate concerning them, there has been a surprising lack of empirical research on their actual operation. Only recently have scholars begun to remedy what Professor Herbert Jacob characterized well over a decade ago as a "shortage of accurate factual information" on elective judicial selection. Much of the debate over judicial selection rests upon normative value preferences regarding the proper role of courts and judges in the political system. These are differences not subject to empirical resolution. But to the extent that empirical inquiry allows a better understanding of how governmental institutions and political processes truly operate, systematic research should be undertaken. It is the thesis here, then, that before judicial elections are sacrificed upon the altar of the merit plan the various criticisms raised against them should be subjected to a more searching scrutiny than previously has been attempted.

It is in this vein that this book was written. Its central purpose is the collection and analysis of empirical evidence on the operation of state judicial elections. Its scope is ambitious, encompassing all statewide elections held from 1948 to 1974 for justices of state courts of last resort in nonsouthern states. Because this is the first attempt to systematically collect and analyze empirical data on state judicial elections from a large number of states over an extended period of time, readers may occasionally feel consumed by detail. It is hoped, however, that the detail provided lends essential strength to the generalizations which emerge in this text concerning the conduct of judicial elections in the American states after World War II.

The initial chapter reviews the three central counts on which judicial elections have been faulted: for lowering the quality of the bench, for impairing the independence of judges, and for failing to secure judicial accountability. On the issue of judicial quality, a review of the existing evidence suggests that the alternative selection systems have not dramatically improved the recruitment process in terms of placing "higher quality" individuals in judicial positions. And that portion of the debate over judicial selection which tips on the conflict between the principles of judicial independence and judicial accountability is not resolvable by empirical demonstration. Thus, this research primarily addresses the third of the major criticisms against judicial elections—their ability to secure the popular accountability of judges.

Once the meaning of accountability and the limits of elections (whether judicial or nonjudicial) in securing it are defined, empirical attention is turned to those aspects of judicial elections bearing on the issue of accountability: the behavior of judicial electorates, the extent of electoral competition, the patterns of gubernatorial vacancy appointments and the electoral fates of appointees, and the behavior of state supreme court judges chosen under a variety of selection systems.

On a number of dimensions, the analysis clearly establishes the superiority of partisan over nonpartisan judicial elections. And, granted certain definitional concessions on the accountability-conferring function of elections, a good case can be made that partisan judicial elections do fulfill this essential function. Readers should not read this argument, however, as necessarily asserting the superiority of partisan judicial elections over the alternative nonelective methods of selection. That conclusion rests upon the resolution of a number of explicit value choices, such as the proper balance to be struck between independence and accountability, and the primacy to be accorded the goal of maximizing the quality of the bench. The tensions underlying the alternative modes of elective and appointee methods of selection among competing values and goals are given explicit attention in the final two chapters.

Throughout the research and writing of this book I have tried to be mindful of the warning of E. E. Schattschneider in *The Semi-Sovereign People* that "the compulsion to know everything is the road to insanity." Although much remains to be known about judicial elections, I repeat Professor Schattschneider's admonition for the benefit of scholars who may travel the road which has so worn my shoes.

This book took its first form as my doctoral dissertation at the University of Wisconsin. Two people were most instrumental in its research, writing, and revision. My special thanks are due Professor David Adamany, presently Vice-President of Academic Affairs at California State University, Long Beach. His influence upon my professional career extends far beyond these pages. He has served by example and direction as a constant source of encouragement and inspiration. An earlier joint research effort with him (1976 *Wisconsin Law Review* 731) provided the impetus for the development of this work. And his diligent and conscientious direction of my thesis research gives him a rightful share to whatever positive contribution this book may make to the literature on state judicial selection. I, alone, of course, am wholly responsible for its shortcomings.

My foremost personal debt is to my wife, Lisa Lewis Dubois. Though this formal acknowledgment and the dedication cannot capture the true measure of her contribution, I can only recognize her here for her patience, counseling, and good humor as a wife, her sharp pencil and skills as an editor, and her critical eye and natural suspicion of social science as a lawyer. She rejuvenated fading morale, kept our home intact, and sharpened the final product.

Many other hands helped write this book, some of them close to home. My parents, Fred and Germaine Dubois, selflessly supported my undergraduate and graduate education. My brother, Dr. Paul F. Dubois, of the Numerical Mathematics Group Computation Department of the Lawrence Livermore Laboratory, served as an indispensable consultant. He developed the computer routines and the statistical adaptations used in the preparation of Chapters 6 and 7. Though he bears no responsibility for errors in either the use of these statistics or the conclusions drawn therefrom, he deserves full credit for making it possible for me to misuse them.

My institutional debts are to the Graduate Research Committee of the University of Wisconsin and the Institute of Governmental Affairs at the University of California, Davis, for financial assistance to fund the costs of keypunching and computer time. Their support is gratefully acknowledged.

Valoyce Gage and Pat Johnson of the Department of Political Science at the University of California, Davis, typed the final manuscript with efficiency and good humor. And many teachers, colleagues, and friends at both Wisconsin and Davis can be thanked inadequately by mere mention of their names for supporting my efforts: Professors David Fellman, Joel B. Grossman, and David Trubek at Madison and Professors Larry Berman, George Downs, Alexander Groth, Clyde Jacobs, Robert Lieber, Lloyd Musolf, and Randolph Siverson, all at Davis.

Finally, Barbara Burnham, former Executive Editor at the University of Texas Press, pursued the publication of this book with forbearance, flexibility, and good will, all for which I am deeply grateful.

P.L.D.

**From Ballot to Bench**

# 1. Judicial Elections and the Debate over State Judicial Selection

## INTRODUCTION

In the early years of the Republic, election by the legislature or appointment by the governor with confirmation by the legislature (or a special council) were the two favored methods of judicial selection. And up until 1845 all the new states entering the Union followed that brief historical tradition by adopting one or the other of these basic modes of selecting judges.[1]

Seeds of dissatisfaction with these systems of judicial selection had been germinating, however, since before the election of Andrew Jackson in 1828. "The concept of an elected judiciary emerged during the Jacksonian era as part of a larger movement aimed at democratizing the political process in America. It was spearheaded by reformers who contended that the concept of an elitist judiciary . . . did not square with the ideology of a government under popular control."[2] Additionally, there was widespread belief that the appointive system of judicial selection had degenerated into a political spoils system for elected public officials to reward loyal party workers.

These concerns found expression in political reform in 1832 when Mississippi became the first state to provide for a completely elective judiciary. New York followed Mississippi's example fourteen years later and the movement toward popular elections gained momentum. Existing states abandoned their judicial selection systems for direct elections and every new state from Iowa in 1846 to Arizona in 1912 provided for an elective judiciary. At their zenith, popular judicial elections were used by over 70% of the states.

Concomitant with the rise of political parties, judicial elections were conducted on partisan ballots along with the elections for other public officials. Candidates for judicial office were nominated by party conventions and campaigned with fellow partisans on the same ticket. Dissatisfaction with partisan judicial elections developed quickly, however. Culminating in the establishment of organized bar associations in the closing decades of the 1800s, the legal profession early expressed both its resentment of the control exercised by parties and party leaders over the selection of judges and its intent to promote reforms which would curb the use of judicial posts as patronage and sources of preferments to be distributed by political bosses.

By the turn of the century, concern over the adverse effects of partisan politics on the quality and operation of the judiciary led many states to replace partisan elections with systems of nonpartisan nomination and election, a reform championed by the Progressives and later extended in many local jurisdictions to the selection of nonjudicial public officials. Many states, unwilling to abandon partisan judicial elections completely, sought to minimize party control over judicial recruitment by eliminating partisan nominating conventions and adopting another Progressive reform, the direct primary.

The result of these various waves of judicial selection reform was a curious patchwork across and within the states in the methods used for selecting state judges. But the quilt was not quite complete. A new method for selecting state judges was being developed and promoted by segments of the legal profession unhappy with the operation of partisan and nonpartisan judicial elections. In 1937, the American Bar Association endorsed a plan for the "merit selection" of state judges, a plan said to combine the benefits but avoid the weaknesses of both the elective and appointive procedures.

In its present form, the merit plan calls for the establishment of a judicial nominating commission composed of lawyers and lay persons who suggest a list of qualified nominees (usually three) to the governor.[3] The state's chief executive makes the final selection but is limited in choice to the nominees submitted by the nominating commission. After a short period of service on the bench (usually a year), the new judge stands uncontested before the state's voters solely on the question of whether he or she should be continued in office: "Should Judge 'X' be retained in office?" If the incumbent gathers a majority of affirmative votes of those cast, he or she earns a full term of office.[4] Each subsequent term is secured by the incumbent through this uncontested "retention ballot." If a sitting judge is rejected by the voters, the process of appointment begins anew.

Because it was sparked primarily by the continuing widespread dissatisfaction with direct popular elections, the reform drive for merit selection was aimed at those states utilizing partisan and nonpartisan judicial selection. The plan quickly found a home in 1940 in Missouri, where it was adopted to cover the selection of all the state's appellate court judges and the trial judges in the state's two major metropolitan areas.[5] During the 1950s and 1960s, reform efforts in several states met with success and the merit plan (or Missouri Plan, as it came to be called) gained increasing acceptance, invariably at the expense of popular elections and especially of those conducted on partisan ballots. By 1970, six states in addition to Missouri had adopted the merit plan for the selection and retention of judges to sit on their highest appellate courts; five of the six abandoned partisan elections for the merit plan while one state adopted the merit plan to replace its nonpartisan contests. The trend toward the merit plan continued in the first half of the 1970s and gained momentum as four more states sacrificed their partisan and nonpartisan elections. By 1976, twelve states had fully adopted the merit plan for the selection and retention of their state supreme court judges.[6]

The growing importance of the merit plan, moreover, extends far beyond the raw number of states in which it has found formal adoption. Although half of the nation's state supreme courts are formally staffed by elections, all state governors in these states are vested with the power of appointment to fill judicial vacancies which occur by virtue of the mid-term death, retirement, or resignation of a sitting judge. A number of governors have, accordingly, instituted "voluntary merit plans" whereby an informal merit nominating panel is established to make nonbinding recommendations to the chief executive for filling court vacancies.[7] In still other states, the mandatory use of a merit nominating commission to assist the governor in making these vacancy appointments has been formalized in statutory or constitutional provisions. By 1976 eleven of the twenty-five states utilizing partisan and nonpartisan elections had some elements of the merit plan in operation within their borders on either a voluntary or mandatory basis.[8] Thus, even though popular elections remain in half of the states for the selection of appellate judges, the merit plan has been steadily growing in significance and all recent indications are that the reform movement has yet to see its summit.

The debate over the best method of state judicial selection has, therefore, by no means ended. And popular elections continue to suffer sharp criticisms along lines which have not much changed over the last several decades. In general, a three-pronged attack has been leveled against the elective method of judicial selection. State judicial elections are criticized for failing to recruit the best legal talent available to serve on the courts, for impairing the independence of judges, and for being ineffective instruments of popular control over judges and judicial policy. These lines of attack require careful review.[9]

## THE QUESTION OF JUDICIAL QUALITY

Popular elections first are criticized because they do not result in the recruitment of the most qualified lawyers to sit on the bench. Successful lawyers are said to be reluctant to set aside their lucrative law practices to pursue election to the judiciary. Clients and cases must be set aside temporarily while the attorney conducts a campaign with no assurances that his or her practice will be intact if the bid is unsuccessful. Even the lawyer offered an interim judicial appointment by the governor to fill a vacancy may be unwilling to serve despite the opportunity subsequently to seek election with all the advantages of incumbency. The uncertain tenure of an elected judge, therefore, is said to discourage the most successful members of the legal profession from risking damage to their established careers.

Qualified attorneys are also said not to seek elective judicial office because they are unwilling to engage in the electioneering and campaigning required for a successful bid for office. Such activities in the grubby world of politics are said to be abhorrent to the persons most qualified to staff the judiciary. Additionally, lawyers are reluctant to participate in a selection process which, in their view, more frequently rewards individuals skilled in politics than it does those who possess superior professional qualifications.

In sum, the uncertainty of tenure in an elective system and the demands of election campaigning combine to deter the recruitment of the most highly qualified legal professionals to sit on the state courts. Critics point to the quality of the federal bench as evidence that superior lawyers are willing to accept judicial positions when guaranteed a secure tenure and freed of "the hazards and distractions incident to the prospect of periodical elective opposition."[10]

In addition to the process of self-selection which keeps highly qualified individuals off the bench, critics assert that the realities of electoral politics also prevent the recruitment of many qualified legal professionals. In states dominated by one political party, for example, those affiliated with the minority party will not be seriously considered for service on the bench either by the governor in filling court vacancies or by the loyal partisan voters on election day. In other states only those candidates with well-recognized names can expect to win election to the court.

On the other side of the coin, critics argue that elections not only keep the best legal talent off the courts but also allow individuals of uncertain ability to be selected. Critics claim that where political party organizations effectively control access to the ballot candidates for judicial office are recruited often to balance a party ticket, to pay off party workers for service to the organization, to promote ethnic or religious representation in the judicial branch, or to repay political obligations to special interests—reasons unrelated to the professional merit of the prospective judge. In states where the parties do not control the recruitment of candidates for the judiciary, such as where a nonpartisan primary is used, each candidate is responsible for securing a place on the ballot by circulating a nominating petition. Critics argue that in these circumstances "the only guarantee the voters have is that the candidate wanted the position badly enough" to take the time and trouble to collect the signatures necessary to qualify for the general election.[11]

The general election ballot is also scored for being no more discriminating among the professional abilities of the opposing candidates than the nominating process. Where party labels are provided, voters select their judges according to the party they happen to favor; the fortunes of qualified candidates for the judiciary are tied to the fortunes of the party's presidential, gubernatorial, and legislative hopefuls. Likewise, if by some chance a person of demonstrated competence has been selected to serve on the judiciary, he or she may be removed from office in an election defeat for reasons unrelated to performance on the bench. In the situation most abhorred by critics, sitting judges are caught in the middle of partisan shifts sparked by political events connected with executive and legislative politics in which the officials of one party, including judges, are swept out of office and replaced by candidates affiliated with the other party. As one who was both a beneficiary and a victim of this process once observed, "I was elected in 1916 because Woodrow Wilson kept us out of war—I was defeated in 1920 because Woodrow Wilson hadn't kept us out of war."[12]

The nonpartisan general election ballot also allows an individual with a familiar name, great personal or political appeal, a good campaign, or even just a good place on the ballot to be elected to the state judiciary regardless of individual qualifications or capabilities. In fact, combined with the nonpartisan primary, critics argue that, despite the hopes of Progressive reformers that nonpartisan elections would allow the selection of qualified judges on the basis of nonpolitical considerations, they are in many respects worse than partisan judicial elections. At least under the system of partisan nomination and election, a party that sponsors a judicial candidate is responsible in the eyes of the voters for the quality of the candidate.

The merit selection process has been promoted by its supporters as a vast improvement over popular elections for recruiting qualified judges. The nominating commission is designed to survey the field of available legal talent and, on the basis of nonpolitical considerations, recommend three highly qualified nominees to the governor. The lawyer members of the commission provide expert judgment on the legal training, skills, and experience of those individuals who might be recruited to occupy judicial office. The lay members of the commission temper the lawyers' concern for professional competence with a consideration of the nontechnical qualifications relevant to judicial service. The governor is able to make the final decision in the selection process and may indeed consider political factors in making a choice. The diffusion of responsibility between the commission and the governor, however, is thought to ease the political pressure upon the state's chief executive to appoint someone with less than superior professional credentials. Limited to the list of nominees submitted by the commission, the governor's eventual appointee is certain to be of high quality.

The merit retention election is also said to be essential to securing a high quality judiciary. The uncontested merit retention election virtually guarantees the long tenure of the judge and thus serves as an encouragement for successful lawyers to sacrifice their legal practices in exchange for the prestige and security of a judgeship. And even if the merit selection process does not dramatically improve the quality of the individuals selected as judges, it is argued that it nonetheless improves the operation of the judiciary by enabling judges to devote full time to their duties without the constant distractions imposed by the necessity to campaign for re-election.

At the same time, the merit retention election is touted by supporters as ensuring significant public participation in the process of judicial selection. Although incapable of making an informed judgment on the professional qualifications of those seeking judicial office, the voters are said to be able to remove judges who have demonstrated inferior or unethical behavior while on the bench during their probationary period.

The merit plan, therefore, is most highly praised for the improvement it will bring to the overall quality of the state judiciary by eliminating political factors from the process of judicial selection and substituting considerations of professional qualifications and technical competence. Based upon the available evidence regarding the merit plan in practice, however, the claims of its supporters seem considerably overrated. In the first place, as Watson and Downing note in their pioneering study of the merit plan in Missouri, the question of whether the merit plan "removes politics" from judicial selection is really "a false issue. Instead, the Plan is designed to bring to bear on the process of selecting judges a variety of interests that are thought to have a legitimate concern in the matter and at the same time to discourage other interests. It may be assumed that these interests will engage in the 'politics' of judicial selection, that is, *they will maneuver to influence who will be chosen as judges*" (emphasis added).[13] Rather than eliminating politics, the merit plan "has changed the nature of that politics to include not only partisan forces but also those relating to the interests of the organized Bar, the judiciary, and the court's 'attentive publics.'"[14]

These interests have found expression in several crucial aspects of the judicial recruitment process under the merit plan. In the selection of the lay and lawyer members of the nominating commissions, in the commissions' internal deliberations, and in the pattern of judicial nominations and appointments the influence of "politics" in the merit selection process is clearly visible.

First, political party affiliation has been a central consideration of the governor in appointing lay members to sit on the nominating commission. Not only does the governor want to influence the nominating process so that individuals with acceptable policy views will be recommended by the commission, but appointment to the commission itself may be used as a reward for political supporters. Despite the constitutional or statutory language existing in most merit plan jurisdictions requiring governors to make commission appointments without regard to partisan affiliation, those individuals appointed usually share the governor's party affiliation and have past close ties, either as former campaign workers or as personal friends.[15] Some states have taken steps to curb this overt expession of partisanship by requiring bipartisan representation on the nominating commission and by limiting and staggering the terms of commissioners. In addition, many states prohibit nominating commissioners (whether lay or lawyer) from holding public governmental office and/or an official position in a political party.[16] But these various sanctions do nothing to mitigate the influence upon decision-making of the political backgrounds and loyalties of the lay commissioners who are selected.

Analysis of the operation of the merit plan in Missouri has also documented political competition in the election campaigns conducted to select the lawyer members of the judicial nominating commission.[17] Since the years of the Great Depression, the metropolitan bars in Kansas City (Jackson County) and in St. Louis have each been split into separate professional organizations. Attorneys practicing in small firms or as solo practitioners representing personal injury and other civil plaintiffs, criminal defendants, and other "have not" interests came to dominate one organization in each metropolitan area while the attorneys from large law firms customarily representing civil defendants (usually insurance companies) and other corporate clients and "have" interests dominated the other bar group. These rival bar associations adopted opposing positions during the original campaign for the adoption of the merit plan—the plaintiffs' organizations opposed the plan while the defendants' organizations supported it.

The adoption of the merit plan did not eliminate the basic rivalry between the two groups, however. Rather, they adapted to the new selection system, with each trying to place "their" representatives on the judicial nominating commission and thereby indirectly promoting the selection of "their" kind of lawyer to the bench. As Watson and Downing note, "the stakes of these elections for lawyers relate both to the perceived policy 'payoffs' in the terms of judges' rulings that affect their clients' economic interests and to symbolic 'payoffs' for the contending bar groups in matters involving prestige and ideology."[18]

In the races for posts on the judicial nominating commissions, a small caucus of officers and activists in each of the competing bar associations in each locality has informally nominated and endorsed a single candidate: ". . . word goes out about the man who will represent each group in the election, and organizational loyalty is sufficient to prevent other nominations that would split the vote of the members of the association."[19] These informal processes have become so firmly rooted that there is rarely an election which goes uncontested and, at the same time, rarely one with more than just two candidates, despite nominal requirements for access to the ballot. The supporters of each candidate then engage in campaign activities and strategies designed to tap the respective sources of their support and secure the election of their "nominee" to the commission. In short, Watson and Downing conclude, the elections to select the lawyer members of the judicial nominating commission are effectively conducted within a "competitive 'two-party system'" where the "parties" are rival bar organizations, representing distinct social status groups in the profession and broader socioeconomic interests outside the legal community which utilize the services of attorneys and the political forum of the courts.[20]

Given the nature of the processes by which the lay and lawyer members of the nominating commission are selected, the introduction of political considerations into the commission's internal deliberations is not surprising. A survey of merit commissioners in several states revealed that nearly half (49%) admitted that political influences or considerations were introduced into commission deliberations at one time or another. Most of the commissioners admitting the influence of politics into the selection process said the occasions were infrequent and then rarely decisive in the results of commission decision-making.[21] But even in the minds of those who would most likely deny the influence of politics in what ostensibly is a "nonpartisan" process, political factors are not totally an irrelevant dimension of merit selection.

More detailed analysis of the inner workings of the nominating commission and the relationship of the commission to the governor also suggest that political maneuvering is not unknown. Watson and Downing have documented the existence of bargaining and logrolling among the commissioners over the names to be sent to the governor. Further, depending upon the political composition of the commission and its relationship to the governor, the panel of names sent to the governor might be "rigged" or "loaded" in such a way as to force the governor to choose a particular nominee favored by the commission majority or, alternatively, the names might be "stacked" or "wired" so that the commission nominates the governor's hand-picked choice and two other individuals as "panel-fillers" or "window dressing." These "nominating and appointing games," as Watson and Downing describe them, reflect the political dimensions of the merit selection process.[22]

The failure of the merit plan to remove politics from the judicial selection process is not a fatal flaw, of course, even though its supporters deserve to be chided for continuing pretensions as to the nonpolitical nature of the plan and its supposed narrow concern for professional qualifications and technical competence. Although political considerations seem an inevitable part of judicial selection, the merit selection process might nevertheless be defended if it does result in the recruitment of more highly qualified individuals to the judiciary than would be possible under an elective system. The security of tenure provided by the merit plan and the elimination of the necessity for judges to campaign for re-election, combined with the screening of potential judges by the nominating commission, are thought by supporters of the plan to promote the recruitment of the highest quality lawyers to staff the state judiciary. Despite these lofty claims, however, there are both philosophical objections to and empirical doubts about the claims posited by advocates of the merit plan that it can dramatically improve the quality of the judiciary.

First, it is not clear that the abandonment of popular judicial elections for the merit plan can be justified because of the ill effects upon judicial recruitment caused by the rigors of electioneering.

> Physical effort of campaigning, candidate's time consumed in a political race, campaign expenses, and general indignities of direct exposure to the voting public are the inconveniences most frequently named. Standing alone, these are not asserted to be sufficiently objectionable to support adoption of a nonelective plan, but when considered in light of their discouraging effect on prospective judges, the case is thought to have been made. It may be easily overlooked, but uncertainty, inconvenience, and sacrifice have gone hand in hand with service to country, and no citizen has reason to be assured that their removal guarantees, or even suggests, dramatic improvement in public service or public servants.[23]

Further, there is no empirical evidence on the extent to which the elective method of judicial selection actually has served as a deterrent to some individuals seeking judgeships. It may be that many qualified individuals have not sought the judiciary because of the insecurity of tenure and the "inconveniences" associated with elections. But it is not clear that the effects upon recruitment have been any greater in the case of the judiciary than for the executive and legislative branches of government. Relatively low salaries, modest fringe benefits, and inadequate retirement allowances compared to those available in the private sector have served to discourage many talented individuals from public service, judicial or otherwise.

Finally, the advocates of the merit plan have not successfully resolved an inconsistency in their own argument. On the one hand, the merit plan is said to encourage successful lawyers to sacrifice lucrative law practices to accept judicial appointments by guaranteeing them security of tenure once on the bench. On the other hand, the merit retention election is supposed to provide the electorate with a meaningful opportunity to remove judges after a short period of probationary service. If the merit retention election is a genuine public review of judicial performance and not a mere genuflection toward public participation in the merit selection process, then many established lawyers might find it to be an effective deterrent to judicial service. Short of a provision granting life terms, any system of judicial selection contains some uncertainty of tenure which might dissuade some attorneys from accepting seats on the bench.

Apart from the question of the effect of elections on discouraging the recruitment of legal talent to the bench, it is most difficult to either substantiate or refute the assertions by critics that the elective method has permitted the empaneling of judges of lesser quality and that the merit plan results in the selection of higher-quality judges than is possible under the elective system. In the first place, the meaning of "quality" as it applies to the tasks confronting trial and appellate judges is extremely elusive. "Without having reliable information on what judges do in the many state and local courts, the selection of criteria used to evaluate how well they carry out their responsibilities (or will do so) must, by necessity, involve substantial guesswork."[24] Formal qualifications for judicial office, such as citizenship, age, residence, and length of law practice, are typically set by constitutional or statutory provisions. But the formal provisions are usually silent as to those backgound experiences or personal characteristics which would ensure a quality bench. Legal practitioners provide little guidance either. When judges and lawyers are queried as to those qualifications and qualities most essential in a judge, "the qualities mentioned are stated in broad generalities and often fail to focus on the attitudes that a judge, as compared to persons in other pursuits in society, should possess if he is to do his job properly."[25] The American Bar Association's *Code of Professional Responsibility*, for example, advises only that judges "ought to be persons of integrity, competence, and suitable temperament."[26]

In an attempt to isolate the qualities essential to judicial service, Professor Maurice Rosenberg surveyed American trial judges as to the qualities which they thought best equip a lawyer to perform the duties of a judge.[27] Highest on the judges' list of valued qualities were, in descending order, moral courage, decisiveness, reputation for fairness and uprightness, patience, good physical and mental health, and consideration for others. As Rosenberg notes, these factors are concerned with personal character and temperament and are not related uniquely to the study or practice of law or the tasks performed by judges. Most importantly, the attributes listed are essentially subjective and difficult to recognize, measure, and apply on a comparative basis. The judges in Rosenberg's survey were much less concerned with the more objectively evaluated qualifications relating to formal legal training, knowledge, and professional achievement by which lawyers might be compared and which might predict future quality performance on the bench.

Given the highly idealized criteria of judicial quality usually suggested by members of the bench and bar, it is perhaps not too surprising that in screening potential candidates for selection to the judiciary, merit nominating commissions have relied most heavily upon subjective evaluations of individual character and personality and not objective indicators or even subjective estimates of professional competence. In a survey of merit nominating commissioners on the specific qualities and qualifications viewed as the most important considerations in the screening of prospective nominees, Ashman and Alfini discovered that the most important background characteristics were "mental health" and "physical health," far outranking in importance previous judicial service, a superior law school record, and previous professional, civic, or political experience.[28] In terms of professional skills, the commissioners most valued a "reputation for fairness" and "professional reputation," considerations related more to subjective estimates of personal character than professional skill. Indeed, 70.3% of the commissioners acknowledged that even subjective evaluations of "professional skill" were more important in their decisions than objectively ascertainable information about the applicant.[29] Among the most highly valued character and personality traits were that the nominee not be "susceptible to influence," possess moral courage, demonstrate openmindedness and objectivity, and be emotionally stable.[30] In sum, despite the stress of the merit plan upon recruiting the most capable legal technicians, the main emphases of merit screening are upon extremely vague qualities of personality and character not strictly related to legal knowledge, abilities, or skill and factors that require evaluations which essentially "are subjective in nature and can only be measured by the complex interdependence of community and individual prejudices, perceptions, and pressures."[31]

Relying upon the opinions of lawyers and judges, moreover, may not reveal those qualities, qualifications, or characteristics truly essential, in some existential sense, to the successful performance of judicial functions. Even if these professional opinions as to the elements of judicial quality are accepted and the experience of merit nominating commissioners in screening potential judges is acknowledged, it is not clear that the lay and lawyer members of these commissions possess any special expertise or experience which make them "more likely to sense greatness in a candidate than the subjective common sense values of an electorate."[32]

Beyond these general doubts about the asserted benefits of the merit plan, there is very little empirical evidence to substantiate or refute the claim that the merit plan improves the quality of the bench. Indeed, as difficult as it is for the members of judicial nominating commissions to apply vague criteria related to personality and character, so also has it been difficult for scholars to research the ability of the merit plan to recruit superior judges.

One technique has been to survey members of the legal profession regarding the performance of sitting judges. This approach is fraught with methodological difficulties, however, since the evaluative criteria being applied by each lawyer surveyed are unknown and, as noted earlier, estimates of judicial quality may not be independent of the political, economic, and social values held by individual members of the profession. Watson and Downing, for instance, surveyed Missouri lawyers regarding the performances of sitting circuit and appellate court judges.[33] The survey *did* reveal that judges selected under the merit plan received more favorable ratings than judges who had originally reached the bench through the partisan election system used in Missouri prior to 1940. But there was also shown to be a positive relationship between the lawyers' evaluations of judicial performance and their a priori support for the merit plan. Lawyers who supported the merit plan rated judges selected by the merit plan more favorably than they did the elected judges; those lawyers who favored the elective method of selection rated the merit plan judges and elected judges almost identically. Similarly, attorney evaluations of judicial performance were colored by the basic rivalry between the "plaintiffs" and "defendants" segments of the profession.

Given the inherent subjectivity of these surveys, scholars have turned to more-objective measures of judicial quality. But the very elusiveness of the concept has forced reliance upon readily available and quantifiable information regarding the prior educational and legal training of judges and their professional experiences before assuming the bench. Based upon the claimed advantages of the merit plan, however, reasonable hypotheses have been formulated to test empirically the differences between elective and merit plan selection systems in the characteristics of individuals recruited to judgeships.

For example, as discussed earlier, the critics of elections have argued that the quality of the bench has suffered because state and local political organizations have used judgeships as incentives for party work and as rewards for loyal party service. In addition, whether the elective system is partisan or nonpartisan, elections place a premium upon the ability of the candidate to tap local sources of political support and to capitalize upon his or her recognition among the voters. It might be expected, therefore, that those individuals selected under the elective method will have distinct ties to the local community as evidenced by in-state birth and education. Presumably, the merit plan promotes the accession of high-quality individuals regardless of their attachment to the community, either as local party activists or as "hometown folks." Similarly, the merit plan might be thought to improve the overall level of educational attainment among members of the judiciary as the merit nominating committee promotes the selection of candidates with more-impressive academic credentials than those selected under the elective system. Finally, it might be expected that the elective system, with its stress upon prior political activity, would disproportionately recruit individuals with experience in elective political positions. The merit plan, in contrast, would more frequently recruit individuals who have shunned political careers and who have assumed public or private positions related to law enforcement or the administration of justice and, in the case of appellate court positions, those with prior judicial experience at the trial level.

Despite such expectations, however, empirical comparisons of the background characteristics of judges have not confirmed many of these hypotheses. Jacob's comparison of trial and appellate judges in twelve states revealed few differences associated with the merit plan.[34] While partisan elections were found to favor slightly the recruitment of locally born individuals, the merit plan attracted those who had attended in-state law schools. In terms of education, Jacob found no particular advantage among merit plan judges. Indeed, while the merit plan states were found to have the largest proportion of judges who had earned law school honors, these states also had a disproportionate number of judges who had attended proprietary and night law schools, institutions which most observers believe provide inferior or substandard training when compared to the major public and privately endowed law schools. Finally, although elected judges were much more likely than merit plan judges to have held prior political office, most of these positions were in elected law enforcement, primarily as public prosecutors, training and experience not unrelated or irrelevant to the tasks which the individual might someday face as a judge.

In the most complete study to date, Canon compared the characteristics of the judges sitting from 1961 to 1968 on each of the state courts of last resort.[35] Judges selected in partisan elective states were slightly more likely than judges selected under the nonpartisan elective or merit plan systems to have been born in-state and to have received their undergraduate and legal educations in the state. But virtually no differences separated the elective and merit plan systems in terms of the proportion of judges with undergraduate and law degrees and with public legal or prior judicial experience.

Importantly, Canon noted the close correspondence between methods of judicial selection and regions of the country. By examining the characteristics of judges selected by methods atypical of the region, Canon was led to conclude that those differences in the judges' background characteristics which could be observed were as much the product of regional factors related to the processes of political recruitment as of the formal judicial selection system. As Canon concluded, "It seems clear that institutional mechanisms surrounding recruitment to state supreme courts do not have the impact on personal characteristics which advocates of competing selection systems often imply they have."[36]

The use of gross characteristics as crude estimates of background qualifications for judicial office may not, of course, bear a close relationship to actual performance on the bench. Partial documentation of this point has been provided by Watson and Downing's comparison of the background characteristics of the best and worst judges as determined in a survey of Missouri attorneys. The authors found very few differences in the background characteristics of "superior" and "inferior" judges in terms of age, birthplace, education, political experience, or prior judicial service.[37]

It is exceedingly difficult if not impossible, therefore, to verify or refute the assertion that the merit plan improves the quality of the bench. The qualifications and qualities essential to a "good" judge are vague and uncertain; needless to say, choosing the "best qualified" individuals to sit on the judiciary is a problematic endeavor.

It is also doubtful that the merit retention elections serve the purposes claimed by the proponents of merit selection. While some commentators acknowledge that the provision for retention elections was a palliative designed to mollify popular opposition to the plan, others steadfastly maintain that such elections allow the electorate to remove judges who, after a short period of service, have proved themselves incapable of competent performance on the bench. Thus, while the uncontested election protects the incumbent of demonstrated quality from being turned out of office for "political" reasons unrelated to performance, it is said to focus voter attention on the judge's competence, without the distraction of party labels and the vicissitudes of partisan politics, and to allow the removal of judges who lack the temperament or abilities required for judicial office. But both by design and in actual operation, the retention election has proven to be a superfluous provision of the merit plan.

Few judges have ever been defeated in merit retention elections. In Missouri, for example, only one judge was defeated in the 179 retention elections held from 1942 to 1964.[38] In 1972, when 308 judges from eleven states sought retention, only 4 were defeated.[39] And in 1976, 353 judges in thirteen states sought re-election on the retention ballot; all but 3 were returned to office.[40]

This remarkable success rate for incumbent judges might be testimony to the success of the merit selection process in recruiting well-qualified individuals to staff the state courts. But upon closer inspection of the operation and results of merit retention elections, the merit retention ballot seems ill-suited to the task assigned to it. In the first place, the record of an incumbent judge is not likely to come under serious public scrutiny under the merit retention system. Without a self-interested challenger to bring to light the professional failings of a sitting judge, re-election is virtually assured.

> Who will spend the time and money to bring such a record to the attention of the people? It will not be done by lawyers who must face such a judge if they should lose; nor will other officeholders who would consider it an invasion of the judicial process and separation of powers. Other judges will remain silent, if only to guarantee that they will not be a target for retaliation. Other candidates will not criticize because the defeat of an incumbent will not guarantee that the candidate will replace the defeated judge. The nominating commission will not confess the fallacy of the selection process by offering criticism. There will be no constitutional or statutory means to provoke criticism; civic organizations and churches have never mobilized their resources to meet the alleged deficiencies in this state's judiciary. The press may be the only means of effective mass education. Yet it has never . . . tried to do so.[41]

Indeed, as one commentator has noted, "Who is to tell the queen she is old and fat" or "who among the mice will bell the cat."[42]

In an informational vacuum, voters will tend to support the incumbent and vote for his or her retention. Voters support the incumbent because they have no other cues to guide them in their voting decision. There are no party labels, no opposing personalities or familiar names from which to choose, and, even less than is usually the case in judicial elections, no issues. The voters know little about the incumbent judge except that he or she is the incumbent. Given the low visibility of the work of the judiciary, voters have little reason to remove a sitting judge unless some outrageous legal offense or moral indiscretion committed by the judge should come to their attention.[43] For most voters, a judge's performance is satisfactory by virtue of its inconspicuousness. In addition, voters may naturally gravitate toward the unopposed incumbent, unsure of the consequences of a "no" vote or fearful that the choice to be made by the merit nominating commission and the governor may give them a judge worse than the one they might remove. Voters find it difficult to vote *against* someone without a reasonable alternative candidate to vote for.

Recent analyses of the results of merit retention elections indicate quite predictably that under these conditions "voters have not been very discriminating in their ballots on individual judges."[44] Most judges poll favorable majorities of over three-fourths of the participating electorate, with from one-fifth to one-quarter of the votes cast consistently opposing the retention of the incumbent, regardless of the particular judges seeking to be returned to office.[45] Similarly, the results of published polls of the legal profession regarding the performance of sitting judges provide consistent endorsement for virtually all incumbents, giving "little guidance for the electorate in deciding whether individual judges should be retained in office."[46] Even when the opinion of the bar is less than overwhelmingly favorable or even unfavorable regarding particular judges, bar ratings have been shown to bear little relationship to the results of the retention elections.[47]

The provision for retention elections has succeeded in achieving one of the major goals of the merit plan—secure and lengthy tenure for the holders of judicial office. Based upon the actual operation of retention elections under the plan, though, they are more properly characterized as "plebiscites rather than meaningful decisions by the electorate."[48] The evidence produced thus far "raises doubts as to the validity of the merit retention election as an accurate barometer of competent performance on the bench."[49]

Advocates of the merit plan argue in response that though removal from the bench via the retention election is extremely unlikely "this problem can be avoided by placing the emphasis on judicial selection and thereby preventing unqualified judges from getting on the bench in the first place."[50] But this answer virtually begs the question of the necessity of the retention elections. Moreover, what often remains unrecognized in the debate over merit selection is that the forces behind the drive for merit selection are precisely the same ones advocating the creation of special disciplinary and removal commissions, the adoption of mandatory retirement laws, and the upgrading of state judicial pension plans.[51] The first of these proposed reforms is necessary to force the removal of incapable or unethical judges who have "slipped through" the selection process; the latter two are necessary to require or encourage the retirement of judges who, by virtue of advanced age accompanying uninterrupted tenure on the court, have developed mental or physical disabilities which prevent their efficient service. Thus, though these reforms are aimed at all states utilizing a variety of selection methods, the proponents of the merit plan appear to concede, at least implicitly, that the merit selection process itself might be faulty, that the public review provided by the retention election format is more imaginary than real, and that significant problems related to the quality of the bench accompany systems which virtually guarantee life tenure.

In sum, the "merits" of the merit plan and its superiority to elective systems of judicial selection in raising the quality of the state judiciary have not been clearly demonstrated. Of course some of the virtues of the merit selection and retention plan, such as the security of tenure which it provides, relate to guaranteeing the principle of judicial independence and are not solely directed to the issue of recruiting high-quality lawyers to sit on the bench. It is to the issue of judicial independence that we now turn.

JUDICIAL INDEPENDENCE

The second major part of the attack on popular elections is based upon a philosophic and normative argument not likely to be resolved by empirical research. Critics assert that elections are inherently inconsistent with the principle of "judicial independence," a value which critics insist is fundamental to the successful operation of the judicial process.

This part of the debate over judicial elections has been clouded some because the concept of judicial independence has not benefited from a single definition. By one definition, independence refers to the freedom of the judge from any external influences which might impair his or her *impartiality* toward the opposing litigants and his or her ability to decide each case "on its own merits." In a much broader view of the concept, judicial independence refers to the ability of the judiciary to perform its functions of judicial review, statutory construction, and common law development without fear of retribution by the elected branches or the population at large.

Depending upon the meaning ascribed to the general term "judicial independence," subsumed beneath its mantle are three distinct objections to judicial elections. First, by creating political obligations, elections are said to interfere with the role of the judge as an unbiased and objective decision-maker. Second, critics assert that elections, which are intended to hold judges accountable, merely interfere with their independent performance of technical duties; judges need not be held accountable by elections because they, unlike other public officials, are not engaged in the formulation or implementation of public policy. Finally, it is argued that even if it is admitted that judges make political decisions and engage in the making of public policy, the special place of the judiciary in the political system demands that judges not be held accountable for their actions. These arguments may be reviewed in turn.

Criticism is initially aimed at judicial elections for impairing the position of the judge as an impartial and objective decision-maker. The requirement that judicial candidates campaign for election means that the successful candidate carries to the bench a list of obligations and favors owed. Where a position on the bench has been secured with the political, organizational, and financial assistance of party leaders, the judge "will find it almost impossible to resist completely the importunities of his creditors for payment through judicial favors," including favorable treatment of certain litigants and the distribution of patronage.[52] The system of nonpartisan selection, designed to eliminate the more pernicious practices associated with partisan judicial politics, does not secure the impartiality of the judge either, however. Unable to obtain campaign contributions from the political parties, the nonpartisan judicial candidate is compelled to solicit funds from fellow members of the bar, thereby incurring obligations to some of those individuals who will appear before his or her court if he or she is elected. These kinds of real or potential conflicts, critics say, impinge upon the ability of a judge to hear cases and render decisions without the outcome being predetermined by the judge's need to repay past political debts and to build credit for future re-election bids. It is perhaps the most quoted passage in the literature on judicial selection that "there is no harm in turning a politician into a judge . . . the curse of the elective system is that it turns every elective judge into a politician."[53] And whether or not a judge is actually unduly influenced is unimportant since public perception of the courts as impartial forums for the resolution of disputes is said to be essential to the effective operation of the judicial process.

This challenge to popular elections is insufficient by itself to justify the abandonment of the elective method for selecting judges. Political corruption, including the undue influence of campaign contributors upon elected public officials, is a problem not limited to the forum of the courts. But even if it is conceded that the adjudicatory setting of judicial decision-making presents a particular problem with respect to the impartiality of the decision-maker, means much less drastic than the abolishment of elections are available. Strict enforcement of the relevant provisions of the *Code of Judicial Conduct* (which replaced the *Canons of Judicial Ethics* in August 1972) and the exploration of alternative means for the financing of judicial campaigns are but two examples.[54] Similarly, the abuses of political patronage are not unique to elective courts. The substitution of a civil service system for the filling of courthouse administrative positions and the appointment of individuals to profitable positions as referees, guardians, receivers, and the like would alleviate direct pressure on judges for the repayment of campaign obligations.[55]

Critics also object to popular judicial elections because they see the judicial function as essentially nonpolitical. Elections are merely bothersome devices which interfere with the judge's performance of technical duties. As nonpolitical agents who apply the law but do not make it, judges need not be held accountable to the electorate. "A judge has no constituency except the unenfranchised lady with the blindfold and scales, no platform except equal and impartial justice under law."[56] Closely related to the desires of reformers to recruit "more qualified" judges, this argument focuses on the nonpolitical aspects of judging and the need for individuals who possess the professional competence necessary to apply the law with fairness and dispatch. In one of the clearest expositions of this argument, a former state jurist observed:

> The judge's equipment, like his task, is different from that of a chief executive. . . . The latter need not—indeed, probably should not—be a technician, unless in an incidental sense. The judge is also much more of a technician than the legislator. The judge is in fact less akin to the political executive and legislator than he is to the medical doctor, engineer, professor, military leader, or scientist. He must be, in the higher sense, an expert. There is little more "democratic" necessity to choose a public expert called a judge by direct popular election,

open to all comers having the minimum or formal requirements, than there is to choose another kind of expert such as
an admiral or university president.[57]

The political and policy-making nature of legislative and executive
positions requires popular selection in order to assure the accountability of these policy-makers to majoritarian sentiments. But because judges are thought to perform purely technical and narrow
legal tasks, not only are the voters incapable of intelligent selection,
but also their participation in the process of staffing the courts is
wholly unnecessary.[58]

Central to the conception of judges as legal technicians is the
belief that the sole function of the judge is to apply the law as it is
expressed in constitutional provisions, statutes, and previous judicial interpretations. Law-making and the determination of policy
are exclusively duties and privileges of the legislature and executive.
Although judges do possess considerable discretion, its exercise is
constrained by the adjudicatory setting which requires the application of legal principles to particular fact situations. Sound legal
traditions requiring the use of syllogistic legal reasoning and the
application of *stare decisis* also govern and confine judicial decision-making. Both the nature of the tasks and the tools of the trade
require individuals who possess the professional qualifications and
technical knowledge necessary for the successful performance of judicial duties.

Whether judges are mere oracles of fixed and known legal principles is a question which most social scientists thought resolved
more than fifty years ago by the Realist revolution. The battle need
not be fought again here. In the modern view, well established
among political scientists, sociologists, and eminent legal thinkers,
judges not only make conscious policy choices in the adjudication of
cases and in the exercise of the power of judicial review, but also engage in political decision-making as a matter of function. "The
judges are [political] actors charged with special responsibilities,
and their decisions . . . allocate values in society such as opportunity, liberty, money, protection, or representation in other types of
decision-making. Like other political decision-making, this alloca-
tion of values is differential; that is, some individuals and groups are
favored and others are disadvantaged. These policy outputs are
called 'justice.'"[59]

At the appellate court level, judges are likely to confront policy
choices directly in the course of developing common law principles
and in interpreting state constitutional and statutory provisions.

Even in the process of reviewing lower court decisions for procedural irregularities or substantive errors, however, appellate court decisions may serve to favor some kinds of interests while disadvantaging others, demonstrating thereby the political nature of the judicial function.[60]

This view of the judicial process does not posit that judges are merely "politicians in robes" or that judicial policy-making is exactly like that engaged in by legislatures and executives; these oversimplifications do not withstand even casual analysis.[61] Nor does it deny that relatively few cases are explicitly partisan or ideological in nature[62] or that many times judges are called upon to make relatively minor and technical adjustments in long-settled principles of law. But it does emphasize that judicial discretion is extensive and that judges are aware of the options available to them and the differential effects alternative choices will have upon individuals and groups affected by the litigation before them. Finally, of course, this conception of the political nature of judicial decision-making recognizes that judges frequently are able to develop common law, to interpret statutes and administrative regulations, and to adjudicate constitutional disputes—all opportunities which allow judges explicitly to make, veto, legitimize, or reinforce public policies.

Not all the critics of judicial elections, however, rely upon the position that judges perform nonpolitical functions. Many commentators, willing to concede the policy-making dimensions of judicial decision-making, nonetheless argue that judges *should not* be held accountable for their decisions. Dean Dorothy Nelson, for example, argues: "The principle of independence of the judiciary involves not merely independence from personal or private influence, such as financial, religious, race, and other social and political considerations, *but the independence from the influence or control of any other branch or officer of government. The courts should be free from control of the executive or legislative branches of government and should be removed from the influence of temporary public majorities*" (emphasis added).[63]

The reasons supporting the policy-making independence of the judiciary are well known and do not require a detailed canvassing here. The independence of the courts from the coordinate branches of government guarantees that governmental power will be limited in its exercise by maintaining the principle of the separation of powers. The independence of the judicial branch from control by the other branches and by the people is also said to guarantee that the essential rights of political minorities will not be trampled by the political majority of the moment. Finally, in an argument reminiscent of the perception of judges as neutral oracles of fixed law, some commentators argue that judges are the only governmental officials with sufficient objectivity, wisdom, and competence to decide the meaning and application of provisions of the constitution, the ultimate check upon majoritarianism and guarantor of limited government.

Whether the judiciary should have this independence is essentially a normative question which politicians, scholars, and jurists have debated since before the formation of the Republic. Most of the controversy has focused on the exercise of the power of judicial review by the United States Supreme Court, the independence of which is secured by the provision for the continued tenure of justices "during good behavior."[64]

The debate over the independent performance of judicial review centers on the question of whether policy-making by a small group of individuals who are effectively insulated from public control is consistent with the principles of democratic government: ". . . when the Court holds unconstitutional an act of Congress, we are confronted by the fact that the one non-elective and non-removable element in the government rejects the conclusion of the two elective and removable branches."[65] Much of this debate can be characterized by what Professor Leonard Levy has called the "principle of the gored ox"; viewpoints on either the merits or the demerits of independent judicial review depend upon whether particular commentators have found the decisions of the Supreme Court to be agreeable.[66] Nevertheless, fundamental arguments both for and against the principle of judicial independence have been advanced which transcend the content of specific policy decisions made by the Court and are equally applicable to the question of whether state court judges should be independent.

Initially, the advocates of judicial accountability deny that courts require independence in order to give proper interpretation to constitutional and statutory provisions—to administer "a supernal code to which it has infallible access."[67] Judicial review is not the product primarily of special legal erudition or the objective views of constitutional and legal oracles; if it were, "divine appointment would then be the proper method of recruitment."[68] The independent exercise of the power of judicial review is undemocratic because it allows judges to make public policy without being responsive to, or held accountable by, the people or their representatives. In a democracy, the people, through the principle of majority rule, should be able to decide all questions of public policy, including those which bear upon the unfolding meaning of their constitution.

The advocates for an independent judiciary counter that the courts provide an important check against the excesses of majoritarianism by serving to restrain majorities in the other branches of government and direct popular majorities from interfering with the personal rights of political minorities, particularly those liberties essential for effective participation in the democratic political process.[69] Some have argued that the essentially undemocratic nature of independent judicial decision-making might "lose its spots" when exercised in a way which promotes the integrity of the democratic process.[70] The protection of fundamental liberties, such as those guaranteed by the First Amendment, might be counter to majoritarian sentiments but nevertheless consistent with the principles of democracy. At this point, however, critics charge that "whether judicial review is democratic . . . depends largely on the results it achieves."[71]

Advocates on both sides of the judicial independence–judicial accountability controversy are in fundamental disagreement over the record of the Supreme Court in using its powers to protect the fundamental rights of minorities. Beyond this, they differ over the extent to which the existing institutional and political checks upon the Court are, and have been, sufficient to keep the Court generally in tune with majoritarian sentiments while allowing it sufficient independence to serve as the guardian of minority rights.[72] For the advocates of accountability, however, the potential for an independent judiciary to serve as the bastion of the essential rights of minorities does not justify the general independence of the judicial branch, particularly since it does not confine its constitutional decision-making to those questions bearing on the protection of the rights of minorities and, moreover, when, outside the brief period of the Supreme Court under Chief Justice Earl Warren, the historical record is "practically barren" of instances of such protection.[73] Further, though an independent judiciary may be responsive to majoritarian sentiments on public policy issues, there is no guarantee or necessity that it be so.

The advocates of judicial accountability further assert that whatever justifications there might be for the independence of the Supreme Court they are not wholly relevant to the question of whether or not state supreme court judges should be held accountable. A large majority of the Supreme Court's docket is devoted to the resolution of constitutional questions, many of which bear on alleged infringements of personal rights and the proper limits of governmental power and official exercises of authority. The highest state courts also decide important federal and state constitutional issues but, at least quantitatively, these are but a whisper in the winds compared to these courts' responsibilities in common law development, statutory interpretation, and supervision of lower courts —policy-making activities for which state judges should be held accountable.[74]

Regardless of the case for or against judicial independence, it is perhaps enough to note that the principle is deeply engrained in Anglo-American legal tradition and finds expression in both federal and state provisions relating to the judiciary. Several arrangements in use in nearly every state have been designed to safeguard judicial independence. Immunity from civil liability for decisions on the bench is a common law principle designed to protect the independence of the judge from disappointed litigants. Constitutional provisions prohibiting the reduction of judicial salaries and granting to judges terms of office considerably longer than those enjoyed by other public officials are clearly intended to secure the independence of the judiciary from the imposition of penalties by the other branches of government or by popular majorities. In addition, a handful of states, modeling on the federal system, provide for their judges to serve "during good behavior"; their removal can then be accomplished only by conviction after impeachment, a procedure requiring an extraordinary legislative majority and reserved, at least by historical tradition, to the case of the corrupt, incompetent, or incapable judge and not invoked against judges who have made unpopular rulings or policy decisions.[75]

Life tenure is perhaps the surest protection of judicial independence. Dean Robert F. Drinan's perceptive statement about the role of life tenure for judicial decision-making reflects the concern which critics of judicial elections have for the insulation of judicial decision-makers. "The qualities imputed to judges with life tenure are a kind of impartiality and even a certain infallibility with regard to the basic norms of justice; these qualities are possible, presumably, only because judges with life tenure are liberated from the fear that public officials adversely affected by their decisions might remove the judges whose decisions are contrary to their interests."[76]

Against this background it is not surprising that advocates of the merit plan see it as the selection method most likely to ensure judicial independence by securing for judges long terms of office and insulating them from the vicissitudes of current political controversies. Competitive elections are seen as inconsistent with judicial independence because they threaten to interrupt a judge's tenure.

Whether judges should be independent or held accountable for the exercise of their powers is a value-laden question that empirical research is ill-equipped to resolve. But it is noteworthy that only a few states have awarded life tenures to their judges.[77] Instead, most states provide for their judges to hold fixed terms of office but terms which are considerably longer than those served by executive and legislative officers,[78] reflecting the simultaneously powerful strains in American thought which support both the value of judicial independence and the periodic accountability of a policy-making branch to the electorate or its representatives.

## JUDICIAL ACCOUNTABILITY:
## DO ELECTIONS GUARANTEE POPULAR CONTROL?

The critics of judicial elections do not rest their case solely on the requirement of judicial independence. Additionally, they argue that even if the need for judicial accountability is recognized elections are nevertheless ineffective mechanisms for securing popular control over the courts.

This is the most fundamental and damning of the criticisms leveled against popular judicial elections. If elections do not hold judges accountable, as they are intended to do, then little else may commend them over other methods of selection. Although elections might serve other functions in terms both of individual voters and the larger political system, their role in enabling the public to assert control over the course of judicial policy-making is the mainstay of the argument which supports the selection of state judges by election and not by some other method. If judicial elections do not provide for such accountability, then some of the more credible claims of advocates of alternative selection systems might on balance assume greater importance. Though the asserted claim of the merit plan to improve the quality of the judiciary is most certainly overrated and while the concept of "quality" remains nebulous, it might nevertheless be the case that a nominating commission and a governor (or even a governor on his or her own) can, by virtue of the informational resources at their disposal, do a better job than the voters in successfully eliminating from consideration those individuals whose personal character or qualities make them ill-suited to hold any office of public trust, judicial or otherwise. Similarly, owing to their greater familiarity with the pool of available talent, appointing officials might be able to actively recruit qualified people to accept judicial posts. Disposing of judicial elections would also most assuredly eliminate whatever threat to judicial impartiality that might be posed by the need to repay political creditors.

The defense of popular elections must rely, therefore, upon the position that the risks which accompany popular elections in terms of the potential for the selection of judges of inferior quality as well as actual or possible threats to the impartiality and integrity of the judicial process are outweighed by the popular accountability of the judiciary secured by elections.

Before reviewing the specific arguments raised by the critics skeptical of the ability of judicial elections to hold judicial policy-makers accountable, the precise meaning of accountability and the role of elections in securing it should be made clear. Judicial elections should be measured against a standard no more, but no less, exacting than that which applies to other kinds of elections.

As Professor Gerald Pomper has so perceptively noted, elections can be viewed as producing both direct and indirect effects.[79] Classical democratic theory has centered upon the potential direct effect of elections in recruiting individuals who will carry out the specific directives of the voters on the major policy issues of the moment. Direct control of policy through the electoral process demands that voters make well-informed, principled, and rational decisions in the choice of political leaders. In order to make such decisions, voters necessarily have to possess intense feelings about political issues, accurate information about the policy views of competing candidates, and the ability to evaluate at subsequent elections the performance by public officials on specific issues.[80]

The results of empirical research conducted during the 1950s on the characteristics of voters and the nature of their voting behavior were disappointing to the classical view, however. The evidence pointed to "a citizenry ... demonstrably inattentive to public affairs, uncertain of the principles of democracy, and unsophisticated in its attitudes toward parties, politicians, and policies."[81] Only a small proportion of the population were found to have opinions on the major political issues about which they felt intensely and for which they could perceive party or candidate differences that might determine their voting choice. Indeed, there was but a limited consensus among voters about which party favored which approaches or solutions to the major public policy problems.[82]

For some political observers these results confirming the inadequacy of the voting citizen portended the failure of democratic government.[83] For others, the theory setting forth the prerequisites of democratic political systems required revision.[84] For others still, like Pomper, the results only had to be interpreted in light of different criteria.[85] As E. E. Schattschneider once pointed out, "the beginning of wisdom in democratic theory is to distinguish between the things the people can do and the things the people cannot do."[86] Elections should not be evaluated in terms of their role in permitting the citizenry to directly control public policy, something they are neither equipped nor disposed to do. Indeed, it is doubtful whether elections could serve as instruments for securing direct popular control over policy even if voters did possess the necessary qualities.[87] The choices between competing candidates made by a majority of voters cannot serve as a mandate for specific policy initiatives by those elected; such choices do not reflect the multitude of issues at stake in an election, the distribution of voter preferences over the spectrum of issues, and the intensity of preferences voters display among issues. Accordingly, the indirect effects of elections need to be appreciated.

Among the indirect virtues of elections are the legitimacy and power they invest in governmental institutions and officials and the contribution they make to the personal development of the members of the polity. But the most important of the indirect effects is the check which elections allow voters to impose upon the exercise of governmental power.[88] Admittedly, voters do not and probably cannot inform themselves on the details of the wide range of problems facing government and the merits of the variety of proposed solutions which government officials might adopt. But the important point is that voters *need not* be interested enough and informed enough to choose their leaders on the basis of specific policy issues. Though they cannot control the details of policy, voters can influence the *direction* of policy formulation. By exercising their control over the selection and tenure of public officials, voters can set effective limits upon the policy initiatives of government. "The voters play an indirect role in the determination of public policy. The actual decisions about the actions of government must be left to the initiatives of officials and their complex bargaining. Voters, however, can meaningfully intervene to support a leadership group which is seeking to enact a particular program. By their endorsement of particular contestants in the bargaining process, the voters can have the final word. The choice of governors can thereby become a choice of governmental policy."[89] Or, as Pomper noted elsewhere, "The electorate does not decide policy; it accepts or rejects politicians associated with policies."[90]

Those scholars who have evaluated elections in terms of their indirect effects have viewed the empirical evidence concerning the nature of the electorate with greater approbation. Voters are not the "philosophical citizens" demanded by classical democratic theory, but neither are they "manipulated subjects," driven in their voting behavior by irrational considerations unrelated to policy. Voters are best characterized as "meddling partisans" guided in their behavior to a greater or lesser degree by their psychological identification with a political party.[91] Early voting research concluded that this psychological allegiance is developed early in life, primarily the product of parental imitation. Nevertheless, party affiliation provides voters with an internal mechanism for organizing and understanding political information and serving to structure their perceptions and choices. Scholars who performed the pioneering studies of voting behavior concluded that though voters are not well informed on specific policy issues and only a fraction of them see the parties in highly ideological terms, most are at least capable of making political evaluations in terms of the group interests advanced by each party and their (the voters') satisfaction with the "nature of the times" under the party in office.[92] "The electorate does not determine the full governmental program, but it can judge its effects later."[93]

The ability of the electorate to pass this kind of retrospective judgment upon the performance of elected officeholders on election day does not end their indirect influence over the course of policy, however. Elected officials must anticipate the policies which they believe the voters want and then act accordingly.[94] Though free from specific instructions from the electorate, the officeholders know that, whatever they do, they will be called to account for their actions. Thus, though voters may not demonstrate a great deal of interelection attention to political issues, they can have a continuing interelection influence upon the resolution of those issues.

More-current evidence suggests that at least in recent presidential elections voters have been more frequently drawn away from their traditional partisan affiliations when their evaluations of candidates and issues have warranted it. The relatively high salience of presidential campaigns has meant that candidates are being evaluated less in terms of their partisan ties and more in terms of voter perceptions of candidate competence and issue positions. To some extent, voting in presidential elections has become prospective in nature as voters cast their ballots "in expectation of future performance on the part of the candidate."[95] But in balloting below the presidential level, in races which do not stimulate voter interest in specific candidates and issues, the party cue remains a preeminent factor in structuring the vote and one which allows voters to exercise indirect control over the past and future direction of governmental policies.[96]

Utilizing a standard which focuses on the indirect effects of elections, electoral accountability has several conditions. First, the electorate must be able to pass judgment upon the performance of elected officials at regular and periodic intervals. Second, the electorate must be provided with the opportunity to express a choice between opposing candidates; in expressing dissatisfaction with the performance of an incumbent, an alternative choice must be available. Third, the voters must be able to identify officials with the policies they have made and, concurrently, to know in a general way what kinds of policies the challenger can be expected to promote once in office. Finally, those who win public office by election must behave "in accordance with their pre-election attitudes . . . If voters prefer the more conservative candidate but if, once elected, he behaves as his more liberal opponent would have, the electorate has been deceived in its efforts to exercise control of policies."[97]

When these conditions are satisfied, elections may be said to secure the popular accountability of elected officials. Indirect control over policy is maintained by voters who can pass a retrospective judgment upon the performance of elected officials as well as exercise a prospective influence on the course of policy through the choice of officials who either share the interests, attitudes, and values of their constituency or possess a realistic fear of the electorate's power of removal and adjust their behavior accordingly.

Against these standards of accountability, several damning indictments have been filed against judicial elections. In the first place, it has been argued that popular control over the judiciary is inhibited by the fact that judicial election campaigns do not involve a discussion by opposing candidates of substantive issues of judicial policy. Indeed, most critics would view the discussion of judicial philosophies by candidates or their positions on policy issues which have or are likely to come before them while on the bench to be a violation of legal ethics and informal norms governing the conduct of judicial campaigns. In order to protect the integrity and impartiality of the adjudicatory process, it is thought that the kind of information which voters need to make an informed choice between judicial candidates and to evaluate past judicial decisions must necessarily be withheld. At best, therefore, judicial candidates must appeal to the electorate on the basis of their respective professional qualifications and debate questions of judicial administration and court reform, matters unrelated to the policies made by judicial decision-makers in the course of deciding disputes between particular litigants.

Second, due to the issueless and lackluster campaigns, critics urge that public attention to judicial election contests is low. And due to this lack of interest, it is argued that the public is not interested in informing itself about the qualifications of those candidates seeking judicial office. Thus, in a vicious-circle phenomenon, many people are unlikely to vote in the judicial election. Drawn to the polls by the salient races on the ballot, such as those for president, governor, and congressman, voters leave blank the choices for judicial officers, contests about which they know nothing and care less. Those voters who do vote, moreover, have no rational basis for making a choice between opposing candidates. Critics point to numerous public opinion surveys documenting voter ignorance about judicial campaigns and candidates. Uninformed, the electorate must vote blindly and rely upon indiscriminate voting cues provided by a party label, a familiar name, or a vague campaign image. Popular control over the judiciary and the maintenance of the principle of judicial accountability are impossible, say the critics, if voters know not for whom or what they are voting.

Third, it is argued that popular control over the judiciary is threatened by the fact that judicial elections are rarely seriously contested. Incumbents are often re-elected with no opposition; even when challengers are present, incumbents tend to win runaway victories. Representative of a dominant party in the state or possessing a name and reputation more familiar to the voters, incumbents enjoy secure tenure in elections which "resemble plebiscites" and "do not seriously threaten the judge's tenure or force him to defend his decisions,"[98] conditions which would appear essential to permit voters to pass retrospective judgment upon the judicial performance.

Infrequently challenged and rarely defeated, the incumbents of judicial office enjoy long careers of service on the bench. In addition to serving formal terms of office much longer than those awarded to elected executives and legislators, the realities of judicial politics allow judges to serve well into the later years of their lives. As a result, many judges either die in office or are forced by the infirmities of old age to retire in the middle of an elected term. The power to fill these interim vacancies, however, rests not with the electorate but with the state's governor, a power which goes unchecked by the state legislature or any other confirming body. At the first election following appointment, the governor's choice may be subject to the electorate's direct check and removed. Given the nature of the judicial election process and the character of the judicial electorate, however, the incumbent is nearly certain to be retained. Thus, say the critics, effective control over the process of judicial selection and tenure really rests with the governor. Direct popular accountability is an illusion. Nor is an electorate, incapable or unwilling itself to remove an appointee of whom it disapproves, likely to exercise secondary control by electorally punishing the governor who made the initial selection.

## THE NEED FOR EMPIRICAL RESEARCH

The attacks leveled against judicial elections would be their death toll were they well supported by empirical evidence. But the descriptions of judicial elections offered by critics have more often than not consisted of the unsystematic personal accounts and anecdotes of observers. When in those few instances empirical evidence drawn from the experience of particular state or local jurisdictions has been offered, the results have too often been uncritically extrapolated to characterize judicial elections generally. Students of the electoral process are painfully aware, however, that neither the characteristics of elections nor the behavior of electorates is subject to a single generalization. Elections conducted under different institutional and structural arrangements and in varying political environments exhibit distinctive qualities. And apart from the psychological and sociological determinants of the individual vote, the behavior of voters in the aggregate is likewise affected by election structures and political circumstances. Generalizing about judicial elections, therefore, from the experiences of separate jurisdictions is extremely misleading.

As the preceding discussion suggests, recent empirical analyses of the merit plan in actual operation make it clear that the expectations of reformers have not been fully realized. Indeed, the goals of "eliminating politics" from the process of judicial selection and recruiting the "highest quality" bench are considerably overrated. Alternatively, it is not unrealistic to expect that once judicial elections are subjected to a comparable searching empirical inspection their alleged defects may be revealed as exaggerations and their positive role in securing judicial accountability can then be more fully appreciated.

The data collected and analyzed here seek initially to document the level of participation, the extent of competition, and the patterns of the vote in state judicial elections. Beyond that, an inquiry into the consequences of judicial elections for the behavior of elected judges will be launched in an attempt to test the strength of the linkage between the electorate and judicial policy-makers.

This linkage might be forged in any one or combination of several possible ways. First, voters might select judges on the basis of their (the voters') understanding of the qualifications and specific policy stands of opposing judicial candidates. However, if judicial campaigns are typical of other subpresidential contests, the candidates for state supreme court judge are not likely to attract much attention and, consequently, the level of specific voter awareness and knowledge about the qualifications and policy positions of judicial hopefuls is not likely to be very high. Voters may thus have to rely upon less-direct indicators and cues to guide them in their choice between competing judicial candidates. Where a party label is available, voters are most likely to call upon it to help them cast their ballots. If the results of previous research are considered, such voting behavior is not irrational from the standpoint of the individual voter since party labels identify, in a general way, the kinds of policies voters can expect from individual judges on the bench wearing each label. Where no party label is present, voters may be forced to rely upon more problematic guides to the policy orientations of judicial candidates, such as incumbency or name familiarity. A final link between the electorate and their judicial policy-makers may be closed only after a successful candidate has assumed his or her position on the bench. If elected officials who occupy the judicial branch are like elected officials in the other branches, they can be expected to observe the rule of anticipated reactions by behaving in ways which will satisfy those segments of the electorate that campaigned and voted for them (and, it is hoped, will do so in the future) and, more importantly, which will forestall the dissatisfaction of the general electoral constituency that secured their victory.

# 2. Turnout in State Judicial Elections

## INTRODUCTION

Critics of judicial elections have most frequently pointed to low voter turnout as the leading indicator that voters lack the necessary interest in, and knowledge about, contests for judicial office. The low level of voter participation in judicial elections is cited as evidence that an indifferent, apathetic, and ignorant electorate is unwilling and incapable of holding its judiciary accountable through elections.

This argument is based upon the observation that large numbers of voters who go to the polls to cast ballots in the major federal and state executive and legislative races opt to leave their ballots blank for the choice of judges. In reports from several separate states utilizing partisan or nonpartisan elections, observers have suggested that anywhere from one-fifth to one-half of those attending the polls regularly fail to vote in the judicial balloting. Even in those states where political party organizations actively promote their judicial candidates, many voters simply ignore the less familiar judicial contests.[1]

Low voter turnout has also plagued those states utilizing the merit retention ballot. Ostensibly designed to permit the electorate to remove judges appointed through the merit selection process but who subsequently have demonstrated their unsuitability for judicial office, the merit retention election draws few voters. Watson and Downing found that only 54% of the votes cast in the 1964 race for Missouri state attorney general were cast on the retention question for each of two supreme court justices; circuit judgeship retention elections drew a more dismal turnout still.[2]

Generally, then, the picture painted of state judicial elections by most critics is that low voter turnout is the natural response of voters to elections about which they know nothing and care less.

Surveys, moreover, confirm that the saliency for voters of the judicial contests and the level of voter information regarding judicial campaigns are extremely low. Most frequently cited are the findings of a 1954 survey in three New York counties where voter inattention and apathy concerning the races for judge resulted in a loss of from 12% to 25% in the proportion of persons who had voted in the partisan contests for governor and congress member. More importantly, however, of those who *did* vote in the judicial races, at the very most less than one-half had paid attention to the judicial campaign and less than one-third could name even one judicial candidate for whom they had voted.[3] Comparable findings have characterized subsequent surveys of the judicial electorate.[4]

The low level of voter participation in state judicial elections is not particularly surprising when one considers the nature of these electoral contests. They are, in the words of two observers,[5] "uninteresting" and "placid" events, rarely featuring the kinds of visible candidates, controversial issues, and spirited campaign activity and accompanying media attention which draw voters to the polls for the major executive and legislative races.

Despite what appears to be the general state of the judicial electorate, however, it is not necessarily the case that the level of voter attention to and knowledge about judicial elections cannot be elevated. Some of the recent proposals to accomplish this will be reviewed in the chapter which follows. Nor is it certain, moreover, that the low level of voter interest in judicial elections is the sole determinant of the size of the participating electorate. Most of what is known about turnout in judicial elections has come from isolated reports in separate states. But in evaluating these reports, little attention has been paid to the variety of electoral arrangements and political conditions under which these elections have been conducted. Systematic attention to the determinants of judicial election turnout in the tradition of electoral analysis of the most salient national and state elections has only recently been of scholarly interest.[6] Only one, rather limited, comparative multistate perspective on judicial election turnout has been attempted,[7] and no study has addressed in detail those factors which might contribute to variations in the level of participation.

If judicial election turnout in the various states consistently lags by a large margin behind the turnout for the more-salient statewide races, then the position of the critics of popular election is strengthened considerably. But if significant variations in judicial election turnout are detected, and these variations are found to be the product primarily of the same factors which affect turnout for the other kinds of elections, then reformers must re-evaluate at least this aspect of their assault on popular elections. "The null hypothesis would be that no substantial difference exists between participation in judicial contests and participation in other races. . . . If the null hypothesis could not be rejected, it would indicate that whatever the turnout rate was in judicial contests, it reflected a 'normal' rate of participation for the electorate. In this scenario, the argument that voters are unattuned or apathetic about judicial races would lose its vitality since it would reflect a malaise of the system, not one kind of political office."[8]

To the extent that the level of popular participation in state judicial contests can be manipulated by institutional arrangements relating to the conduct of elections, then that portion of the case for the abolition of popular election based on the low level of public participation in the selection of state judges is most certainly undermined. Equally important is the possibility that election arrangements which affect the size of the judicial electorate may also shape its composition and, at least potentially, the overall preferences of the electorate with respect to issue orientation and candidate choice. Election procedures may, therefore, determine not just the size of judicial electorates but the results of judicial elections as well. Finally, election arrangements may be found to affect the quality and not merely the quantity of public participation. If elections are the instruments by which citizens select those who will judge them, the channels through which their policy preferences are indirectly expressed, and the vehicles for the expression of discontent, then certain election arrangements may allow them to perform these functions better than others. These inquiries must be reserved for at least partial consideration in the next chapter.

## THE DETERMINANTS OF VOTER TURNOUT

Students of the electoral process have devoted a substantial portion of their efforts to developing propositions to explain the level of voter turnout in national, state, and local elections. A major portion of the academic literature has focused on the relationship of personal motivational patterns to the act of voting. At the individual level, survey research has paved the way to understanding the inclination of the voter to vote or not to vote.[9] At the aggregate level, inferences about individual voter motivations are drawn from the differential association of certain socioeconomic and demographic profiles of the electorate with voting rates.[10]

An equally fundamental approach has been to investigate the importance of various elements of "the political system" to the level of voter turnout in national, state, and local elections. Students have focused in particular on the effects of electoral arrangements and legal structures and the impact of the political party system upon election participation. This approach has called primarily upon aggregate level data, but the theoretic tie to individual voter motivation has been implicit.[11] For example, state election laws which require all persons to meet certain minimal requirements before being permitted to vote have been viewed and tested as an important factor influencing voter turnout. Requirements of citizenship, age, and residency define the eligible electorate. But complex registration procedures buttressed by such familiar devices as literacy tests and poll taxes are among the additional restrictive legal and administrative barriers to the exercise of the franchise which have been erected.[12] Moreover, the relative ease of voting on election day, affected by such factors as the length of voting hours and provisions for the casting of absentee ballots, may facilitate or retard voter participation.[13] The "high cost" of voting created by these laws may simply discourage the eligible voter from going to the polls by making voting inconvenient, difficult, or even impossible.

Elements of the party system have also been viewed as influencing voter turnout. Indeed, the relationship of interparty electoral competition to turnout may have been, at least until recently, among the most revered of political science propositions. Under conditions of competition between the political parties for the control of public offices, it is thought that each party will have an incentive to encourage participation among its supporters, hence raising the overall level of voting.[14] Moreover, "party competition probably affects participation by stimulating interest in a campaign and giving citizens the impression that their individual efforts affect the outcome."[15]

In addition to a milieu of competition which encourages turnout, the characteristics of specific elections may have an influence on whether those who are eligible choose to go to the polls. When voters perceive that an election is important or that their individual votes are crucial to the outcome, they are more likely to participate than when they view an election as unimportant in its consequences or their votes as unessential.[16]

Thus, American presidential elections typically produce the highest turnout of the electorate, nationally about 60% of the voting-age population.[17] Voters perceive the office and the issues as important, close contests are usually anticipated, relatively clear alternative choices are provided, and other campaign stimuli (like party activity, media attention, and the clash of the candidates' personalities) combine to spark voter interest and participation every fourth year. State and local elections held concurrently with the presidential contest are high-turnout elections as well, riding primarily on the "coattails" of the main event.[18] When these state and local contests are scheduled in nonpresidential years, however, not even those most salient for the voters, such as the races for governor, U.S. senator, or congress member, can draw the attention of the voters witnessed in the quadrennial sweepstakes.[19] The host of conditions which combine to produce high turnout in presidential years and lower turnout in nonpresidential years have been collected by scholars under the rubric of electoral effects due to election scheduling.

A further decline in turnout has been observed in elections where the competition between the political parties has been formally removed. For instance, turnout in primary elections for president, governor, and U.S. senator has been found to lag far behind the levels observed in general elections for these offices.[20] Initially, of course, election laws and procedures governing the conduct of primary elections restrict voter participation. Beyond the usual requirements of voter registration, for instance, many states require registered voters to formally specify a party affiliation in order to vote in a party's primary, a requirement disenfranchising those who choose not to specify a party preference. But apart from the restrictions which accompany the closed-party primary, turnout is lower in primaries among the eligible pool of party registrants than turnout in general elections among those eligible to vote.[21] It may be that the nominating process is not perceived by voters to be as important as the final selection of public officials.[22] Moreover, since primaries are intraparty struggles, clear alternatives which inspire participation may not be perceived by the voter without the guiding cue of party identification to separate the candidates both during the campaign and on the ballot.[23] Finally, since primary elections are scheduled in the months preceding general elections, they do not benefit from the concurrence with a more salient race which draws voters to the polls.

Similarly, turnout declines in nonpartisan general elections. Primarily used for the selection of local public officials, the nonpartisan ballot has been associated with low rates of voter participation.[24] Researchers have been unclear as to whether the turnout in nonpartisan elections is attributable to the ballot form or to the complex of political and socioeconomic factors which accompany such contests.[25] But it can be safely concluded that local elections generally lack those conditions which produce an election that stimulates voter interest and participation. Additionally, local non-partisan races are most often scheduled so as not to coincide with the contesting of the major partisan races; elections held in the November of odd-numbered years or, more commonly, elections held in the spring are designed to insulate these contests from the influences of party politics.[26] Even when they are scheduled concurrently with the biennial fall elections, however, turnout in non-partisan elections is lower.[27] The nonpartisan ballot probably functions much like a primary, removing the clash of party candidates and the guidance of party labels from the consideration of potential voters.

Finally, electoral analysts have devoted some study to the influence of ballots on election day. This has been an important question because although high-stimulus elections, like those for the presidency, may be most responsible for drawing voters to the polling place in the first place, other important national, state, and local races are often determined at the same time and on the same ballot. The ballot form has been viewed as an important factor which may facilitate or impede voter "turnout" for the offices listed below the top of the ballot. V. O. Key estimated that the length of the American ballot discourages perhaps as much as 30% of the voters from reaching the bottom of the ballot where the less conspicuous offices and popular referenda are decided.[28] Other students have examined the extent to which various balloting techniques and ballot formats contribute to or relieve "voter fatigue" or "roll-off," the tendency of weary or confused voters to refrain from voting on offices or measures located near the bottom of a lengthy ballot.[29]

## TURNOUT IN STATE JUDICIAL ELECTIONS

With but two recent exceptions, scholars have not applied to the study of judicial elections the propositions which contribute to an explanation of variations in electoral turnout.

Susan Blackmore Hannah examined the levels of voter participation, electoral competition, and the political and socioeconomic bases of voting patterns in Michigan's nonpartisan elections for supreme court and circuit court judges from 1948 to 1968.[30] Hannah's analysis of turnout confirmed that Michigan judicial elections follow the general rule that participation is affected by election scheduling. Judicial elections held concurrently with the quadrennial presidential election had the highest turnout, followed by those held concurrently with the biennial gubernatorial elections in the mid-term years, with the lowest turnout observed in the spring elections. Further, as other studies had found, Hannah's results indicated that judicial election turnout in any given election year lagged far behind that for the more visible races at the top of the ticket. The mean turnout by county in supreme court races ranged from 60% to 81% of the turnout in the partisan statewide office drawing the most voters in the election.[31]

Finally, Hannah found no significant differences in turnout in state supreme court races which could be explained as a function of judicial election competition. Because candidates for the Michigan Supreme Court are nominated by party convention, judicial elections are always contested and thus voters are consistently given the opportunity to express a preference. But Hannah's rank-order comparison of the statewide turnout (measured as a percentage of the turnout in the top partisan race) in seventeen supreme court races and the degree of competitiveness (measured by the closeness of the vote) yielded an unexpected slightly negative correlation.[32]

A recent examination of voter turnout in five states during the 1960s also suggests in a comparative context the effects of scheduling arrangements and ballot forms upon the levels of judicial election participation.[33] This analysis first affirmed the general proposition that election scheduling appears to have a major impact upon turnout in judicial elections. Judicial elections held concurrently with the presidential elections drew a higher turnout than elections held in the mid-term November elections. The mid-term elections likewise attracted more people to participate on the judicial ballot than did elections held in the fall of odd-numbered years, as is done occasionally in Pennsylvania and New York. Voter turnout was found to be lowest in the nonconcurrent spring judicial contests held in Wisconsin and Michigan.[34] Second, the partisan ballot form allowed a higher level of voter turnout than did the nonpartisan ballot form. In Pennsylvania and New York, where the partisan ballot was used, voters participated at about the same rate as in the concurrent high-salience gubernatorial races. The nonpartisan ballot had the effect of dramatically reducing turnout in the selection of judges.[35]

Finally, it was found that salient races which attract public attention may pull voters to the polls who then incidentally vote for judicial candidates. In Wisconsin, for instance, where the spring judicial election coincides every fourth year with the presidential primary, turnout jumped dramatically above its usual level.[36] The

Wisconsin data also suggested that highly salient referenda decided in Wisconsin's spring election could increase voter turnout in the judicial race.[37] The importance of concurrent scheduling was also confirmed by the finding that turnout in Wisconsin supreme court races was insignificantly altered by the existence of a competitive judicial race; competitive presidential primaries, however, pulled judicial turnout up considerably.[38]

These research efforts suggest that a comparative, multistate examination of turnout in judicial elections conducted under a variety of partisanship systems, scheduling arrangements, and ballot formats would be particularly fruitful. The application to the study of judicial contests of those general propositions developed by scholars to explain why people vote should indicate the extent to which the level of participation in state supreme court elections is typical or atypical of the pattern of participation for other kinds of elections and whether judicial election turnout is a function of the same or different variables that affect voting in other contests.

## PARTICIPATION IN STATE JUDICIAL ELECTIONS, 1948–1974

This study examines voter turnout in elections held for justices of state courts of last resort in twenty-five nonsouthern states from 1948 to 1974.[39] All the nonsouthern states utilizing partisan, non-partisan, and merit retention ballots on a statewide basis during this period were included.[40] The essential focus of this analysis is cross-sectional and comparative. Unlike previous studies, the data also allow a longitudinal perspective on the determinants of judicial election turnout in a number of states. Several of the states studied changed their judicial election system during the 1948 to 1974 interim. It is thus possible to examine the immediate effect of these changes, in most states from a partisan judicial ballot to a merit retention ballot, upon the level of turnout in judicial elections.

No attempt will be made here to explain all of the interstate differences in judicial election turnout. Among other things, the analysis indicates that the general level of judicial election turnout in any one state is in large measure the product of those factors which draw voters to the polls for the most salient partisan races. As analysts have begun recently to explore, turnout is the result of a complex of individual and systemic variables that are legal, political, and socioeconomic in nature. The contribution of each set of factors to turnout in the major statewide ballotings is now getting increased and well-deserved systematic attention.[41] The analysis here is more limited in its objectives, recognizing the interstate variations and setting as its primary goal the preliminary mapping of the dimensions of participation in state supreme court elections. These are races which are probably not foremost in the minds of most voters when they go to the polls. Rather, drawn to the election to cast ballots for a major partisan office like president, governor, U.S. senator, or congress member, the voter is asked to make additional choices among competing candidates for statewide offices like lieutenant governor, attorney general, secretary of state, and state supreme court judge, as well as for state legislative and local government posts. The goal here is to understand the level of turnout in state judicial elections and the variation among states not attributable to differences in turnout for the major races at the top of the ballot.

### Aggregate Level of Turnout in Judicial Elections

As scholars have demonstrated with respect to the level of turnout in major statewide elections, great variation characterizes the level of participation in elections for justices to sit on state courts of last resort. For judicial elections held in presidential election years, the mean turnout in the states ranges from a high of 72.8% in Utah's partisan judicial elections to a low of 27.7% in Indiana's merit retention election in 1972. A similar variation can be observed for elections held in the mid-term election years, from Utah's mean turnout of 67.1% to Indiana's dismal turnout of only 19.9% of the state's population of voting age casting ballots in the uncontested retention elections.

The turnout in judicial elections is considerably more variable among these states than the turnout levels observed for major national and state elections.[42] In turn, we can now consider the extent to which this variability is attributable to election scheduling, the type of election system, ballot formats, and the extent of electoral competition.

### The Effects of Election Scheduling

Previous studies have consistently shown that the stimulus attaching to presidential elections draws more voters to the polls than for any other election. Participation in presidential election years is heightened by the participation of both "peripheral" and "core" voters.[43] "Core" voters are those individuals "whose level of political interest is sufficiently high to take them to the polls in all national elections," even those held in the mid-term where the amount of stimulation is low.[44] The core voters are joined in the presidential election years by the "peripheral" voters "whose level of political interest is lower but whose motivation to vote has been sufficiently increased by the stimulation of the election to carry them to the polls."[45] According to Angus Campbell, the absence of the peripheral voters in the low-stimulus mid-term elections and their presence in the high-stimulus presidential elections accounts for the predictable "surge and decline" of turnout. In those elections held in the off-year or in the off-season, only the most politically interested voters from among the "core" electorate, what we euphemistically might call the "hard core" voters, are motivated enough to go to the polls to vote in electoral contests which provide only minimal political stimulation to the rest of the population.

These expectations with respect to state judicial elections are confirmed in a state-by-state inspection of the impact of scheduling upon voter participation. In every state but one, the mean turnout in presidential years exceeds turnout in the mid-term election years.[46] The differences between the mean turnout in presidential and mid-term election years range from a low of .7% in South Dakota to a high of over 23% in Iowa.

Turnout declines further still in judicial elections scheduled in off-years or off-seasons. In New York and Pennsylvania, for example, turnout in supreme court elections conducted in odd-numbered years fell an average of 5.5% and 8.6%, respectively, below turnout in the mid-term elections. In Michigan, where until 1963 some judicial elections were conducted in the spring, mean turnout dipped to 18.2%, cutting the mean turnout witnessed for the state's mid-term judicial elections almost by half. Finally, in Wisconsin, where state supreme court posts have been scheduled only in the spring, mean turnout has averaged about 29%, but it has dipped as low as 18.6% and has climbed as high as 43.0%, generally rising when the judicial race has been accompanied by a presidential primary or salient referenda balloting; the average turnout in the presidential primary years has been 37.8%.

Election scheduling, therefore, explains a great deal about judicial election turnout. Indeed, it is logical to assume that the overall level of participation in a state's judicial elections is largely a reflection of turnout for the major statewide and national contests which pull voters to the polls in the first place. It is also true, however, that those states with high levels of participation in the major races of president, governor, and U.S. senator are not necessarily the same as those with high judicial election turnout. Further, the range among

**Table 1. *Mean Turnout in State Judicial Elections***

|  | Concurrent Elections | | Nonconcurrent Elections | |
| --- | --- | --- | --- | --- |
|  | Presidential Years | Mid-Term Years | Odd-No. Years | Off-Season |
| Partisan ballot | 62.4% (N = 58) | 50.3% (N = 56) | 43.1% (N = 11) | None |
| Nonpartisan ballot | 45.0% (N = 145) | 38.7% (N = 141) | None | 25.7% (N = 31) |
| Merit retention ballot | 38.2% (N = 44) | 32.4% (N = 54) | None | None |

NOTE: Turnout is measured as a proportion of the population of voting age in each state. These figures are not substantially altered when the data are averaged across states instead of by elections as has been done in this table and in every other presentation of tabular data in this chapter.

the states in the rate of turnout in judicial elections is nearly twenty percentage points wider than in the major partisan contests found at the top of the ballot. Judicial election turnout, then, is not merely "the tail on the electoral kite"; factors other than the scheduling of judicial elections concurrently with high-salience races must be considered as possible determinants of judicial election participation.

Table I suggests that judicial election participation is, at least to some extent, independent of the turnout for the major partisan nonjudicial races. Table I displays the mean level of judicial election turnout in partisan, nonpartisan, and merit retention elections held under a variety of scheduling arrangements. Though confirming the effects of election scheduling upon judicial election turnout, the data also suggest that the election system may have an important separate impact upon the level of voter participation. Regardless of the scheduling of the election, the mean level of judicial election turnout is higher under the partisan ballot than under the nonpartisan or merit retention ballots.

Unfortunately, as long as judicial election turnout is measured as a proportion of the voting-age population, the contaminating effect of those races at the top of the ballot which pull voters out on election day obscures the impact of the judicial election system upon the level of participation. Measuring judicial election turnout in a slightly different manner, therefore, allows further exploration of this branch of analysis.

## The Effects of the Election System

When judicial election turnout is calculated not as a percentage of the adult population of voting age but as a percentage of the vote cast for the "major partisan office" at the top of the ballot in each election year, the data more clearly suggest that judicial election turnout is not solely the result of election scheduling and turnout at the top of the ballot.[47] Rather, there is a considerable variation among the states in the proportion of voters who manage to complete their ballots and to cast their votes for state supreme court justice. And among these states, it appears that a greater percentage of voters complete their judicial ballots in the states utilizing partisan ballots than in those utilizing the nonpartisan or merit retention ballot forms. Among the partisan states, in both presidential and mid-term election years, an average of from approximately 87% to 99% of the voters casting ballots in the major partisan race also cast ballots in the supreme court contest. Among the nonpartisan states, however, there is a much larger variation in the proportion of voters completing their ballots in the judicial race, ranging from an average of slightly over 84% in Idaho to a mere 52% in South Dakota's non-partisan supreme court elections. Finally, among the states utilizing the merit retention ballot, anywhere from nearly 90% of the voters (in Alaska) to well less than half of the voters casting ballots in the major partisan contest also expressed some opinion on whether or not sitting judges should be retained in office. Table 2 summarizes these observations. Among states utilizing the partisan judicial ballot, the mean proportion of voters completing their judicial ballots is over 90% in both presidential and mid-term election years. This proportion drops substantially among the nonpartisan states on the average, however, to about 70% and declines further still among the merit retention states to the 60% level. Clearly, therefore, the type of election system has some independent impact upon the level of judicial election turnout apart from election scheduling.

Though there is a significant amount of variation among the individual states within each kind of election system type that requires explanation, the clear difference between the rate of participation in judicial elections conducted under the partisan ballot, on the one hand, and those held under nonpartisan or merit retention ballots, on the other, is easily understood in light of the principles of voter behavior uncovered by previous electoral research.

First, it is well established that the nature of the nonpartisan ballot discourages voter participation. Studies have repeatedly docu-

**Table 2.** *Mean Roll-off in State Judicial Elections*

|  | Presidential Years | Mid-Term Years |
|---|---|---|
| Partisan ballot | 91.5% (N = 58) | 91.6% (N = 51) |
| Nonpartisan ballot | 67.6% (N = 145) | 71.7% (N = 130) |
| Merit retention ballot | 59.8% (N = 44) | 63.9% (N = 50) |

NOTE: The percentages displayed here represent the number of voters casting ballots in each state judicial election as a proportion of the total number of voters casting ballots in the "major partisan race" in that year. The "major partisan race" was defined as the presidential, gubernatorial, or U.S. senatorial contest which attracted the most voters in each election year.

Judicial elections held under nonconcurrent scheduling arrangements have been excluded since "major partisan races" (as defined above) were not widely contested at the same time. Similarly, judicial elections held in mid-term years in which no partisan race at the top of the ballot was decided have been excluded as well.

mented that the single most important cue for voting for the American voter is the individual's partisan affiliation.[48] And the voter's psychological attachment to one or the other of the major political parties is constantly reinforced by partisan messages released during the election campaign. Moreover, it is clear that as the office being contested is less important to the voter and the candidates competing for such low-salience offices are less familiar and the issues less visible, the voter will rely less upon short-term considerations of particular candidates and issues and more upon long-term psychological attachment to a political party.[49] If the voter is not familiar with a particular race and has not previously decided upon a choice before entering the voting booth, the partisan label provides a cue on which a vote can be based. The nonpartisan ballot removes this all-important cue. For contests like those for state supreme court which do not attract a greal deal of public attention and in the absence of the party cue for voting, voters may become confused and bewildered. Some voters may spot a familiar name on the judicial ballot or recognize the name of the incumbent and cast a vote "reassured in those rare cases by the warmth of recognition that they can do their civic duty [vote] in a not altogether meaningless way."[50] But other voters may respond to their confusion by withdrawing their participation in the judicial race.

A similar logic would seem applicable to voters facing the uncontested merit retention ballot. In addition to lacking the cues of political party absent from the nonpartisan ballot, however, voters in the merit retention states also lack a choice between competing candidates. Of course, the psychology of the voter who is faced with an uncontested ballot can only be surmised. But it is probably the case that an uncontested race draws even less attention from the electorate than the usually low-salience judicial races do under contested circumstances. Alternatively, once in the polling booth, many voters may fail to mark the retention ballot believing that their vote will have little impact upon the final result. Others might have some kind of principled objection to casting a ballot in a race in which they are offered no choice.

Similar psychological motivations would apply of course to voters facing uncontested races in partisan or nonpartisan judicial elections. And a comparison of the rates of voter participation in contested and uncontested races in the partisan and nonpartisan states supports this proposition. In the only two partisan states experiencing uncontested races, Iowa and New Mexico, turnout in uncontested judicial elections lagged approximately 35% behind the level of participation in the contested ones. Among the nonpartisan states the roll-off from the top of the ballot was increased by uncontested ballotings in varying amounts from 5.6% to 27.5%.[51]

Thus, perhaps one of the major effects of the judicial election system upon turnout is not just the actual form of the ballot and the cues it provides to the voter but the difference in the extent of competition provided in partisan as compared to nonpartisan and merit retention ballotings. As Table 3 demonstrates, judicial elections in the partisan states are much more often contested and more frequently competitive than judicial contests in the nonpartisan states. Indeed, the incentives available for the task of recruiting candidates for judicial office under each type of system make it only natural that this should be so. In those states where judicial candidates are nominated by partisan convention or endorsed at preprimary conventions, contested races are virtually assured. The party organizations in these states are not likely to pass up the opportunity to capture a major statewide public office or at least appear to suggest an alternative to the candidate offered by the favored party.[52] Moreover, where candidates are nominated at partisan primaries, candidates may be persuaded to run for public office knowing that the party organization is willing and prepared to back their candidacy with the necessary financial and organizational resources.[53] In the nonpartisan states, however, where the parties play no formal role in nominating or recruiting judicial candidates, it may be more difficult to ensure that every supreme court race will be contested.[54] A potential candidate may be unwilling to begin the drive to collect signatures on the nominating petition without certain financial and organizational campaign assistance. Moreover, even where a campaign

**Table 3.** *Patterns of Competition in State Judicial Elections*

| State | Uncontested[a] | Noncompetitive[a] | Competitive[a] |
|---|---|---|---|
| Partisan states | | | |
| Indiana | 0.0% (N = 0) | 23.8% (N = 5) | 76.2% (N = 16) |
| Colorado | 0.0% (N = 0) | 25.0% (N = 5) | 75.0% (N = 15) |
| West Virginia | 0.0% (N = 0) | 61.1% (N = 11) | 38.9% (N = 7) |
| Kansas | 0.0% (N = 0) | 61.1% (N = 11) | 38.9% (N = 7) |
| Utah (1948–1950) | 0.0% (N = 0) | 50.0% (N = 1) | 50.0% (N = 1) |
| Iowa | 4.2% (N = 1) | 37.5% (N = 9) | 58.3% (N = 14) |
| New Mexico | 20.0% (N = 4) | 55.0% (N = 11) | 25.0% (N = 5) |
| Pennsylvania[b] | 33.3% (N = 4) | 8.3% (N = 1) | 58.3% (N = 7) |
| New York[b] | 52.2% (N = 12) | 8.7% (N = 2) | 39.1% (N = 9) |
| Nonpartisan states | | | |
| Michigan | 0.0% (N = 0) | 68.8% (N = 22) | 31.3% (N = 10) |
| Ohio | 12.2% (N = 5) | 70.7% (N = 29) | 17.1% (N = 7) |
| Montana | 20.0% (N = 5) | 56.0% (N = 14) | 24.0% (N = 6) |
| Wisconsin | 27.3% (N = 6) | 40.9% (N = 9) | 31.8% (N = 7) |
| Utah (1952–1974) | 28.6% (N = 2) | 42.8% (N = 3) | 28.6% (N = 2) |
| Minnesota | 41.7% (N = 15) | 50.0% (N = 18) | 8.3% (N = 3) |
| Wyoming | 46.7% (N = 7) | 26.7% (N = 4) | 26.7% (N = 4) |
| Idaho[c] | 52.6% (N = 10) | 36.8% (N = 7) | 10.5% (N = 2) |
| Arizona | 57.1% (N = 16) | 35.7% (N = 10) | 7.1% (N = 2) |
| North Dakota | 57.9% (N = 11) | 21.1% (N = 4) | 21.1% (N = 4) |
| Nevada | 68.4% (N = 13) | 10.5% (N = 2) | 21.1% (N = 4) |
| Washington[c] | 82.4% (N = 42) | 9.8% (N = 5) | 7.8% (N = 4) |
| Oregon[c] | 96.9% (N = 31) | 3.1% (N = 1) | 0.0% (N = 0) |
| South Dakota | 100.0% (N = 25) | 0.0% (N = 0) | 0.0% (N = 0) |

[a] An uncontested race is one in which a candidate ran unopposed in the general election for the state supreme court. A noncompetitive race is a contested election in which the winner collected more than 55% of the vote. A competitive race is a contested election in which the winner captured 55% of the vote or less. The vote totals of third-party candidates, if any, were excluded from these calculations.

[b] In both Pennsylvania and New York, candidates may in reality be unopposed but the ballot may make it appear as though a contested race is underway. Hence, turnout in these states in "uncontested" races is not depressed as it is in other states. See n. 52.

[c] These data are slightly misleading for the states of Idaho, Oregon, and Washington. In Idaho, a candidate receiving a majority of the votes cast in the nonpartisan primary is declared elected and is not required to face election in November. In Oregon and Washington, a candidate receiving a majority of primary votes runs unopposed in the general election. Thus, in each of these states the primary is often, in essence, the election, and the general election goes "uncontested."

committee and workers have been assembled to encourage a particular individual to run, few will relish the role of challenging a well-entrenched incumbent. In the partisan states, an individual may be willing to accept an apparently hopeless bid for the state judiciary out of loyalty to the organization, in hopes of a more promising future nomination, or in response to the honor bestowed by the party and its workers. But the temporary and ad hoc political organizations which form to promote judicial candidates in the nonpartisan states have none of the more permanent incentives available to the party to recruit candidates to contest judicial elections. As a result, many of the elections in the nonpartisan states feature an unchallenged incumbent.

A re-examination of the level of participation in judicial elections considering only the contested races in each state reveals that at least part of the lower level of turnout (and higher amounts of roll-off from the top of the ballot) in the nonpartisan states is due to the prevalence of uncontested races. Table 4, which displays these results in summary form, shows that in the partisan states over 90% of those voters who go to the polls to vote in the major partisan race also cast ballots in contested judicial elections. In the nonpartisan states, an average of over 75% of the voters participating in the top partisan race voted in the contested judicial balloting. If one compares these proportions with those reported in Table 2 where both contested and uncontested races were included, it is apparent that the elimination of uncontested races results in an average decline among the nonpartisan states in roll-off from the top of the ballot of about nine percentage points.

Despite this recalculation of roll-off with the exclusion of uncontested races, it is apparent that the presence or absence of a party label has the major effect upon the rate of voter participation. Even when only contested races are considered in both the partisan and nonpartisan election systems, a much larger proportion of voters going to the polls cast ballots in the judicial races held in the former than in the latter. As Table 4 shows, in presidential years 92.6% of the voters in the partisan states who voted in the top partisan race also voted in the contested judicial race. But in the nonpartisan states nearly 25% of those going to the polls and voting in the top partisan race in the presidential election year did not cast a vote in the contested nonpartisan judicial race. Similarly, in mid-term election years, nearly one-fifth of the voters abstained from voting in the nonpartisan judicial election while barely over 6% of the voters in the partisan states failed to indicate a choice in the supreme court elections.

**Table 4. *Mean Roll-off in State Judicial Elections, Contested Races Only***

|  | Presidential Years | Mid-Term Years |
|---|---|---|
| Partisan ballot | 92.6% (N = 54) | 93.8% (N = 45) |
| Nonpartisan ballot | 76.3% (N = 66) | 81.5% (N = 60) |
| Merit retention ballot | No contested elections | |

NOTE: See Table 2 note.

The extent of the differences between partisan and nonpartisan judicial election turnout is appreciated further in Table 5, where voter participation is once again measured as the percentage of the adult population of voting age in each state. The data clearly indicate that even when uncontested elections are eliminated from the analysis turnout in partisan judicial elections runs markedly ahead of turnout in nonpartisan judicial contests in both presidential and mid-term election years. In the partisan states, where over 90% of those going to the polls also vote for state supreme court justice, turnout averages 63.6% in presidential years while dropping, as expected, to 51.8% in the mid-term elections. In the nonpartisan states, however, where between one-fifth and one-quarter of the electorate who vote in the top partisan race fail to vote in the judicial race, turnout is only 50.5% in presidential years and 43.3% in the mid-term. Election turnout in those states which use the merit retention ballot falls even lower, in large measure because the voters must always face the equivalent of an uncontested election in a nonpartisan setting. Thus, on the average less than 40% of the adult population of voting age in these states express their views on the judicial retention question while less than a third do so in the retention elections held in the mid-term years.

**The Effects of the Ballot Format**

Although there are demonstrable differences which distinguish the mean turnout of the states utilizing each kind of election system, there remains a significant amount of variation among the states *within* each kind of system. Undoubtedly, differences in the socioeconomic composition, political culture, and political competition which affect voter turnout for the major partisan offices in the states also affect the general level of judicial election turnout. As noted earlier, however, the states also differ in the amount of roll-off or voter fatigue from the top of the ballot to the judicial contest. Certainly many of the factors which contribute to an explanation of

**Table 5. *Mean Turnout in State Judicial Elections,
Contested Races Only***

|  | Concurrent Elections | | Nonconcurrent Elections | |
|---|---|---|---|---|
|  | Presidential Years | Mid-Term Years | Odd-No. Years | Off-Season |
| Partisan ballot | 63.6% (N = 54) | 51.8% (N = 50) | 44.8% (N = 7) | None |
| Nonpartisan ballot | 50.5% (N = 66) | 43.3% (N = 69) | None | 25.6% (N = 25) |
| Merit retention ballot[a] | 38.2% (N = 44) | 32.3% (N = 55) | None | None |

NOTE: See Table I note.

[a] None of the merit retention ballots are contested, of course.

turnout, particularly those relating to the nature of the electorate, might also explain differential amounts of roll-off. But a major possible explanation is that differences among the states in ballot format, whether the ballot is partisan, nonpartisan, or merit retention, may explain differing amounts of voter fatigue.

Among the partisan states, two basic ballot forms are in use and each is believed to have some effect upon the amount of voter fatigue.[55] The party column ballot lists the candidates of each party for all offices in a single column or row. Usually called the Indiana ballot, this format allows the voter to vote for all of the candidates of one party with a single motion, either by marking a "party circle" at the top of the column or by pulling a single lever on the voting machine. The party column ballot is thought not only to facilitate straight-ticket voting,[56] but also to minimize voter fatigue because it requires less effort on the part of the voter to make a choice for offices listed far down on the ballot.[57] The alternative ballot form, the office block ballot, groups candidates of both major parties by the office which is being contested. Often referred to as the Massachusetts ballot, this format is believed to facilitate if not encourage split-ticket voting. Additionally, the office block ballot might contribute to voter fatigue because it requires the voter to express a number of individual choices along a lengthy ballot. For races well down on the ballot and for public measures being decided about which the average voters have not informed themselves, the voter may become frustrated and simply fail to complete the ballot.

A third basic ballot format, called the Pennsylvania ballot, is in actuality a hybrid of the two major ballot forms. Voters using a

Pennsylvania-type ballot face the typical office block format, but at the same time a party circle or lever is available for those voters who choose to cast a straight party ballot. It is to be expected that the amount of split-ticket voting and roll-off due to this ballot form would fall somewhere between that experienced under the two major ballot forms.[58]

In a major study of ballot forms and their relationship to voter fatigue, Jack L. Walker confirmed that the amount of roll-off is greater in states utilizing the office block ballot than in states with the party column ballot format.[59] Comparing the amount of roll-off in thirty-six states during the period from 1950 to 1962 from the election race with the largest turnout in a given election year (usually president, governor, or U.S. senator) to the statewide totals registered in the races for U.S. House of Representatives, Walker found that states utilizing the party column experienced a mean percentage of voter fatigue of from 0.2% to 2.0% less than the states with the office block format.[60]

Walker also tested the hypothesis that the office block format works its greatest toll in voter fatigue among the less well-educated who are more likely to become confused and thus fail to finish the ballot. Utilizing both aggregate and survey research data, Walker confirmed that the higher one's level of education and the more one had been exposed to various forms of mass media, the less will be the tendency for the voter to fatigue and fail to complete the ballot.[61] By extension, one can hypothesize that the concentration of peripheral voters in the presidential electorate accounts for the greater amount of roll-off which Walker observed in these years. Angus Campbell confirmed that peripheral voters are distinguishable from the core voters not only in terms of their lower political interest and involvement but also by their somewhat lower status in terms of occupation, income, and education—socioeconomic characteristics associated with lower rates of voter participation.[62] Campbell also found that the peripheral voters were less likely to complete their voting tasks on the ballot. Drawn to the polls by the high stimulus of the presidential election, the peripheral voter is less likely to vote in the low-stimulus elections lower on the ballot; the result is a greater overall amount of roll-off in presidential years than in mid-term years.[63]

Using aggregate data on state judicial elections, it is also possible to examine the effects of ballot format upon voter fatigue. Table 6 presents the mean percentage of roll-off from the top partisan office to the contested state supreme court elections held in presidential and mid-term election years. These data indicate the consid-

**Table 6.** *Mean Judicial Election Roll-off in Partisan States, Contested Races Only*

| State | Mid-Term Years | Presidential Years | All Years | Ballot Format[a] |
|---|---|---|---|---|
| Utah (1948–1950) | 1.0% | 1.6% | 1.3% | PC |
| Indiana (1948–1970) | 2.2% | 3.0% | 2.6% | PC |
| Pennsylvania | 3.7% | 1.9% | 3.0% | Hybrid |
| New Mexico | 5.6% | 5.9% | 5.8% | PC |
| West Virginia | 3.6% | 7.6% | 6.6% | PC |
| Colorado (1948–1966) | 6.9% | 7.9% | 7.4% | OB |
| New York | 7.3% | 8.0% | 7.6% | OB |
| Iowa (1948–1962) | 9.3% | 10.0% | 9.7% | PC |
| Kansas (1948–1958) | 10.1% | 12.7% | 11.4% | OB |

NOTE: For this table, roll-off has been calculated as the proportion of voters casting ballots in the top partisan race who failed to vote in the contest for state supreme court.

ᵃ PC = party column, or Indiana, ballot.
 OB = office block, or Massachusetts, ballot.
 Hybrid = office block ballot with straight-ticket device, or Pennsylvania ballot.

erable variation in voter fatigue among the partisan states from a low of 1.3% in Utah to a high of over 11% in Kansas.

Many factors undoubtedly contribute to this variation. Certainly, if Walker's analysis applies to judicial elections, then the general educational and social composition of a state's population can be expected to have some impact upon whether its voters are capable of completing their ballots. The overall length of the general election ballot and the location of the judicial race on it also might easily influence the amount of roll-off. Obviously, a judicial race located relatively close to the top of a short ballot would more readily attract voter attention than one listed low on a long ballot. Additionally, the extent to which a state employs voting machines in place of paper ballots will affect the statewide amount of voter fatigue. Several studies have confirmed that voting machines increase roll-off by confusing voters with "their mechanical mysteries."[64] Finally, the general salience of state judicial elections will affect voter participation: judicial races in some states are exciting and highly visible events while in others they spark little voter attention. Depending upon the stimulation, voters will be more or less diligent in marking a choice in the judicial contest.

Considering all these possible explanations, however, and for the moment invoking the social scientist's plea that all other things remain equal, Table 6 indicates that voter fatigue is, indeed, generally greater in the states utilizing the office block ballot than in states utilizing the party column ballot except Iowa. And mean roll-off from the top partisan office to the state supreme court was slightly greater in the presidential years than in the mid-term years in every state but Pennsylvania, a finding which parallels Walker's results. Not all things are always equal, but as a general proposition the party column ballot form seems best able to encourage full participation in judicial elections; the office block ballot makes participation more difficult.

Among the states utilizing the nonpartisan or merit retention judicial ballots, the use of either the party column or office block ballot form for the major partisan races is of little relevance for a consideration of roll-off. But these states do differ in the format of their judicial election ballots and these formats may also affect the extent to which voters are inclined or able to complete their voting tasks.

The major difference among the nonpartisan and merit retention states with respect to ballot format is whether the judicial election is located on a separate part of the general election ballot or whether it is a physically separate paper ballot or specially marked section or line of the voting machine. A major problem, however, is to know whether to expect voter fatigue to be increased or lessened by such a separate ballot arrangement. A separate nonpartisan or merit retention ballot might encourage voter fatigue since it requires the voter to address still one more choice after having completed a lengthy partisan ballot. Alternatively, the separate ballot could minimize roll-off by calling special attention to the judicial race, making it unlikely that the voter will overlook the opportunity, or indeed may feel an obligation, to express a choice.[65]

Table 7 presents the mean roll-off in contested nonpartisan supreme court races in twelve states from 1948 to 1974. The amount of roll-off varies from a mean of 11.3% in Wyoming to 34.4% in Michigan. No systematic relationship between the extent of voter fatigue and the presence of a separate judicial election ballot appears from these data, although in a general way states with the lowest amounts of roll-off are more likely to have the separate ballot than not.[66]

In eight of the eleven states for which comparison is possible, mean roll-off was greater in presidential years than in the mid-term years. The increased roll-off in the presidential year ranged from a low of 2.9% in Minnesota to 16.5% in Washington. In the states of Wyoming, North Dakota, and Idaho, however, the amount of roll-off

**Table 7.** *Mean Judicial Election Roll-off in Nonpartisan States,*
*Contested Races Only*

| State | Mid-Term Years | Presidential Years | All Years | Separate Ballot |
|---|---|---|---|---|
| Wyoming | 11.4% | 11.2% | 11.3% | Yes |
| Utah (1952–1974) | 7.5% | 12.5% | 11.8% | Yes |
| Nevada | 10.4% | 13.5% | 12.0% | No |
| North Dakota | 15.1% | 13.8% | 14.7% | Yes |
| Montana | 12.1% | 18.0% | 15.1% | No |
| Idaho | 16.5% | 13.8% | 15.6% | Yes |
| Oregon | None | 16.9% | 16.9% | No |
| Minnesota | 18.1% | 21.0% | 19.1% | No |
| Ohio | 21.1% | 25.5% | 23.4% | Yes |
| Arizona | 23.5% | 27.0% | 26.7% | No |
| Washington | 21.1% | 37.6% | 31.4% | No |
| Michigan | 32.8% | 36.1% | 34.4% | No |
| South Dakota | None | None | None | Yes |

NOTE: As in Table 6, roll-off is calculated here as the proportion of voters casting ballots in the major partisan race who failed to vote in the contest for state supreme court.

was 0.2%, 1.3%, and 2.7% less in the presidential years than in mid-term years. The concentration of peripheral voters in presidential years might, indeed, contribute to an overall increase in voter fatigue in each state in these years, a proposition confirmed by the evidence here from sixteen of the twenty states with partisan and nonpartisan ballots.[67]

Table 8 repeats the preceding analysis for those states utilizing the merit retention ballot. Among the states, Alaska stands out as experiencing very little voter fatigue even with its separate judicial ballot. But Alaska is easily distinguishable from the others because it features an extremely short partisan ballot; voters who go to the polls are not overburdened with voting tasks, casting ballots on a statewide basis only for the offices of president, governor, lieutenant governor, and U.S. senator. Among the remaining merit retention states, there once again appears to be no connection between voter fatigue and the presence or absence of a separate judicial ballot.

In distinct contrast to the partisan and nonpartisan states, however, roll-off was not found to be greater in the presidential than in the mid-term years. In fact, in all but two of the nine merit retention states, the results were precisely the reverse, with voter fatigue in the mid-term anywhere from 0.3% to 5.4% more than that wit-

**Table 8.** *Mean Judicial Election Roll-off in Merit Retention States, Uncontested Races Only*

| State | Mid-Term Years | Presidential Years | All Years | Separate Ballot |
|---|---|---|---|---|
| Alaska | 11.2% | 9.3% | 10.4% | Yes |
| Wyoming (1974) | 23.2% | None | 23.2% | Yes |
| Utah (1968–1974) | 25.1% | 24.7% | 24.9% | No |
| Kansas (1960–1974) | 33.1% | 32.8% | 33.0% | Yes |
| California | 33.2% | 35.7% | 33.7% | No |
| Colorado (1968–1974) | 38.7% | 33.8% | 36.7% | No |
| Missouri | 32.0% | 45.5% | 43.8% | Yes |
| Iowa (1964–1974) | 59.2% | 53.8% | 56.0% | Yes |
| Indiana (1972–1974) | 59.2% | 54.4% | 57.6% | No |

NOTE: As in Tables 6 and 7, roll-off is calculated as the proportion of voters casting ballots in the major partisan race who did not cast a ballot on the merit retention question.

nessed in the quadrennial balloting. Only in California and Missouri did the amount of roll-off reflect prior expectations based upon the composition of the presidential year electorate.[68] The reasons for this reversal among most of the merit plan states are elusive. It may be that the uncontested merit retention ballot attracts so little attention from the voters that even the core voters fail to participate in large numbers; under these conditions, the addition of the peripheral voters in the presidential years would have little impact upon the aggregate level of roll-off.

Thus, the partisan judicial ballot encourages voters to participate in the selection of their state supreme court justices, particularly when the ballot is equipped with a device which allows the voters to make all of their electoral choices in a single motion. The nonpartisan ballot presents the voters with a choice of unlabeled names which are likely to bewilder them. Unless the voters recognize a familiar name or are perhaps guided by some other label on the ballot, such as one which indicates incumbency, they may respond to this bewilderment by failing to make a selection altogether. Moreover, in many nonpartisan races, judicial candidates run unopposed and the voters may withhold their votes either because they react to this "nonchoice" or because they believe their participation unnecessary to the final result. A similar set of perceptions affect the voters under the merit retention ballot. However, these voters can at least express their dissatisfaction with the lone candidate by registering "no" votes on the retention question, and their votes will bear upon

**Table 9.** *Mean Roll-off Differentials in Four States Switching from Partisan to Merit Retention Ballots*

| State | Partisan Ballots | Retention Ballots[a] | Difference |
|-------|------------------|---------------------|------------|
| Presidential Years | | | |
| Colorado | 7.8% | 33.8% | +26.0% |
| Indiana | 3.0% | 54.4% | +51.4% |
| Iowa | 10.0% | 53.8% | +43.8% |
| Kansas | 12.8% | 32.8% | +20.0% |
| Mid-Term Years | | | |
| Colorado | 6.9% | 38.7% | +31.8% |
| Indiana | 2.2% | 59.2% | +57.0% |
| Iowa | 16.4% | 59.2% | +42.8% |
| Kansas | 10.1% | 33.1% | +23.0% |

NOTE: As in Tables 6–8, roll-off is measured as the proportion of voters casting ballots in the major partisan race who also voted in the supreme court contests.

[a] The merit retention ballot was first used in Colorado in 1968, in Indiana in 1972, in Iowa in 1964, and in Kansas in 1960.

the final outcome of the election. Nevertheless, many voters abstain from indicating their preferences in the merit retention balloting, perhaps uncertain about the effects of either a "yes" or a "no" vote.

The cumulative impact of these factors affecting judicial election participation can be demonstrated most clearly in a comparison of roll-off in states which altered their selection system during the 1948 to 1974 period. Seven states included in this study abandoned their partisan or nonpartisan judicial selection systems during this period and adopted the merit plan and its retention ballot. A comparison of voter fatigue in four of these states under each kind of election system is possible and reveals the dramatic depressing effect upon participation associated with the retention ballot.[69]

Table 9 shows that in those states switching their selection system one of those most notable effects has been to restrict the size of the participating electorate. The mean increase in roll-off has ranged from 20.0% in Kansas (in presidential years) to a staggering 57.0% increase in Indiana (in the mid-term years). The result has been that in Colorado and Kansas a full third of those who attended the polls to cast ballots in the top partisan nonjudicial race failed to complete the merit retention question. In Indiana and Iowa the effects have been even more complete as less than half of the voters going to the polls bothered to express their views on the retention of a sitting judge.

## The Effects of Judicial Election Competition

It was seen earlier in this chapter that the existence of competition affects judicial election participation. But it has also long been thought that the closeness of electoral competition can have a stimulating effect upon turnout.

Two major explanations have been offered to account for this often stated but less frequently verified relationship. At the simplest level, it is believed that the closeness of an election, or rather the anticipated closeness of a contest, will heighten voter interest and hence stimulate popular attendance at the polls.[70] A second explanation, offered first by the dean of modern political science, V. O. Key, has been termed the "competitive threat theory."[71] Key asserted that where the political parties are highly competitive in their battles for public office, party leaders will be more active in mobilizing and organizing the party faithful on election day than will be party leaders where the results are likely to be a foregone conclusion. Aggregate-level support for this proposition has been provided in several comparative state and intrastate analyses,[72] though more-recent studies, attempting to determine the relative contribution of socioeconomic, legal, political, and regional influences to levels of voter turnout, have cast some doubt upon the general proposition.[73] In any event, no published study has yet investigated at even the simplest level the relationship of turnout to competition in state judicial elections.[74] Only in our analysis of Wisconsin judicial elections did David Adamany and I suggest such a possibility. The results there indicated that turnout in the spring judicial contests was only slightly affected by the existence of a close contest, though competitive presidential primaries held every fourth year did have the effect of drawing additional voters to the supreme court races.[75]

For this analysis the differences in roll-off in competitive and noncompetitive judicial elections held in presidential and mid-term election years were compared. A competitive race was defined as one in which the winner captured 55% of the votes or less; elections in which the winner attracted more than 55% of the votes cast were considered noncompetitive.[76]

Among the partisan states the differences in roll-off between the competitive and noncompetitive races were found to be negligible. In presidential years, the mean roll-off in competitive elections was from 0.6% more to 2.8% less than in the noncompetitive ones; in the mid-term, participation in competitive elections ran from 1.5% ahead to 4.8% behind that observed in those contests not closely contested.

Similarly, in the nonpartisan states there appears to be virtually no relationship between judicial election competition and participation. Closely competitive judicial elections held in the presidential years were attended by a mean of from 11.8% fewer to 7.0% more voters than the noncompetitive races; the comparable range for the mid-term years was from +5.8% to −3.5%.

In sum, within the states there appears to be little, if any, relationship of electoral competition to participation in state judicial elections. Actual election results, such as those used here, are but a crude estimate of the electorate's perception of the closeness of a race before and on election day.[77] But the results here are not surprising if judicial elections are of as little importance to the voters as they appear to be. As noted earlier, whether or not an election is contested in the first place does have a significant impact upon whether voters choose to mark their ballots. But drawn into the voting booth by the stimulation of the major partisan contests, whether or not a judicial election is truly competitive makes very little difference in a voter's decision to participate or to abstain.

It does not make much sense to compare, as previous studies have done, the relationship between judicial election competition and turnout across the various states. To do so would require careful procedures to control for differences in the socioeconomic composition of the electorates in each state. Additionally, the "competitive threat" thread of the interparty competition thesis which supports such cross-sectional comparisons is not relevant to the analysis of nonpartisan judicial elections where there are no permanent political organizations like parties with an incentive to promote the participation of organizational followers in the electorate. Nevertheless, even among the partisan states, where competition between competing political organizations is guaranteed, there is only a modestly positive 0.46 correlation between state rankings on judicial election competition and participation in contested races. This correlation is well below the levels of association reported in previous studies investigating the relationship between party competition and turnout in partisan nonjudicial races.[78]

## TURNOUT IN JUDICIAL ELECTIONS: SOME CONCLUSIONS

Critics of judicial elections have long pointed to the low level of voter turnout in the contests to select state judges as evidence that the electorate is unwilling and incapable of meaningful participation in the selection of judges. But the evidence offered here suggests that the level of participation in state supreme court elections is not universally low and that it is very much a function of the same set of factors which affect turnout for other statewide elections. Election scheduling, the existence of competition, the presence of a meaningful voting cue on the ballot, and the nature of the ballot format each affect the level of judicial election participation as they do in other elections. The low level of voter turnout which many critics have observed in state judicial elections is easily explained by those propositions developed in electoral research to account for the levels of turnout observed in elections generally. The scheduling of the election to coincide with high-saliency races, the presence of partisan voting cues during the campaign and on the ballot, and the existence of electoral competition combine to boost turnout in judicial elections. At the other extreme, elections held in the off-season, apart from the more salient partisan contests, where partisan voting cues and electoral competition are lacking, dramatically combine to reduce the size of the participating judicial electorate.

Given the comparable level of turnout in state judicial elections held under partisan arrangements with the level of participation in the major races for president, governor, and senator, the critics of judicial elections necessarily must premise their arguments for reform more upon the basic ignorance of judicial voters and less upon their low rate of participation. As the analysis here demonstrates, the level of voter turnout in judicial elections is primarily a function of the institutional arrangements under which they are conducted and is not reflective of peculiar voter behavior in these kinds of elections.

Such results, of course, do not defuse the criticism that the judicial electorate is hopelessly ignorant and lacking in the kinds of information required to make a rational choice from among competing candidates for judicial office. But they do suggest that, at the very least, an assessment of the level of voter intelligence in judicial elections ought to rest in part upon a comparison with the voters' level of knowledge of candidates and issues in nonjudicial races, especially those which do not occupy a pre-eminent place on the ballot. If, for example, voters know as little about their state legislative candidates as they do about their state judicial candidates, critics would have to either advocate the abolishment of popular elections generally or "premise their arguments more upon intrinsic differences between courts and other public institutions and less upon the inability of the electorate to meet its democratic obligations in selecting judges."[79] Further, even conceding that voters do not currently possess a great command of specific campaign information, some inquiry into the underlying basis of voter decisions in judicial elections ought to be made before the electorate's behavior is condemned as irrational and inappropriate for the selection of judges. Such is the task of the chapter which follows.

# 3. Voting Behavior
# in State Judicial Elections

INTRODUCTION

Low voter turnout has not been the only evidence mustered by critics to demonstrate the nature of the judicial electorate. Rather, public opinion surveys have consistently demonstrated that voters in judicial elections are not only indifferent and apathetic but also ignorant about the competing candidates and issues featured in judicial campaigns.

The results of a poll conducted of New York voters shortly after the 1954 election, for example, revealed that although a large majority of those persons interviewed had voted in the election only a small minority said that they had paid attention to judicial candidates before the election and fewer still could name just one of the candidates for whom they had voted.[1] A similar poll conducted after the 1960 election revealed that only 1% of the voters in New York City, 3% in Buffalo, and 4% in Onondaga County knew the name of Judge Stanley H. Fuld, a candidate for the state's high court nominated by both of the major political parties.[2]

The results of a poll in Wisconsin painted an equally discouraging portrait of the judicial electorate. Conducted a few months after the second of two highly controversial judicial election campaigns in 1964 and 1965, the poll revealed that only 30% of the total electorate could correctly identify the incumbent candidate and only 9% could recall any of the substantive issues of the 1965 campaign. Moreover, approximately 85% of those polled could not correctly identify the political parties with which the candidates had been associated. The study revealed further that, aside from details of specific campaigns and candidates, the judiciary in Wisconsin suffered from low salience in the minds of the state's citizens; less than half of the citizens polled were even aware that the state's judges are elected.[3]

Despite this rather dismal view of the judicial electorate, it has been shown that controversial judicial campaigns can, on occasion, arouse a fair proportion of the electorate from its usual state of quiescence. Following a heated campaign in 1973 for the chief judgeship of the New York Court of Appeals, for instance, a survey of voters attending the polls on election day revealed that two-thirds of those queried had heard about the race, the only statewide office being contested that year. More importantly, of those who knew about the race, about 85% could name the major party candidates and three of every four voters correctly associated each candidate with his party.[4]

Even with the comparatively high level of public attention which the 1973 race attracted, however, nearly half (49%) of those aware of the contest indicated that they would have desired more information about the race before casting their ballots.[5] And of those voters who went to the polls but did not cast a vote in the election for chief judge,[6] 72% indicated that they refrained from voting because they "didn't know enough" about the candidates.[7]

Notwithstanding the low turnout in some judicial elections and the low levels of information possessed by voters, it is not true, as some have suggested, that the public does not want the responsibility of electing its judiciary. In the Wisconsin survey, 64% of those polled thought that state judges should be elected.[8] An earlier survey conducted after the 1963 Wisconsin judicial election revealed similarly high public support for an elective judiciary with well over 80% of those polled saying judges should be elected.[9] In the most recent New York survey, voters were queried as to what they thought was the best way to choose the chief judge of the New York Court of Appeals. When offered a list of alternative methods of judicial selection, an overwhelming majority of 73% favored election.[10]

Even though voters want to select their judges, both the formal restrictions placed upon judicial candidates and the informal norms of behavior governing the conduct of judicial election campaigns so restrict the flow of information concerning candidates and issues to the voters that their meaningful participation is rendered problematic. The American Bar Association's *Code of Judicial Conduct* limits the extent to which judicial candidates can discuss alternative viewpoints on the resolution of public policy issues likely to come before the justices of the state's high court. A candidate for judicial office is instructed by the *Code* to "not make pledges or promises of conduct in office other than the faithful and impartial performance of the duties of the office" and not to "announce his views on disputed legal or political issues."[11] Incumbent judges are prohibited from engaging in political activity generally (except their own re-election campaign), though they may campaign "on behalf of measures to improve the law, the legal system, or the administration of justice."[12]

As a result of these formal limits on judicial candidates, the campaigns for office do not focus on the competing judicial and political philosophies of the candidates or substantive questions of law and public policy. Instead, judicial candidates stress their personal qualifications for the bench and their views on such subjects as the administration of justice and court reform. If judicial candidates compete on partisan ballots, they are permitted by the *Code* to acknowledge a connection with a political party, but the campaign necessarily must remain formally nonprogrammatic. And in states utilizing the nonpartisan nomination and election method of selection, state law usually prohibits political party organizations from offering endorsements to the candidates and from engaging in direct or indirect campaign activity on behalf of a candidate.

The formal ethical standards which determine the nature of judicial election campaigns are reinforced by powerful informal professional norms of proper judicial campaign activity. Strictly enforced by incumbent judges, most opposing candidates, the organized bar, and the press, these norms are a weighty deterrent to the substantive discussion of legal philosophies, judicial decisions, and public policy. Programmatic election appeals are considered to be a violation of the basic rules of the judicial election game, inconsistent with the dignity of judicial office, and a threat to the independence of the judiciary.[13]

Thus, voters in judicial elections know little about the candidates and issues confronting them. Both the formal and informal rules governing judicial campaigns are strong centripetal forces which confine the election debate primarily to the candidates' qualifications, extending at most to a discussion of judicial administration and a debate over alternative proposals for court reorganizations and reform, issues which generally do not spark voter interest. Sayre and Kaufman's description of New York's judicial politics is an apt characterization of judicial elections generally: "[Thus,] whereas much of the maneuvering and negotiation elsewhere in government are overtly and explicitly oriented toward shaping the substance of decisions, the visible foci of judicial politics are selection of personnel and design of organization and procedures. The forces concerned with the substantive aspects of political questions are hampered . . . Public policy is often affected or formed by judicial decisions, but the policy questions are rarely highly perceptible or widely discussed. In appearance, at least, judicial politics is a politics of personnel or procedure rather than of program."[14]

Under these conditions and within the formal and informal constraints governing judicial election campaigns, it is not particularly surprising that voters have preciously little information upon which to base their voting decisions. Indeed, judicial campaigns are so uninteresting that voters scarcely take advantage of those sources of information that *are* available.

In response to the deficiencies in the judicial election process noted by critics, some efforts have been made to help educate the judicial electorate. But because of the prevailing view that substantive policy issues have no place in judicial campaigns, nearly all of the current proposals for reform have been aimed at improving potential voters' knowledge about the professional qualifications and personal characteristics of those seeking judicial office. The most widespread of these educational efforts are polls of members of the legal profession concerning their preferences among the candidates competing for election to the bench. Some of the bar polls are designed solely for public consumption while others are used as the basis for an official endorsement from a local or state bar association. These bar associations also frequently maintain "rating committees" designed to provide the electorate with an informal professional certification of a candidate's qualification (or lack thereof) to sit on the state's high court.[15]

Without questioning the need for devices to help voters learn more about judicial candidates, experience has shown bar polls, ratings, and endorsements to be questionable instruments for informing the voting public. In the first place, bar polls and endorsements do not often attract much more publicity or attention from the public than the campaign itself. In the 1973 New York survey, less than half of those who had voted in the race for chief judge could correctly identify the candidate who had been endorsed by the New York State Bar Association and the Association of the Bar of the City of New York; barely a quarter of those voting knew which of the candidates had been found unqualified by these two powerful bar associations.[16]

A second criticism of bar polls in particular is that most lawyers must base their votes on the general reputation of the candidates or their general reaction to court decisions, possessing virtually no more information on which to base a judgment than a well-informed voter.[17] Additionally, the experience of many state and local bar associations has been that as many as half and often more of the lawyers queried are not interested enough to return their ballots in the bar poll.[18] Moreover, where bar poll ballots are distributed only to members of a particular voluntary professional association, the results cannot possibly reflect a broad cross-section of professional opinion even if the turnout is high.[19] Similarly, where rating committees are used, the members of the association serving on the committee are not representative of the profession serving the community, especially where bar association membership is voluntary and not compulsory.

Aside from their questionable basis, bar polls and association endorsements rarely provide the public with information based upon an objective and detached estimate of professional qualifications. Critics have argued that lawyers tend to favor incumbent judges, fearing that offending a sitting judge with an adverse rating may have a detrimental effect upon future litigation. Though these polls usually are conducted by mailed secret ballot, many lawyers apparently are afraid that their votes are not kept entirely secret.[20]

Whether or not the bar poll is secret, it is nonetheless true that these polls and bar association endorsements usually result in the support of incumbents,[21] perhaps because lawyers consider judicial experience an important qualification for office[22] or perhaps because "there is strong conservative bias among lawyers in favor of continuity under almost any circumstance."[23] Ironically, both low voter participation and the tendency to favor incumbents uncritically are among the traits of judicial electorates most attacked by those who would do away with judicial elections and provide for the legal profession to play a more central role in judicial selection.

It can also be argued that the results of bar evaluations of judicial candidates amount to no more than a reflection of the political and socioeconomic cleavages within the legal profession. In some jurisdictions, these cleavages are manifested in rival bar groups, while in other places the conflicts are internally contained within a single association.[24] In either situation, bar association endorsements and the results of polls of association members may merely mirror the outcome of the conflict among opposing political-legal and socioeconomic interests and will not represent the considered opinion of legal practitioners on those characteristics of judicial candidates thought to be within the special province of lawyers to appraise. Attorneys support and endorse candidates whose philosophy and views are most likely to coincide with their own and the interests of their clients.[25] The bar's claim to provide an objective evaluation of professional qualifications is often no more than a facade for the desire to see judges with sympathetic attitudes nominated and elected to the bench.

Apart from the publication of the opinions, endorsements, and ratings of candidates offered by the legal profession, other general solutions to the problem of voter awareness and knowledge about judicial candidates have been suggested. One possibility is to distribute to voters a "Statement of Qualifications" in a pre-election packet of election materials.[26] Unfortunately, voter information pamphlets are in use in few states. In 1975, only five states distributed such materials, usually containing information about ballot propositions.[27] Only in Oregon and California do the pamphlets contain biographical information and the issue positions of those candidates who pay a nominal fee to purchase the space.

Empirical research on the effects of such voter materials reveals that voters usually find this information helpful to them in reaching their voting decisions.[28] A survey of Oregon voters showed that pre-election materials were thought to be most valuable with respect to ballot measures, but 59% of the voters also found them "very" or "somewhat" useful in deciding how to vote in statewide and congressional races. Of direct relevance to judicial elections, a study in California has shown that, after laws were adopted to allow candidates in the nonpartisan judicial races for municipal and superior court positions to file biographical statements, voter fatigue from the top of the ballot in those districts where a statement was filed averaged 16.8%, while those where the statement was not filed had an average roll-off from the top of the ballot of 20.6%. Moreover, candidates who filed the statement fared better than those who did not.[29]

In sum, voters in judicial elections know little about the candidates and issues confronting them. Formal and informal rules of judicial campaigning serve primarily to keep the voter uninformed and at arm's distance from the candidates and issues. Those issues which are discussed are far removed from the basic questions of law and public policy which the elected justice must ultimately address while on the bench. Additional information provided the public by bar ratings, endorsements, and the results of bar polls probably have little educational impact and that which they might have is decidedly nonprogrammatic in content. Nor is it clear that they should have any impact when professional estimates of candidate qualifications seem to amount to not much more than the expression of particular political-legal viewpoints entitled to no special audience before the voters.

## THE PARTISAN DIVISION OF THE VOTE

If voters in judicial elections do not base their voting decisions upon some knowledgeable assessment of the candidates and the issues, then on what basis are these decisions made? The starting point for an investigation into this question is the realization that for most individuals party identification is the major organizing device of political life. It is, therefore, the logical starting place for analyzing the patterns of electoral behavior in state judicial elections.

The concept of the "normal vote," developed by Philip E. Converse for the analysis of national elections, is also a useful analytic device for the study of state supreme court elections.[30] The normal vote concept recognizes that the voters' long-term psychological attachment and loyalty to a political party is the most powerful and enduring determinant of voting behavior. "The normal vote is simply the vote that would have been cast if party identification were the only political factor relevant to partisan vote choice."[31]

But party identification is not, of course, the sole element in a voter's electoral calculus. Short-term forces also operate on each individual. Responding to particular candidates and issues in a given year can pull a voter away temporarily from a long-term party attachment. Nevertheless, party allegiance is remarkably stable, constant, and resistant to change, forming the base from which voting decisions will be made in each new election year.

Not all voters are influenced equally by these short-term factors. Those with stronger and more intense party loyalties are less likely to defect from their party. The intensity of long-term party identification is like an "elastic cord tying each voter to a preferred party," one which stretches to a greater or lesser degree in response to the short-term political variables.[32]

The impact of short-term factors varies, of course, with the particular candidates and issues in a given election. Candidates and issues play a consistently more influential role in some kinds of elections than in others. Scholars have been giving most of their attention to deviations from the normal vote in presidential elections produced by variations in presidential candidate appeal and the extent of issue voting by the voter.[33] At the same time it has been recognized that deviations from the normal vote are likely to be both less frequent and of smaller magnitude in elections below the presidential level where voters are less aware of particular candidates and the issue positions taken by those candidates. As Cowart has noted, it seems probable that "the relationship between basic partisan loyalties and voting is stronger in state political contests than in presidential contests, since the higher saliency level usually accompanying presidential contests yields greater opportunities for particular issues to stimulate partisan defections."[34] A small but consistent body of literature supports this proposition, demonstrating that in subpresidential balloting voters rely most heavily upon their party identification in casting their ballots.[35] Recent research suggests that basic party loyalties may be either reinforced or attenuated by the presence of an incumbent seeking re-election. In low-salience races, the recognition by voters of an incumbent may induce some partisan defections among those voters not sharing the party of the incumbent, particularly those voters with only a weak attachment to their party.[36] But the predisposition of their long-term party allegiance dominates electoral decision-making at the subpresidential level, even in ballotings for such visible offices as governor, U.S. senator, and U.S. representative.[37]

By extension, a similar perspective on the normal vote can be applied to the behavior of electorates in races for state supreme court justices. Because short-term factors are unlikely to play any significant role, voting for state judges is likely to closely approximate the normal vote. The issues and the candidate personalities involved in a judicial campaign are of such low salience for voters that there exists no powerful short-term stimulus for them to temporarily abandon their long-standing partisan allegiance.

Whether voters divide along basically partisan lines depends on whether they are aware of the party affiliations of the candidates. In states utilizing the partisan ballot, the ballot itself contains this information. And during the campaign, party organizations will be working hard to disseminate this information to their followers in the electorate.

In some of the states utilizing the nonpartisan judicial ballot, voters may also become aware of the partisan affiliation of the opposing candidates because the political parties have a formal, legal role in making nominations for the nonpartisan general election contest. In Michigan, candidates for the state supreme court are nominated in statewide party conventions. In Ohio, judicial candidates compete on a nonpartisan ballot after winning nomination in partisan primaries; a similar system was used in Arizona until 1974 when a merit selection system was adopted to replace it. In each of these states the nomination process may help some voters to make the connection between candidates' names and their respective partisan affiliations. Additionally, the general election campaigns in these states are often conducted with strong partisan overtones.[38] As Ulmer once remarked of Michigan's judicial elections, "no one in the state need have any doubt as to who is what" in terms of the candidates' partisan affiliations.[39] Nevertheless, with the low visibility and attention attached to supreme court contests generally, it is not likely that the party cue in those states which use the system of partisan nomination but nonpartisan election, hereinafter called "mixed" states, is as strong as it is in those partisan states where party is clearly labeled on the general election ballot.

On the other hand, party is likely to be of greater importance in the decisions of voters in the states which used the mixed partisan nomination–nonpartisan election system than it can be in those states which utilize both the nonpartisan nomination and election of their high court justices. There are usually no pre-election campaigns in the latter where the candidates can be identified by party; indeed, such identification typically is prohibited by state constitutional provisions or state statutes. Candidates are further restrained, either by legal provisions or by informal norms of proper nonpartisan campaign behavior, from claiming or receiving the direct or indirect support or endorsement of an organized political party.[40] Because the parties exert no formal control over the nominating process, it is by no means certain, moreover, that judicial election races will be contested between candidates of opposing party affiliations or involve individuals who have more than just a nominal attachment to one party or the other. Unable to call upon the party label on the ballot or to make a connection between candidates and partisan affiliations, the voters in states utilizing nonpartisan nomination and election of state supreme court justices will be forced to rely upon whatever voting cues are available.

These propositions on partisan voting in judicial elections could be tested at the aggregate level by comparing the proportion of the statewide vote captured by candidates for judicial office and for the top partisan offices who share the same party label or affiliation. But as Barber has noted, "statewide election statistics may obscure significant variations in patterns of partisan support."[41] A more revealing aggregate approach, therefore, is to examine the voting behavior of the judicial electorate by counties. Thus, in this study the Democratic percentage of the two-party vote was calculated in each county in each state for the contested races for state supreme court and governor. These percentages were then subjected to a simple correlational analysis.[42] Due to the consistency and stability of party identification and the predominance of partisan voting in gubernatorial elections, the correlation technique should reliably assess the extent of partisan voting in judicial elections.

High positive correlations would tend to indicate that the electorate in each county divided their votes between the candidates for justice by party much like they divided their votes between the opposing partisan candidates for governor. Low positive or negative correlations would tend to suggest that the voter divisions by county were not strictly along partisan lines and that some other, nonparty factor formed the basis for the electorate's division.[43]

Among the states utilizing partisan nomination and partisan general election ballots, ballot labels were used to identify the party affiliations of the opposing candidates in both the gubernatorial and supreme court races. In those states featuring partisan nomination processes but nonpartisan general election ballots (the "mixed" states), convention nominations (in Michigan) or party primary ballots (in Arizona and Ohio) openly identified the opposing partisans in the judicial election contests. In states utilizing both the nonpartisan nomination and election of high court justices, the party affiliations of opposing judicial candidates were ascertained according to several predetermined criteria and researched using standard biographical sources and research questionnaires.[44]

The analysis of the partisan division of the vote was performed in every judicial election in which the candidates had different partisan affiliations. Thus, every contested race conducted in the partisan and mixed states was analyzed. In the nonpartisan states, judicial races in which neither candidate could be identified by party were eliminated as were those between candidates sharing the same partisan identification. Where one candidate's partisan background could be established but the opponent's could not, these races were included on the assumption that the voters need only perceive one candidate's partisan affiliation in order to be stirred to vote along partisan lines. If a candidate has a name familiar to the voters and, at the same time, one closely identified with partisan politics in the state, the voters may be provided with a voting cue which will structure their response along partisan lines. Unless an opponent's name is familiar to the voters for some reason unrelated to partisan identification, the candidate with the recognizable "party name" will cue fellow partisans to express their support at the polls and will simultaneously warn away opposition party voters.

To be sure, the correlations of the partisan division of the vote in supreme court races might be affected by the nature of the gubernatorial balloting in each state. Generally, partisan voting patterns in each state are quite stable from year to year. However, particularly salient issues or attractive candidates in any year might disrupt the usual partisan division. Population shifts or slight changes in the partisan loyalties of the electorate over time, moreover, might impact upon the normal voting divisions. As a check on the possible instability of the gubernatorial vote, the correlations among temporally contiguous gubernatorial races have been prepared. A parallel matrix of intercorrelations among the contiguous contested supreme court races has also been constructed.[45]

The customary warnings about drawing inferences concerning individual voting behavior from aggregate voting data are applicable here.[46] In addition, because of the amount of voter roll-off from the gubernatorial race to the judicial race, especially severe in states using the nonpartisan ballot, one must be particularly cautious about these data. Some of the voters in each county who cast their ballots in the governor's race "dropped out," failing to make a choice in the judicial race. The county-by-county percentages used in the correlational analysis, therefore, were not drawn from precisely the same base of data.

Table 10 presents in summary form the results of the correlational analysis of the partisan division of the vote by county for governor and supreme court justice. Initially, it should be noted that only a fraction of the judicial elections held in the nonpartisan states could be subjected to this analysis. Over half of the nonpartisan ballotings were, as noted in the last chapter, uncontested. And an additionally large proportion of these races could not be analyzed because the judicial candidates shared the same party identification or because the partisan affiliations of the opposing candidates could not be determined. In all, only from one-fourth to one-third of all the nonpartisan elections were included in the correlational analysis.

Two major patterns emerge from the data in Table 10 and deserve special attention. First, it is clear that, on the average, voters in the partisan states are more likely to cast their votes along party lines than voters in the mixed and nonpartisan states. In states utilizing the partisan ballot, voters who cast their ballots for the Democratic gubernatorial candidate are likely also to vote for the Democratic judicial candidate; Republican candidates for justice and governor draw similarly from the same partisan base of support. In eight of nine states considered, the mean correlation between the races for governor and justice is comfortably over 0.75; for all nine states together the mean correlation is 0.84.

An examination of the elections in each state shows the correlations for the partisan division of the vote to be consistently high in Indiana, Iowa, New York, Pennsylvania, and West Virginia, nearly always registering over 0.85 and frequently over 0.90. The correlations for Colorado, Kansas, and Utah trail only slightly behind, usu-

**Table 10.** *Correlations between Partisan Division of the Vote, by County, for Supreme Court Justice and Governor*

| State | Mean Correlation[a] | Range High | Low | Standard Deviation[b] |
|---|---|---|---|---|
| Partisan States | | | | |
| West Virginia | 0.92 (N = 20) | 0.98 | 0.78 | 0.068 |
| Indiana (1948–1970) | 0.92 (N = 21) | 0.99 | 0.74 | 0.071 |
| Pennsylvania | 0.91 (N = 10) | 0.98 | 0.86 | 0.036 |
| New York | 0.89 (N = 12) | 0.99 | 0.70 | 0.076 |
| Iowa (1948–1962) | 0.88 (N = 23) | 0.95 | 0.82 | 0.040 |
| Colorado (1948–1966) | 0.80 (N = 20) | 0.92 | 0.64 | 0.058 |
| Kansas (1948–1958) | 0.79 (N = 18) | 0.90 | 0.64 | 0.078 |
| Utah (1948–1950) | 0.78 (N = 2) | 0.80 | 0.76 | * |
| New Mexico | 0.67 (N = 13) | 0.97 | 0.39 | 0.192 |
| Mixed States | | | | |
| Ohio | 0.47 (N = 36) | 0.81 | −0.42 | 0.210 |
| Arizona | 0.44 (N = 10) | 0.77 | −0.02 | 0.275 |
| Michigan | 0.40 (N = 29) | 0.73 | −0.23 | 0.305 |
| Nonpartisan States | | | | |
| Montana | 0.37 (N = 15) | 0.74 | −0.42 | 0.302 |
| Minnesota | 0.34 (N = 5) | 0.65 | −0.01 | 0.284 |
| Nevada | 0.32 (N = 4) | 0.66 | 0.03 | 0.314 |
| Utah (1952–1974) | 0.32 (N = 4) | 0.42 | 0.18 | 0.106 |
| Washington[c] | 0.18 (N = 8) | 0.66 | −0.30 | 0.322 |
| Wisconsin | 0.18 (N = 12) | 0.46 | 0.03 | 0.128 |
| Wyoming | 0.15 (N = 7) | 0.60 | −0.49 | 0.332 |
| North Dakota | 0.07 (N = 3) | 0.18 | −0.05 | * |
| Idaho[c] | 0.03 (N = 4) | 0.10 | −0.06 | 0.069 |

[a] The entries in this column represent the mean correlation of the partisan division of the vote for all elections included in the correlation analysis in each state. For example, in West Virginia the mean correlation of the vote between governor and supreme court justice in twenty elections was 0.92. In the remaining columns it can be seen that these correlations ranged from a high of 0.98 to a low of 0.78, with a standard deviation among the twenty correlations of 0.068.

[b] The designation * indicates N ≤ 3; standard deviations in such instances have been omitted as unreliable.

[c] In the states of Idaho and Washington, a candidate who collects a majority of the votes cast in the primary election is either declared elected (Idaho) or entitled to run unopposed in the general election (Washington). The correlation analysis was performed only upon the contested judicial elections held concurrently with the November elections. Oregon, which uses the same arrangement as that in Washington, has not been included in this analysis since only one such contested race has been held in the postwar general elections.

ally remaining above the 0.75 mark and climbing on occasions to quite impressive levels.

Only New Mexico presents major problems for this analysis with a relatively low mean correlation for the partisan division of the vote and a wide variation among the state's elections in the extent of partisan voting by the electorate. Beginning with the 1956 election, in which the correlation for the partisan division of the vote registered only 0.47, New Mexico's judicial elections have not been consistently structured along partisan divisions in the electorate.

In his major study of New Mexico politics, Professor Jack E. Holmes discovered that beneath the relative calm of statewide results (which have consistently favored Democratic judicial candidates) there is a considerable variation among the counties in the state's elections which may account for the apparently inconsistent results of the correlational analysis attempted here. According to Holmes: "The several counties are by no means alike in their reactions to campaigns and candidates. Variations in the percentage of the vote to a series of a party's gubernatorial candidates are quite limited in some counties, but others have consistently shown a disposition to make relatively radical shifts in the percentage of the vote going to a party's candidates."[47] In addition, Holmes detected a trend beginning in the 1950s for "a high degree of ticket-splitting that differentiated between president and governor, with a second level of splitting between gubernatorial and other state and local candidates."[48] The reasons for the existence of some large shifts in voter sentiment in some of New Mexico's counties from one election to the next and from one level on the ballot to another are complex and do not especially concern us here. All that need be noted is that population movements, the composition of the electorate, the nature of political competition and party organization in the various counties, and the quadrennial pull of national politics all contribute something to an explanation of the variability of the party vote in New Mexico. The unique circumstances of political change in the state combine to disrupt the correlational analysis of the party division of the vote.[49]

In contrast to the high correlations observed in the states using partisan judicial ballots, the correlations in those states using nonpartisan ballots in the general election race for justice are much lower. For the three mixed states, the overall mean correlation is only 0.44. They are even lower in the nonpartisan states, averaging only 0.22 for all nine states. Indeed, the state with the highest mean correlation for the partisan division of the vote under a nonpartisan ballot, Montana, registers a mere 0.37.

Perhaps a more intriguing result presented in Table 10, however, is the fact that the variation among the mixed and nonpartisan states in the correlations for the partisan division of the vote is considerably greater than among the states using the partisan judicial ballot. In the states of Ohio, Arizona, Michigan, and Montana, correlations indicating a considerable amount of partisan voting occasionally have been demonstrated. On the other hand, the analysis of party voting in the states using nonpartisan judicial ballots reveals correlations which sometimes fall to very impressive depths. In Ohio, Montana, and Wyoming, for instance, negative correlations for the partisan division of the vote of −0.42, −0.42, and −0.49, respectively, were observed. The wider variation in the extent of party voting by the electorates in the mixed and nonpartisan states than in the partisan ones is confirmed not just by a comparison of the range of correlation coefficients but also by calculation of the standard deviations of the correlations for each state.[50] Only in New Mexico among the partisan states does the variation in the pattern of partisan voting compare with that for the mixed and nonpartisan states. Among the nonpartisan states, only in Idaho, where the partisan division of the vote seems clearly and consistently unimportant for understanding the lines of division in the judicial electorate, does the deviation in correlations compare to the low level demonstrated in most of the partisan states.

As a check upon these observed relationships, an inspection of the intercorrelations of the gubernatorial and judicial races in each state confirms that the relationship between the type of judicial election ballot and the degree of partisan voting by the electorate is not a spurious one due to excessive instability in the voting for governor. Table 11 presents the means and standard deviations of these intercorrelations.

The gubernatorial intercorrelations reveal a high degree of stability from one election to the next in the partisan patterns of the vote in virtually every state, regardless of the type of judicial election system. The intercorrelations among the gubernatorial races are slightly lower in the nonpartisan states than in the partisan or mixed states, but among the former are a number of western and mountain states which, for various reasons, frequently experience split-ticket voting.[51] Additionally, some instability in the pattern of the vote from one election to the next is also indicated by the relatively low gubernatorial intercorrelations in the partisan states of

**Table 11.** *Mean Judicial and Mean Gubernatorial Intercorrelations, Partisan Division of the Vote, by County*

| State | Judicial Contests | | Gubernatorial Contests[a] | |
|---|---|---|---|---|
| | Mean | Standard Deviation[b] | Mean | Standard Deviation[b] |
| Partisan States | | | | |
| West Virginia | 0.95 | 0.045 | 0.90 | 0.061 |
| Indiana (1948–1970) | 0.93 | 0.019 | 0.81 | 0.095 |
| Pennsylvania | 0.92 | 0.029 | 0.88 | 0.048 |
| New York | 0.92 | 0.060 | 0.79 | 0.188 |
| Iowa (1948–1962) | 0.91 | 0.024 | 0.83 | 0.051 |
| Utah (1948–1950) | 0.87 | * | 0.61 | * |
| Kansas (1948–1958) | 0.84 | 0.037 | 0.72 | 0.060 |
| Colorado (1948–1966) | 0.83 | 0.087 | 0.76 | 0.101 |
| New Mexico | 0.68 | 0.150 | 0.53 | 0.158 |
| Mixed States | | | | |
| Arizona | 0.58 | 0.195 | 0.90 | 0.068 |
| Ohio | 0.50 | 0.169 | 0.85 | 0.026 |
| Michigan | 0.33 | 0.256 | 0.93 | 0.050 |
| Nonpartisan States | | | | |
| Nevada | 0.73 | * | 0.57 | * |
| Montana | 0.21 | 0.281 | 0.80 | 0.083 |
| Wisconsin | 0.17 | 0.187 | 0.85 | 0.054 |
| North Dakota | 0.13 | * | 0.89 | * |
| Utah (1952–1974) | 0.07 | * | 0.68 | * |
| Washington | 0.02 | 0.395 | 0.75 | 0.115 |
| Idaho | −0.07 | * | 0.63 | * |
| Minnesota | −0.10 | 0.331 | 0.76 | 0.124 |
| Wyoming | −0.11 | 0.425 | 0.77 | 0.093 |

NOTE: Intercorrelations are of temporally contiguous contested races, e.g., 1948–1950, 1950–1952, 1952–1954, etc. See n. 10.

[a] Includes only gubernatorial races held in years with contested supreme court races included in correlation analysis.

[b] The designation * indicates N ≤ 3; standard deviations in such instances have been omitted as unreliable.

New York, Utah, Kansas, Colorado, and New Mexico. In any event, the magnitude of the differences between the partisan and nonpartisan states does not seem sufficient to account for the extremely low correlations for the partisan division of the vote in the nonpartisan and mixed states reported in Table 10.

A secondary and crucial check is provided by the intercorrelations of the judicial races. This exercise, displayed also in Table 11, reveals that there is a high similarity in the partisan division of the judicial vote from one election to the next among the partisan states. In fact, the mean judicial intercorrelations exceed the mean gubernatorial election intercorrelations in every state. Moreover, the standard deviations of the intercorrelations are less in each partisan state for the judicial races than for the gubernatorial, a phenomenon consistent with the view that in gubernatorial races short-term influences may partially disturb otherwise stable partisan voting alignments. In judicial contests, however, where candidates and issues provide the voters with very little stimulus to abandon their traditional partisan affiliations, ballots are cast along more predictable party lines.

In contrast, the judicial intercorrelations in the mixed and non-partisan states pale by comparison to the gubernatorial intercorrelations. The standard deviations confirm, moreover, that the judicial intercorrelations are more variable than those in the gubernatorial races, precisely the reverse of the relationship in the states utilizing the partisan judicial ballot.

## VOTING IN JUDICIAL ELECTIONS UNDER THE NONPARTISAN BALLOT: AN OVERVIEW

Both the overall high level and the marked consistency of the correlations produced by this analysis confirm the sharp division of the electorate along party lines in states utilizing a partisan ballot for the conduct of their judicial elections. On the other hand, the analysis of the party division of the vote in states using nonpartisan judicial ballots confirms that it is much more difficult for voters to cast their votes along partisan lines in the absence of an explicit partisan cue. Even where the nomination process is partisan and voters might have the opportunity to learn the party affiliations of the nominees and where the political parties actively promote their candidates during the campaign, the nonpartisan ballot makes it very difficult for the average voters to cast their ballots consistent with their partisan preferences.

Those who once hoped for the fulfillment of the Progressive ideal behind the adoption of the nonpartisan judicial ballot might be greatly encouraged by these results. By removing the influences of the party label and the partisan campaign, the nonpartisan ballot was designed to free voters to give more sober and thoughtful consideration to the qualifications and qualities of the competing candidates. Indeed, preceding its subsequent widespread adoption for the election of many nonjudicial officials at the local level, the nonpartisan ballot was developed first for the election of judges because Progressive reformers viewed the qualifications for the bench and the functions of judicial office to be such that competing candidates should not be evaluated within the context of partisan politics.

Regardless of whatever well-intentioned impulses resulted in the adoption of nonpartisan judicial elections, however, it is probably not possible for most voters to behave in the ideal fashion once envisioned. Given the low-stimulus nature of these contests, voters must look for cues to guide them in their voting. Under the partisan ballot, of course, one major cue is readily provided. Under a nonpartisan format, though, voters are compelled to rely upon other sources of guidance. Two such major guides available to the voter are incumbency and name recognition.

Incumbency and name familiarity are often, of course, the same thing. In congressional elections, for instance, voters are more familiar with and will more readily recognize the name of the incumbent. Congressional officeholders are privy to many privileges, such as the frank, which enable them to keep their names continually before the electorate. Another aspect of incumbency, however, is the reputation incumbents enjoy with their constituencies, including popular perceptions of their personal qualities, stands on the issues, and performances in office.[52]

For the election of state supreme court justices, the name recognition aspect of incumbency is likely to be of most importance in structuring voter choice. With the exception of the campaign efforts of supporters to publicize an incumbent's qualifications and experience, judges engage in none of the basic kinds of activities between elections which other public officials use to enhance their reputations with voters.[53] If an incumbent's name becomes known to the voters, it is likely to be the result of the campaign. Indeed, in those states which directly or indirectly label on the ballot the current occupant of a seat on the state's high court, the cue of incumbency may reveal itself to some voters only after they have stepped inside the voting booth.

Name familiarity, of course, is not solely a function of incumbency. Previously unknown candidates will of course have a difficult time getting their names before the judicial electorate without massive publicity efforts. But a candidate who has served before in public office or one who has been a frequent contender for public office, particularly at the statewide level, will be recognizable to some and perhaps many voters. Even a candidate who has previously served in a visible appointive office will be familiar to the judicial voters. Finally, some candidates will benefit from sharing the surname of some well-known political figure in the state even if unrelated by family or political affiliation. If a candidate possessing high name familiarity with the voters is also strongly associated (or the name is associated) with one political party or the other, voters might call upon this cue.

In addition to incumbency and name recognition, voters may call upon any number of other cues in nonpartisan judicial elections. Voters in some areas of the state, for example, may give disproportionate support to candidates whose familial, political, or professional roots extend into their region, a phenomenon V. O. Key called "friends and neighbors" voting. The local candidate "gains support, not primarily for what he stands for or because of his capacities, but because of where he lives."[54]

Other cues may be drawn directly from the ballot itself. The surname of a candidate may have an ethnic or religious significance for segments of the electorate.[55] Ballot labels indicating the occupation of a candidate may serve for some voters as an indirect measure of a candidate's qualifications for the bench.[56] Finally, vote choices might be determined by the sex of a candidate, the presence of an eye-catching nickname, or even the relative position of candidates on the ballot.[57]

It would be an impossible task to attempt to estimate the precise effects of each of these nonparty cues in nonpartisan judicial elections. But their impact may be partially assessed by examining disruptions in the partisan division of the vote which occur when the party cue is removed in these low-visibility and low-salience contests and replaced by other factors which inspire voter choice.

### Voting Behavior in the "Mixed" States

The role of voting cues in structuring the behavior of the judicial electorate is best initiated in those states using nonpartisan general election ballots following partisan systems of nomination. It is in these "mixed" states that the stimuli for partisan voting are the strongest, with partisan cues emanating both from the formal nomination processes and in the conduct of the general election campaigns. Nevertheless, the low visibility of judicial contests has meant that the partisanship of the pre-election process has not penetrated to the electorate, leaving voters to call upon alternative nonparty voting cues, often with haphazard results.

The importance of name familiarity and incumbency as voting cues is most clearly demonstrated in Ohio judicial elections.[58] For example, the name of Matthias has appeared on the supreme court ballot in Ohio virtually every six years since 1914. Edward S. Matthias was first elected to the supreme court in that year and was subsequently re-elected six times, leaving the bench by death in 1953. He was succeeded by his son, John M. Matthias, who won an initial election bid in 1954 and won re-election three times before his resignation in 1970. The correlations for the partisan division of the vote for elections in which one of the popular Republican justices was involved in the postwar years are among the most consistently low reported for the state. One of the two Matthiases ran in contested elections in 1950, 1954, 1956, and 1962; the reported correlations of 0.39, 0.46, 0.44, and 0.39 are all below the average correlation of 0.47 for the state's judicial elections during the 1948 to 1974 period. Since Matthias is a name traditionally associated with not only the supreme court but also Republican politics in the state, some voters probably cast their ballots along lines consistent with their partisan preferences. Other voters were probably more influenced by the long-term incumbency of the candidate and the familiarity of the family name vis-à-vis those of opposing candidates.

Races involving long-time Democratic incumbents have been even less frequently decided along partisan lines. The electoral staying power of such Democratic justices as Carl V. Weygandt and Charles B. Zimmerman attests to their widespread recognition and popularity among the voters of both parties. Weygandt won five full terms as chief justice beginning in 1932, losing only in his sixth attempt in 1962 to popular Republican Associate Justice Kingsley Taft. Only when Weygandt was challenged by an equally well-known Republican, such as Taft in 1962 and Francis B. Douglas in 1950, were the elections even moderately partisan in nature ($r = 0.70$ and $0.57$, respectively). Similarly, Zimmerman won six election campaigns after his initial appointment in 1933. In two of the three races occurring after 1948 this long-time incumbent faced only weak opposition; most voters gave their loyal support to the incumbent in contests clearly decided along nonparty lines ($r = 0.19$ in 1958 and $0.34$ in 1964). It required a 1952 challenge from the same recognizable Republican opponent to Weygandt in 1950, Francis B. Douglas, to spark some partisan behavior within the electorate ($r = 0.55$).

Though incumbency and name recognition have often encouraged Ohio voters to abandon their traditional partisan allegiances in casting their votes in the judicial elections, the previous examples also suggest that a name strongly associated with the state's partisan politics can evoke a partisan response from the voters despite the nonpartisan ballot. The name of Taft, for example, which is virtually synonymous with the Ohio Republican party, invariably produces a partisan electoral response. In 1948 and in several races thereafter, Kingsley Taft ran successfully for the position of associate justice (1948, 1954 [unopposed], 1960) and chief justice (1962, 1968). In the four contested races involving Taft, the correlations for the partisan division of the vote were 0.63, 0.60, 0.70, and 0.55, indicating a moderately deep partisan division in the Ohio electorate. And in 1974, a candidate by the name of Sheldon A. Taft ran in a very partisan race ($r = 0.69$) against a well-known Democratic incumbent, Frank D. Celebrezze.[59]

Elections involving other candidates possessing names usually associated with Republican politics in the state have also resulted in a relatively high degree of partisanship among the voters. C. William O'Neill served as governor of Ohio from 1957 to 1959. Initially elected as an associate justice to an unexpired term in 1960, O'Neill was re-elected in 1964, elevated by the voters to the position of chief justice in 1970 to fill out the term left vacant by the death of Chief Justice Taft, and returned in 1974. In the four races involving O'Neill, the party divisions resulted in correlations of 0.60, 0.55, 0.42, and 0.63, the last in a race against an opponent with the same last name where the opportunity for name confusion was great.

Herbert is also a well-known Republican name. Thomas J. Herbert was elected to a single term in 1956; his race against his Democratic opponent correlated at 0.60 with the gubernatorial race. In 1962, Paul M. Herbert ran successfully for a single term ($r = 0.49$). Finally, Thomas M. Herbert was elected in 1968 ($r = 0.57$) and again in 1974 ($r = 0.45$) in a race against a Democrat named Brown, an anomaly in Ohio politics.

Brown is another of the many names familiar to Ohio voters as being associated with Republican partisan politics. Paul W. Brown, who ran successfully in 1964, 1966, and again in 1972 after a brief retirement (from 1968 to 1972), attracted a partisan response from the voters in each of these three elections, well above the average for the state ($r = 0.56, 0.63, 0.58$).

Undoubtedly well aware of the fondness of Ohio's voters for candidates named Brown, Democratic candidates holding the Brown surname have occasionally attempted to win election to the supreme court. As a result, some Republican voters, unaware of this "switch," have probably "crossed over" to vote for the candidate whose name they associate with their party, while some Democratic voters "cross over" to avoid voting for the candidate they think is a Republican. In 1966, Democrat Clifford Brown opposed incumbent

Republican Louis J. Schneider, Jr.; the correlation for that race was a low 0.38. Schneider was once again opposed in 1972 by a Democratic Brown (William B.) but this time Schneider was defeated; the party division of the vote in this race correlated at only 0.21 with the 1970 gubernatorial race.

Two other races featuring Democrats named Brown, however, did not result in a serious disruption of the moderately partisan voting habits of Ohio's judicial electorate. Democrat Lloyd Brown attempted but failed in 1972 to unseat the popular Republican Paul Brown: $r = 0.58$. And in 1974, Thomas M. Herbert was challenged by Democrat Clifford Brown; Herbert was re-elected in a race attracting an average partisan response from the voters ($r = 0.45$). Thus, it might be argued that many voters react to the familiar name which they associate with Republicanism but many others are confused by the contradictory signals they are receiving from the campaign and the parties. When a Democrat named Brown faces a particularly well-known Republican (like P. Brown or Herbert), some of the Republicans who might ordinarily have defected to the Democratic candidate to vote for the name of Brown are held to their party's nominee by an equally attractive Republican name. Similarly, in the 1974 race when Chief Justice C. William O'Neill was opposed by a Democratic O'Neill, many voters were kept in the appropriate column by the pulling power of the Republican O'Neill.

The dramatic effect of name confusion under the nonpartisan ballot in Ohio was clearly demonstrated in the 1970 race between a Democratic Brown (Allen) and J. J. P. Corrigan, a Republican appointee of Governor John Rhodes. In this race, a Democratic candidate associated by name with Republicanism faced a Republican candidate possessing a "Democratic name" in Ohio politics. The correlation between this judicial race and the 1970 gubernatorial contest was an astounding $-0.41$; many Democratic voters obviously voted for Corrigan and many Republicans for Brown, resulting in a moderately partisan vote in the wrong direction!

Michigan's supreme court elections should follow the basic pattern observed in Ohio. Judicial candidates in Michigan are nominated by party convention and the parties take an active role in promoting the candidacy of their nominees. The ballot, however, is nonpartisan; no indication of the nominees' partisan affiliations can be discerned once the voter steps inside the voting booth.

The analysis of the partisan division of the vote is somewhat complicated by the manipulation of data required to perform the correlational analysis. With the exception of elections to fill the portion of a term left unexpired by the death or retirement of a judge, judicial elections in Michigan have been contested on an "at large" basis. When more than one full-term position on the court has been contested in a given year, all the opposing party nominees compete in one "pool" of candidates from which the voters choose. Each voter can cast as many votes as there are positions to be filled. The pairing of opposing candidates, described in note 42 accompanying this text, is admittedly an artificial construct, one complicated by the fact that each voter might not cast the number of votes to which he or she is entitled. In addition, several of the elections analyzed were held in the spring of odd-numbered years, unaccompanied by the gubernatorial race. These spring elections have been correlated with the closest gubernatorial election.[60] While somewhat crude, the method offered here yields a reasonably accurate representation of the extent of partisan voting under Michigan's mixed judicial election system. Caution has to be exercised, of course, in attaching meaning to the correlation for the partisan division of the vote to any one of the artificial pairings without considering the correlation for the other pairing as well.

Although the correlations for each and every election are not always easily understood, the general principles made clear in the discussion of the Ohio experience are applicable in Michigan as well. For example, the relatively partisan judicial race of 1953 ($r = 0.48$, 0.69) involved easily identifiable Republicans, John M. Dethmers and Harry F. Kelly. Dethmers was originally appointed to office in 1946 while serving as the state's attorney general. Elected to the court in 1946 and re-elected in 1953, the former attorney general (who had previously served as the chief assistant attorney general and as chairman of the Republican State Central Committee from 1942–1945) was probably recognized by many voters. The other position was won by Kelly, who was perhaps even more familiar to voters, having served as governor from 1943 to 1947 and previously as secretary of state from 1939 to 1942. It is interesting to note that eight years later, in 1961, when both Kelly and Dethmers sought re-election, their partisan attachments had apparently not waned in the minds of the voters ($r = 0.65$, 0.41).

In the 1955 election ($r = 0.60$, 0.65) three of the four candidates competing for the supreme court were well-known partisans before the election. D. Hale Brake, one of the Republican nominees, had served as state treasurer from 1943 to 1954, losing his re-election bid only a few months before the 1955 spring contest. Brake had also made an unsuccessful bid in the 1954 Republican gubernatorial primary. Each of the Democratic nominees previously had been attorney general: Eugene Black served from 1947 to 1948 and Stephen

Roth from 1949 to 1950. Only incumbent Justice Leland Carr, the other Republican nominee, appointed to the supreme court in 1945 (by Governor Kelly) after twenty-four years on the circuit bench, might not have stirred the partisan memories of the voters.

One of the 1962 vacancy races also drew a relatively partisan response from Michigan's voters. The Democratic nominee, Otis M. Smith, a Black, was appointed by Governor John Swainson to the supreme court in 1961 and elected in 1962 ($r = 0.60$). Smith had previously served as chairman of the Public Utilities Commission and had won election in 1960 as the state's auditor general after his initial appointment to that post in late 1959. The other vacancy race contested in 1962 involved another recognizable partisan, Paul L. Adams, who had won election on the partisan ballot to the University of Michigan Board of Regents in 1955 and had been appointed attorney general in early 1958 by Governor G. Mennen Williams, subsequently winning election to that post in 1958 and 1960. Adams served as attorney general until his appointment by Governor Swainson to the supreme court in early 1962. He was defeated in his bid for election to the court in the 1962 election, however, losing to attorney Michael D. O'Hara in a race not characterized by a high degree of partisan voting by the electorate ($r = 0.34$). Adams' 1963 race (with Eugene Black as the other Democratic nominee) was fairly partisan, however ($r = 0.58, 0.56$); the Republican nominees were circuit judges at the time of the election, one a former state legislator.

Finally, the 1970 supreme court race was also decided along marked party lines ($r = 0.64, 0.71$). Few voters could fail to respond in partisan fashion to the candidacy of G. Mennen Williams, Michigan's Democratic governor for over a decade (1949–1960), and John B. Swainson, Williams' lieutenant governor from 1959 to 1960 and successor to the governorship in 1961.

In addition to electoral contests which spark a partisan response from the voters, Michigan's judicial elections have, on occasion, been decided along electoral lines which do not appear to have their basis in partisan identification. Long-term incumbency or name familiarity which do not reinforce partisan emotions are usually present in these elections. In 1949, for example, two Democratic incumbents who each had served on the bench since 1933 were easily re-elected against weak Republican opposition in contests clearly not decided along partisan lines ($r = 0.18, -0.17$). Similarly, in 1968, Democratic nominee Thomas Giles Kavanaugh narrowly defeated sitting Justice Michael D. O'Hara; the correlation for the partisan division of the vote for this race, $-0.22$, was the lowest observed for Michigan's supreme court elections in the 1948–1974 period. Many voters apparently confused Thomas Giles Kavanaugh with Thomas M. Kavanaugh, the enormously popular incumbent chief justice first elected in 1957 and former Democratic attorney general from 1955 to 1957.

Name confusion was also a major factor in the 1959 race when two candidates with identical last names were among the five-man field competing for two positions. The Republican party nominated William H. Baldwin and Maurice F. Cole, a circuit court commissioner from Oakland County. Also on the ballot, however, in addition to the two Democratic incumbents seeking re-election, was the name of Kenneth P. Cole, an attorney and a nominee of the Prohibition party. Third-party candidates had previously made supreme court bids in Michigan with but the limited level of success which usually befalls such efforts. But although the candidates were labeled on the ballot by occupation, Kenneth Cole gathered 199,123 votes compared to Maurice Cole's total of 209,155; Kenneth Cole captured over 30% of the votes cast for the three non-Democratic candidates. An inspection of the county returns reveals that the Prohibition party nominee led Maurice Cole in sixty-two of the state's eighty-three counties and competed closely in virtually all the remainder. Only a winning margin of over 11,000 votes gathered in his home Oakland County preserved a plurality for the Republican Cole. This is an extreme, but enlightening, example of the dramatic effects which name identification and/or confusion can have upon the voting response of the electorate faced with a nonpartisan ballot. It confirms, moreover, that what V. O. Key called "friends and neighbors" voting is also present in state judicial elections, serving as a meaningful cue for some voters in the absence of the party label.

Finally, one additional possible basis for voting in state judicial elections not related to party, incumbency, or name familiarity must be entertained. An inspection of the correlations for the analysis of the partisan division of the vote produced in Michigan reveals that some voters might respond favorably to ethnic or religious cues present in the surnames of judicial candidates. In particular, Irish Catholic candidates, both Democratic and Republican, have been fairly successful in their bids for election to the state supreme court. Moreover, the party correlations for the party division of the vote in races involving Irish Catholic candidates reveal a greater than average disruption of the partisan alignment in the electorate. Michael D. O'Hara's competitive but unsuccessful bids in 1956 and 1957 were clearly decided along nonparty lines in the electorate ($r = 0.23$ and $-0.01$, respectively). In a successful try in 1962 against the former Democratic attorney general Paul L. Adams, the correlation for the division of the vote reached only 0.34. And in 1968, when O'Hara was narrowly defeated by Thomas Giles Kavanaugh, the correlation dropped to −0.22. As noted earlier, Kavanaugh, also an Irish Catholic, probably benefited from some voter confusion with the popular Thomas M. Kavanaugh, but it is also possible that voters responding to an ethnic-religious cue found themselves torn between equally desirable alternatives.

Other races involving other candidates with Irish Catholic names have similarly low correlations for the partisan division of the vote when partisan cues for voting are absent.[61] It is not entirely clear why this particular ethnic-religious cue might be important in Michigan. And indeed, without supporting data from survey research, these speculations must remain untested. But it could be that some voters, confused by the directionless ballot, call upon one of the few cues for voting available to them.

Arizona follows the general pattern set by the other states utilizing partisan nomination systems but nonpartisan general election ballots. Some voters undoubtedly become aware of the candidates' party affiliations during the primary election campaign. The candidate with a well-known political personality or name can stir the partisan emotions of the electorate. Alternatively, the incumbent judge or the candidate with a familiar name may pull voters away from their usual partisan preferences.

It must be initially remembered that a large proportion (57.1%) of Arizona's judicial elections in the postwar period have gone uncontested, with Democratic justices holding a decided advantage in the state's balloting. However, the rise of Republican fortunes since the mid-1960s has resulted in more contested and competitive judicial races.[62] When supreme court races have been contested, they have been moderately partisan affairs, at least in terms of the patterns of the vote.

Notable among the races is the 1964 contest between Republican Edward W. Scruggs and Democrat Ernest W. McFarland which sparked a strongly partisan division in the electorate ($r = 0.77$) despite the nonpartisan ballot. But McFarland was a political landmark in Arizona politics during the 1940s and 1950s, serving first for two terms as U.S. senator and then as governor for two terms from 1955 to 1959. McFarland made an additional unsuccessful attempt to unseat Barry Goldwater from his senate seat in 1958. Republican and Democratic voters alike were able, in this instance, to cast votes consistent with their partisan preferences; few voters could have been unaware of McFarland's partisan background.

At the other extreme are two races notable for the absence of party voting. In 1960, Jesse A. Udall, a Republican, won election to the state supreme court, the only Republican elected in the postwar years until 1968. Appointed in June 1960 by Governor Paul Fannin, Udall managed to keep his seat in the Democratically dominated state because he shared the Udall name, one associated historically with a pioneer Mormon family and with Democratic politics in the state to this day. The confusion of the voters in electing a Republican Udall is clear from the slightly negative correlation for the partisan division of the vote, −0.02. It is confirmed by the intercorrelation of the 1960 judicial race with one held in 1952 in which a Democratic Udall (Levi S.) was elected to the court, −0.61.[63]

Finally, the power of incumbency is demonstrated by the 1972 race between Harold Riddel, a Republican, and Fred C. Struckmeyer, Jr., a Democrat and a member of the Arizona Supreme Court since 1954 seeking his fourth term; the correlation for the party division of the vote was a mere 0.03.

The results from Ohio, Michigan, and Arizona are noteworthy because, although each state uses the nonpartisan general election ballot, partisanship is a central feature of their formal nomination processes and, at least in Michigan and Ohio, of the general election campaigns. Yet it is clear that even in these states, where the stimulus for partisan voting is strongest, the nonpartisan ballot results in unstructured and often idiosyncratic voting patterns. Identifiable names on occasion provide voters with indirect cues for voting along party lines but not always in the "correct" direction.

### Judicial Election Voting in Nonpartisan States

These general observations about the effect on voting patterns in the mixed partisan-nonpartisan states due to the factors of name identification and incumbency are seen also in the nine states utilizing both the nonpartisan nomination and election of their supreme court justices. Unlike the mixed states, however, the parties have no formal role in nominating candidates or campaigning on their behalf. In most nonpartisan states, candidates are prohibited from being identified by partisan affiliation. And in some, the parties are legally restrained from offering judicial campaign endorsements. Whether or not the parties are limited in the formal role they can play in judicial campaigns, however, they might nonetheless engage in informal, sub rosa, activity on behalf of specific candidates.[64] But even then the parties are probably not as visible to the judicial electorate as they are when they have an institutional responsibility for choosing party nominees to run on the nonpartisan general election ballot.

It is thus most unlikely that voters will be able to ascertain the partisan affiliations of the opposing candidates. Indeed, as I have pointed out before, because the parties have no legal role in recruiting candidates for judicial office, there is no guarantee that the opposing candidates in a judicial election will offer the voters a choice between candidates of differing partisan allegiances. When opposing partisans do contest a judicial race, voters are usually unaware of it. Thus, the overall level of the correlations for the partisan division of the vote are below those observed in the mixed states. In only a few isolated instances discussed below do the correlations rise to even moderate levels and these occasions are consistent with the principles outlined thus far.

The 1950 race in Minnesota ($r = 0.65$) was contested between Theodore Christianson, Republican governor from 1925 to 1931, and Mark Nolan, a former state legislator and Democratic party activist. In 1956, Democratic appointee William P. Murphy was challenged by Leslie L. Anderson in a race decided along moderately partisan lines ($r = 0.49$). Anderson happened to share the last name of C. Elmer Anderson, the state's Republican governor from 1951 to 1955 and the party's unsuccessful gubernatorial candidate in the 1954 election. Similarly, the 1966 race was contested between candidates whose partisan affiliations were probably familiar to many voters and thereby prompted some partisan voting. Thomas Patrick Gallagher was running for the seat on the high court being left vacant by the retirement of his father, Thomas Francis Gallagher, a well-known Democratic leader and former unsuccessful candidate for governor. The junior Gallagher lost his bid for the high bench, however, to Republican C. Donald Peterson, a state legislator and unsuccessful Republican candidate for lieutenant governor in 1962.[65]

In Montana, the effects of nonparty cues are also clearly observable. The 1948 race ($r = 0.48, 0.54$) involved the sitting Democratic attorney general, R. V. Bottomly, and a former Democratic attorney general, Harrison J. Freebourn. Freebourn also ran for a full term in 1950 in another relatively partisan race ($r = 0.57$). In 1956, James D. Freebourn ran unsuccessfully for the bench in a four-way race but his pairing indicates moderate partisanship from the voters ($r = 0.52$). James Freebourn had made a previous unsuccessful attempt in the 1952 Democratic primary for attorney general; some voters might have remembered his name from that contest, but name confusion with Harrison Freebourn is the more likely explanation.

In 1958, Montana experienced its two most partisan judicial races in the postwar period. Democrat Arnold Olsen squared off in one race against recent Republican appointee James T. Harrison

($r$ = 0.74) while James D. Freebourn challenged another Republican appointed to the bench in 1957, Wesley Castles ($r$ = 0.71). Olsen, a Democrat, was quite familiar to Montana voters, having served as attorney general from 1948 to 1965. Harrison had tried once unsuccessfully in 1954 for the Republican nomination for Congress from the Second District in Montana. Freebourn's Republican opponent, Wesley Castles, had lost a 1952 bid for attorney general. Thus, each of the candidates in these two races had been more or less active in partisan politics prior to attempting to win election to the state supreme court. Their names rang partisan bells among the voters.

Former Democratic attorney general and governor John W. Bonner sparked a partisan response from the voters in his 1968 bid ($r$ = 0.56). And Democrat Gene B. Daly, appointed in April 1970, evoked an above average degree of partisan voting after having been an unsuccessful candidate for attorney general just two years previously ($r$ = 0.49).

The power of name confusion is dramatically evident in Montana's election in 1966 for the state supreme court where John M. McCarvel, a Republican, challenged incumbent Justice John Conway Harrison, a Democrat. Harrison had been elected in 1960, defeating that perennial candidate James D. Freebourn, when many voters apparently confused him (John Conway Harrison) with James T. Harrison, a Republican. In any event, the correlation for party division of the 1966 vote was sent plunging in a negative direction ($r$ = −0.42).

In Nevada, judicial candidates have sometimes also stimulated party voting. In 1950, incumbent Justice Charles Lee Horsey, on the court since 1945, was defeated by Charles M. Merrill, a lawyer in private practice ($r$ = 0.50). Some of the voters might have remembered that Horsey served as a Democratic state senator until 1940. In 1968, Republican Governor Paul Laxalt's appointee, Cameron Batjer, won election to the court ($r$ = 0.66); Batjer was a former unsuccessful Republican candidate for attorney general in 1958 and again in 1962. Batjer's opponent, John F. Mendoza, ran unsuccessfully in the 1962 Democratic primary for Congress. Four years later when Batjer faced re-election against a weak opponent, the voting response was decidedly nonpartisan ($r$ = 0.07).[66]

Among Washington's supreme court elections, the race of 1950 stands out as the most partisan ($r$ = 0.66). Republican Frederick G. Hamley, appointed in 1949 by Governor Arthur B. Langlie, fought off a challenge by Hugh J. Rosellini, a Democratic state legislator from 1939 to 1945 and a sitting superior court judge. In addition to public exposure in partisan politics, Rosellini shared the name of Albert D. Rosellini, a three-term Democratic state senator later to be elected governor in 1956.

Partisanship among the voters in Wisconsin's judicial elections has been virtually unknown. Only in 1973 did the correlation for the partisan division of the vote climb as high as 0.46 for reasons unknown. The standard deviation of the correlations for the partisan division of the vote in Wisconsin is among the lowest of those reported for the nonpartisan states in Table 10, attesting to the consistently low amount of partisan electoral vote in the state's judicial elections.

In Wyoming, the 1960 supreme court balloting stands out as the most partisan race in the postwar years ($r = 0.60$). The race featured a former attorney general, Harry Harnsberger, against John J. Spriggs, Wyoming's perennial candidate for the high court. The next most partisan race occurred in 1962 when two former attorneys general faced off. Despite near ideal circumstances for a partisan showdown in the electorate, the party-line voting was inexplicably weak ($r = 0.31$).[67]

The modestly negative correlation of $-0.49$ for the 1956 race between Spriggs and Republican Glenn Parker has defied explanation. The next lowest correlation for the partisan division of the vote is perhaps more understandable. In 1960, Frank O'Mahoney (whose partisan affiliation could not be ascertained) faced John J. McIntyre, a former Democratic congressman, deputy state attorney general, and state auditor. While McIntyre's partisan affiliation was familiar to many voters, O'Mahoney might have been confused in the minds of some with the popular Democratic U.S. Senator Joseph C. O'Mahoney who, with the exception of a two-year break in tenure from 1952 to 1954, held office from 1934 until 1961.

## THE VOTER IN STATE JUDICIAL ELECTIONS: SUMMARY AND IMPLICATIONS

It is clear that "the division of the vote is structured by the degree of partisanship in electoral arrangements and campaign resources."[68] In states utilizing the partisan nomination and election of judges, electors respond in a highly partisan fashion both to the campaign efforts of the parties on behalf of their nominees and to the cues of party identification found on the ballot. In the states with a mixed partisan-nonpartisan judicial election system, voters divide only moderately along partisan lines. During the campaign, the parties aid and promote their nominees (to a greater or lesser extent, depending upon the state), but the generally low visibility of judicial candidates and campaigns mitigates most of their efforts to make known the partisan affiliation of their candidates. One might be tempted to rush to the simplistic conclusion that the parties in the mixed states are simply less effective in promoting their candidates than are the parties in the partisan judicial states. But it is much more probable that a large proportion of the voters make no decision until inside the voting booth. Without the party label on the ballot, these voters turn to other cues to help them cast their judicial votes in ways they find meaningful.

Voters in the states with the nonpartisan nomination and election of their judges rarely divide along partisan lines. In the first place, the nomination process in the nonpartisan states does not guarantee competition between candidates with opposing party affiliations. In fact, as observed in Chapter 2, the nonpartisan system often does not produce any competition at all. Even when offered the choice between a Democrat and a Republican, the judicial electorate may be unaware of the candidates' partisan backgrounds. Neither the campaign nor the ballot is likely to help stimulate the division of the electorate along partisan lines.

Voters in states with the nonpartisan general election ballot must rely primarily upon nonparty cues for voting. Often bewildered and confused, some voters are unable to reach a decision and simply refrain from voting. Those who do vote may base their choice upon any number of signals received either during the campaign or in the ballot booth. Some voters may recognize the name of the incumbent; some states even help the voters in this regard by designating the incumbent on the ballot. Candidates might also be recognizable as former elective or appointive partisan officeholders or contestants for public office. In such circumstances, voters may rely upon a candidate's name as an indirect cue for party identification and divide in a remarkably partisan alignment despite the nonpartisan ballot. Reliance on name recognition, however, may result in a vote for a candidate totally unrelated by family or politics to the individual originally responsible for the name stamped in the memories of the voters.

Voting cues other than incumbency and name familiarity, of course, undoubtedly determine the judicial choices of some voters at some times. Unfortunately, the data collected here do not allow a full exploration of the relative importance of the myriad of nonparty voting cues available to the voter. But the effects of such cues in other low-visibility and low-salience elections have already been documented. And among the elections studied here, examples of voting based upon religious-ethnic cues and the existence of "friends and neighbors" balloting have been seen.

These results undoubtedly provide some comfort to the opponents of popular judicial selection. The analysis of the voting behavior of the electorate in nonpartisan judicial contests merely confirms their worst suspicions that voters have no rational basis for casting their ballots in these low-salience races and often have to resort to idiosyncratic decision rules in making voting choices. Even under the best of conditions, the critics might say, where voters are guided by a party label, no necessary relationship exists between the qualifications and competence of those who seek high judicial office and the respective partisan labels they wear. In this view, partisan and nonpartisan judicial elections are nothing more than periodic occasions for voters to demonstrate their ignorance.

Party labels are, admittedly, poor guides for comparing the qualifications of those seeking election to the bench. On the other hand, there is little reason to criticize a partisan ballot for conveying less information to the voter in judicial contests than it does in the election of other public officials. What supports this criticism in the context of judicial elections, however, is the belief that the formal minimum qualifications for office typically provided in constitutional and statutory provisions are inadequate and that judicial recruitment requires more stringent control over the professional qualifications of those selected than for the filling of legislative and executive positions. As discussed in Chapter 1, underlying this belief is a conception of the judicial function as essentially nonpolitical and technical in nature, requiring the recruitment of the most qualified technicians, in contrast to those offices which require occupants to possess and demonstrate essentially political skills.

Unfortunately, despite the Realist revolution and empirical verification that judges not only make political decisions as a matter of their function to allocate societal values and goods but also make conscious policy choices in the process of adjudication, this traditional view of the nature of judicial office continues to be held by a wide segment of the legal profession. And it supports the persistent claim that the need to find the best qualified individuals to be judges is too crucial a decision to be left to the uninformed whim of the electorate. Rather, elections should be replaced by some form of appointive system of judicial recruitment, either where governors are given the sole power of selection or, better yet, where governors are assisted in their task by the work of a merit nominating commission. By virtue of the greater informational resources at their disposal, it is argued that governors and merit nominating commissions can do a much better job in actively recruiting high-quality people to fill judicial posts and in eliminating from consideration those individuals ill-suited by training or temperament to hold judicial office.

Unfortunately for the advocates of appointive judicial recruitment, however, little empirical evidence has been mustered to support their claims regarding the ability of appointive systems to dramatically improve the quality of the judiciary. As discussed in Chapter 1, governors and merit nominating commissioners have found the establishment, measurement, and comparative application of criteria of "quality" to prospective judges to be exceptionally difficult tasks. Further, the results of empirical studies of the consequences of the various systems of judicial selection make it clear that the objectively measured characteristics of those judges selected by partisan and nonpartisan elections do not differ in many fundamental respects from the characteristics of those selected by the appointive methods. Finally, with particular reference to the merit plan, studies of the process by which nominating commissioners screen potential nominees indicate that the most salient factors in the decisions regarding nominations are subjective evaluations of individual character and personality and not objective indicators or even subjective estimates of professional competence.

The question, then, of whether an elective or an appointive selection system is most capable of recruiting the most qualified individuals to staff the courts is, at best, unresolved and perhaps entirely unresolvable. But even assuming arguendo that appointive officials are better situated than the voters actively to recruit high-quality judges or at least to prevent the accession of those individuals of questionable ability or character, the direct popular accountability of the judiciary secured by popular judicial selection may nevertheless outweigh the risks which attend popular elections in terms of selecting judges of less than superior quality.

Of course not all students of the judicial process, particularly those who view the judicial function as nonpolitical, accept accountability as a normative value properly applied to the courts. However, if popular accountability is recognized as a primary value to be achieved by the elective method of selection, the central issue is whether voters in fact are able to hold their judges accountable. Even those critics who accept the value of judicial accountability point out that the low level of public attention to and information about judicial elections makes it extremely doubtful that accountability can be achieved in any meaningful way. How are judges to be held accountable for their actions when no one is paying attention?

When voters cast their votes "blindly" along party lines or rely upon other irrational voting cues, accountability is being achieved perhaps only in theory.

Initially, it must be noted that critics also find judicial elections to be poor instruments for securing judicial accountability for reasons unrelated to the abilities of the electorate. The frequency with which incumbents go unchallenged and the infrequency of incumbent defeat, for example, have meant that under normal circumstances judicial elections "do not seriously threaten the judge's tenure or force him to defend his decisions,"[69] conditions which would seem essential to permit voters to pass retrospective judgment upon judicial performance and to secure judicial accountability. However, as demonstrated in Chapter 2, the vast majority of uncontested judicial races are the product of the nonpartisan format where there are no permanent and regularized channels for the recruitment of candidates as under the partisan system. The frequent re-election of incumbents, moreover, can hardly be considered as damning evidence of the malfunctioning of the judicial election process when incumbents in nonjudicial offices at all levels of government are typically returned.

The principal inquiry, therefore, is whether the voting behavior of the electorate in judicial elections is "irrational," as the critics assert, or whether it bears some relationship to the process of holding judges accountable for their decisions.

Of the cues available to the voter in nonpartisan elections, voting for (or against) the incumbent would appear to be the surest way for voters to hold their judges accountable. Voters can choose to exercise their retrospective control over the judiciary by rewarding with re-election those judges whose performance they approve while punishing with defeat those whose decisions displease them. As discussed earlier, however, the low visibility of the judiciary and judicial elections means that voting based on the factor of incumbency probably does not follow a careful evaluation of judicial performance. Rather, the familiarity of the incumbent's name draws voter attention, or a ballot label indicating the incumbent guides the uncertain and previously undecided. Voting based upon name recognition, a ballot label, or any of the many possible nonparty cues available is an uncertain means for voters to exercise retrospective judgments concerning judicial performance, to say nothing of attempting to influence prospectively the decision-making behavior of judges.

The same cannot be said of party identification. The party label provided on the partisan ballot may perform an important function in structuring voter choice along partisan lines. In so doing, party may serve as the instrument by which voters can guarantee the accountability of their state judicial policy-makers. In the first place, there are both theoretical and empirical reasons to support the conclusion that in casting their ballots along party lines the voters in judicial elections are neither blind nor irrational, as the critics suggest, but are in fact able to use the party label as a meaningful guide to express their general preferences on the resolution of public policy issues.

As discussed early in this chapter, party identification has been identified by scholars as the single most important determinant of individual voting behavior, a conclusion supported in the context of partisan judicial elections by the results of data collected here. The earliest voting research focused on the stable role of party affiliation, its inherited character, and its effects on structuring voter perceptions of candidates and issues. But even then scholars recognized that the party label allows voters to express their general impressions of, and to fix responsibility for, the conduct of government under the party in power. Subsequent, ground-breaking research by V. O. Key demonstrated, moreover, that the voters' retrospective judgments are not the product of blind partisan loyalties but are, in the vast majority of instances, related to voter policy preferences in broad issue areas.[70] Key confirmed that most voters do support "their" party from one presidential election to the next. In part, this party loyalty is attributable to the impact of the "perceptual screen" which voters' psychological attachment to a party provides with respect to evaluating competing candidates. But in substantial part, partisan voting occurs because, in Key's words, "this strong partisan attachment seems to be associated in high degree with compatible policy outlooks and expectations."[71] Key also found that although a relatively small proportion of the voters switch their partisan voting preference from one election to the next those who do usually make "choices congruent with their policy preferences."[72]

More contemporary studies have cast a small shadow upon this usual portrait of the voter. Observing a drop in the high association between partisan affiliation and the vote and a rise in ticket-splitting between the presidential race and the rest of the ballot, scholars have argued that voters are less concerned today with the partisan affiliation of candidates than with their stands on public issues and their personal abilities to handle the demands of the presidency.[73]

The heightened impact of nonparty factors on the presidential vote has been attributed to several factors. Many scholars point to the growing number of voters who fail to identify themselves with one or the other of the major political parties. Some attribute the growth in the proportion of self-identified "independents" to a decline in public faith in the abilities of parties to faithfully represent their interests in the conduct of government.[74] Other observers cite the recent entry into the electorate of new voters who possess only weak or nonexistent ties to the established parties; these voters are, therefore, less influenced in their perceptions of political events by a partisan allegiance and must make independent assessments of candidate competence and issue stands.[75]

Another explanation offered for the decline in importance of partisan affiliation in presidential voting is the increasing educational level of the population combined with the widespread impact of the mass media, especially television; these developments have presumably served to enhance the ability of voters to perceive differences between candidates on issue positions, to directly appraise differences in the personalities and characters of the candidates, and to vote on the basis of these differences.[76]

Apart from these explanations which focus on the characteristics of the electorate, other scholars have suggested that the changing character of presidential election contests explains a great part of the increasing importance of voter evaluations of candidate qualifications and issue positions. More than one analyst has suggested that the emergence in the mid-1960s of salient national political issues which cut across the traditional lines of interparty cleavage pulled voters away from their normal partisan loyalties which were formed along another set of issues in another time.[77]

Each of these possible explanations for presidential election voting behavior might be valid. But they tend to underestimate the continuing high correlation between party affiliation and electoral choice and the rise in issue awareness among individuals maintaining a partisan identification.[78] The heightened concern of voters with presidential candidates and issues seems most probably related to the increased clarity of the alternatives in candidates and issue stands presented to the electorate since the presidential contest of 1964.[79] Further, whatever the explanation might be for increases in deviations from the normal partisan division of the vote in presidential elections, the continuing preeminent role of partisan affiliation in structuring the vote in electoral contests below the presidential level cannot be gainsaid.

In subpresidential contests, such as those for congress member, governor, and lower state offices, the candidates and the issues are not as salient to the voters as those presented in presidential elections. In the absence of short-term stimuli which affect their voting decisions, voters must look to other cues to help them cast their ballots. The party label attached to each candidate provides the most familiar and readily available voting cue. And if one evaluates the role of elections in terms of their indirect effects, such behavior by the electorate does allow the voters to control the direction of policy.

Accompanying the development of voter awareness of specific issues has been an increase in the ability of voters to distinguish between the parties on policy and ideological grounds.[80] Thus, though they may be faced with a lack of specific information about candidates and issues in subpresidential campaigns, voters may be able to express their policy preferences in the choice of political leadership by utilizing the party label which most appeals to them.

It is clear that at least since the mid-1960s voters are aware of differences between the parties on those issues that are most salient to them and they tend to be identified with the party that most closely reflects their own positions on the issues.[81] There is, of course, still evidence that some voters rationalize their own issue positions to be consistent with their partisan affiliation or attribute to their party issue stands which are incorrect. But, as RePass has noted, there is "a strong strain toward a correct perception of party positions," particularly "in policy areas where the parties have taken opposing stands over a long period of time or on issues on which the candidates have taken clearly opposing positions."[82]

Voters who identify themselves with the Democratic party are considerably more likely than Republican party identifiers to maintain the liberal position on a series of domestic issues, particularly those related to matters of economic well-being.[83] Further, voters' attitudes on different issues are more consistently related than ever before; "as politics has become more pressing and more relevant, Americans have developed a more coherent, constrained belief system."[84]

Paralleling this development of issue awareness and consistency, voters across the political spectrum have developed sharper perceptions of differences between the parties on major domestic issues. At the most fundamental level, the parties present distinctive images to the voters:

> The strength of the Democratic party is its domestic policies and the connections to social groups these policies have created. The party is liked because it is good for "the common man" or the "working people," because it opposes the interest of "big business," and because of its association with popular

policies. . . . The positive qualities ascribed to the party clearly date to the times of the Great Depression and the New Deal. That they persist to the present, when the voters and leaders of the earlier period have largely passed from the scene, is testament to the stability of strongly felt popular attitudes. A mirror image of Democratic attractiveness is found in the features of the Republican party disliked by the voters.[85]

Additionally, however, voters are also quite able to agree on the relative position of the parties in their specific approaches to solving public problems. "There is a high degree of consensus on the more liberal position of the Democrats, with even the most ardent Republicans agreeing to this characterization. On the bread and butter issues, voters of all tastes know which side has their favorite spread."[86]

That the partisan judicial ballot structures voter choices in politically meaningful directions would be a hollow finding if judicial decision-making is unrelated to the labels upon which voters are basing their decisions. However, though further research is needed and will be offered later in this book, there is a demonstrable relationship between partisan affiliation and judicial policy-making. In scholarly studies of the relationship between social background characteristics and the patterns of individual judicial behavior, political party has emerged as the single most powerful factor which accounts for the differences in the decision-making tendencies of state supreme court justices.[87] Moreover, case studies of patterns of judicial behavior on state supreme courts suggest that the extent to which partisanship is important in judicial decision-making varies with the partisanship of the nomination and election system.[88] There is a growing literature, therefore, to link the judicial election constituency to the behavior of judges selected under the partisan system. At present, the results of previous analyses provide only inferential support for this linkage. But if the inferences gleaned from the case studies can be more firmly established in future research, a task which is taken up in Chapters 5, 6, and 7, then party identification may be seen as the chief mechanism by which voters can indirectly influence the course of judicial policy-making and secure the accountability of the third branch of state government.

# 4. Appointment and Election: Patterns of Accession to Elective Courts

## INTRODUCTION

One of the major criticisms of popular election as a means of selecting judges to state courts has been that most state judges do not reach the bench initially through the electoral process but are, in fact, appointed to their positions. In every state in which popular elections are the central method to select judges, the governor possesses the power to appoint a temporary successor to fill the untimely vacancy left by the death, retirement, or resignation of a sitting judge. Unlike in states using gubernatorial appointment as the primary means of judicial selection, these vacancy appointments are not subject to confirmation by any other body, such as the state legislature, state senate, or special commission. Persons appointed to a vacancy usually serve on the bench until the next general election when they may run for election to fill either the unexpired portion of their predecessor's term or for a full term of their own, depending upon state provisions.

Writing in 1962, Glenn R. Winters charged that "if a count were made it would certainly show that a very substantial percentage, if not an actual majority, of the judges of all courts of record in the United States actually were chosen for the job by an act of appointment and not by vote of the people."[1] James Herndon supported Winters' claim by reporting that nearly 56% of the judges serving on thirty-six elective state courts of last resort during the period from 1948 to 1957 had reached the bench initially by appointment. In fact, half of these courts were composed of a majority of judges who had been initially appointed rather than elected to office.[2] Subsequent studies and reports from separate states also reported that a large proportion of the judges serving on state courts at all levels had been appointed to office, despite the formal designation of each state's judicial selection system as elective.[3]

Most state judges on elective courts, it seemed, were not the product of the electoral process but of gubernatorial choice. And, as Winters noted, these judges are selected through an appointment process not subject to an external check from any confirming body. This system of "one-man judicial selection," said Winters, allows the governor to exercise an unrestricted power to choose whomever he or she wishes to fill judicial vacancies and to respond without consequence to the demands of partisan politics or to exercise unchecked personal whim.[4]

A governor's choice for a judicial vacancy is, of course, always subject to the check of the electorate when the appointed incumbent seeks election to the post. But critics claim that appointed incumbents are almost always re-elected to office, often without opposition; the electorate's check is ineffective. "Checks and balances to be effective," said Winters, "must be applied at the time of and in connection with the appointment itself, and not a year or two later after the appointee has become entrenched in the job and voters have gotten used to calling him 'Judge.'"[5]

Because of these arguments, it is a common assumption about the elective state judiciary that the usual path to the bench is by appointment followed by an automatic, often uncontested, election of an entrenched incumbent. Once elected, the power of incumbency is multiplied with each re-election so that the appointed judge can expect to remain through many terms without facing any substantial electoral challenge. Father Time is more likely to end a judge's career by death or by forcing resignation or retirement than is an electoral adversary. A new judge is then appointed by the governor to fill the untimely mid-term vacancy and the cycle begins anew.

All of this might remain undisturbed amidst other political science folklore were it not for significant inconsistencies in the evidence and a fair amount of contrary data. In Herndon's study of initial accession to elective state supreme courts, nearly 56% of all the judges sitting on these courts were initially appointed. But the nationwide total obscured the large variation among individual states ranging from 12.5% to 100% in the proportion of judges reaching the bench by appointment.[6] Barber's study of the Ohio judiciary also revealed that slightly less than 20% of the initial accessions to the supreme court from 1852 to 1970 had been by appointment.[7] Kenneth Vines' study of the Louisiana courts also reported that a vast majority of the state's judges had reached the bench by election.[8]

These variations in the extent to which various elective courts were dominated by gubernatorial appointees remained unaccounted and, with but one exception, largely unexplained. Only Herndon has attempted to determine why some elective state supreme courts are, in fact, appointive while other states actually elect most of their judges. Herndon hypothesized that the "normal" pattern of judicial appointment followed by successive election and re-election might be disrupted and the number of initial accessions by election correspondingly increased if judicial candidates facing re-election happen to be the victims of a "realigning election" where "wholesale shifts of electoral sentiment take place and substitutions of one party's candidates for the incumbents of the opposition occur as a result."[9] Herndon argued that in such circumstances and where the judicial candidates' partisan attachments are well known, such as on a partisan ballot, incumbent judges are more likely to share the adverse electoral fates of other members of their party facing re-election to executive and legislative positions. In contrast, judges competing on nonpartisan ballots are less likely to be affected by partisan electoral shifts occurring elsewhere on the ballot. These judges are more likely to be able to serve until death or resignation, events which will result in the appointment of a replacement. Thus, Herndon advanced the hypothesis that "appointment as a means of initial accession occurs more frequently than election in the case of 'Semi-' and 'Non-Partisan' elective courts owing to the greater isolation of the electoral fates of judges on these courts (relative to that of judges on the 'Partisan' courts) from the vicissitudes of interparty competition."[10]

Utilizing the statewide two-party vote for governor as a measure of "stable," "proximate," and "gross" shifts in electoral sentiment,[11] Herndon was able to demonstrate that appointment as a means of initial accession to state supreme courts was least frequent in those states experiencing the greatest amount of change in partisan control of the governorship and which utilized partisan judicial ballots. In those states using nonpartisan elections, sitting judges were relatively secure, insulated from even the most severe partisan shifts occurring in the state's other elections.[12]

Herndon's study provided ample ammunition for both the supporters and the critics of judicial elections. Advocates of partisan judicial selection could argue that the partisan ballot was most effective in keeping an elective judiciary truly elective. Critics could and did assert that the partisan election system allowed highly qualified and able sitting judges to be swept out of office by the electorate for reasons related more to the tides of partisan politics than an individual judge's record of performance.

From either perspective, however, Herndon's explanation of the patterns of initial accession is not entirely satisfactory. In the first place, the conclusions drawn from the data are not entirely supportable. While Herndon does demonstrate that appointment is less common in partisan judicial election systems than in the non- or semipartisan systems, his evidence also shows that "gross" electoral shifts at the top of the statewide ballot have a proportionately greater impact (when compared to "proximate" and "stable" shifts) in reducing the percentage of appointed judges in the semi- and nonpartisan states than in the partisan states.[13] This kind of evidence is inconsistent with Herndon's theory about the relative insulation of nonpartisan electoral systems from the pull of party politics. If the partisan ballot is more effective than the nonpartisan ballot in removing sitting judges on election day, then gross electoral shifts should have their greatest impact in states utilizing the partisan ballot which closely ties the electoral fates of candidates for the state supreme court to those for the top statewide offices.

Second, Herndon's presentation masks a considerable degree of inter- and intrastate variation. Barber, for example, found that a "gross" electoral shift in Ohio's 1962 race for governor in the direction of the Republicans resulted in the defeat of the only judicial appointee to the state's intermediate appellate court running for election, a Democrat. In contrast, when Democrat John Gilligan swept into the governor's office in 1970 with 55.5% of the vote (a gross shift by Herndon's standards), all four of the appointees of his Republican predecessor to the supreme court and all three appointees to the appeals court were elected.[14] Thus, at least in Ohio, the effect of partisan shifts at the top of the ballot have been variable and not subject to a single generalization.

Finally, Herndon failed to consider other relevant variables which are important for understanding the patterns of judicial appointment and election to state courts. Herndon did not consider the nature of competition in judicial elections and its relationship to the pattern of initial accession. As Chapter 2 showed, due to the activity of the political parties and party activists in recruiting and campaigning on behalf of party candidates, partisan judicial elections are more often contested and more often competitive than nonpartisan contests. Under these circumstances, judges in partisan states are more likely to lose their seats than judges who sit on nonpartisan courts where electoral competition is weak or nonexistent. Herndon also made no allowance for the length of judicial terms of office in considering the pattern of initial accession. It is not unreasonable to expect that, where judicial terms are lengthy and where the opportunity for a convenient retirement at the end of an expired term is distant, judges are more likely to resign, retire, or die in the middle of their terms.[15]

Using a slightly different set of data, Herndon's thesis can be subjected to a more rigorous examination in light of these factors. In addition, fresh information concerning the electoral fates of appointed judges makes it possible to determine whether, as Winters suggested, gubernatorial appointments go completely unchecked by the electorate. Finally, in an attempt to verify Herndon's assertions about the impact of realigning elections upon the patterns of initial accession, the conditions under which incumbents have been defeated can be explored.

## PATTERNS OF INITIAL ACCESSION TO STATE SUPREME COURTS

Table 12 presents the patterns of initial accession to elective nonsouthern state courts of last resort by election system for the years 1948 to 1974.[16] In the twenty-two states studied, a bare majority (52.7%) of the over four hundred judges initially reached their courts by appointment. This is a slightly lower proportion of appointed judges than that reported by Herndon (56.4%), but the results from the two studies are quite comparable considering the differences in the data bases.[17] Moreover, as in Herndon's study, this mean statistic masks a considerable range among the states in the percentage of initially appointed judges, from a low of 27.8% in Arizona to a high of 81.8% in Wyoming.

Though their impact cannot be dismissed entirely, it is doubtful that constitutional and statutory differences for filling judicial vacancies account for much of this variation.[18] All states provide that in the case of a vacancy the governor is empowered to appoint a successor. In nearly every instance, the appointed judge serves until the next general election when he or she may run for election against competing candidates. Only in Idaho and South Dakota do vacancy appointees serve the balance of an unexpired six-year term; in West Virginia, an appointee may serve out the unexpired portion of a twelve-year term if fewer than two years remain on that term. In most other states, a judicial appointee must face the electorate at the next general election and, if successful, will serve out the portion of the term left unserved by the predecessor. In a handful of states, the successor is elected to a full term of his or her own.[19] Obviously, the former arrangement increases the frequency of elections

**Table 12.  *Initial Accession to Elective State Courts of Last Resort***

| | Type of Judicial Election System | | | |
| | Partisan | Mixed | Nonpartisan | Total |
| --- | --- | --- | --- | --- |
| Number of justices | N = 172 | N = 74 | N = 190 | N = 436 |
| Percentage elected | 58.1% | 58.1% | 33.2% | 47.2% |
| Percentage appointed | 41.9% | 41.9% | 66.8% | 52.7% |
| Herndon[a] percentage appointed | 51.0% | 54.7% | 70.5% | 56.4% |
| | (N = 138) | (N = 27) | (N = 86) | (N = 445) |

[a] See Herndon, "Appointment as a Means of Initial Accession to Elective State Courts of Last Resort," p. 66 (Table V).

and thus, at least potentially, makes greater the possibility that some recently appointed judges will leave the bench because of electoral defeat. If more judges are defeated in elections, fewer will serve until an advanced age and the opportunities for gubernatorial appointment brought on by the mid-term retirement or death of an incumbent will decrease correspondingly.

Another factor which might affect the percentage of appointed judges is the extent to which state law requires or encourages the retirement of sitting judges.[20] Mandatory retirement provisions may compel, or generous retirement provisions may encourage, the mid-term departure of a sitting judge, thus necessitating the appointment of a replacement. On the other hand, where there exists no constitutional or legal obligation to retire, where a minimum age or number of years of service must be achieved in order to qualify for pension benefits, or where the financial benefits of retirement are relatively unattractive judges may have a powerful incentive to stay on in office during their later years, making more probable the occurrence of an untimely mid-term vacancy due to death.

Unfortunately, the precise effect of compulsory retirement requirements and judicial retirement plans is most difficult to gauge. Few areas of judicial administration have undergone such widespread and frequent alteration in the states over the past twenty-five years. Further, it is impossible to know with certainty how the various age and service requirements and benefit levels affect the patterns of judicial retirement from state to state. A comparative state analysis of individual cases of retirement might provide some indications but these data are not currently available.

Any of these factors might partially determine the relative frequency of the appointment of judges to elective state supreme courts. But Herndon's results suggest that perhaps the most important factor affecting the pattern of initial accession is whether a judicial election system is partisan or nonpartisan. While recognizing that the type of election system is not the sole determinant of variations in initial accession, Table 12 does confirm Herndon's finding that the proportion of initially appointed judges is smaller where partisanship is a significant element in the nomination or election of judges. In the partisan and mixed systems, a sizable majority (58.1%) of the judges reached their courts by election. In contrast, two of every three judges (66.8%) in the nonpartisan states were initially appointed to the bench.

These differences survive beneath the overall percentages presented in Table 12. Though there is wide variation among the states in the proportion of initially appointed judges, from a low of 27.8% in Arizona to over 80% in Oregon, South Dakota, and Wyoming, the impact of election type upon initial accession patterns remains clear. With but two exceptions (North Dakota and West Virginia), the partisan and mixed states have a smaller percentage of appointed judges than the nonpartisan states. Moreover, only West Virginia among the partisan-mixed states has had more than half (52.9%) of its judges appointed, while in every nonpartisan state except North Dakota (41.2%) *at least* half of the judges have been initially appointed.

Herndon's explanation for these differences focuses on the relative frequency of incumbent defeat. Under the partisan systems, Herndon suggested, the electoral fates of judges are tied to those of their fellow partisans at the top of the ticket. Judges not identified by party will escape the ebb and flow of partisan tides. Hence, in the partisan states a larger proportion of sitting judges can be expected to leave the bench at election time rather than in mid-term due to retirement or death. And the more judges who leave the bench due to election defeat, the fewer who will serve repeated terms until advanced age or death causes their removal and necessitates the appointment of a replacement.[21] Taking Herndon's analysis one step farther, then, it should be the case that states in which a large number of incumbents have met with defeat have a relatively small proportion of appointed judges.

Table 13 considers in detail the relationship between the patterns of initial accession and the frequency of incumbent defeat, with the length of the judicial term held constant. As noted earlier, the length of judicial terms must have some effect upon the proportion of initially appointed judges.[22] Where terms of office are long, judges are more likely to die in office or to be forced by illness to resign or by age to retire. Where shorter terms are provided, sitting judges have comparatively more-frequent opportunities to give up their seats at the end of completed terms.

Table 13 exhibits the fact that the partisan and mixed states have a smaller proportion of initially appointed judges than the non-partisan states. And, as Herndon suggested, incumbents have most frequently met with defeat in the partisan and mixed election systems. Electoral defeat cuts short the careers of sitting judges, making it impossible for them to serve for extended periods of time, to die or to be forced into retirement at mid-term, and to begin the cycle of gubernatorial appointment.

On the other hand, the relationship between the proportion of appointed judges and the frequency of incumbent defeat is far from being a perfectly inverse one. Indeed, states like Kansas and South Dakota, which feature the same number of defeated incumbents (none), display a vast difference in the proportion of initially appointed justices. Clearly there are other factors which contribute to the frequency of gubernatorial appointments on a state supreme court. Additionally, the incidence of incumbent defeat is but an imperfect indicator of judicial tenure. In the first place, it does not reveal the extent to which incumbents have voluntarily left the bench to pursue other personal and professional goals. Nor does it highlight those occasions when an incumbent has been denied renomination to office or has been persuaded by political or community leaders not to seek re-election.[23] Alternatively, as the analysis below will demonstrate, in some states the importance of gubernatorial appointment to a state judicial selection system can be grossly underestimated, depending upon the particular patterns of incumbent defeat.

PATTERNS OF INCUMBENT DEFEAT IN STATE JUDICIAL ELECTIONS

Though the relationship is not perfect, it remains true as a general proposition that incumbents are more frequently defeated by election in the partisan and mixed states than in the nonpartisan states, perhaps partially verifying Herndon's explanation for the relative infrequency of gubernatorial appointment in the partisan states. But a thorough test of Herndon's thesis requires an examination of the conditions under which incumbent justices have been defeated in re-election bids. In doing so, three basic goals can be achieved. First, closer attention can be given to those factors which result in the defeat of incumbent justices and which thereby in-

**Table 13.** *Proportion of Initially Appointed Judges and Incidence of Incumbent Defeat, by State, Election System, and Length of Term*

| Length of Term States | Total No. of Judges[a] | % of Judges Appointed | Election System | No. of Incumbents Defeated[b] |
|---|---|---|---|---|
| Six-Year Terms | | | | |
| Arizona | 18 | 27.8% | Mixed | 3 |
| Indiana | 21 | 28.6% | Partisan | 4 |
| Kansas | 17 | 41.2% | Partisan | 0 |
| Ohio | 28 | 46.4% | Mixed | 10 |
| Idaho | 18 | 50.0% | Nonpartisan | 0 |
| Nevada | 10 | 60.0% | Nonpartisan | 1 |
| Washington | 30 | 73.3% | Nonpartisan | 1 [2] |
| Minnesota | 21 | 76.2% | Nonpartisan | 0 |
| Oregon | 21 | 81.0% | Nonpartisan | 1 |
| South Dakota | 16 | 81.3% | Nonpartisan | 0 |
| Eight-Year Terms | | | | |
| Iowa | 18 | 38.9% | Partisan | 2 |
| New Mexico | 22 | 45.5% | Partisan | 5 |
| Michigan | 27 | 48.1% | Mixed | 5 |
| Montana | 16 | 50.0% | Nonpartisan | 2 |
| Wyoming | 11 | 81.8% | Nonpartisan | 1 |
| Ten-Year Terms | | | | |
| Utah | 6 | 33.3% | Partisan | 0 |
| Colorado | 22 | 36.4% | Partisan | 6 |
| North Dakota | 17 | 41.2% | Nonpartisan | 1 [1] |
| Utah | 6 | 50.0% | Nonpartisan | 1 |
| Wisconsin | 24 | 70.8% | Nonpartisan | 2 |
| Longer Terms[c] | | | | |
| New York | 25 | 48.0% | Partisan | 2 |
| Pennsylvania | 25 | 48.0% | Partisan | 3 [2] |
| West Virginia | 17 | 52.9% | Partisan | 2 [1] |

[a] Entries in this column indicate the total number of judges serving on each state supreme court from 1948 through 1974, excluding judges appointed to newly created positions.

[b] Figures in this column reflect the number of incumbents defeated in general elections. Where known, the number of incumbents defeated in primary contests has been noted in brackets.

[c] The judicial terms in New York and West Virginia are 14 and 12 years, respectively. Pennsylvania used a 21-year term until 1968, when the term was reduced to 10 years.

crease the proportion of judges reaching the bench by election and decrease the number of those who are appointed to office. Second, it is possible to test the vitality of Herndon's proposition that incumbent justices running for election under the partisan ballot are more likely to be affected by the "vicissitudes of interpartisan competition" occurring at the top of the ballot. Thus, it will be important to consider not only the circumstances surrounding the defeat of incumbents but also the general relationship between partisan trends occurring at the top of the ballot and the outcome of judicial elections. Finally, this analysis permits us to evaluate the strength of Winters' contention that appointed justices are only infrequently defeated and thus the ability to fill interim vacancies gives the governor an unchecked power in staffing the state's judiciary.

Table 14 displays the patterns of incumbent electoral defeat by states grouped according to election system and by the partisan affiliation of the defeated justice. As previously noted in Table 13, incumbents most frequently meet with defeat in the partisan and mixed states but only rarely in the nonpartisan states. More importantly, however, are the emergent patterns of incumbency defeat. In several states, most notably New Mexico and Ohio, defeat has fallen principally upon previously appointed justices seeking their first election. Moreover, electoral misfortune appears to have a partisan bias—against Republicans in New Mexico and against Democrats in Ohio. In other states, such as Colorado, Indiana, and Michigan, most of the incumbents meeting with election defeat could claim at least one previous victory to their credit. In concert with an analysis of the relationship between the outcomes of the major statewide partisan races and those for the supreme court in each state, these basic patterns of incumbency defeat will now be explored in detail.

### Judicial Elections in One-Party Partisan States: New Mexico, West Virginia, Iowa, and Kansas

In partisan states dominated by one political party, electoral defeat falls most frequently upon members of the minority party who have been appointed to judicial office. The best examples are from the states of New Mexico and West Virginia, both predominately Democratic states. In each state, Democratic candidates have dominated the outcome of supreme court elections. If Republican gubernatorial candidates had not managed to capture the governor's office on several occasions in the postwar years and to appoint some of their fellow partisans to the bench, Democratic control over the high court in each state would have been total.

In contrast, in Iowa and Kansas, Republican candidates for the judiciary have been overwhelmingly favored. In Kansas, only one Democrat could win a state supreme court race from 1948 to 1958, the year in which the state abandoned its partisan election system. Iowa Democrats were similarly unrepresented on the state's high court for most of the postwar years prior to 1962 when Iowa voters approved a constitutional amendment adopting the merit selection plan. In both states, only a short-term surge of Democratic electoral sentiment which carried a Democrat into the governor's office and some Democratic judicial candidates on the bench in the late 1950s temporarily marred the near perfect Republican record.

*New Mexico.* In New Mexico, five Republican justices were appointed to the state supreme court from 1948 to 1974, but not one of them survived their first bids for election. Although the New Mexico electorate has frequently elected Republican governors in the postwar years (1950, 1956, 1960, 1966, 1968, 1972), the appointees of Republican governors to the state supreme court have in each case lost their seats in their first appeals to the electorate.

Whether these election defeats are attributable to the effect of partisan swings at the top of the ballot or to the general partisan preferences of the state's voters is not immediately clear. In four of these contests in which an appointed Republican justice was defeated, Democrats were at the same time regaining control of the statehouse;[24] in the fifth instance, the Republican judge had been appointed by a Democratic governor but lost his election chance as the Democrats retained control of the governorship.[25] This would tend to suggest that partisan results at the top of the ballot, combined with the party column ballot which links the electoral fates of those at the top and the bottom of the ballot, serve to make judicial incumbents in the partisan state more vulnerable.

It is crucial to note, however, that no Republican candidate for justice has ever defeated a Democratic candidate in New Mexico, even in those years where the Republicans have won the gubernatorial race. In fact, only 25% of the state's judicial elections could be considered competitive; the mean Democratic percentage of the two-party vote in contested races from 1948 to 1974 was 56.9%. In contrast, gubernatorial contests in the state have been quite competitive between the parties. As noted, Republican gubernatorial candidates captured six of the thirteen postwar contests, all but two of which were decided by a winning margin of less than 55% of the two-party vote.

New Mexico gubernatorial politics have been heavily linked to the tides of national politics. In six gubernatorial races held in presi-

**Table 14. Patterns of Electoral Defeat of Incumbent Judges**

| State | All Defeated[a] | | Appointed[b] | | Other[b] | |
|---|---|---|---|---|---|---|
| | Democrats | Republicans | Democrats | Republicans | Democrats | Republicans |
| **Partisan States** | | | | | | |
| Colorado | 2 | 4 | 1 | 1 | 1 | 3 |
| Indiana | 1 | 3 | 1 | 0 | 0 | 3 |
| Iowa | 1 | 1 | 0 | 0 | 1 | 1 |
| Kansas | 0 | 0 | 0 | 0 | 0 | 0 |
| New Mexico | 0 | 5 | 0 | 5 | 0 | 0 |
| New York | 0 | 2 | 0 | 2 | 0 | 0 |
| Pennsylvania | 2 | 1 | 2 | 1 | 0 | 0 |
| West Virginia | 0 | 2 | 0 | 2 | 0 | 0 |
| **Mixed States** | | | | | | |
| Arizona | 1 | 2 | 0 | 2 | 1 | 0 |
| Michigan | 3 | 2 | 1 | 0 | 2 | 2 |
| Ohio | 7 | 3 | 6 | 1 | 1 | 2 |
| **Nonpartisan States** | | | | | | |
| Idaho | 0 | 0 | 0 | 0 | 0 | 0 |
| Minnesota | 0 | 0 | 0 | 0 | 0 | 0 |
| Montana | 0 | 2 | 0 | 2 | 0 | 0 |
| Nevada | 1 | 0 | 0 | 0 | 1 | 0 |
| North Dakota | 1 | 0 | 1 | 0 | 0 | 0 |
| Oregon | 1 | 0 | 0 | 0 | 1 | 0 |
| South Dakota | 0 | 0 | 0 | 0 | 0 | 0 |
| Utah | 0 | 1 | 0 | 0 | 0 | 1 |
| Washington | 1 | 2 | 0 | 1 | 1 | 1 |
| Wisconsin | 0 | 2 | 0 | 1 | 0 | 1 |
| Wyoming | 0 | 1 | 0 | 0 | 0 | 1 |

[a] In the partisan and mixed states, the incumbents' partisan affiliations were established by the party label under which they sought nomination and/or election. In the nonpartisan states, judges' party affiliations were established by reference to standard biographical sources. Where a judge's partisan affiliation could not be so established, the party of the governor who made the initial appointment was used.

[b] The designation "Appointed" refers to judges seeking their first election following appointment. The designation "Other" refers to judges who won election to the bench at least once prior to meeting with electoral defeat, including those judges who initially may have reached the state's high court by appointment.

dential years from 1948 to 1968, the state's voters failed only in 1960 to award the presidential vote and the governorship to candidates of the same party.[26] Extremely close balloting in the state gave the 1960 presidential vote to John Kennedy (50.4%) while awarding the governorship to Republican E. L. Mechem with a similarly slight margin (50.3%). In six of seven off-year elections, however, the voters selected gubernatorial candidates not of the party of the incumbent president, "a result likely to occur when margins of victory are small, and state issues most readily dominate national attention."[27] The result of this highly competitive environment in New Mexico gubernatorial politics has been an alteration in party control of the governorship virtually every two years since 1948. Only Republican E. L. Mechem (1951–1955) and Democrat Jack Campbell (1963–1967) were able to serve more than a single two-year term consecutively.[28]

In contrast, for statewide offices below the level of governor and for legislative and local offices, Democratic candidates have consistently led the Republican candidates and fellow Democratic candidates at the presidential and gubernatorial levels.[29] The result of competitive elections at the gubernatorial level and noncompetitive, Democratic-dominated legislative races has been extended periods of divided control of the state's executive and legislative branches.[30] Similarly, the dominance of Democratic candidates below the top of the ticket has meant that no Republican has ever reached the New Mexico high court except by appointment and none of these appointees has survived the first election bid.

The effects of New Mexico judicial election politics upon the pattern of initial accession can now be seen more clearly. Table 13 indicates that less than half (45.5%) of New Mexico's justices sitting since 1948 have been appointed to office, a relatively low figure although not as low as one might expect given the frequency of incumbent defeat. What is not revealed by these statistics is the underlying pattern of incumbent defeat. The result is that the importance of appointment to the New Mexico judicial system is severely underestimated. The election of five Democratic justices to replace five previously appointed Republican justices has in effect "cancelled out" the frequency of appointments made to fill vacancies on the bench. As the analysis offered demonstrates, Democrats in New Mexico hold a decided electoral advantage; they may easily serve several terms without facing any substantial challenge from the Republicans. When advanced age forces their departure from the bench, a vacancy appointment must be made by the governor. The competitiveness of partisan politics for the major statewide races, however, has allowed the frequent election of Republican governors. When vacancies have occurred, these Republican executives have appointed their fellow partisans to the bench. But at the first general election when the appointee must gain the electorate's approval in order to stay on the court, the predisposition of New Mexico voters for Democratic candidates below the top of the ballot has always resulted in the defeat of the Republican incumbent. If the effects of the defeats of newly appointed Republican justices are removed statistically, then it is clear that appointments play a major part in staffing the New Mexico judiciary.[31]

*West Virginia.*    A similar phenomenon can be observed in West Virginia where two of three appointees of Republican governors have been defeated for election to their posts. In the first of these contests, appointed Republican Justice Robert T. Donley lost in his 1958 attempt for election after his appointment by Governor Cecil H. Underwood. Donley lost to Democrat Harlan M. Calhoun by a margin of nearly three to two; Democratic candidates also captured two U.S. Senate seats contested in that year with similar margins of victory.

West Virginia's gubernatorial elections are held concurrently with the quadrennial presidential balloting. In 1956 Underwood became the first Republican governor elected in the state since 1928, courtesy of Dwight Eisenhower's presidential coattails. But Underwood's appointee, Donley, could not survive an electoral challenge in a mid-term election, nor could Underwood himself secure a seat in the U.S. Senate in 1960.

Democratic control of the governorship was restored in 1960 and retained until 1968 when Arch M. Moore, Jr., narrowly defeated Democrat James M. Sprouse despite Hubert Humphrey's victory in the state's presidential voting. Moore placed three appointees on the Supreme Court of Appeals during his first term, two of whom sought election in 1972. Though Republican candidates dominated the voting at the top of the ticket in that year (Richard Nixon trounced George McGovern by winning 63.6% of the vote and Moore won re-election with a comfortable margin of 54.7% of the two-party vote), appointed Republican Justice John Carrigan lost in a four-way race for two positions on the state's high court by finishing third in the field behind two Democratic candidates. The other Moore appointee, Charles Haden, narrowly won his seat in a separate contest for the unexpired portion of the term to which he had been appointed. As in New Mexico, the importance of partisan affiliation for voter choice in races below the top of the ballot strongly militates against the judicial appointees of minority-party governors.

*Iowa.* A variant of the pattern observed in New Mexico and West Virginia typified Iowa Supreme Court elections during the period that the state used the partisan judicial ballot (1948–1962). Iowa was securely within the Republican column during this time. Republican candidates dominated the presidential, senatorial, and gubernatorial ballotings by winning 75% of the presidential races, 83.3% of the U.S. Senate contests, and 62.5% of the gubernatorial. The state, however, has been considered by analysts to be among the two-party competitive states because Democratic candidates frequently come close to winning and, on occasion, are successful. For example, of the eight gubernatorial races held from 1948 to 1962, six (75%) were competitive and the Democratic candidates were victorious in half of these. Nevertheless, below the top of the ballot the state has been more completely and decidedly Republican. In twenty-four races for state supreme court, for instance, twenty-two (nearly 92%) were won by GOP candidates.[32]

The only Democrats elected to the supreme court during this period were elected in 1958. Democrat Harry F. Garrett narrowly defeated his Republican opponent in an election to fill the vacancy left on the court by the death of Justice William A. Smith in June of that year. Neither candidate was an appointed incumbent, however. Democratic Governor Herschel Loveless had previously appointed a third lawyer, Luke Linnan, to fill the Smith vacancy with the mutual understanding that Linnan would not seek election in November. Linnan reportedly said that he could not afford to serve permanently and the governor apparently perceived the political liabilities in prejudicing the outcome by appointing one of the candidates.

The other Democratic victory in the 1958 supreme court races occurred in a six-person contest for three positions. This election was very keenly contested with a mere 8,939 votes (out of approximately 780,000 cast) separating the highest from the lowest vote totals for the candidates. Republican Theodore G. Garfield led the balloting, followed by Democrat T. Eugene Thornton. Third place was a virtual toss-up with Republican Justice Ralph A. Oliver squeaking by a Democratic challenger named Messer with a thin 114 vote margin. The fifth-place finisher was another Democrat, with incumbent Republican Charles F. Wennerstrum finishing last and losing his place on the state's high bench.

These victories for Democrats Garrett and Thornton accompanied the successful bid of Democratic Governor Loveless for a second term. Loveless originally had won a narrow victory in 1956 by defeating incumbent Leo Hoegh, thus becoming the first Democratic governor in Iowa in twenty years despite the overwhelming victory for Eisenhower in the presidential balloting. Loveless was unable to help Democratic judicial candidates in this first campaign, however, as three incumbent Republican justices easily won re-election in a six-person contest; each justice collected a comfortable share of approximately 57% of the vote. In 1958, however, Loveless collected 54.1% of the vote and led the Iowa Democratic party to "one of its most complete victories . . . since the depression."[33] Loveless apparently helped carry Democrats into half of the state's eight congressional seats, a number of minor state offices, and judicial candidates Garrett and Thornton onto the supreme court. This Democratic surge was short-lived, however. Iowa voters put Republican Norman Erbe in the governor's office in 1960 with 52.1% of the vote, rejected two of the Democratic congressmen elected in 1958, and gave all three supreme court positions to Republican candidates, each of which attracted over 54% of the two-party vote. Justice Garrett lost his seat by finishing last in the field of six.[34]

An examination of the statewide vote totals in the races for supreme court justice and governor reveals that during the 1948 to 1962 period Republican judicial candidates outpolled the party's gubernatorial candidate in six of seven election years. With the exception of 1948, when Republican William Beardsley led the average Republican judicial candidate by 4.4% of the total statewide vote, Republican candidates for the supreme court have consistently run ahead of the party's gubernatorial candidate by an average of 4.5%, from a low of 0.6% to a high of 9.0%. This slightly stronger commitment of the Iowa electorate for Republican judicial candidates explains a great deal about the outcome of the races for the state's high court.

In 1956, when Loveless was elected to his first term, Republican Governor Leo Hoegh collected 48.8% of the vote. The average Republican judicial candidate, however, ran 5.5% ahead of Hoegh statewide and thus each won election. In 1958, however, the Republican challenger to Loveless could muster only 45.9% of the vote. As expected, the Republican judicial candidates outpolled the gubernatorial candidate (William G. Murray) by 3.8%, resulting in an average Republican statewide vote of only 49.7% and the defeat of two Republican candidates in extremely close contests.[35]

Iowa, therefore, fits within the general pattern of New Mexico and West Virginia. Judicial candidates from the major party typically outdistance their own party's gubernatorial candidate's share of the vote. In New Mexico and West Virginia, the dominance established by Democratic judicial candidates has virtually closed off access to the bench for Republican candidates except by gubernatorial appointments from Republican governors who have managed to achieve office. In Iowa, a similar dominance of one party virtually precluded the accession by election of minority-party candidates. And in Iowa, the only Democratic governor to serve during the period under study made only one appointment to the court but, as indicated, his appointee did not seek election.

As Herndon suggested, however, where the partisan loyalties of judicial candidates are known, "wholesale shifts in electoral sentiment [may] take place and substitutions of one party's candidates for the incumbents of the opposition occur as a result."[36] In the year when Democratic gubernatorial fortunes were at a maximum, Iowa Democrats did capture some of the available slots for the state supreme court, perhaps benefiting from their governor's coattails. But when Republicans recaptured the executive office, those coattails were unavailable to help the elected Democratic judges stay in office.

*Kansas.*   During the postwar years from 1948 to 1958 in which the state utilized partisan elections for the selection of its high court judges, judicial elections in Kansas followed a pattern nearly parallel to the one observed in Iowa. Since the end of the Populist era in Kansas at the turn of the century, Republicans have dominated state government.[37] In the judicial branch, the Republican hegemony was reflected in the fact that only 8.3% of the judges appointed or elected to the supreme court between 1900 and 1958 were Democrats. In the postwar years, only one Democrat was selected to serve on the court.

Republican candidates continued their control of state government by winning the governor's office and all the statewide constitutional offices from 1948 to 1954 by comfortable margins. Of eleven supreme court positions contested, all were won by Republicans collecting an average share of 57.9% of the vote.

In 1956, however, Democrat George Docking collected an astounding 56.8% of the vote to defeat his Republican opponent, the survivor of a bitter and divisive GOP primary battle.[38] Docking's victory was a lonely one, though, for he carried no fellow Democrats into office with him at the statewide level. The Republican judicial candidates continued the party's ironclad grip on the supreme court as none of the four GOP candidates attracted less than 54.2% of the vote.

During his first term, though, Docking did have the opportunity to appoint a fellow Democrat, Schuyler Jackson, to fill a vacancy on the supreme court; Jackson was only the third Democrat to sit on the court since 1900 and the first since 1943.

In 1958, Docking became the first Democratic governor in the state to win a second term. In this campaign, however, Docking helped to elect Democratic candidates to three statewide offices (lieutenant governor, treasurer, state printer) and to three of the six seats in Congress. Additionally, Justice Jackson won re-election, though trailing Docking by nearly 5% of the vote statewide. In a separate race, however, incumbent Republican Harold R. Fatzer did manage to hold his seat in a narrow victory (50.4%). The relatively low correlation for the partisan division of the vote for this race ($r = 0.64$) suggests that a number of voters split their tickets to re-elect the Republican incumbent.

As in Iowa, further examination of the trends of judicial elections in Kansas was made impossible and unnecessary by the constitutional change in selection system approved by the voters in the 1958 election. But based upon the results of statewide elections held since that time, it is most likely that the Democratic surge would have been short-lived. Republican control of the governor's office was returned in 1960, 1962, and 1964. George Docking's son, Robert, returned Democratic control of the statehouse in 1966 and won re-election an unprecedented three times. But despite the preference of Kansas voters for Democratic Dockings, the electorate's subgubernatorial voting has been consistently and overwhelmingly Republican. Over 90% of the statewide races below the office of governor contested between 1960 and 1974 were captured by Republicans. It is not likely that Democratic judicial candidates, whether previously appointed or not, would have been very successful. Had Robert Docking's Democratic appointees been forced to face the electorate on the partisan ballot, they most certainly would have been turned out of office.

## Judicial Elections in the Competitive Partisan States: Indiana and Colorado

The states discussed thus far only partially confirm Herndon's thesis. It is true that incumbents frequently face electoral defeat in the partisan systems. But many of these defeats would never have occurred had not minority-party governors appointed fellow partisans to vacant supreme court positions. It remains to be seen whether a similar pattern has occurred in those states in which the two major parties have been more closely competitive.[39]

*Indiana.* Elections for the supreme court in Indiana represent most clearly the pattern suggested by Herndon. Election results in the judicial contests parallel the results in the other partisan races on the ticket; incumbent justices of both parties often fall prey to partisan trends.

Indiana elects its governor, lieutenant governor, and attorney general every four years in the presidential election years; the other statewide offices (secretary of state, auditor, and treasurer) are filled every two years. In five of the seven presidential elections held between 1948 and 1972, Hoosier voters awarded their presidential votes and all the major statewide offices to candidates of the same party, preferring Republican candidates in each election except 1964. In 1948 and 1960, the state's voters selected presidential and gubernatorial candidates of different parties, preferring Republican presidential candidates but Democratic governors. However, Democrats made a sweep of the other statewide offices in 1948, while these positions were captured by Republicans in 1960. In each of the postwar presidential elections, Republican gubernatorial candidates have trailed the party's presidential candidate by an average statewide vote of 4.4%, win or lose.

The Republican dominance of the postwar presidential and statewide races has been repeated in the state's supreme court races. Republican judicial candidates campaigning in presidential years failed only twice to win their elections. In 1948, Democrat Paul G. Jasper defeated incumbent Republican Justice Mart O'Malley to accompany the Democratic sweep. In 1964, Democrat Amos Jackson swept to a similar victory against a Republican incumbent in that Democratic year. In 1960, the voters of Indiana gave a narrow victory to Democratic gubernatorial candidate Matthew E. Welsh. But their presidential sentiments were with Richard Nixon by a wide margin (55.2%) and they awarded each of the other statewide offices to Republican candidates, including the sole supreme court position filled in that year. Thus, in presidential years, judicial election outcomes have generally followed the partisan trend occurring at the top of the statewide ballot.

Similarly, in the mid-term elections, judicial elections are linked to the other statewide contests. In 1950, 1954, and 1966, Republican candidates captured the statewide offices and the available supreme court positions. In 1958 and 1970, Democratic candidates, led by Vance Hartke in the U.S. Senate race, swept all the statewide and judicial offices, albeit in competitive races. In 1962, Democrat Birch Bayh won a seat in the U.S. Senate by an extremely narrow margin, gathering 50.3% of the vote, but the balance of the state-wide offices were taken by Republicans. In this closely contested year, Republican candidates were victorious in two of the three supreme court races, but neither of these winners attracted more than 50.5% of the vote. Republican Justice Archie N. Bobbitt was defeated, losing to Democrat Walter Myers, Jr., who gathered 50.3% of the vote. Bobbitt's defeat was attributed by some observers to the efforts of the Indiana State Teachers Association (ISTA), which opposed Bobbitt because he had authored an opinion holding unconstitutional a law which had been sponsored and supported in the state legislature by the executive secretary of the ISTA.[40] For whatever reasons, Bobbitt's loss represents the only time in over forty years that one party has not won all the supreme court races contested in a given year.[41]

Thus, Indiana voters overwhelmingly cast their ballots for supreme court justice along the party line. With but the one exception noted above, the incumbents who have been defeated in re-election bids were victims of partisan sweeps occurring all along the ballot. The party column ballot has facilitated this result. The extremely high correlations for the partisan division of the vote reported in Chapter 3 reflect this close connection between the fates of judicial candidates and those of their fellow partisans elsewhere on the ballot. Overall, this phenomenon has favored Republican judicial candidates, who have won 71.4% of the judicial positions contested, a reflection of Republican dominance in eight of the twelve (66.7%) biennial statewide elections held from 1948 to 1970.[42]

*Colorado.* Unlike the partisan states of New Mexico, West Virginia, Iowa, and Indiana, Colorado does not utilize the party column ballot in the selection of its public officials. Split-ticket voting has been facilitated if not encouraged to some extent by the office block ballot form. Moreover, although the major parties have played an influential role in the nomination of candidates at preprimary conventions (called assemblies), party discipline has been weak and candidates have been most successful making personalistic rather than partisan political appeals to the electorate.[43]

The result has been a frequent division of statewide offices and ballotings between the parties. From 1948 to 1966, Republican presidential candidates were successful in three of five contests, while the parties split the biennial gubernatorial races at four each. More notably, only once (in 1948) did one party (the Democrats) sweep all six major statewide offices. In the remaining elections, the party winning the gubernatorial race has usually won a majority of the statewide offices, but the losing party has often captured at least one, two, or even three of these positions.[44] Similarly, divided party control of the two houses of the state legislature is not unknown either historically or during the postwar years prior to 1966.[45] As one pair of observers has noted, "Colorado voters have always been extremely independent, critical, and unpredictable."[46]

This extremely close competition between the parties' candidates was also characteristic of the state's supreme court elections. Of twenty high court races contested in the period, fourteen (or 70%) were decided in competitive races in which the winner averaged only 52.1% of the vote; 60% of all races were won by Democrats, 40% by Republicans.

The effects of intense competition, ticket-splitting, and the office block ballot upon judicial elections are best seen in the 1956 presidential election year. Eisenhower swept the presidential ballot with 59.9% of the statewide vote, but the gubernatorial voting was narrowly captured by Democrat Stephen L. R. McNichols with 51.3%. Democrats also won the U.S. Senate race, half of the four-member Congressional delegation, and the statewide offices of secretary of state and treasurer. Nevertheless, Republican candidates captured the statewide offices of lieutenant governor, attorney general, and auditor.

The supreme court races reflected a similarly intense competition as the voters turned one incumbent from each party out of office. Democrat Felix Sparks, an appointee of Governor "Big Ed" Johnson, was running for the final six years of the ten-year term started by his predecessor. Sparks was narrowly defeated, though, by Frank H. Hall (51.5%). At the same time, however, three Democrats were winning election to the supreme court. Leonard V. B. Sutton, another Johnson appointee, won his seat to an unexpired eight-year term with 53% of the vote. And newcomers Edward Day and Albert Frantz won election in a four-way race for two positions; incumbent Republican Justice Wilbur Alter was cast out of office by finishing a close third to Frantz.

Another instructive instance occurred in 1966 when Republican Hilbert Schauer, an appointee of Governor John Love, was defeated for election by finishing fifth in a field of six candidates competing for three positions. At the same time, Governor Love easily won re-election against a former governor and lieutenant governor, Robert Knous; Love attracted 55.4% of the vote. Moreover, Republican candidates captured four of the other five statewide offices and recouped nearly all their losses suffered in the 1964 Democratic landslide in races for Congress and the lower house of the state legislature. All was not lost for the party's supreme court candidates either, as two other Republican candidates, neither an incumbent, finished first and second in the at-large balloting, ousting incumbent Democrat Frantz, who placed fourth. Only 9,000 votes out of approximately 595,000 cast separated the third-place finisher (Democratic Justice Edward Day), Democrat Frantz, and Republican Schauer.

Thus, if aggregate statewide election results are any indication, a highly competitive electoral environment, the tendency of some voters to split their tickets, and a facilitative ballot format apparently combined to loosen the generally strong connection of the electoral fates of judicial candidates with fellow partisans competing for office higher on the ticket.

Further evidence can be considered in an examination of the outcome of Colorado judicial elections during periods of major partisan shifts at the top of the ballot. During the 1948 to 1966 period, there were, in Herndon's terms, one gross shift and two proximate shifts. In 1962, Republican John Love defeated incumbent Governor McNichols with over 57% of the vote. But Democrats managed to hold two of the other statewide offices and one of two judicial positions. Republican Frank Hall won re-election easily (55.3%), but Democratic appointee Edward Pringle survived by capturing a 51.9% share of the vote.

In 1950, Republican Dan Thornton defeated Walter Johnson with 52.6% of the statewide vote in the gubernatorial contest, but long-time Democratic Justice Benjamin C. Hilliard held on to his post by outpolling Johnson by over 4% statewide despite the "proximate" shift to the GOP.

Only the second proximate shift, occurring in 1954, might have contributed to the defeat of a sitting Republican justice. Johnson captured the gubernatorial race with 53.6% and Democratic candidates recaptured the offices of lieutenant governor and secretary of state from Republican hands, although the auditor and attorney general remained in Republican control. At the same time Democrat Henry S. Lindsley defeated Justice Mortimer Stone by attracting nearly the same statewide percentage as Johnson. But it is not likely that Johnson's coattails were entirely responsible for Lindsley's victory; the correlation for the partisan division of the vote for this race was only 0.71, the second lowest of the correlations reported for Colorado.

Generally, then, Colorado judicial politics only partially fit the Indiana pattern. More-competitive elections, personal rather than party politics, an independently minded electorate, and frequent ticket-splitting are the major differences. In years of overwhelming partisan strength across the ballot, such as the Democrats enjoyed in 1948 and 1964 and the Republicans in 1952 and 1960, judicial candidates of the winning party shared in the fruits of victory. But in other election years, though the general trend favored the party winning most of the statewide contests, the outcome of the judicial races was not so closely tied to the results at the top of the ticket.

### Judicial Elections in the "Mixed" States: Ohio, Arizona, and Michigan

In the mixed states, where a nonpartisan ballot is used in the contest between partisan nominees, we might expect a greater insulation of the judicial races from trends in partisan politics observed at the top of the ticket. Some voters may be aware of the partisan affiliation of the candidates, but a great many voters are probably not. The results of the correlational analysis for the partisan division of the vote offered in Chapter 3 confirm this probability. The overall partisan sentiments of the electorate at the top of the ticket for the major partisan races will not always penetrate to the nonpartisan judicial races. Hence, the results of the contests for the supreme court can be expected to exhibit a greater independence from the results of the major partisan races, even in years of large shifts in partisan sentiment among the voters.

*Ohio.* The characteristic disadvantage of the judicial appointee from a minority party may not be limited to states selecting their judges by partisan election. As Table 14 indicated, appointed Democratic justices in Ohio have had a very difficult time winning election to their seats. Between 1948 and 1974, each of six Democratic justices appointed by Democratic governors lost in their first bid for election. In contrast, four of five Republican appointees were elected.

This is a particularly interesting result in light of some contradictory data. On the one hand, the postwar Ohio electorate has consistently regarded itself as more Democratic than Republican. In separate surveys conducted in 1958 and 1968 reporting identical results, 42% of the electorate identified themselves as Democrats, 31% as Republicans, and the remainder as Independents.[47] Accordingly, Democratic candidates have captured seven of ten gubernatorial races conducted in the postwar years. Alternatively, however,

Republican candidates have won most of the elections for every statewide office except governor as well as the statewide ballotings for president. Not including races for the state supreme court, Republican candidates won 77% of the statewide offices other than governor between 1950 and 1970.[48] Moreover, Ohio Democrats "have been relegated to an on-going minority status in both the state legislature and in Ohio's delegation in Congress."[49] Thus, although most observers rank Ohio among the "two-party competitive" states, Ohio is "fairly securely Republican but within a two party framework,"[50] because "the Democrats frequently almost win."[51]

While the higher turnout rate of Republicans would clearly not explain the success of Democratic candidates in gubernatorial and U.S. senatorial races, the fact remains that Ohio voters have favored Republican candidates for lower statewide office and in the aggregate for legislative positions in the state legislature and Congress. Accordingly, 76.2% of the state supreme court posts decided in the years 1948 to 1974 were won by Republican candidates. Only three Republican incumbents suffered re-election defeats while seven Democrats, including six appointees, lost their places on the bench.

Moreover, most of the Democratic victories either have involved long-term incumbents or candidates who possess a high degree of name familiarity. Unlike the situation in those partisan states which are predominately one-party below the top of the ticket (New Mexico, West Virginia, and Iowa), the nonpartisan ballot in Ohio has permitted the occasional election or re-election of candidates traditionally disadvantaged in the state's Republican-oriented balloting by allowing factors like name familiarity to play some part in the voting decisions of some voters. Where those factors are absent, as they usually are when gubernatorial appointees must face the electorate for the first time, Democratic candidates have been defeated without exception. Ohio judicial elections reflect, therefore, the strength of Republican voting witnessed in other, nongubernatorial electoral contests.[52] They appear to be determined more by the underlying partisan preferences of the voters, mediated on occasion by certain idiosyncratic factors, than they do by major partisan trends at the top of the ballot.

During the 1948 to 1974 period, four "gross shifts" in the control of the governorship and one "proximate shift" occurred in the state. The first gross shift occurred in 1956 when Republican C. William O'Neill (who would later serve as an associate justice and chief justice of the Ohio Supreme Court) captured control of the statehouse with 56% of the two-party vote after a decade of Democratic control. Eisenhower swept the state's presidential balloting by an even larger margin (61.1%), while Democratic Governor Frank Lausche sought and won a seat in the U.S. Senate. Of three judicial races contested in that year, two were won by Republicans, each of whom received over 73% of the vote, while long-time Democratic incumbent Carl V. Weygandt, first elected chief justice in 1932, won re-election with a comfortable 58.4% share of the vote.

Democrat Michael DiSalle defeated O'Neill in the 1958 gubernatorial race in a second "gross shift" of the period; one long-term incumbent from each party won re-election in the supreme court contests.

DiSalle made three appointments to the supreme court before he met defeat in 1962. But all three of his Democratic appointees were defeated in their subsequent election bids. Whether these defeats were due to partisan shifts occurring at the top of the ballot or merely represented the traditional attachment of the Ohio electorate to Republican candidates might be debated. Justice John Peck, the first of DiSalle's appointees, lost in 1960 to former Governor O'Neill, who was making his first bid for a seat on the court. Associate Justice Kingsley Taft, one of the famous Republican Tafts, easily won re-election, too. Democrat James Bell, however, won re-election to his second full term on the court, easily defeating his Republican challenger by capturing 54.5% of the vote. The only major partisan race at the top of the ballot conducted in 1960 was the presidential balloting, which Nixon won with 53.3%.

In 1962, after serving thirty years on the state's high court, Chief Justice Weygandt was defeated by Associate Justice Kingsley Taft by a mere 1,775 votes of over 2.66 million cast. In that same year Republican John Rhodes captured the governorship with 58.9% of the vote, the third gross shift in Herndon's terms. Yet two other Republican incumbent justices won re-election in that year, both by margins considerably larger than Rhodes could muster. All three of the Republican candidates in that year, Taft, Matthias, and Herbert, had names well recognized in Republican politics in the state. Matthias and Herbert even outpolled the party's gubernatorial candidates by 4.5% and 6.7%, respectively. It is likely that Taft would have done so also if he had challenged anyone but Weygandt, a thirty-year incumbent with high name recognition among the voters. Thus, it is unlikely that the "gross shift" occurring toward Republicanism at the gubernatorial level in 1962 had much to do with Republican victories at the supreme court level. Rather, the long-standing commitment of Ohio voters to Republican candidates below the gubernatorial level was most responsible. Candidates for judicial office affiliated with the dominant party need not rely upon gross electoral shifts to be elected.

Additional evidence can be taken from the 1964 supreme court race in which the second of DiSalle's appointees, Rankin Gibson, was defeated by Republican Paul W. Brown, another name familiar to Ohio Republicans. Two other Republican candidates, incumbent O'Neill and newcomer Louis J. Schneider, Jr., also won election, although O'Neill won in a runaway while Schneider faced close competition against the third of DiSalle's luckless appointees, Lynn B. Griffith. Despite these Democratic losses, however, incumbent Democrat Charles B. Zimmerman, first appointed in 1933, won a healthy victory with 59.9% of the vote. Republican judicial candidates, therefore, captured three of four slots contested in 1964 though Lyndon Johnson dominated the state's presidential vote (62.9%).

Republicans retained control of the governorship in 1966 and controlled the state's presidential balloting in 1968.[53] Five Republican candidates for justice, including four incumbents, won election. In every case but one the Republican judicial candidates outpolled the party's gubernatorial or presidential candidate elected in the same year. Only Louis Schneider, running for re-election in 1966, failed to match Governor John Rhodes' performance, in which Rhodes collected over 62% of the vote. Schneider could manage a mere 56%, but it is crucial to note that Schneider was opposed by a Democrat named Brown (Clifford), a name traditionally associated with Ohio Republican politics. As the correlations reported in Chapter 3 suggested, it is not unlikely that some Republican voters, accustomed to voting for Republican candidates by the name of Brown, may have cast their votes for Democrat Brown though not in sufficiently large numbers to cause his election.

The fourth gross shift in the state's gubernatorial voting occurred in 1970 when Democrat John Gilligan was elected with 55.5% of the vote. Gilligan was unable to pull any Democratic judicial candidates into office with him, however, as four Republican justices, including three appointees of Governor Rhodes, were elected; two of the appointees, in fact, won uncontested races, while appointee J. J. P. Corrigan captured 56% in defeating another Democratic Brown (Allen). Justice O'Neill, elevated by appointment to the chief justice position by Governor Rhodes in 1970, won election with a stunning 69% share of the vote.

At first glance, the electoral developments in 1972 somewhat confuse the picture of Ohio judicial politics. In the only top partisan race contested in 1972, President Nixon overwhelmed the challenge by George McGovern. But two of the three judicial slots contested were captured by Democrats. A Democratic Brown (William) defeated incumbent Republican Schneider, a member of the court since his election in 1964. Democrat Frank D. Celebrezze defeated another of Rhodes' appointees, Robert Leach, in a highly partisan race ($r$ = 0.81).[54] It is not likely, however, that this election represented a Democratic surge of any consequence. Rather, it is best explained by the attractiveness of candidates with high name recognition. Democrat Brown capitalized upon the name he shares with so many Ohio Republicans. And Democrat Celebrezze benefited from sharing the familiar surname of Anthony J. Celebrezze, mayor of Cleveland for a decade beginning in 1952 until his appointment first as secretary of the Department of Health, Education, and Welfare by President Kennedy and then as federal appeals court judge for the Sixth Circuit by President Johnson. Republican Paul W. Brown was also a victor in 1972, defeating Democrat Lloyd Brown by a wide margin (66.3%).

In 1974, the state's voters returned Rhodes as governor in an extremely narrow victory over Gilligan, a "proximate shift" for Herndon. At the same time, former astronaut John Glenn outdistanced his Republican challenger by a margin of over two to one in winning election to the U.S. Senate. In the supreme court races, Ohio voters faced a situation where there were many opportunities for idiosyncratic voting. Chief Justice O'Neill faced a challenge by Democrat Joseph E. O'Neill, but voters were not fooled and returned the chief justice. Incumbent Democrat Celebrezze faced another Republican Taft (Sheldon), but Celebrezze won an easy victory as well.[55] Only the race between incumbent Republican Thomas J. Herbert and Democrat Clifford Brown was closely contested, with Herbert capturing 51% of the vote for victory amidst some voter confusion.

Thus, the normal pattern of Ohio supreme court elections appears to be a high degree of support for Republican candidates, regardless of partisan swings either toward or away from Republican candidates at the top of the ballot. Democratic candidates who either are long-time incumbents or possess high name recognition may be able to win election even in those years when the state leans toward Republicanism at the top of the ticket. But Democratic appointees who lack these advantages will most likely suffer defeat in their first appearances before the electorate.

Republican margins of victory tend to be customarily large, but they may be increased when the Republican judicial candidate possesses such names as Taft, Herbert, Brown, or O'Neill, which are familiar to Republican voters. Republican margins of victory are, on the other hand, often narrowed when the Democratic challenger possesses the name of Brown and can capitalize on voter confusion. It is unlikely that what is occurring at the top of the ballot affects the fortunes of Republican judicial candidates one way or the other since, all other things being equal, Republican candidates for the state's high court usually outdistance Republican candidates in the statewide ballotings for president, U.S. senator, and governor. In this respect, the pattern of Ohio's judicial elections is quite similar to the pattern observed in the one-party partisan states of New Mexico, West Virginia, Iowa, and Kansas.

*Arizona.* Arizona judicial elections very closely fit the pattern witnessed in Ohio. The major difference between the two states is that, while persistent one-partyism below the top of the ticket has characterized Ohio, Arizona has gradually experienced a fundamental shift in the overall partisan balance of its electorate as the result of the in-migration of Republican identifiers. This shift has had a correspondingly gradual impact on the outcome of the state's supreme court elections.

Until the election of Republican Howard Pyle as governor in 1950, Arizona was an overwhelmingly Democratic state. Democrats had captured every presidential, senatorial, gubernatorial, and statewide balloting for twenty years.[56] The Eisenhower victory in 1952 gave Pyle his second term and also gave the state its first Republican U.S. Senator, Barry Goldwater, and Congressman, John J. Rhodes, since the state had received its second Congressional representative a decade earlier. Pyle lost in his bid for a third term in 1954 to Democratic former U.S. Senator Ernest W. McFarland (who had lost in 1952 to Goldwater). McFarland served one additional gubernatorial term in the face of Eisenhower's landslide 1956 victory but stepped down from the governor's office in 1958 to unsuccessfully challenge Goldwater for his old Senate seat. The Democratic gubernatorial banner was left to Attorney General Robert Morrison, who was soundly defeated by Republican businessman Paul Fannin; Fannin was subsequently re-elected to two more terms by comfortable margins.

The years from 1950 to 1960 appeared, therefore, to be Republican watersheds in Arizona. Republican candidates had captured five of seven gubernatorial races, all three presidential ballotings, and Republican Senator Goldwater and Congressman Rhodes had managed to hold half of the state's delegation in the nation's capital. Yet Republican successes below the top of the partisan ticket had remained extremely limited. Only in 1952, 1960, and 1962 could Republican candidates capture just one other statewide position, the office of the attorney general. Five other statewide offices remained solidly in Democratic hands as did that of the attorney general from 1954 to 1960.

The reason for Republican success in the major partisan races during the decade of the 1950s might be attributed to a number of factors, but a basic change in the state's partisan make-up is not one of them. In 1958, Democratic voter registration was over twice that for the Republican party; over two-thirds of the registered voters identified themselves as Democrats.[57] The dominance of Democratic candidates in the statewide races below the gubernatorial level also attested to the long-term dedication of most of the state's voters to the Democratic party. Notably, however, Republican registration was on the rise, particularly in populous Maricopa and Pima Counties, which contained nearly three-fourths of the state's registered voters.[58] Moreover, many Republicans (euphemistically referred to as "pinto Democrats") apparently registered with the Democratic party so as to be able to participate in the usually hotly contested closed Democratic primaries.[59]

Divisive Democratic primary contests were most frequently cited to explain Democratic losses at the top of the ticket despite a wide advantage for the party in voter registration. As one observer noted, "The winner of a hard-fought Democratic primary race may not necessarily be opposed actively by the vanquished and their supporters, but may find that the defeated may simply sit on their hands and render him no effective aid against the Republican nominee."[60] Despite the party column ballot, "registered Republicans remain cohesively behind their party nominees, while a considerable numer of registered Democrats are likely to split their tickets for some of the Republican nominees at the top of the ballot."[61] One other scholar humorously has noted that the Democratic party in Arizona has always really been two parties in one organizational shell, one of which has been very much in line with the national Democratic administrations since the New Deal, while the more conservative Democratic group "tends to regard Grover Cleveland as its logical patron saint."[62]

Eventually, however, the increasing influx of Republican-oriented voters, especially in the state's urban areas, "began to make inroads into Democratic strength at the statewide level."[63] In 1964, the state's voters honored favorite-son Goldwater with the presidential vote, elected Governor Fannin to Goldwater's Senate post, and returned Rhodes to his own seat in Congress. Democrat Sam Goddard defeated Richard Kleindienst in the gubernatorial race, but for the first time Republican candidates captured two of the other state-wide offices, the attorney general and the superintendent of public instruction. In 1966, more convincing evidence of a major shift in the partisan balance in the electorate emerged when Republican candidates captured two of the state's three-member Congressional delegation and five of seven statewide offices. This trend continued during the 1966–1972 period with Republican candidates sweeping the quadrennial presidential ballotings, all the U.S. Senate contests, every Congressional seat except the position held by Morris Udall, all the gubernatorial races, and every statewide office except secretary of state and auditor. Only a Democratic resurgence in the first post-Watergate election in 1974 blemished the near perfect Republican record in the preceding decade.

This extended discussion of the general patterns of Republican voting in Arizona has been necessary to understand the outcome of the state's judicial elections. Prior to the rise of Republicanism among the electorate, several characteristics of Arizona judicial elections were clear. First, Democratic supreme court candidates typically ran unopposed or were only minimally tested. In the 1948 to 1974 period, only two races were competitive; both of these occurred after 1966 and both were won by Republicans. Second, as in the other states dominated by one party, Republicans were virtually precluded from reaching the state supreme court except by gubernatorial appointment. Once appointed, these Republican justices faced uncertain futures when forced to face the predominately Democratic electorate. In 1960, Robert Lesher, a partisan appointee of Republican Governor Fannin, was defeated in his bid for election despite the overwhelming endorsement of the electorate for Fannin's second term. Republican Jesse A. Udall, however, another Fannin appointee, was able to keep his seat, outpolling his opponent with a whopping 73.1% of the vote, outdistancing even the popular governor. As noted in Chapter 3, Udall unquestionably capitalized upon voter recognition and allegiance to the Udall name in Arizona. Another Fannin appointee, Edward W. Scruggs, sought his seat by election in 1964 but fell victim to the electorate's partisan preference for Democrats. In addition, Scruggs faced the handicap of being opposed by former U.S. Senator and Governor McFarland who easily bested Scruggs by collecting 58.7% of the vote.

Since 1966, Republican judicial fortunes have improved, just as they have elsewhere on the ballot. Up until 1968 only Jesse Udall provided Republican representation on the bench. But in 1968, Jack D. H. Hays narrowly defeated incumbent Democrat Charles Bernstein by a narrow margin in one of the more partisan of the state's judicial elections ($r$ = 0.66). In 1970, James Duke Cameron ran away from Charles L. Hardy with a 56.1% share of the vote. Finally, in another relatively partisan contest in 1972 ($r$ = 0.70), William Holohan narrowly defeated Howard V. Peterson. Only long-time Democratic incumbent Fred C. Struckmeyer, Jr., seeking his fourth six-year term, survived a challenge from a Republican opponent in 1972. Idiosyncratic factors still played a part in the state's nonpartisan elections but, given the partisan preference of the voters for Republican candidates, these factors worked most profitably to the advantage of the Democrats.

*Michigan.* Judicial elections in the third state utilizing a mixed election system, Michigan, present some special problems of analysis; consequently, a complete comparison with those in Ohio and Arizona is difficult. In the first place, all but one of the eight appointments to the state's high court from 1948 to 1974 were made by Democratic governors. Moreover, each of these Democratic appointments occurred prior to 1963, with the sole Republican appointee of the postwar years taking office in 1973. In part, this fact reflects Democratic control of the governor's office during the years 1948–1962 in the persons of G. Mennen Williams (1949–1960) and John Swainson (1961–1962). The Republicans controlled the position after George Romney's election in 1962, but Republican governors have had only one opportunity since then to fill a vacancy on the supreme court, a quirk of fate more than anything else.[64]

All but one of the eight appointees to the bench during the period 1948–1974 earned their seats by subsequent election. In 1962, Paul L. Adams, a Swainson appointee and attorney general at the time of his appointment, lost to attorney Michael D. O'Hara by a narrow margin. But because of the near total absence of appointments by minority-party governors, it is difficult to compare Michigan with Ohio in this respect.

Another problem of comparison concerns the use in Michigan of spring elections for the selection of supreme court justices. Prior to a 1963 constitutional revision, Michigan provided that all judicial elections for full terms be held in April of the odd-numbered years. Recent appointees to the bench would seek election at the next general election; this meant that they could run for election either in the spring or in the biennial contests for executive and legislative posts in November, whichever came first. With these caveats in mind, it is still worthwhile to compare the overall patterns of incumbent election and defeat as they relate to the outcomes of the major partisan races. At least in this respect, Michigan judicial elections share many of the characteristics of those conducted in Ohio and Arizona.

Since 1948, Michigan voters have favored Democratic candidates for the supreme court, awarding two-thirds of the contested judicial races to them. These Democratic victories appear unrelated to partisan election outcomes, however. The state has experienced only one "proximate" shift at the gubernatorial level when Republican George Romney captured 51.5% of the 1962 vote to oust Governor John Swainson. Republican Michael D. O'Hara did manage, as noted above, to unseat a recent Swainson appointee, but Otis M. Smith, another Swainson appointee and the first Black to sit on the state supreme court, held on to his seat by garnering a 53.3% share of the vote. Moreover, the years of Republican hegemony at the gubernatorial level since 1962 have apparently not dampened the electoral fortunes of Democratic judicial candidates. Since 1962, eight of eleven judicial contests have been won by Democrats.[65]

As the correlations for the partisan division of the vote in Chapter 3 indicated, Michigan voters do respond on occasion in a moderately partisan fashion in the nonpartisan judicial races, particularly when one or both of the candidates are clearly identified with one of the major parties. But the aggregate statewide results also indicate that, as in Ohio and Arizona, Michigan voters often respond to short-term factors like incumbency and name identification in making their vote choices. And it is these factors which explain not only the overall results of the state's judicial elections but also the instances of incumbent defeat.

In the spring election of 1953, Clark J. Adams, originally appointed and elected to an unexpired term in the November 1952 election, was defeated in a four-way race for two full-term positions. Adams finished third in the field as the voters re-elected Republican incumbent justice and former Attorney General John M. Dethmers and elected former Republican Governor Harry F. Kelly. Kelly's astounding collection of 74.1% of the two-party vote suggested the power of name recognition in the state's judicial elections. And Dethmer's narrow victory over Adams (50.1%) was merely the outcome of a close race between two incumbents forced against each other in the at-large balloting.

Incumbent Republican justices have typically polled large margins in winning re-election, even in the face of Democratic gubernatorial victories. Similarly, Democratic incumbents have won their re-election bids comfortably in spite of Republican fortunes in the governor's race. However, incumbent justices of both parties have seen their margins of victory reduced when opposed by well-known candidates of the opposite party. Moreover, as in Adam's defeat in 1953, a sitting justice may be ousted if challenged by a well-known or equally known opponent. Thus, in the spring elections of 1949, 1957, and 1959 and the November elections of 1952, 1956, 1960, and 1962, Democratic incumbents (including six of seven appointees) were successful in their re-election bids. In virtually every one of these races, the Democratic justices attracted a larger proportion of the two-party vote than did the party's candidate for governor in the closest November election. On the other hand, Republican incumbents were equally successful in the spring elections of 1951, 1953, 1955, and 1961, winning with customary runaway margins.

After the Republicans recaptured the governorship in 1962, this description of the state's judicial elections remains accurate but must be qualified. Incumbent Democratic justices were still able to win re-election in the spring election of 1963 and the November elections of 1966 and 1974. However, since 1962, two Democratic incumbents as well as two Republican incumbents have been defeated for re-election.

In 1962, Democrat Paul L. Adams was narrowly defeated by Republican Michael D. O'Hara, who had tried twice previously but unsuccessfully to be elected to the court. In 1966, Black justice Otis Smith, a Democrat, finished a close but losing third in a four-way race. Popular Democratic Justice and former Attorney General Thomas M. Kavanaugh led the balloting, followed by Republican Thomas E. Brennan. These two instances of incumbent defeat are somewhat perplexing inasmuch as neither O'Hara nor Brennan was holding or had held visible public offices prior to the election and neither would appear to possess the kind of widely recognized name sufficient to oust a sitting Democratic incumbent.

As in Chapter 3, one might engage in some speculation that another kind of "name recognition" was operative in these elections. Perhaps some voters found in the Irish Catholic names of O'Hara and Brennan an acceptable and meaningful vote cue. Given the substantial roll-off on the state's ballot, it is not implausible to argue that some voters seized upon this ethnic-religious indicator to assist them in casting their ballots; voters for whom such a cue was meaningless would, absent other kinds of cues, choose not to cast their ballots. It may be that these specially motivated voters were sufficiently numerous to tip the balance in these close races in favor of O'Hara and Brennan.

Similarly, in 1968, when O'Hara sought re-election, he was defeated by another Irish Catholic, Thomas Giles Kavanaugh.

Kavanaugh undoubtedly benefited from some voter confusion with the popular Thomas M. Kavanaugh, but it is also possible that voters responding to the ethnic-religious cue found themselves torn between equally desirable alternatives. The correlation of the party division of the vote for this race was −.22; perhaps the Irishman had been out-Irished![66]

Michigan, of course, has also had judicial races which evoke a partisan response from the voters. In 1970, Republican Justice John M. Dethmers, seeking his fourth term on the bench, finished fourth in the four-way race and, alliteration notwithstanding, became the fourth sitting justice defeated since 1962. The two seats were captured by former Democratic governors, G. Mennen Williams and John Swainson, in an election aligned along relatively strong partisan lines ($r$ = 0.64, 0.71).

As one observer of Michigan's judicial elections has noted, incumbency is a major asset of supreme court justices.[67] Appointed incumbents have been very secure in their first election try and are similarly secure in subsequent election bids. But incumbents have been defeated when challenged by an opponent who is very familiar to the voters or whose name evokes an ethnic-religious response.

As in Ohio and Arizona, the outcomes of Michigan's supreme court elections have been determined largely independent of the ebb and flow of partisan politics in the state. Judicial elections are at least partially affected by the underlying partisan predisposition of the electorate. And with the political parties active in the nomination and promotion of their candidates, a partisan electoral response from the voters is both encouraged and expected. But as in the other mixed states, voters in Michigan rely to a significant but imprecisely measurable extent upon nonparty factors in making their choices for justice of the state supreme court.

### Judicial Elections in the Nonpartisan States

The patterns of incumbent defeat in the states which utilize the nonpartisan judicial ballot are more difficult to characterize, perhaps because the outstanding characteristic is the near absence of instances in which incumbent justices seeking re-election have been defeated. As Table 14 detailed, three states have not had a single incumbent leave the bench by electoral defeat since 1948, while five other states have lost only one and three states only two.[68] Because judicial elections in the nonpartisan states often go uncontested and are usually not competitive, incumbents usually remain undefeated.

At the same time, incumbents in isolated instances have lost their seats under circumstances which appear similar to those in the partisan states despite the nonpartisan ballot. In North Dakota, for example, Republican dominance in the postwar years virtually precluded Democratic representation on the bench despite the formally nonpartisan selection system. Supreme court contests have traditionally been between Republican candidates if indeed there has been any contest at all. Thomas J. Burke, initially elected in 1938 and twice re-elected, was the only Democrat on the state's high court until 1966 when Democratic Governor William L. Guy appointed William S. Murray, a private attorney and former state legislator who had been active in Democratic politics in the early 1960s.

Guy was elected in 1960 and subsequently re-elected in 1962, 1964, and 1968, usually by comfortable margins. Yet despite his success for the Democrats at the gubernatorial level, there was very little spillover to other statewide offices. During the years of Guy's tenure, Democratic candidates were completely shut out from the other five statewide offices except in 1964 when they captured the offices of lieutenant governor and treasurer for one four-year stint. Consequently, when Justice Murray faced the electorate in 1966 against Republican William E. Paulson, Murray could muster only 43.6% of the vote.

No other Democrat reached the bench until 1973 when Governor Arthur A. Link, Guy's successor, appointed Robert Vogel, a former U.S. Attorney and previously unsuccessful candidate for Congress. Vogel was elected in 1974, overwhelming the assistant securities commissioner, Republican Peter Quist, by collecting 77.0% of the vote. The magnitude of Vogel's victory, combined with the election of two Republican candidates in two separate contests fought among Republican candidates, suggests that the nonpartisan ballot in North Dakota does permit a personalistic following independent of the general partisan disposition of the electorate.[69]

Similarly, the only two judicial incumbents to be defeated in Montana's postwar races occurred under circumstances similar to those witnessed in the partisan states. But these elections were clearly atypical of those generally held in the state. In 1948, Republican Governor Sam C. Ford, who was originally elected in 1940, was defeated by Democratic challenger John W. Bonner in a Democratic sweep of the state's presidential and U.S. senatorial ballotings and of all eight statewide offices. Two Ford appointees facing their first election were also defeated, losing by wide margins to Democratic challengers. Justices I. W. Choate, appointed in January 1947, and Fred L. Gibson, appointed in October of the same year, were defeated by no mean Democrats, however. Gibson lost to Harry J. Free-bourn, the state's attorney general from 1936 to 1940 and unsuc-cessful candidate for chief justice of the supreme court in 1946; Freebourn collected 56.1% of the vote. The more impressive victory, however, was registered by the sitting attorney general, R. V. Bot-tomly, who attracted 71.1% of the vote in defeating Choate. To some extent, both Democrats drew from the same partisan base as the party's gubernatorial candidate but clearly capitalized upon the familiarity of their names with the electorate.[70]

Since the 1948 election, no incumbent justice, appointee or not, has been defeated in Montana's judicial elections. From 1952 to 1968, Montana was served by Republican governors, J. Hugo Aron-son (1953–1960), Donald Nutter (1961–1964), and Tim Babcock (1965–1968); all four appointees to the supreme court by these gov-ernors were successful in their subsequent election and re-election campaigns. Similarly, Gene B. Daly, the sole appointee of Demo-cratic Governor Forrest H. Anderson, won election in 1970.

As pointed out in Chapter 3, Montana's supreme court races do, on occasion, evoke a moderately strong partisan response from the voters, most typically when well-known partisans with name famil-iarity run for the court. Incumbents, however, have been quite se-cure; with perhaps the exception of the 1948 election year, electoral trends at the top of the partisan ballot appear to have little relation-ship to the outcome of the contests on the nonpartisan ballot. Can-didates from both parties have reached the bench with equal success even in the face of unfavorable partisan trends.

These conclusions are equally applicable to Wyoming's su-preme court elections. In 1968, incumbent Republican Justice Harry Harnsberger, a member of the court since his appointment in 1953, was successfully challenged by Democrat Leonard McEwan. Mc-Ewan's victory occurred in the same year Richard Nixon swept the presidential voting with 61.0%, the major partisan balloting in 1968. This Democratic victory and two other successful bids by serious Democratic candidates in Wyoming judicial elections, combined with the correlations reported in Chapter 3, confirm that the state's supreme court elections are well insulated from partisan influences. In 1960, former Democratic Congressman, Deputy Attorney Gen-eral, and State Auditor John J. McIntyre, was elected with a 53.6% share of the vote, despite large Republican victories in the presiden-tial and U.S. Senate races. And in 1962, Democratic Attorney Gen-eral Norman Gray defeated former Attorney General John F. Raper, a Republican, by a narrow margin. These Democratic victories are significant in that they occurred at the same time Republican candidates were dominating the races for other statewide offices. From 1948 to 1970, Democratic candidates were successful only once in the gubernatorial race (in 1958) and in only 12.5% (3 of 24) of the contests for four other statewide offices. Inasmuch as Democratic Governor F. F. Hickey (elected in 1958) had no opportunity to fill a vacancy on the supreme court, no Democrat reached the bench by appointment. Serious Democratic candidates, however, with recognizable names were able to curry enough favor with the voters to secure representation on the bench.

Judicial elections in the remaining nonpartisan states follow much the same pattern. Judicial candidates of both parties are able to pursue their judicial fortunes with the assurance that they will be neither helped nor hurt by the "vicissitudes of interpartisan competition" elsewhere on the ballot. Incumbents are defeated only in the rarest of instances, whether the incumbent is seeking an additional term or is a gubernatorial appointee pursuing confirmation by the electorate. With but the possible exceptions from Montana and North Dakota, the defeat of sitting judges and the results of judicial elections seem wholly unrelated to the tides of partisan politics or to the underlying partisan disposition of a state's electorate. In each of the eight defeats of incumbent judges occurring in Nevada, Oregon, Utah, Washington, and Wisconsin, the incumbent was defeated by either a fellow partisan or a challenger with no (or at least nominal) party allegiance. In states like Minnesota, Nevada, Oregon, South Dakota, Washington, Wisconsin, and Wyoming, where judicial appointments are a large majority of all initial accessions to the state's high court, the results of gubernatorial races have as much to do with the representation of each party on the bench as do subsequent judicial elections. When a governor makes an appointment to the state supreme court, he or she can be confident that the electorate will not reverse the decision.

## APPOINTMENT AND ELECTION TO STATE SUPREME COURTS: "ONE-MAN JUDICIAL SELECTION"?

This lengthy excursion into the patterns of state judicial elections may be concluded with some remarks which can also serve to introduce a final area of inquiry related to the initial accession and subsequent retention of judges on state courts of last resort.

First, the patterns of initial accession do not appear to be determined primarily by the absence or presence of shifts in partisan control of the governorship or by the magnitude of such shifts. Rather, it is likely in the first instances that patterns of appointment and election are influenced by a number of relatively invariant factors, such as constitutional arrangements for filling judicial vacancies and provisions governing the length of judicial terms. Indeed, the very length of judicial terms almost dictates that a large number of midterm vacancies will occur and necessitate the appointment of a replacement. Although no data, to my knowledge, has been collected on the point, judgeships are certainly one of the elective public offices most frequently filled by appointment. The lengthy terms of office make it almost impossible to be otherwise. Further, compulsory retirement requirements (where they exist) and the specific provisions of judicial retirement plans may also have some bearing upon initial accession.

As Herndon predicted, the type of judicial election system also affects the extent to which elective state judiciaries are dominated by appointed judges. Judicial elections in the partisan and mixed states are more often contested than supreme court elections held under the nonpartisan ballot. Consequently, incumbents most frequently meet with defeat in the former systems while only rarely in the latter. An analysis of the pattern of tenure on these courts would undoubtedly demonstrate that, all other things being equal, judges in the nonpartisan states are able to serve for longer periods on the bench until their death or retirement at an advanced age; judges in the partisan or mixed states are more likely to lose their positions "prematurely" through the electoral process either at the nomination or election stages.

However, it did not prove true that the victims of electoral defeat in the partisan and mixed states were helpless drifters in a partisan ebb tide. The "vicissitudes of interparty competition" occurring at the top of the ballot do not necessarily penetrate down to the judicial contests. In fact, it is not even necessarily the case that incumbents have most frequently been defeated in competitive judicial elections. A close examination of the instances of incumbent defeat revealed that just as frequently incumbents have been defeated in noncompetitive if not landslide elections. This strange relationship has come about primarily because of the election of "minority party" governors in states usually dominated by one party. The judicial appointees of these governors invariably share the governor's party affiliation but, to their misfortune, they do not share the short-term political appeal. For races below the top of the ballot, like the supreme court, voters rely more upon their long-term partisan affiliation as the major cue for voting and consequently cast these "minority party" appointees out of office. Despite the party column ballot, which links the electoral fates of candidates on the ballot sharing the same party label, voters in states like New Mexico and West Virginia have split their tickets when necessary to express short-term policy preferences at the gubernatorial level while relying upon their more permanent allegiances at the judicial level. So, too, in the nonpartisan states of Arizona and Ohio, the electorate's traditional partisan affiliation is the most powerful explanation of the outcomes of most state supreme court elections, despite the absence of a party label to assist the voters and a ballot device to facilitate party line voting.

Judicial election competition is not totally unimportant for understanding the defeat of incumbents in some states, however. In Colorado, Indiana, and Iowa, for example, incumbent justices have lost their seats in competitive judicial circumstances. But these three states are distinguishable for the underlying electoral conditions which contribute to the defeat of incumbents in the judicial races. In Colorado, for instance, a normally competitive electoral environment, the proclivity of the electorate for ticket-splitting, and the office block ballot format combined to contribute to the defeat of several incumbent justices. In Indiana, judicial outcomes have closely followed the rise and fall of party fortunes elsewhere on the ballot; incumbent defeats accompanied major shifts in partisan sentiment from the top to the bottom of the Indiana party column ballot. In Iowa, the traditional dominance of the Republicans in the state's judicial elections was temporarily broken in one election year (1958) when a Democratic candidate captured one of three slots decided in an at-large balloting while another won a separate contest for an unexpired term. These Democratic advances accompanied the re-election campaign of the state's only Democratic governor in the postwar years prior to 1964, but they were quickly reversed as the Republicans won back the governor's office two years later.

In sum, therefore, within the limits of aggregate data analysis, Herndon's hypotheses have been only partially verified. Appointment as a means of initial accession to state supreme courts is less frequent in states utilizing partisan and mixed election systems. This is partially the result of the fact that incumbent judges are more frequently defeated in these systems. But the occasions of incumbent defeat have not always been linked to what Herndon called the "vicissitudes of interparty competition."

These results also bear upon Glenn Winters' claim that the fre-

**Table 15.** *Partisanship in Judicial Appointments*

|  | Appointments Identified by Party | Appointments Same Party as Governor | Appointments Not Identified by Party[a] |
|---|---|---|---|
| Partisan states[b] | 56 | 96.4% (N = 54) | 0.0% (N = 0) |
| Mixed states[b] | 23 | 100.0% (N = 23) | 3.0% (N = 1) |
| Nonpartisan states[b] | 74 | 93.2% (N = 69) | 25.3% (N = 25) |

NOTE: Includes all judges appointed from 1948 through 1974, including those appointed to newly created positions on each court.

[a] The entries in this column represent the proportion of all appointments for which the partisan affiliation of the appointees could not be ascertained. Thus, for the nonpartisan states, the partisan affiliations of 74 appointees were determined, but those of 25 others (or 25.3% of the 99 appointments) remain unknown.

[b] State-by-state totals may be located in Philip L. Dubois, "Judicial Elections in the States: Patterns and Consequences," Ph.D. dissertation, p. 262 (Table 8).

quency of gubernatorial appointments in ostensibly elective judicial systems amounts to "one-man judicial selection." According to Winters, subject to no immediate check upon appointments by the state senate or other confirming body and given the inability of the electorate to impose a meaningful subsequent check, the governor is, in essence, vested with the total power and responsibility for staffing the third branch of state government.[71]

The evidence offered here, however, appears to undermine Winters' warnings. In the first place, governors are always subject to an indirect check by the electorate when they seek their own re-election; the voters can hold the governor accountable retrospectively for any and all appointments. More importantly, though, conceding the likelihood that the public does not pay much attention to gubernatorial appointments, it is clear that the voters in several states have effectively exercised a more effective direct check over the process of "one-man judicial selection" than Winters recognized.

It is of first importance to recognize that all governors utilize their power to fill vacancies on the judiciary in an attempt to "pack" the membership of the state supreme court with fellow partisans.[72] What is true of the pattern of appointments to the federal judiciary seems equally true of the pattern of vacancy appointments to state supreme courts. Whether the initial election system is partisan, mixed, or nonpartisan, appointing governors usually select individuals who share their partisan affiliation.

Table 15 confirms that in the partisan and mixed states, over

**Table 16.** *Electoral Success of Appointed Judges Seeking First Election*

|  | Elections Opposed | Opposed Appointees Elected | All Appointed Judges Elected[a] |
|---|---|---|---|
| Partisan states[b] (N = 8) | 88.2% | 66.2% | 71.2% |
| Mixed states[b] (N = 3) | 84.2% | 50.0% | 61.3% |
| Nonpartisan states[b] (N = 11) | 55.0% | 81.2% | 95.9% |

NOTE: Includes judges appointed before 1948 but seeking their first election in 1948 or later. The figures in each row and column have been averaged by states so that undue weight would not be given to those states with many appointed judges.

[a] Includes appointees who were opposed in their first bid for election as well as those who were unopposed in their first election after appointment.

[b] State-by-state totals and caveats to data calculation in specific states may be found in Dubois, "Judicial Elections in the States," pp. 267–269 (Table 11).

95% of the vacancy appointments have been along party lines. Similarly, of those appointees in the nonpartisan states whose partisan affiliation could be ascertained, over 93% shared the party identification of the appointing governor. Because they serve in posts which are formally and legally nonpartisan, many of the justices serving on nonpartisan courts are reluctant to provide their party affiliations in the standard biographical publications. But even if we assume that all these judges (slightly over one-fourth of the total) were of a different party than the governor who appointed them or, alternatively, that these judges had no partisan allegiances at all, nearly seven of every ten appointments in the nonpartisan states followed party lines.

Once the partisanship of the appointment process is recognized, the effectiveness of the electorate's check under each kind of election system can be appreciated. Table 16 presents comparative data on the rate of electoral success of vacancy appointees seeking their first election following appointment. It is there seen that Winters' charge of "one-man judicial selection" appears most supportable with respect to nonpartisan judicial elections. As Table 16 indicates, nearly half of all appointed judges in the nonpartisan states faced no competition whatsoever in their first bids for election. Even when opposed, the average incumbent judge is virtually assured of victory

**Table 17.** *Electoral Success of Appointed Judges Seeking First Election, by Party of Appointing Governor*

| State | Democratic Appointees Elected | Democratic Appointees Defeated | Republican Appointees Elected | Republican Appointees Defeated |
|---|---|---|---|---|
| **Partisan States** | | | | |
| Colorado | 2 | 1 | 2 | 1 |
| Indiana | 1 | 1 | 2 | 0 |
| Iowa | 0 | 0 | 3 | 0 |
| Kansas | 1 | 0 | 2 | 0 |
| New Mexico[a] | 4 | 1 | 0 | 4 |
| New York[b] | 0 | 0 | 4 | 2 |
| Pennsylvania | 1 | 2 | 3 | 1 |
| West Virginia | 3 | 0 | 1 | 2 |
| **Mixed States** | | | | |
| Arizona | 1 | 0 | 2 | 2 |
| Michigan | 6 | 1 | 1 | 0 |
| Ohio | 0 | 6 | 4 | 1 |
| **Nonpartisan States** | | | | |
| Idaho[c] | 0 | 0 | 6 | 0 |
| Minnesota | 6 | 0 | 7 | 0 |
| Montana | 1 | 0 | 4 | 2 |
| Nevada[c] | 4 | 0 | 3 | 0 |
| North Dakota | 1 | 1 | 4 | 0 |
| Oregon | 2 | 0 | 8 | 0 |
| South Dakota[c] | 3 | 0 | 5 | 0 |
| Utah | 1 | 0 | 2 | 0 |
| Washington[d] | 3 | 0 | 11 | 1 |
| Wisconsin | 2 | 0 | 8 | 1 |
| Wyoming | 0 | 0 | 4 | 0 |

[a] Augustus Seymour, who was appointed in 1950 by Democratic Governor Thomas Mabry, met with defeat in his first attempt for election in 1954 running on the *Republican* ticket.

[b] One of the two appointees of Republican Governor Malcolm Wilson was Harold Stevens, a life-long Democrat. Endorsed for election by all the parties in the 1974 primary, he was rebuffed by Democratic primary voters, however, and ran on the Republican, Conservative, and Liberal labels in the general election. Stevens finished third in a contest for two seats on the court of appeals.

[c] In Idaho, one of the Republican appointees was a Democrat, while in Nevada and South Dakota, one each of the Democratic appointees was a cross-party appointment.

[d] The sole defeated appointee lost in the primary contest.

with an over 80% chance of winning (col. 2, Table 16). Thus, including the uncontested ballotings, appointees in the nonpartisan states have been successful on the average over 95% of the time (col. 3, Table 16), with no state using the nonpartisan system registering a success rate of less than 80% and a majority of states featuring perfect records for the appointed incumbents. With no significant voting cues, voters are forced to "rubber stamp" the governor's choice.

Under the partisan and mixed election systems, in contrast, the chances of appointed incumbents winning election are quite variable. Though such elections are nearly always contested (col. 1, Table 16), there is a great difference among the states in whether an appointee is likely to survive the first electoral challenge. In Ohio, only 36.4% of the appointed incumbents won their first elections compared to perfect records of success for the appointees in Kansas and Iowa. The mean success rate of 71.2% for the partisan states and 61.3% for the mixed reported in Table 16, therefore, reveals the generally greater vulnerability of incumbents in the partisan-mixed states though it conceals the important variations among them in the danger of electoral defeat.

Table 17 displays by state the record of success for the appointees of Democratic and Republican governors in the first election following appointment. These data confirm the patterns identified earlier. In the one-party partisan states, the partisan ballot has allowed the electorate to effectively counter the appointing power of a minority-party governor. Short-term electoral factors have often permitted the election of a governor from a minority party. But the electorate's long-term allegiances have kept the new governor's power effectively in check by preventing "packing" of the state supreme court with fellow partisans who do not share the voters' overall partisan disposition. The states of New Mexico and West Virginia provide prime examples, as our earlier discussion indicated and Table 16 confirms.

Voters in the mixed states have exercised a similar power as well. Although the general election ballot is nonpartisan, these voters have been effective in reversing the appointments of minority-party governors. Perhaps taking their voting cues from the partisan nomination process and the partisan campaign, enough voters have been able to distinguish between the candidates of the two parties and to cast ballots consistent with their party identification to the extent necessary to remove judges not of a similar persuasion.

# 5. Partisanship and Judicial Accountability

## INTRODUCTION

Previous chapters have shown that partisanship in a judicial election system has important positive consequences for the operation of popular elections as a means for selecting state judges. First, the partisan ballot boosts turnout in judicial elections; approximately 90% of those going to the polls to vote for the major partisan public offices also participate in the judicial race when the ballot provides them with a party label to guide their voting choice. The nonpartisan ballot discourages voter participation, both because nonpartisan judicial races are less frequently contested and because in a low-salience contest many voters will refrain from voting without a party label to help them cast their ballots.

Partisan judicial elections were also found to be more frequently contested and more closely competitive than nonpartisan judicial elections, conditions which are essential if the electorate is to hold its judges accountable.

Additionally, the partisan judicial ballot structures voter choice in politically meaningful directions. In relying upon party labels, voters in the partisan states are able to vote for candidates representing political organizations with different approaches to the resolution of important public policy issues. In the nonpartisan states, voters are forced to rely upon nonparty cues for voting and are not certain to select those candidates sharing their general political and ideological perspective. Moreover, because governors play such a major role in staffing state courts with their power to fill vacancies by appointment, voters under the nonpartisan ballot are generally unable to identify, and thus to remove, appointed judges who do not share their overall partisan disposition. In the partisan states, however, the attempts of minority-party governors to "pack" state supreme courts with fellow partisans have been generally unsuccessful.

All this evidence supports the case for partisan judicial elections as effective instruments for maintaining popular control over the judiciary. But the final link in the chain of accountability depends upon the existence of meaningful distinction by party in the decision-making tendencies of state supreme court judges.

The ability of the partisan ballot to serve as the mechanism which allows the electorate to exercise indirect control over the course of judicial policy depends upon the correlation between the party labels on the ballot and the policy preferences of the opposing candidates associated with each label. As discussed in the concluding remarks of Chapter 3, even in the absence of specific information about judicial candidates, past judicial decisions, and future policy questions which might confront the court, voters may nevertheless rationally and intelligently protect their interests by relying upon the party label. But in relying upon that label, voters must be able to vote to remove judges whose policy views are not consistent with theirs and, at the same time, to select individuals whose political attitudes are more compatible.

The political and policy views of the unsuccessful candidate for judicial office are never put to a test. Confirming the link between party labels and policy depends, therefore, upon a comparison of past performances by judges of differing partisan affiliations. If Democratic judges are no different than Republican judges in the resolutions they bring to judicial policy questions, then the argument supporting popular partisan elections as institutional devices for holding judicial policy-makers accountable is severely undermined.

Popular judicial elections might, indeed, be justified on other grounds, such as the role they play in securing the popular legitimacy of the courts and public acceptance of, and compliance with, judicial decisions. Moreover, to the extent that partisan elections boost popular participation in the judicial selection process, this form of election might be said to have certain salutary effects apart from its impact on the substance of judicial decisions.[1] But in the absence of meaningful policy-making differences between judges of different parties, partisan voting by the electorate will have little impact upon the resolution of individual cases or the overall direction of judicial policy, at least to the extent to which it might be concluded that partisan elections serve as effective agents of accountability.

## PARTY, POLITICAL ATTITUDES, AND JUDICIAL POLICY

There are sound theoretical reasons to expect that partisan judicial elections are capable of forging a strong linkage between the electorate and the policy decisions made by state judges. First, the psychological identification of an individual with a political party is well known to be one of the most powerful influences on the shaping of political attitudes. Assumed largely as the result of parental imitation, party identification nevertheless serves as a lifelong mechanism to help individuals organize, digest, and interpret political information.[2] It is not surprising, therefore, that individual attitudes on political issues are distinguishable by party. While the extent of the differences between loyalists of opposing parties on the resolution of major policy issues varies over time and by issue area, Democratic identifiers tend to be more liberal while Republican identifiers tend to be more conservative.[3]

Party identification, therefore, serves to shape political attitudes and policy views—for judges as well as for other individuals. And, as the Legal Realists early recognized, the attitudes and values of judges play a major role in affecting their perceptions of the various claims brought by opposing litigants for resolution. Thus, to the extent that judges' values are shaped by their psychological identification with a political party and its principles, it can be expected that judicial decision-making will exhibit some party-based differences. Thus, partisan judicial elections may indirectly influence the course of judicial policy by resulting in the selection of individuals who possess different party identifications and who thus hold different viewpoints and issue orientations which, in turn, affect their decisions as judges.

Moreover, to the extent that they attract individuals with personal histories of vigorous involvement in partisan political activities, partisan judicial elections may actually accentuate the influence of partisan attitudes and values in the judicial decision-making process. Studies of political behavior confirm that the intensity of an individual's psychological attachment to a party is as important to the development of political attitudes as the basic party identification itself.[4] The intensity of partisan allegiance has a significant effect in reinforcing partisan values and contributing to the formation of more-consistent political attitudes across several issue areas. Those who strongly identify with each party are more clearly differentiated in their political attitudes than those with only weak or nominal attachments to the parties.[5] Individuals who are strongly committed to their party are also more likely than others to be interested in political affairs and, in turn, to take an activist and participatory role in the political arena.[6] Partisan political activity itself also contributes to the formation of political attitudes by reinforcing those already strongly held beliefs. It is not surprising that studies reveal a greater gap between the political attitudes of Democratic and Republican party activists than between the parties' respective followings in the electorate.[7]

Party identification is thus an important influence in shaping those political attitudes and values which might be brought to bear in the resolution of judicial policy questions. But to the extent also that a judge was a party activist prior to assuming the bench, these partisan attitudes will be strongly held and likely to find more-consistent expression in judicial decisions.

Partisan judicial elections are not, of course, the only method of judicial selection which will recruit party activists to the judiciary. Judges in states employing gubernatorial appointment, legislative election, or even merit selection are likely also to have prior histories of partisan political activity.[8] Likewise, as Chapter 4 showed, individuals appointed by the governor to fill mid-term vacancies in states using nonpartisan (and partisan) elections are likely to be fellow partisans who have a long and faithful record of service to the governor or the party.

Nonpartisan judicial elections might, on the other hand, "encourage lawyers who are not party regulars—and who are, therefore, probably less committed along lines of traditional party cleavages—to run for judicial office."[9] Though nonpartisan elections do not preclude the selection of dedicated partisans (especially through the appointment process), the relationship between the party affiliation of judges and their decision-making might be weakened in a nonpartisan setting because some of those individuals who reach the bench are not strongly committed psychologically to a party, its ideological perspective, or its policy positions.

In sum, partisan judicial elections may have an indirect impact upon the course of judicial policy. Voters, casting ballots along party lines, select judicial candidates who possess attitudes and issue orientations related to the party label under which they compete for election. These attitudes affect judges' perceptions of the issues which confront them on the bench and thereby influence their decisions.

JUDICIAL CONSTITUENCIES AND JUDICIAL POLICY

A partisan election system may also have a more direct effect upon judicial decision-making. Because elections hold the key to continued tenure in office, they establish the dependence of public officials upon the electorate. This means that incumbent office-holders must act in anticipation of the potential reaction by key political supporters and those segments of the electorate which they hope will secure their re-election. Elections may, therefore, prospectively influence judicial behavior as judges anticipate the expectations and reactions of their constituencies.[10]

The nature of a judge's constituency will, of course, vary in different political environments. Where judges are selected in highly partisan circumstances and depend upon a highly partisan constituency for continuance in office, they may act in ways which will cultivate the support of that constituency, that is, exhibit partisan voting tendencies in their judicial decision-making.

The existence of a partisan judicial constituency depends upon the partisanship of the judicial selection process. At the outset, partisan nomination processes may provide judges with a partisan constituency. Where judicial candidates are nominated by party conventions, judges will be dependent upon the support of party leaders and convention delegates for renomination to another term. This dependence may inspire the incumbent judge to demonstrate his or her allegiance to party positions in judicial decision-making between elections. Similarly, where political party organizations effectively control access to the primary election ballot and their endorsements are essential to securing the nomination of the party's followers in the electorate, judges may likewise have a strong incentive to give full expression to party principles in judicial decision-making. Additionally, regardless of the system of nomination, sitting judges depend to a greater or lesser extent upon the support of party organizations to suppy the material and human resources vital to a successful re-election campaign. Finally, judges must consider the possible reactions of the loyal partisans in the electorate. Though voter attention to judicial decisions is low, judges must nevertheless be alert to the potential mobilization of the electorate in response to controversial decisions. When the electorate does awaken from its normal state of quiescence, the judge who is concerned about a partisan constituency must make certain that he or she has taken policy positions which fellow partisans would approve.

The strength of the direct effect of a partisan judicial constituency upon judicial behavior will vary, of course, from state to state depending upon the extent to which judges are dependent upon, or perceive their dependence upon, their party organizations, its workers, and its supporters for renomination and re-election to office. To the extent that the party exercises less-effective control over the future of the sitting judge, partisanship can be expected to diminish in importance for judicial decision-making.[11]

Both formal institutional arrangements regarding judicial selection and the informal characteristics of political party processes can determine the strength of a partisan constituency. Nomination by partisan convention ensures maximum partisan control over judicial officeholders. Not only is the party able to select party activists who are highly committed to the principles of the party, but also convention nomination enables the party to maintain the loyalty of its judges once in office by establishing the judges' clear dependence upon the party for renomination and hence re-election. By its very nature, in contrast, the direct primary reduces the leverage which parties have over judges who wear the party label. "The direct primary undercuts the ability of the party organization to recruit to public office those partisans who share its goals and accept its discipline."[12] Party organizations may, with varying degrees of success, attempt to control the outcome of the primary nomination process by seeking out their own recruits, by their offerings of endorsement (both formal-legal or informal-extralegal) and by their supplying the campaign expertise, personnel, and finances required for a winning campaign. The effective strength of the statewide party organization in controlling the process of nomination will, therefore, have a great deal to do with the willingness of judicial officeholders to adhere closely to party principles and partisan positions.[13]

In the general election campaign, judicial candidates similarly may be more or less dependent upon the party organizations for campaign help. As a rule, judicial candidates are undoubtedly quite dependent upon party organizations. Judicial hopefuls, even incumbent judges, are not likely to be well known on their own and thus will have a most difficult time in building up a personal campaign organization and attracting an independent core of supporters and sources of funding outside the party structure. Nevertheless, one can envision political circumstances which would compel a judicial candidate to maintain a careful distance from the rest of the party ticket during the campaign. In some states, for example, political cultural norms may dictate that candidates for judicial office avoid making purely partisan electoral appeals; candidates must appeal to the electorate on the basis of their personal qualities and not solely on the basis of their partisan affiliation. Similarly, the partisan balance in a state may force a judicial candidate to pursue a nonparty election strategy. Where appointees of a minority-party governor are seeking election, for instance, their fortunes will depend upon their ability to attract voters who identify with the majority party in the state. In such circumstances, judicial candidates may attempt to establish a political identity of their own apart from their party. Their need to attract independent sources of support provides them with an incentive, therefore, to eschew partisan judicial behavior and to establish a record of bipartisan decision-making on the bench which can be cited during the election campaign.

The influence of a partisan constituency upon judicial decision-making is undoubtedly most clearly diminished where the formal or informal processes of judicial selection do not involve partisanship at all. If the judge does not depend upon the party for renomination or election and the parties are not instrumental in providing the judge with vital campaign resources, the judge will be largely freed from the prospective pressures of a partisan constituency.

But the judge is not thereby made independent of all constituency influences. Each judge who must face the possibility of a contested election in order to remain in office has some kind of constituency to which prospective attention must be paid. The precise nature of that constituency will depend upon the kinds of individuals, groups, and organizations which the judge must court in order to secure nomination and election. For example, where nonpartisan primaries and nonpartisan elections are used, the incumbent must construct a "nonpartisan" constituency. Formal institutional provisions for nonpartisan selection have not always effectively suppressed partisan activity. Where such arrangements have been successful and enshrined by tradition, however, judges must seek to build their re-election campaign to cut across normal partisan divisions to attract campaign workers and contributors, to secure political endorsements, and, most of all, to attract voter support.[14] In such an environment, the incumbent has a strong incentive between elections "to act in ways that show he is not a partisan, not a 'liberal' or a 'conservative' but rather a 'nonpartisan' judge" responding to the bipartisan constituency which supported the campaign for office originally and which will support him or her in the future.[15] Where the nomination and election constituency is truly drawn across and not along party lines, even dedicated partisans selected by a governor to fill mid-term judicial vacancies have an electoral incentive to mute their partisanship and to appeal to those bipartisan segments of the community which hold the key to another term in office.

Apart from the partisanship of a judicial selection system, other factors may also influence the extent to which partisan values find expression in judicial decisions. Lengthy terms of office, for instance, may diminish the attention paid by judges to their partisan constituencies. The prospective fear of party disapproval may be quite remote to judges serving terms of ten years or even longer, while "on courts with short terms several judges would be anticipating not very distant re-election campaigns at any given moment." [16] In addition, the psychological attachment of a judge to his or her party may wane with the passage of time; judges who serve long terms are not "continually resocialized into partisan values by involvement with party activists and voters" as are judges who must face re-election more regularly. [17]

Judges in different states also face differing sets of norms and expectations emanating both from the community and from within the court itself which may serve to mitigate the importance of party in their decision-making. The judges' "understanding of the 'rules of the game' may be such as to make party an improper consideration in decision-making." [18] Political, cultural, and professional norms transmitted through various attentive nonparty publics of the court (bar groups, civic organizations, and the press) may impel judges to temper their partisan orientations. Socialization experiences on the bench also vary from state to state. Studies have documented that different perceptions of the importance of traditional legal norms (such as *stare decisis*) to judicial decision-making and the proper role of the judiciary in policy-making vary not just among individual judges but also across different states. [19] In those states where judicial norms emphasize that judges should assume but a limited policy-making role and that they closely adhere to precedent where possible, party orientations undoubtedly assume a diminished importance.

Finally, partisan judicial behavior on a state court may be moderated by informal norms and formal procedural arrangements within each state which facilitate the accommodation of divergent views on the resolution of judicial policy issues. In some states, internal court norms direct that judges avoid public demonstrations of intracourt factionalism and attempt to compromise their differences so that a consensus can be reached. [20] Additionally, certain formal procedures of collegial court decision-making maximize the possibilities for judges to reach a consensus. The existence of a resident court, for example, promotes the face-to-face interaction of judges and the circulation of slip opinions, allowing judges to resolve their differences before the court's collective decision is announced.[21]

Though these factors surely serve to reduce the influence of partisanship in judicial decision-making, they are probably secondary to the primary influence of the judicial constituency. If judges' constituencies are strongly partisan, they have the most powerful incentive to demonstrate partisan loyalty in their voting behavior—to win renomination and re-election. Short terms of office, an environment which accepts the legitimacy of partisan considerations in judicial policy-making, and the absence of informal norms and formal procedures which encourage compromise undoubtedly accentuate (both separately or in combination) the partisan divisions on a court. Alternatively, long terms of office, an environment in which traditional legal norms are emphasized, and the presence of consensus-producing norms and procedures may each serve to further diminish the likelihood of partisan patterns in judicial decisions where judges do not have partisan constituencies. But whether a judicial constituency is essentially partisan or nonpartisan probably has the greatest impact on the extent to which judges make decisions along partisan lines.

In summary, therefore, it can be hypothesized that judicial elections have a twofold impact upon judicial behavior.[22] First, by influencing the extent to which individuals with a deep attachment to a political party, its ideology, and its partisan policy stands are recruited to serve as judges, the election process may have an effect on the extent to which judges vote along partisan lines in their decisions. Presumably, individuals selected through a partisan process are more likely to be dedicated "partisans" than individuals selected in a nonpartisan process.

The second impact of the election system is its prospective influence upon judicial behavior. Regardless of the degree of initial commitment to a political party and its values, the nomination and election system imposes diverse demands upon the incumbent judge, either reinforcing or countervailing his or her predisposition toward the expression of partisan attitudes in judicial decisions. Judges selected through an essentially partisan process have a prospective incentive to demonstrate their loyalty and allegiance to the party while on the bench in order to secure a future renomination and re-election. Moreover, during the campaign incumbent judges are once again brought into close contact with fellow partisans and continually resocialized in the ideology and values of the party. Where the nomination and election constituency is effectively nonpartisan, however, judges are freed to give expression to other strongly held attitudes and values without regard to party and may, indeed, have an electoral incentive to mute their partisanship and to appeal to those bipartisan segments of the community which will support their bid for another term in office.

Accordingly, the partisanship of a judicial election system may have two independent, but reinforcing, effects upon judicial behavior and, hence, upon the course of judicial policy. A partisan judicial election system is probably more likely than a nonpartisan one both to select individuals who are intensely committed to partisan values and to prospectively influence judicial decisions along party lines. In gauging these impacts of the electoral system upon judicial decision-making, it may be most useful to think of election systems along a continuum. At the "partisan" end of this continuum are those states in which judges are nominated by party convention and campaign in highly partisan contests with the endorsement and campaign support of their party organizations. At the "nonpartisan" pole of this continuum are those states in which judges are nominated in nonpartisan primaries, run in nonpartisan general elections, and draw their campaign and electoral support from nonparty or bipartisan sources.

In placing a judicial election system along this continuum, one must consider not just the formal institutional arrangements for selection, but also the informal and less visible aspects of judicial recruitment. In states using the direct primary, for example, notice must be taken of those instances where party organizations are in effective control of access to the ballot and the electoral success of party nominees. In such circumstances, the party may be able to assure the placement of dedicated partisans in judicial office and to guarantee their loyalty with an efficiency usually witnessed only in states utilizing a convention system of nomination. Similarly, while the process of nonpartisan nomination and election allows individuals with no past or present commitment to attain judicial offices, it must also be considered that a majority of the seats on nonpartisan courts are filled initially by gubernatorial appointment. And as the evidence offered in Chapter 4 attests, the governor, a partisan official, is most likely to appoint fellow partisans to fill judicial vacancies.

In addition, the extent to which partisanship in the selection system influences partisanship on the bench may also be affected by a host of factors unrelated to either the formal or the informal dimensions of judicial selection and retention, such as the length of judicial terms, cultural norms within and without the court relating to the appropriateness of partisanship in judicial decision-making, and the existence of informal pressures encouraging, and formal procedures which facilitate, the compromise of divergent viewpoints on the resolution of judicial policy issues.

Whether these possible connections between judicial election systems and the decisional propensities of state judges who possess different partisan identifications have any basis other than in speculation is, of course, a subject for empirical inquiry. Fortunately, some empirical research has already been performed. The results tend to suggest that each of the hypothesized linkages between an election system and judicial voting behavior may hold some vitality. Two strands of scholarly literature suggest this possibility. The first strand of research has examined on an aggregate level the relationship between certain social background characteristics of judges, including political party affiliation, and differences in their voting behavior. These studies have confirmed significant differences in the decisional tendencies of state judges of opposing partisan affiliations. The second research strand consists of independently conducted case studies of judicial decision-making on several state supreme courts. The results of these studies cumulatively suggest that there may be a meaningful connection between the partisanship of a judicial constituency and the propensity of judges on state courts to divide along partisan lines.

## PARTY AS A SOCIAL BACKGROUND CHARACTERISTIC

The aggregate social background studies are based upon the assumption that certain background experiences contribute to the development of attitudes and values which shape decision-making. Background factors do not, of course, directly translate into specific attitudes and values, nor do specific values find direct expression in judicial decisions.[23] The relationships among social background characteristics, personal values, and judicial decisions are "tempered by a host of experiential, institutional, and interpersonal variables."[24]

Nevertheless, there are, as noted before, strong theoretic reasons to expect party affiliation to be fundamental to the development of basic political attitudes and, in turn, for those attitudes to be expressed in judges' decisions. Thus, in studies investigating the relationship between the voting behavior of judges and a host of social background characteristics (including party affiliation, religious identification, ethnicity, age, region, and prior political, legal, and judicial experience), political party has emerged as the single most powerful predictor of the differences in the decisional tendencies of individual judges.

Using the decisions of judges serving on those state and federal supreme courts with bipartisan membership in 1955, Stuart Nagel discovered that Democratic judges were significantly different in their decisional tendencies from Republican judges in nine of fifteen areas of law.[25] Democratic judges were more likely than Republican judges to score above the average of the judges of their own courts on behalf of (a) the defendant in criminal cases; (b) the administrative agency in business regulation cases; (c) the claimant in unemployment compensation cases; (d) the defendant in cases involving claims of constitutional violations in criminal cases; (e) the government in tax cases; (f) the tenant in landlord-tenant disputes; (g) the consumer in sales-of-goods cases; (h) the injured party in motor vehicle accident suits; and (i) the employee in workmen's compensation cases.

Nagel thus noted the tendency for Democratic judges to support "the interests of the lower or less privileged economic or social groups," a liberal viewpoint when compared to the tendency of Republican judges to support the conservative position in support of "the interests of the upper or dominant groups" in society.[26]

To a surprising extent, therefore, Nagel found that the general ideological divisions between Democratic and Republican judges were characteristic of the ideological differences which studies have revealed separate the behavior of elected public officials of different parties in the other branches of government,[27] the attitudes of party activists,[28] and, albeit to a weaker extent, public perceptions of the policy stands of the parties and the attitudes of different partisan identifiers within the electorate.

Subsequent, more methodologically sophisticated studies by Bowen[29] and by Nagel[30] have reconfirmed the importance of party affiliation as the background characteristic most consistently and significantly linked to differences in judicial behavior, even with the effects of other social background characteristics and attitudinal variables statistically controlled.

Partisan affiliation emerged from these aggregate studies, therefore, as the single most important factor associated with the decisional differences among state judges. Aggregate analyses of the decisional tendencies of federal appellate judges have reached generally the same conclusion.[31] As with their counterparts in the legislative and executive branches of government, opposing partisans in the judiciary have been found to divide along party lines most sharply "in those cases where the issue is most clearly economic in nature," issues which touch upon the basic socioeconomic divisions separating the parties' identifiers in the electorate and the parties' divergent approaches regarding the distribution and redistribution of economic resources.[32] In the main, therefore, these aggregate studies support the conclusion that "in their decisional propensities, judges appear to resemble their fellow partisans in the public at large, in Congress, and in the executive."[33]

## PARTISANSHIP ON STATE SUPREME COURTS: CASE STUDIES

Though the aggregate studies confirm that judges do exhibit partisan tendencies in their decision-making, they do not make possible a precise understanding of how the variable of party operates. Indeed, by aggregating the votes of judges serving on both federal and state courts and those state judges selected and retained under different systems and in differing political environments, these studies obscure any significant variations in the strength of partisanship which might exist. Thus, the aggregate studies cannot clarify the extent to which party operates indirectly, as a background factor which contributes to the formation of political attitudes that ultimately influence judicial decision-making, or directly upon judicial behavior, through the prospective influence of a partisan judicial constituency. The second major strand of literature which has investigated the effect of political party on judicial decision-making consists of several case studies of judicial behavior on separate state supreme courts. These analyses make an important contribution to an understanding of the influence of a judicial constituency upon judicial decision-making.

Three separate studies of the Michigan Supreme Court, analyzing over a decade of its nonunanimous decisions, have each confirmed the existence of clear and persistent partisan voting blocs. Schubert[34] and Ulmer[35] found sharp divisions between Democratic and Republican judges in workmen's compensation cases, attesting, as Ulmer said, "to either the strength of party affiliation in Michigan judicial politics or the unusual homogeneity of social attitudes among those judges who wear the party label."[36] In his analysis of the Michigan court, Feeley[37] found nearly perfect party-line division on the court in cases involving the claims of criminal defendants, the power of governmental regulatory authority, claims against companies (including workmen's and unemployment compensation), and domestic law controversies. Significantly, Democratic judges were consistently more liberal than the Republican judges on all issues, not just those "of direct and immediate interest to the state political parties."[38]

While significant as initial explorations into state court decision-making, the results of the studies by Schubert, Ulmer, and Feeley merely confirmed the conclusions of the social background research. Political party is one of the most reliable predictors of judicial decision-making, albeit that party seemed to be an especially powerful predictor in Michigan.

All would have remained undisturbed were it not for Adamany's finding that the party variable was not a major factor accounting for the divisions on the Wisconsin Supreme Court.[39] Examining the behavior of Wisconsin's high court justices in workmen's and unemployment compensation cases from 1957 to 1966, Adamany could find no sharp party line dividing Republican from Democratic justices. His analysis of dissenting blocs showed no strong or stable blocs on the court; those which did form were most often weak, highly fluid in membership, and likely to be bipartisan in composition.

The findings in Wisconsin added a new wrinkle to the explanation of the party variable. Party affiliation had always been thought to be an important background characteristic which shaped the decisional propensities of judges. But clearly the degree of partisanship in judicial voting could be greater or less as the case studies of Michigan and Wisconsin indicated.

Adamany suggested that the main reason for the difference between the two states in the extent to which partisanship emerged in judicial decision-making might rest with the crucial differences in the electoral constituencies of the judges in each state. Supreme court judges in both Michigan and Wisconsin are elected on nonpartisan ballots. But the nature of judicial politics in the two states is fundamentally different. In Michigan, judicial candidates are nominated in partisan conventions and openly campaign as partisans, despite the nonpartisan ballot. Wisconsin's judicial candidates are, in contrast, nominated in nonpartisan primaries and elected on nonpartisan ballots. The legal and institutional arrangements for nonpartisan judicial selection are, additionally, buttressed by a strong Progressive heritage of a nonpartisan judiciary, guaranteeing that Wisconsin judicial elections are nonpartisan in fact as well as form.

Adamany examined Wisconsin's nonpartisan election campaigns from 1957 to 1966. He first observed that these elections are often not contested between nominees of opposing party affiliations.

Moreover, in the three (of seven) elections contested between clearly identified opposing partisans, the candidates drew bipartisan campaign support in the press, in the legal profession, among interest groups, and in the electorate. Adamany concluded that "members of the Wisconsin Supreme Court may accurately view their constituencies as bipartisan and do not need to remain actively engaged with their parties as a method for election or re-election to the bench."[40]

Michigan judges, in contrast, had to act in a partisan fashion "to retain the support of their highly partisan constituencies."[41] Moreover, the contact of the judges with the party during the election campaign and between elections in anticipation of the next campaign also continually reinforced the judges' commitment to the values of the party. The Wisconsin judges, however, suppressed their tendencies in order to retain their appeal to the bipartisan constituency which helped them achieve office and which would help them retain office in the future. The different electoral circumstances, therefore, facing the judges in Michigan and Wisconsin accentuated the saliency of party affiliation for Michigan judges and diminished its significance for the Wisconsin judges.

The pressures toward partisanship on the Michigan court and nonpartisan behavior on the Wisconsin court were additionally reinforced by the absence in Michigan and the presence in Wisconsin of procedural arrangements which encourage the softening of divergent partisan viewpoints. A resident court in Wisconsin creates "a considerable personal interaction between the justices which maximizes the opportunities for accommodation and compromise" compared to the nonresident Michigan court.[42] Michigan's judges, moreover, have ample time to write and submit dissenting opinions while Wisconsin's judges, constrained by fairly rigid time limits on the filing of dissenting opinions, must often forego registering their disagreement with the decision of the majority.

The case studies of state judicial decision-making in Michigan and Wisconsin reveal, therefore, that the influence of partisan affiliation on judicial behavior is not a constant. Though both the Michigan and Wisconsin courts were staffed by individuals with past histories in partisan political activities, the Michigan judges were sharply divided along party lines while party did not explain the lines of division observed among Wisconsin's high court members. The main difference between the two states appeared in the amount of pressure for partisan judicial behavior emanating from the judicial constituency.

Several subsequent studies of state judicial behavior in other states have reported results which by implication support the "constituency theory" of the party variable. Viewed as a whole, these analyses appear to place state supreme courts along a hypothetical continuum reflecting the partisanship of the judicial election system. The more partisan the electoral system is in fact, the greater will be the tendency for divisions on state supreme courts to be drawn along party lines. In each of these case studies, the amount of partisanship observed on the court appears to fall between the extremes of partisan and nonpartisan judicial behavior observed in Michigan and Wisconsin, respectively. In each instance, some institutional or political factor or set of factors is present which appears to account for the extent to which party affiliation influences the judicial decision-making process.

In several studies of the Pennsylvania Supreme Court[43] and the New York Court of Appeals,[44] party identification has been only moderately successful in accounting for the lines of cleavage within each court. Despite systems of partisan nomination and partisan election, party has not emerged in either state as nearly as powerful as it did in Michigan, but it most certainly has been more significant in these states than in Wisconsin. Though the judges on each court are selected through basically partisan processes, institutional and political arrangements in each state mitigate the expression of partisanship on the bench.

Until a constitutional change was adopted in 1968, Pennsylvania supreme court justices were elected for a single twenty-one–year term, the longest fixed term for any high court in the country. Thus, if they lived so long, the elected judges would at most serve one full term. Although the products of a partisan recruitment process, these judges did not have to cultivate their partisan constituency while on the bench nor were they "continually resocialized into partisan values by involvement with party activists and voters in periodic re-election campaigns."[45]

In addition, intraparty factionalism has partially mitigated the strength of the party variable for judicial behavior on the Pennsylvania court. While the parties go to great lengths to try to control the outcome of primary election contests by offering endorsements and campaign support, persistent differences within each party have been a problem in the selection of judicial candidates as they have for executive and legislative nominations. Major political factions in each party are headquartered in Philadelphia and Pittsburgh "and leaders of both city organizations have opposed each other frequently in the selection of supreme court candidates."[46] As a consequence, "serious competition has existed within as well as between political parties and the judges may not be especially attracted to members of their own party on the court."[47]

In New York, candidates for the court of appeals were, until 1967, nominated by state party judicial conventions. But the political parties typically agreed to each nominate any previously elected judge seeking re-election. If more than one position on the court fell vacant in the same election year, party leaders agreed to give mutual support to one candidate from each party.[48] From 1948 to 1967, ten of fourteen (71.4%) of the positions on the court of appeals were filled by candidates receiving endorsements from both of the major parties. No previously elected incumbent failed to secure the nominations of both parties for a re-election bid. Further, from 1926 to 1973, no race for the powerful and prestigious position of chief judge was contested between opposing partisans as the parties observed the tradition of giving bipartisan endorsement to the most senior associate justice, regardless of party affiliation.[49]

Once elected, therefore, the New York high court justices could be virtually reassured of support from both parties in a re-election bid, provided their decisions on the bench did not become too unpalatable to leaders from the opposite party. They did not have to deny partisan allegiance, but they did have an incentive to mute strong party attachment. Moreover, the New York judges had only to face re-election every fourteen years, next to Pennsylvania (twenty-one years) and Maryland (fifteen years) the longest fixed term for state supreme court justices. Like the Pennsylvania judges, their electoral situation required very infrequent contact with their party and its activists; even if the informal practice of bipartisan endorsement had not been present to provide the sitting judges with an incentive to temper partisanship in their decision-making, their commitment to partisan values would inevitably wane over the long term without the regular reinforcement provided by periodic campaigns.

Additional studies of state judicial decision-making on the supreme courts of Iowa and California have also uncovered evidence of considerable, but not perfect, partisan voting. And each state fits rather comfortably along the hypothetical continuum of partisanship being used here.

Although he was unable to identify strong partisan dissenting blocs on the Iowa court, Beatty did find, in accordance with the results of previous studies, that Democratic judges were consistently more liberal than the Republican judges in four major issue areas.[50] But Beatty made no attempt to explain how the results of his study related to those of previous studies in terms of the partisanship of the judicial selection system. He took no notice of the constitutional change adopted by Iowa voters in 1962 abandoning the party convention–partisan election of judges and adopting the merit plan. Nor did he note that of the judges serving on the Iowa court at the time of his analysis, all five Republicans were the products of the partisan selection system used prior to 1962, while all the Democrats were appointees of Democratic Governor Harold E. Hughes under the merit nominating system. Moreover, each of the justices on the court, both Democratic and Republican, had been confirmed in office by the electorate on the merit retention ballot. Apparently, therefore, the merit retention system, which virtually guarantees a judge continued tenure after appointment, served to temper but not totally mitigate the partisan backgrounds of the justices on the Iowa court.

Similarly, Feeley has documented that a moderate amount of partisan voting characterized the lines of cleavage he observed on the California Supreme Court.[51] In fact, while not as significant as on the Michigan court, party was, in Feeley's estimation, more important in California than in either Pennsylvania or New York.

Though the judges of California's high court are not elected, partisanship is nevertheless an essential element of the system of judicial selection. The choice of a new justice is the governor's, though the approval of a majority of the three-member Commission on Judicial Qualifications (consisting of the chief justice, the attorney general, and the presiding judge of the court of appeals) is required. But the members of the commission fully honor the governor's privilege to select a fellow partisan provided the appointee is not objectionable on other grounds. Thus, nearly all the justices appointed to serve on the California Supreme Court in recent history have shared the governor's party affiliation. Partisanship is not a consideration in the re-election of a sitting justice, however. After a year on the bench the appointed justice faces the electorate on an uncontested retention ballot identical to those used in the merit plan states.

Finally, the results of Watson and Downing's study of the effects in Missouri of the transition from partisan elections to the merit plan support the view that the removal of a partisan constituency mitigates the impact of partisan backgrounds upon judicial decision-making. Studying the percentage of interagreement among fellow partisans on the bench immediately before and after the enactment of the plan, Watson and Downing conclude that "the kinds of cleavages that were factors in Supreme Court decision-making in the pre-Plan years no longer affected voting alignments among Supreme Court justices in the Plan era. After 1942 neither partisan affiliation nor the method by which the justices were chosen had any significant bearing upon voting behavior in nonunanimous decisions."[52]

## SUMMARY: THE "PARTY VARIABLE" IN JUDICIAL DECISION-MAKING

In sum, empirical research has confirmed the importance of party affiliation to judicial decision-making. Judges are clearly distinguishable along party lines in their decision propensities. But party is not equally powerful in explaining the divisions on state courts. And the results of a few case studies of patterns of partisan voting on state courts of last resort suggest that the variance may be attributable to the partisanship of the judicial selection system, which has an impact upon judicial behavior. A partisan judicial selection system is more likely than a nonpartisan system both to (a) encourage the recruitment of party activists deeply committed to the policy and value orientations of their party and (b) provide judges with a partisan constituency whose policy preferences the judges must anticipate in their judicial decision-making if they are to realize renomination and re-election.

The dual effects of the selection system in structuring judicial recruitment and in prospectively influencing judicial behavior are simultaneous. Unfortunately, the current state of behavioral research does not allow their independent effects to be assessed. Nor can the relative importance of each linkage to judicial behavior be known with any precision, as each relates either to individual judges or to the courts on which they sit. What is required is, in essence, an intuitive and qualitative estimation of the pressures for partisan judicial behavior emanating from the characteristics of those individuals recruited and the prospective influence of the judicial constituency based upon a consideration of the formal and informal dimensions of judicial selection in each state.

By examining the partisanship of judicial behavior on several state courts under a variety of formal and informal selection arrangements, the respective roles of party as a background-attitudinal factor and as a prospective influence on judicial decisions may be better understood. More importantly, the potential for party affiliation to forge the crucial link of accountability between the electorate and the judiciary can be explored in greater detail.

PARTISAN VOTING ON STATE SUPREME COURTS:
A COMPARATIVE APPROACH

The goal of this chapter and the one which follows is to expand the analysis of the party variable to the supreme courts in several states which utilize a variety of the formal systems which have been adopted for the nomination and election of high court justices. Unlike those case studies just reviewed, this analysis applies one set of measurement techniques to the decisions of all the courts in an attempt to compare the importance of the political party variable in supreme court decision-making. In addition, a comparative measure of partisan voting is developed and applied to each of the courts chosen for study in an analysis which seeks to gauge with some precision the relative strength of the party variable in different states featuring different selection systems.

Eight state supreme courts were selected for analysis. The primary concern in the choice of these courts was to select a sample of courts which demonstrate and are broadly representative of the diversity of the formal and informal aspects of elective judicial selection. In particular, close attention was given to the role which partisanship appears to play in the selection process and an attempt was made to select courts which could be placed along a hypothetical continuum from high to low in the partisanship of the nomination and election processes.

It was also desirable not just to study those state courts selected by elective methods, but also to include states utilizing the merit plan of selection and retention. As indicated in Chapter i, the merit plan does not remove partisanship from the selection process; state high court judges appointed under the merit system usually share the governor's partisan affiliation. But the merit retention system effectively removes the potential influence on behavior of a judicial constituency. Because the retention elections are uncontested and the chances of defeat remote, the merit plan judges have no prospective incentive either to display or mute their partisanship on the bench. They have no constituency of contributors, supporters, or voters whose support they must cultivate by their on-the-bench behavior. In the minds of merit plan supporters, this arrangement gives the judges freedom to decide each case on its own merits without regard to party. But the amount of partisan voting on state courts staffed by judges selected and retained under the merit plan remains for empirical research to determine.

Beyond these basic considerations, specific criteria related to the size and partisan make-up of these courts were applied in the selection of courts. First, the analytical techniques to be applied here require that no court containing less than five members be included; thus the courts selected had to contain from five to nine members, the largest of the state courts of last resort. Second, the membership on the courts selected had to be closely divided between judges of opposing partisan affiliation. It was hoped that, by choosing such courts, the opportunity to observe the existence of partisan voting would be maximized. On a court completely dominated by the members of one party, of course, no division between opposing partisans is possible. Even when just a single member of one party is found voting against the rest of the court controlled by opposing partisans, one cannot be certain that the lone dissent is due to party or to the personal "idiosyncracies" of the dissenting judge. Thus, at least two judges from each party had to be included on a court for its inclusion in this study.

Courts with stable memberships for at least two years were sought out in order to guarantee a sufficient number of cases from each court. In several instances, it was possible to choose a court and examine the extent of party voting by the judges on that court in different time periods under conditions of varying court memberships.

Other standard conventions of judicial research were adopted also,[53] of which only one requires specific mention here. Only the nonunanimous decisions of each court were collected for analysis.[54] Nonunanimous cases do not, of course, fully encompass all the judicial business of a state supreme court. In fact, on most state courts, a great majority of the cases decided gain the unanimous approval of all the judges and no expression of disagreement is registered with the filing of either a dissenting vote or an opinion.[55] The various courts differ, however, in the proportion of cases in which public dissents are provoked.

The causes of dissenting behavior on state supreme courts are undergoing continuing investigation. State court dissent rates appear to be the result of a complex of factors including, but not limited to, the controversiality of the issues confronting each court, the heterogeneity of the political, social, and legal backgrounds of the judges, the norms in each state governing the propriety of public expressions of dissent, and the existence of formal institutional arrangements which promote the private accommodation and compromise of diverse views and the concomitant reduction in the occasions of public disagreement.[56]

The amount of dissent does not concern the analysis here except to the extent that it is recognized that dissenting votes provide the variance in judicial behavior which will be used in the analysis of partisan voting alignments. The central question for this study is whether the cleavages which emerge in nonunanimously decided cases follow party lines. It is hoped that the analysis of voting divisions in nonunanimous cases provides some inferential evidence on the patterns of interaction and influence which control the disposition of those cases in which disagreement is privately felt but which, for one reason or another, is not openly expressed with a dissenting vote.

The eight courts selected, the time periods considered, their respective systems of nomination and election, the partisan division in their memberships, and the rate of nonunanimous decisions during each period are summarized in Table 18.[57]

Because three of these states (Colorado, Indiana, and Utah) changed their selection systems during the periods chosen for study, it was possible to observe changes in partisan patterns of state court decision-making which might accompany alterations in the method of selection and retention. In each instance, a partisan (Colorado and Indiana) or nonpartisan (Utah) elective system was abandoned in favor of the merit plan of selection and retention, making possible an inquiry into the effects upon judicial behavior associated with the removal of the influence of a judicial constituency.

Nearly 1,700 nonunanimous cases from the eight supreme courts were identified, with a mean of 130 cases for each court in each period studied. The cases were then classified and analyzed in six basic categories outlined below.

*1. Criminal Appeals.* These cases concern the postconviction appeals of criminal defendants who have violated some misdemeanor or felony statute. These appellants usually raise questions regarding the legal sufficiency of the evidence leading to their convictions and the constitutionality of the proceedings leading to their arrests and the conduct of their trials. Prisoners may also seek review of the severity of the sentence imposed by the trial court or the review of postconviction proceedings relating to probation and parole. Because the claims in criminal appeals often raise collateral claims of both a constitutional and a nonconstitutional variety, no attempt was made to give separate treatment to cases raising constitutional issues.

*2. Domestic and Private Disputes.* The cases in this area are of three basic types. First are those cases concerning marriage and family relations, including annulments, divorces, alimony settlements, child custody and support, adoption, and the like. The second type of case in this area consists of disputes involving the interpretation

**Table 18. Selected Characteristics of Eight State Supreme Courts Chosen for Analysis**

| State | Selection System | | Partisan Division | | Dissent Rate |
|---|---|---|---|---|---|
| | Nomination | Election | Democrats | Republicans | |
| Colorado (1962–1964) | Preprimary | Partisan | 5 | 2 | 9.8% |
| Colorado (1965–1966) | Same as above | | 5 | 2 | 9.6% |
| Colorado (1967–1968) | Merit selection and retention | | 4 | 3 | 7.4% |
| Indiana (1963–1965) | Partisan convention | Partisan | 2 | 3 | 28.2% |
| Indiana (1969–1970) | Same as above | | 2 | 3 | 40.2% |
| Indiana (1971–1972) | Merit selection and retention | | 2 | 3 | 23.1% |
| Iowa (1972–1974) | Merit selection and retention | | 4 | 5 | 12.4% |
| Kansas (1972–1974) | Merit selection and retention | | 2 | 5 | 12.3% |
| Pennsylvania (1972–1974) | Partisan primary | Partisan | 3 | 4 | 37.8% |
| Utah (1960–1966) | Nonpartisan primary | Nonpartisan | 3 | 2 | 14.3% |
| Utah (1967–1970) | Merit selection with challenge retention | | 3 | 2 | 21.8% |
| Washington (1963–1967) | Nonpartisan primary | Nonpartisan | 5 | 4 | 11.5% |
| Washington (1973–1974) | Same as above | | 4 plus 1 Independent | 4 | 28.0% |
| Wisconsin (1968–1974) | Nonpartisan primary | Nonpartisan | 3 | 4 | 6.8% |

of wills, matters of probate, the disposition of trusts and estates, and so forth. Finally, also included in this category are those cases involving conflicts over the obligations imposed by private contractual agreements and disputes over private property rights related to titles, deeds, and such matters.

3. *Economic Distribution.* These cases encompass the broadest range of legal disputes. But at the same time they contain the common dimension of a conflict between litigants of differing economic status and privilege. Such cases include disputes between landlords and tenants, employers and employees, creditors and debtors, manufacturers and consumers, and so forth. Other cases included in this category involve suits for damages in which one party is an injured or aggrieved individual seeking payment and reparations for some injury done to them or their property by a second party. Thus, such cases typically involve a test of judges' sympathy for the injured and aggrieved and, because the defendant is usually indemnified by an insurance company, offer judges a choice between an economically privileged litigant (i.e., the insurance company) and a disadvantaged and injured party seeking to recover compensatory and punitive damages over and above the monetary limits afforded by personal insurance coverage. These cases are most typically suits for personal injury or wrongful death arising out of motor vehicle and other kinds of accidents, but they also include employment-related injuries covered by workmen's compensation; other negligence actions, such as those involving medical malpractice; and claims by policyholders against their own insurance company under the provisions of auto, home, business, and life insurance policies.

4. *Government Regulation.* The cases classified in this category involve questions concerning the extent and exercise of government powers and responsibilities by state and local government agencies and officers in regulating the activities of private individuals, groups, and companies. Included are conflicts over the imposition of various kinds of income, property, business, and use taxes and challenges to state and local zoning regulations. Also included are suits brought against the government concerning the exercise of its power of eminent domain and matters connected with the condemnation of property and just compensation for private property appropriated by the government. Finally, the power of government regulation of business enterprises and the exercise of administrative agency discretion in the areas of business licensing and regulation are also included.

5. *Civil Rights and Liberties.* A fifth category of cases includes those nonunanimous decisions of state high courts which are primarily decided over the alleged deprivation of state or federally guar-

anteed or protected constitutional rights in noncriminal cases. These may involve claims of infringements with personal liberties covered by the First Amendment of the federal constitution or parallel provisions in the state constitution regarding the freedom of religion, speech, press, and assembly. Or they may be cases in which claims are raised concerning the possible denial of equal protection of the laws or due process of law to some individual or group by the state or one of its arms or instrumentalities. Both federal and state constitutional claims are included in this category.

6. *Residual Category.* As its title implies, this category includes all the nonunanimous decisions of each court not classified in the five other major areas. Among the cases in this category are disputes between different branches or levels of government or their officials, between different governmental jurisdictions or different government agencies, and the like. Also in the residual class of cases are reapportionment decisions and judicial resolutions of election contests. Finally included are those cases involving supreme court supervision over the lower courts, their judges, and the members of the legal profession.

The five major categories were defined broadly enough that a vast majority of the nonunanimous decisions of each court are included within one or another of them. For all eight courts during all time periods, a mean of 90.5% of all the nonunanimous cases could be classified, with the proportion of cases categorized in the five major areas ranging from 76.5% to 97.0%.[58]

MEASURING PARTY VOTING ON STATE SUPREME
COURTS

Various analytical techniques have been brought to bear on the study of the patterns of voting on state supreme courts. The most common method involves the calculation of support scores for each judge, that is, the proportion of times each judge voted in favor of one litigant or the other in the various areas of law. Some analysts have been content to find party voting when the Democratic judges more frequently support the liberal position than do the Republican judges.[59] Others have required that a majority of one party oppose a majority of the other in order to support an inference of partisan judicial voting.[60]

A refinement of this simple roll call type analysis, usually called Guttman or cumulative scaling, arrays the judges and their votes along a liberal-conservative continuum over a series of cases.

Scaling has been put to a variety of uses in judicial research, most prominently to identify the existence of a single underlying dimension which characterizes judicial attitudes in a series of cases which appear to present the judges with a choice between competing value positions. As a purely descriptive technique, however, scaling is useful for identifying those judges whose voting behavior is most similar. As with support scores, judges can be ranked from the most liberal to the most conservative, based upon their apparent sensitivity to the claims of certain litigants.[61] Moreover, if the criteria for the construction of an attitude scale can be satisfied, a judge may be placed along the scale continuum even if he or she failed to participate in some of the decisions, an impossibility when simple support scores are used.

The use of either support scores or Guttman scaling is a necessary first step for inferring the influence of partisan affiliation upon judicial voting behavior. Political party would not be a particularly valuable electoral cue for the voters in making their choices in judicial elections if, once elected, judges did not behave in the directions which voters associate with the ideological and policy stances of each major party. Thus, Guttman scaling has been applied here to the decisions of the judges of each state court in each area of law in which the cases lend themselves to a meaningful liberal-conservative classification.

No attempt was made to scale the judges along a liberal-conservative dimension according to their voting behavior in either the domestic law or residual categories defined earlier. The cases contained in the domestic category, involving questions of divorce, family relations, trusts and estates, and the like, do not appear to present judges with a basic choice between litigants of competing political, social, or economic status nor do they revolve around alternative approaches to the solution of important public policy issues associated with each of the major parties. The cases in the residual category, while often containing cases raising issues of importance to the political parties, like reapportionment and election disputes, were much too diverse to be scaled along a single dimension. Fortunately, in no state did the cases contained in these two areas jointly constitute more than about 30% of the nonunanimous decisions.

Thus, a large majority of the cases could be subjected to cumulative scaling analysis and the judges ranked according to their relative commitment to a "liberal" or a "conservative" resolution of the nonunanimous decisions of each court. As other studies have done, judges were considered here to adopt a "liberal" position when they

supported the claims of the less privileged political, economic, or social group or individual.[62] In the major case areas, therefore, a "liberal" vote was one in which a judge supported:

*Criminal*
  1. The claims of criminal defendants or prisoners
*Economic Distribution*
  2. The tenant in landlord-tenant disputes
  3. The debtor in creditor-debtor cases
  4. The claimant in unemployment and workmen's compensa-
     tion cases
  5. The claimant in cases involving suits for personal injury,
     wrongful death, negligence, malpractice, other insurance
     claims for liability and other damage actions
  6. The consumer in sale of goods cases
  7. The employee or labor union in labor-management dis-
     putes, both private and governmental
*Civil Rights and Liberties*
  8. The position favoring the free expression of speech, press,
     and religion
  9. The claims of those asserting a deprivation of some right
     guaranteed or protected by the equal protection and/or due
     process clauses of the Fourteenth Amendment of the feder-
     al constitution or like provisions of the state constitution
*Government Regulation*
  10. The position of the state or local government agency or its
      officers

The cases in the government regulation area involve such diverse
questions of eminent domain, tax, business regulation, and administrative agency authority that no single liberal or conservative position or one readily attributable to either of the parties is easily discerned. Generally, the Democratic party has promoted policies
supporting progressive taxation and government spending to solve
social problems and redress economic imbalances. And the Democrats have supported the close regulation of business enterprises in
order to protect competition in the economic marketplace to assure
as nearly as practicable the fair and equitable distribution of goods
and services to the population.

But in judicial decisions, the liberal-conservative dimensions
may vary with the litigants opposing the government in particular
suits. Liberal judges might not be particularly concerned about voting to support the government's imposition of a business tax upon a

major company, but they might feel some reticence about supporting the government's position in a similar case against a small-
business owner upon whom the tax burden may fall with particular
severity.

Similarly, it is usually true that, with respect to business regulation, state agencies exercise their regulatory power to control the activities of business corporations; liberal justices have no trouble
supporting the government in such litigation as part of their basic
attitudes relating to economic liberalism and the desire to protect
the marketplace from uncontrolled laissez-faire. And, as a rule,
judges generally can be expected to support the judgments of administrative agencies; judicial deference to the exercise of administrative discretion absent a clear violation of constitutional provisions
or statutory guidelines is a settled maxim of both federal and state
administrative law. But Spaeth has demonstrated that judicial responses to the value of economic liberalism often become entangled
with judicial attitudes toward the deference to be accorded the exercise of state administrative power when the agency's position is in
support of the business corporation; as Spaeth notes, "choice between them is inescapable."[63]

Thus, scalogram analysis is handicapped by the diversity of parties and issues involved in cases concerned with the exercise of state
regulatory and administrative power. In the cases involving criminal
appeals, economic distribution, and civil liberties, the parties advocating the "liberal" position are, virtually by definition, the disadvantaged and less privileged political, economic, and social groups.
But where the power of government is involved, it is invoked against
a variety of parties, some of which represent the powerful and the
privileged segments of society and some of which represent underdog groups and individuals. Thus, the liberal-conservative dimension which characterizes the voting options of judges in the other
areas often becomes blurred in cases involving the government and
the exercise of its regulatory authority.[64]

For this analysis, therefore, the votes of state judges were coded
as being either in support of or in opposition to the position of the
government, regardless of what the government position was or the
nature of the opposing litigants on appeal. Thus, the statistic reported in association with the scale analysis in the government regulation area represents the proportion of cases in which each judge
supported the position of the state or local government agency or
official. For ease of discourse, a progovernment stance will be assumed to be a more liberal position, but the validity of this assumption as it applies to each court depends heavily, of course, upon the

distribution of the kinds of cases and the nature of the litigants raising such appeals against the exercise of government regulatory authority.

The two major statistical criteria for testing the existence of a single attitude scale, the coefficient of reproducibility and the coefficient of scalability, were applied to the scales produced in each of the four case areas on each state court during each of the periods of stable court membership.[65] Acceptable scales were, with but few exceptions, achieved for the criminal, economic distribution, and civil liberties decisions of most of the state supreme courts studied, providing empirical confirmation for the basic classification of cases adopted. The government regulation cases consistently failed to satisfy the minimum criteria for scalability, owing as expected to the heterogeneity of the parties and issues involved in such cases.[66]

Based upon the results of the scalogram analysis, the judges of each state court will be arrayed in descending order based upon the proportion of times they supported the liberal position in those cases in which they participated in each of the four major areas.[67] Since the notions of liberal and conservative are purely relative, there is no necessity that a Democratic judge support the liberal position more than half the time while a Republican judge supports the liberal position less than half the time. For inferring the importance of party, it should be enough that the Democratic judges are, in a relative sense, more liberal and less conservative than the Republican judges.

## PARTISAN VOTING BLOCS ON STATE COURTS

However helpful, the analysis of partisan voting patterns by Guttman scaling and support scores is like the blood test for paternity. It is an important initial test to identify the cause of some observable effect. But just as blood type does not conclusively identify fatherhood, so too are these techniques of judicial behavior analysis inconclusive indicators that party affiliation is the significant variable accounting for the observed judicial voting patterns. As Adamany has noted, these methods regard a judge's vote as related to his or her party affiliation even when fellow partisans "on the same bench in the same case are voting for a contrary disposition of the matter. If party affiliation were the primary variable, it should affect most or all of the members of the same party in approximately the same way."[68]

A research method which yields stronger inferences of party

voting is Rice-Beyle cluster-bloc analysis or, simply, bloc analysis. There are several variants to this technique but its basic purpose is the same: to identify groups of judges within a court who tend to vote alike in the same cases.[69] Bloc analysis relies essentially upon some measure of interpersonal agreement among all possible pairs of judges; a matrix of interagreement is then prepared according to one of several established procedures. Groups or "blocs" of judges who have voted together in a significant proportion of cases according to some predetermined criteria may then be identified from an inspection of the bloc matrix.

The major use of bloc analysis in the study of state court behavior has been to identify those pairs of judges who frequently join together in casting dissenting votes in state court decisions. Most commonly referred to as "dissenting bloc analysis" this technique suffers from the same problem which Adamany identified with respect to the analysis of support scores. Those judges in a dissenting minority might claim the same partisan affiliation, but the analysis of dissenting judges says nothing about their fellow partisans who might be part of the majority in a decision.[70] For instance, on a court divided in membership between four Democrats and three Republicans, the joint dissent of two of the Democrats is not particularly strong evidence of the influence of party when two of their colleagues joined with the Republicans to form a solid bipartisan majority. The study of dissenting blocs ignores fully half of the information on judicial voting patterns at the disposal of the analyst.

A more satisfactory approach is to utilize all the interagreements of pairs of judges, whether they agreed in dissent or agreed as part of a larger majority.[71] A number of measurement techniques have been devised for this purpose, but the simplest, most comprehensible, and most widely accepted measure is the Index of Agreement (IA). Often called the Interagreement Index, this measure is simply the proportion of times two judges have voted alike based upon the total number of cases in which they jointly participated.[72] In simplest terms, $IA = f/t$, where $f$ is the frequency or number of agreements and $t$ is the total number of cases in which both judges participated. This index is unrelated to the direction of the judges' votes either for or against particular litigants and it matters not whether the judges agree in the majority or in dissent. After the Index of Agreement is computed for each pair of judges on the court, a matrix of interagreement is constructed.

Though several different techniques have been developed for constructing the matrix of interagreement, no single method has yet gained universal acceptance as the best way to arrange the judges to reveal all the significant voting pairs and groups within the court.[73] Nor have scholars been able to agree upon a minimum level of inter-agreement from which it can be inferred that any two judges have voted alike more frequently than could be expected as the result of chance alone. As two researchers in this field have observed, political scientists have set about this latter task "with an admitted degree of arbitrariness."[74]

For this research it is sufficient to adopt the widely used method of matrix construction developed by David Truman for his study of congressional voting blocs.[75] And the analysis here calls upon a comparatively powerful statistical technique which has been developed in recent years for identifying patterns of bloc voting. This method sets as its criterion for significant agreement that inter-agreement score which is significantly larger than any value that would be likely to occur by random voting. Its derivation is not important here, except to note that it is based upon the binomial distribution of sampling probabilities and relies upon the simple principle that the probabilities of agreement between any two individuals change with the size of the sample of roll calls or votes considered.

Consider, for example, two judges, X and Y, voting on a single case. The probability of these two judges agreeing upon the disposition of this case would be 0.50. Thus, if we actually did observe X and Y to agree, we would not be led to make sweeping inferences based upon the similarity of their behavior. After all, it is just as likely as not (i.e., 50–50) that their agreement could have been produced by chance.

But suppose now that in a series of ten cases X and Y are observed to vote alike in seven, producing an interagreement score of 0.70. Based upon the binomial distribution, the chances of the two judges agreeing in seven of ten cases by chance are only about 0.17. Yet if one were testing the null hypothesis that the voting of Judges X and Y was the product of chance alone, the null hypothesis could not be rejected at the customary 0.05 level of significance. Indeed, the two judges would have to agree in nine of the ten cases to show that their voting agreement could have been the product of random voting less than five times in a hundred.

If one collected and analyzed twenty cases, however, and Judges X and Y still agreed in 70%, one might be more impressed that they had formed a significant voting pair. The probability of any two judges agreeing in fourteen of twenty cases by chance is only 0.058, a level which might lead one closer to rejecting the null hypothesis and to conclude that their voting agreement was not the product of random chance.

Levels of interagreement based upon these principles have been developed by Professor Peter Willetts for the different number of roll calls or votes one might include in a cluster-bloc analysis.[76] Willetts developed cut-off points for levels of agreement at significance levels between 0.001 and 0.05, the latter of which shall be adopted here.[77] In addition, because the same probabilistic principles work on the other tail of the binomial sampling distribution, Willetts has developed interagreement levels for each of the sample sizes which indicate when a pair of judges voted alike so *in*frequently that it could not have been the product of random voting. That is, not only can one determine when two judges are in *significant agreement*, but one may also determine whether they are in *significant disagreement* which could have occurred only as often by chance five times in a hundred.

Thus, for example, given a hypothetical five-member court deciding fifty cases, the Willetts criterion for significant agreement requires two judges to agree in at least 64% of the cases in which they participated together. Alternatively, any two justices agreeing no more than 36% of the time could be said, according to the Willetts criterion, to be significantly in disagreement. Given the results:

|   | A | B | C | D | E |
|---|---|---|---|---|---|
| A | — | | | | |
| B | 0.76 | — | | | |
| C | 0.72 | 0.70 | — | | |
| D | 0.50 | 0.46 | 0.48 | — | |
| E | 0.34 | 0.20 | 0.34 | 0.68 | — |

Judges A, B, and C could be said to have been in agreement among one another in a significant proportion of cases; the same could be concluded for Judges D and E. Alternatively, by agreeing with A, B, and C less than 36% of the time, Judge E can be said to have been in significant disagreement with those members of the court. Judge D is in neither significant agreement nor significant disagreement with those judges, since D's interagreement with each of them falls between the values of 0.36 and 0.64.

The final methodological concern is to determine how a significant voting *bloc* of justices can be identified from the interagreement scores among all pairs of judges. Most scholars have relied upon a computation of the mean interagreement of all the pairs of an hypothesized voting bloc; if the mean score among all pairs of judges in the bloc exceeded the minimum criterion for significant agreement set by the researcher, a significant voting bloc was thereby identified.

Grossman has pointed out, however, that bloc analysis based on the analysis of the interagreement of *pairs* of justices is not an accurate indicator of "when a bloc votes as a bloc."[78] Judges A and B may be each strongly linked by their interagreement scores with Judge C but only moderately or weakly linked to each other. Nevertheless, the mean interagreement among the three judges may exceed the minimum criterion set by the analyst by the strength of C's independent agreement with A and B separately. It produces a classic example of spurious correlation. As a bloc of three judges they may have voted together only infrequently or certainly much less frequently than originally supposed. To attempt to remedy this problem, it has been proposed that "no judge should be included in a bloc if his average interagreement with other bloc members is lower" than the minimum level of significant agreement used by the analyst, a modification which usually "prevents a pair of judges with a very high percentage of interagreement from pulling into a bloc a contiguous judge who agrees with one of them considerably less often than with the other."[79]

Insisting that all pairs in a hypothesized bloc of judges have interagreement scores which exceed the minimum level of cohesion does not, of course, indicate the extent to which the bloc members voted as a bloc. Similarly, the analysis of interagreement pairs is insensitive to those occasions when members of a bloc may join or are joined by "outsiders." Only an inspection of the actual voting patterns in a series of cases can provide a truly accurate accounting of the frequency with which members of a hypothesized bloc join together exclusive of the other members of the court. Such an inspection will be called upon to highlight apparent patterns suggested by the bloc analysis.

It is important here to note that the label "bloc" indicates "nothing more than that a group of judges had a specified level of interagreement."[80] The inferences to be drawn to explain the existence of empirically observed voting blocs do not find their origins in the data. Where, as here, the goal is to investigate the strength of the influence of political party upon the voting behavior of state supreme court justices, Adamany's proposition for inferring the existence of party bloc voting seems most appropriate: "Where party identification is largely coterminous with a voting bloc, there is a strong likelihood that party plays a significant role in the voting."[81]

Precisely the nature of the role which party affiliation plays is, as discussed at length earlier, quite uncertain. Shared attitudes and values are undoubtedly part of the influence of political party. But party also serves as an important reference and friendship group. Moreover, where judges are selected by partisan processes, dedicated partisans may be recruited for service on the bench. Finally, to the extent that the nomination and election process exerts a prospective influence upon judicial decision-making, judges, with their judicial votes, may either confirm their dedication to the principles and values of the party or mute their partisan attachment and loyalty, depending upon the pressure for partisan behavior originating from their judicial constituencies in the party and in the electorate.

# 6. Partisan Voting on State Courts: Eight Case Studies

## INTRODUCTION

A systematic comparison of the extent of partisan judicial behavior on state supreme courts is an extremely difficult task. In part this difficulty is a function of the lack of useful measures which are simultaneously comparative in nature but not suffering from inherent methodological flaws, a concern addressed in the next chapter. Additionally, however, a precise cross-state comparison of judicial voting is rendered especially hazardous by the presence of several sources of interstate variation in the environment of judicial decision-making. Prudence dictates that any examination of partisan voting on state courts be preceded by an appreciation of the dangers of comparative analysis.

First, the frequency of nonunanimous decisions, which comprise the data base for an examination of the lines of intracourt cleavage, ranges from 6.8% to 40.2% for the courts chosen for this study. It is difficult to make truly comparative statements about the importance of party to judicial voting on a given court without considering the overall frequency with which party bloc voting is, or can be, observed. Similarly, not only the frequency but also the sharpness of dissent exhibits considerable variation among the states. On some courts, most of the nonunanimous decisions involve just a single dissenting justice; on other courts, multiple dissents are more regularly filed and the occasions for observing partisan voting divisions are more frequent.

The frequency and sharpness of intracourt divisions are, of course, at least partially the result of the conflict of judges of opposing partisan dispositions. But other, nonparty factors both internal and external to each court undoubtedly affect the extent to which judges disagree and the frequency with which such disagreements are publicly acknowledged. These include, but are not limited to, the nature of the cases flowing to the high court for final disposition, the heterogeneity of the court's membership in terms of social background characteristics and attitudes unrelated to partisan affiliation, and the nature of the court's collegial decision-making procedures.[1]

A second major difference among state courts that makes a comparison of partisan voting patterns difficult is the variation in the kinds of questions reaching each supreme court for resolution. The courts in this study, and in the states generally, differ in the distribution of the kinds of cases which they decide. State supreme courts exercise varying amounts of discretion over the cases they hear, with some courts able to choose not to hear or to avoid certain cases or issues. But just as importantly, differences in the political, socioeconomic, and cultural environments of state legal systems generate interstate variations in both the amount of litigation and the kinds of controversies to be resolved by judicial decision-makers.[2]

Similarly, the case categories used in this and other studies of judicial behavior are only broad classes designed to provide some general indication of the choices facing state judges. They do not, however, reveal systematic differences among the states in the specific kinds of parties and issues confronting state judges, nor do they account for variations in formal legal and judicial standards and the existence of controlling legal precedents. Additionally, the judges serving on the various state appellate courts operate within different sets of decision-making norms governing the review and disposition of cases, differing particularly in the importance they accord to *stare decisis* as a value in judicial decision-making, not to mention their general approaches toward the proper role of courts and judges in state policy-making.[3]

Precise cross-state comparisons of the extent of party bloc voting also must take into consideration the host of social background and attitudinal factors not subsumed under the label of party which affect individual judicial decision-making. With but perhaps the exception of religious affiliation, most social background characteristics (such as ethnicity, age, region, prior legal and judicial experience) have been found to be only weakly related to differences in judicial decision-making.[4] But one or more of these factors (or, more properly, the attitudes which are believed to flow from them) may assume a heightened importance in any one judge's hierarchy of attitudes and values (including those related to partisan affiliation) which affect his or her judicial decision-making.

Finally, comparative study of partisan judicial voting patterns must also take into account those formal and informal aspects of collegial judicial decision-making which may sharpen or mitigate the tendency for judges to divide along party lines. As noted earlier, formal decision-making procedures may encourage compromise and accommodation and thereby curb the instances of public expressions of dissent. Similarly, the procedures of collegial decision-making may affect the direction and substance of the court's decisions and the lines of intracourt cleavage when dissent cannot be contained. The use of oral argument, the nature of internal conference proceedings, and the processes used in the assignment and circulation of written opinions may have an impact, to a greater or lesser degree, upon the patterns of interaction and influence on the court and the resolution of divergent viewpoints on the proper disposition of cases.[5]

In addition to formal decision-making procedures, the decision-making process on collegial courts may be affected by the influence exerted by a specific judge or judges who occupy positions of leadership on the court, either by virtue of their formal command over the decision-making process of the court, as is often possessed by the chief justice, or as a result of their personal qualities of intellect or personality which enable them to persuade colleagues on the bench to adopt a particular point of view.[6]

The cumulative effects of these formal institutional procedures and the informal dimensions of personal influence upon the patterns of party bloc voting are not precisely known. While their general impact upon collegial decision-making is widely recognized, whether they serve to reinforce partisan division or to blur party lines would most probably depend upon the specific constellation of procedures and personalities on each court.

With these caveats appropriately noted, a state-by-state consideration of the patterns of partisan voting on the selected state courts should prove fruitful. In Chapter 7 a comparative measure will be applied simultaneously to the voting patterns on all the courts. Taken together and subject to the qualifications just discussed, these analyses should provide a reliable assessment of the extent of partisan judicial voting on the various courts and the impact upon judicial behavior of different formal and informal arrangements of judicial recruitment and retention.

## THE PARTISAN COURTS: INDIANA, PENNSYLVANIA, AND COLORADO

### Indiana

Until 1971, partisanship was a dominant feature of the Indiana judicial election system. Candidates for the state supreme court were nominated at state party conventions and then competed alongside party nominees for the other statewide offices on the party column ballot which structured voter response along partisan lines. In short, Indiana's judicial selection system invited partisan behavior on the bench. As in Michigan, the party convention system allowed the party to select dedicated partisans to sit on the state's high court. Moreover, once elected, these partisans had a partisan constituency in their party and in the electorate on which they depended for renomination and re-election every sixth year.

In the 1970 election, however, Indiana's voters ratified a constitutional amendment calling for the merit plan of selection and retention. In the years immediately following adoption of the plan, judges selected under the "old" partisan system continued to serve on the court but had been freed from the prospective influence of their partisan constituencies. One could expect, therefore, a decline in the importance of party to judicial decision-making on the Indiana court after the removal of the partisan system and its replacement by the merit retention system.

The analysis offered here traces the patterns of judicial behavior on the five-member court in three periods: 1963–1965, 1969–1970, and 1971–1972.[7] The partisan balance on the court remained stable throughout these time periods at three Republicans and two Democrats despite changing individual membership. All the justices serving on the court during these periods were selected originally through the partisan system, but those serving in the last period were not required to seek re-election through the partisan system because the merit plan had been adopted.

Table 19 presents the results of the scalogram analysis performed on the nonunanimous decisions of the Indiana supreme court during the first period (1963–1965). The data do not indicate dramatic differences between the judges by party. In the area of criminal appeals, the distinguishing characteristic of the voting behavior of the judges is the total support of Judge Amos Jackson for the claims of the criminal defendant; the support of the remaining court members for criminal defendants pales by comparison. Jackson's distinctive behavior is primarily a function of his place on the

**Table 19. *Percentage of Liberal Votes in Nonunanimous Cases,* Indiana Supreme Court, 1963–1965**

| Criminal Appeals | | Economic Distribution | | Government Regulation | |
|---|---|---|---|---|---|
| Jackson (D) | 1.00 | Arterburn (R) | 0.64 | Arterburn (R) | 0.86 |
| Myers (D) | 0.09 | Achor (R) | 0.58 | Achor (R) | 0.79 |
| Achor (R) | 0.02 | Jackson (D) | 0.58 | Myers (D) | 0.69 |
| Arterburn (R) | 0.02 | Myers (D) | 0.58 | Jackson (D) | 0.64 |
| Landis (R) | 0.02 | Landis (R) | 0.50 | Landis (R) | 0.54 |
| Mean court | 0.38 | | 0.58 | | 0.70 |
| Mean Democrats | 0.55 | | 0.58 | | 0.67 |
| Mean Republicans | 0.02 | | 0.57 | | 0.73 |
| (N = 47) | | (N = 12) | | (N = 14) | |

court as a lone dissenter; of forty solitary dissents cast in criminal cases, thirty-nine were cast by Jackson and each time in support of the criminal defendant.

In the areas of economic distribution and government regulation, the scale scores of the judges are not sharply distinguished along partisan lines. Part of the reason is the plethora of solitary dissents; only one of twelve economic cases and three of fourteen government regulation cases involved more than just one dissenter.

Bloc analysis of the Indiana court for this first period is severely limited by the absence of cases with more than a single dissent. Judge Jackson was clearly alienated from the rest of the court, agreeing no more than one-fourth of the time with any other member. Nevertheless, considering only those cases involving more than a single dissent, it is clear that in particularly close decisions the Indiana court divided along party lines. Jackson joined with fellow Democrat Walter Myers, Jr., in 80% of these split decisions. Among the Republicans, Norman Arterburn and Frederick Landis agreed in 94% of the cases and were joined in a substantial majority of cases by fellow partisan, Harold E. Achor.

In the second period (1969–1970), single dissents by Jackson once again isolate him from the decisional tendencies of the rest of the court. The results of the scale analysis (Table 20) in the criminal appeals area reflect Jackson's nearly total commitment to the cause of the criminal defendant. Jackson was joined in about half of these cases by fellow Democrat Roger O. DeBruler, who was appointed to office in 1968 by Democratic Governor Roger Branigan and elected in 1970. The Republican members of the court, including Judges Donald Hunter and Richard M. Givan (elected in 1966 and 1968, re-

**Table 20.** *Percentage of Liberal Votes in Nonunanimous Cases,*
*Indiana Supreme Court, 1969–1970*

| Criminal Appeals | | Economic Distribution | | Government Regulation | |
|---|---|---|---|---|---|
| Jackson (D) | 0.92 | DeBruler (D) | 0.91 | Givan (R) | 0.86 |
| DeBruler (D) | 0.57 | Jackson (D) | 0.64 | Arterburn (R) | 0.79 |
| Hunter (R) | 0.17 | Arterburn (R) | 0.64 | Hunter (R) | 0.64 |
| Givan (R) | 0.09 | Hunter (R) | 0.55 | Jackson (D) | 0.50 |
| Arterburn (R) | 0.03 | Givan (R) | 0.50 | DeBruler (D) | 0.43 |
| Mean court | 0.36 | | 0.65 | | 0.64 |
| Mean Democrats | 0.75 | | 0.78 | | 0.47 |
| Mean Republicans | 0.10 | | 0.56 | | 0.76 |
| (N = 98) | | (N = 11) | | (N = 14) | |

spectively), supported the criminal defendant only rarely. The two
Democrats supported the criminal defendant in an average of 75% of
the cases while the mean support score of the three Republican justices was only 10%.

In the economic distribution area, the average Democratic support score for the economic underdog exceeds the mean Republican
score, but four solitary dissents by Jackson in the "wrong" direction
once again contribute to his relatively low score. Finally, in the government regulation area, Republican judges were more sympathetic
to government claims than the Democratic judges.

Since 70% of the nonunanimous decisions in the 1969–1970 period were criminal appeals, bloc divisions in this area are clearly of
prime importance. Bloc analysis confirms the implication of the
scale scores that Justice Jackson was clearly isolated from his brethren on the court in most cases, agreeing no more than one-fourth of
the time with any of the Republican judges and only in half of the
cases with fellow Democrat DeBruler. But if only closely divided
cases are considered, it is clear that the lines of division on the Indiana court were decidedly partisan in nature. Not only do the observed blocs satisfy the stringent criterion of interagreement suggested by Willetts (IA = 0.65) and used here, but the members of the
respective Republican and Democratic blocs also demonstrated
significant levels of disagreement. Party bloc voting on the court
was clear, sharp, and unmistakable. When criminal defendants
raised controversial questions, the court was most likely to divide
along straight party lines. In these closely decided cases, the two
Democrats voted on the same side of the issue 98% of the time as
did two of the Republican judges, Arterburn and Givan. The remain-

ing Republican judge, Hunter, joined his fellow Republicans in about three of every four cases (mean IA = 0.84) crossing party lines to help the Democrats control the majority in the remaining one-fourth of the decisions.

Criminal appeals once again constituted a significant proportion of the nonunanimous decisions of the supreme court during the 1971–1972 period, accounting for seven out of every ten cases. The court's membership remained stable except that Judge Jackson was replaced by Democrat Dixon W. Prentice, who was elected in the November 1970 contest. But Jackson's departure did not stem the tide of single dissents. Democrat Roger DeBruler took over the role of "the great dissenter" on the Indiana court. Of the 73 nonunanimous criminal cases decided in this final two-year period, 53 (72.6%) were single dissents; over 60% of these were filed by DeBruler, all but one in support of the criminal defendant.

Thus, in Table 21, it can be observed that DeBruler supported the claims of the criminal defendant in 89% of the cases in which he participated. His fellow Democrat, Prentice, was not nearly so supportive of the liberal position, voting in favor of the defendant's claims in barely over half of the cases. Nevertheless, both of the Democratic judges were far more supportive of the defendant than were the three Republicans; the most liberal Republican, Judge Hunter, voted for the defendant in only 30% of the cases.

Bloc analysis of all of the nonunanimous criminal decisions does not reveal sharply drawn partisan blocs; the three Republican judges were linked in a significant proportion of cases (mean IA = 0.76), but Democrats Prentice and DeBruler agreed just 53% of the time, a proportion insufficient to satisfy the Willetts criterion of significant agreement (IA = 0.62). However, when only the most closely divided cases are considered, clear partisan blocs do emerge. Thirteen of these twenty cases (65%) were decided along straight party lines; Republican Judge Hunter joined the two Democrats on five other occasions to form a liberal majority.

In sum, therefore, the prevalence of solo dissents during each of the three time periods examined was perhaps the most distinguishing characteristic of the nonunanimous decisions of the Indiana Supreme Court uncovered here. Whether these solitary expressions of disagreement were the result of personal "idiosyncracies" or representative of the extent of the attitudinal and ideological differences among the judges cannot be known with certainty.

Even with the large number of solo dissents cast by a single judge, however, the Democratic judges were found to be more liberal than the Republican judges in those cases brought by criminal de-

**Table 21.** *Percentage of Liberal Votes in Nonunanimous Cases,*
*Indiana Supreme Court, 1971–1972*

| Criminal Appeals | | Economic Distribution | | Government Regulation | |
|---|---|---|---|---|---|
| DeBruler (D) | 0.89 | DeBruler (D) | 0.56 | Givan (R) | 0.77 |
| Prentice (D) | 0.53 | Givan (R) | 0.56 | Arterburn (R) | 0.69 |
| Hunter (R) | 0.30 | Hunter (R) | 0.56 | Hunter (R) | 0.69 |
| Givan (R) | 0.18 | Arterburn (R) | 0.44 | DeBruler (D) | 0.50 |
| Arterburn (R) | 0.12 | Prentice (D) | 0.44 | Prentice (D) | 0.42 |
| Mean court | 0.40 | | 0.51 | | 0.61 |
| Mean Democrats | 0.71 | | 0.50 | | 0.46 |
| Mean Republicans | 0.20 | | 0.52 | | 0.72 |
| (N = 73) | | (N = 9) | | (N = 13) | |

fendants. The judges of different party affiliations were not so distinguishable, though, in cases concerned with issues of economic distribution and the extent of government regulatory authority. The reasons for this inconsistency across issue areas are, like the causes of solo dissenting behavior, elusive.

The patterns of judicial decision-making on the Indiana court in criminal appeals may, nevertheless, be of the greatest consequence inasmuch as these cases contributed the vast majority of the court's nonunanimous decisions and its docket as a whole. It is in these cases, particularly those decided by a one-vote margin, that the members of the Indiana Supreme Court were observed to divide consistently along partisan lines.

These results are consistent with the amount of partisanship one would expect given the extent to which the selection and retention of judges are intertwined with the partisan political process. Selected by party conventions, the judges selected are likely to have had a long and faithful record of service to the party and its officeholders. And elected judges must return to the party at the end of their term with their judicial record in hand to win the renomination of the party and pledges of support in the general election contest. Thus, as a product of both their partisan backgrounds and the continuing pressures of a partisan constituency, Indiana's high court judges often voted along partisan lines in highly contested cases.

There is some indication from this analysis that the impact of the selection process in recruiting active partisans to sit on the court is more important than the prospective influence of the judicial constituency in affecting the patterns of judicial behavior. Even after Indiana had adopted the merit plan of selection and retention, the judges of the state supreme court, all previously recruited through the partisan system, continued to give expression in the most controversial cases to strongly held partisan attitudes and values.

## Pennsylvania

Prior to 1968, Pennsylvania required that its supreme court justices run for and retain their offices through the partisan selection process. After nomination in a partisan primary and election on a partisan ballot, a justice of the Pennsylvania court would serve for a single twenty-one–year term.

In 1967–1968, the Pennsylvania Constitutional Convention created a new judicial article calling for, among other things, the merit selection and retention of all state judges. The voters approved the new judicial article in the 1968 primary, but the adoption of the merit selection provision was contingent upon voter approval of a referendum on the question in the 1969 primary. The voters rejected the merit selection plan, however, and the results left Pennsylvania with a curious hybrid of partisan selection and merit retention.[8]

All supreme court justices must run initially on the partisan ballot to attain office. After a ten-year term, however, incumbent judges can retain their office by filing a declaration of candidacy for a retention election. They then run unopposed on a separate judicial ballot (or column on the voting machine) solely on the question of whether they should be retained in office. A majority of affirmative votes secures an additional ten-year term.

When vacancies occur on the high court, the governor as before is empowered to appoint a successor. Since 1964, Pennsylvania governors have been guided in their choices by the recommendations of a nominating commission voluntarily established by the governors themselves. Appointees must face the electorate at the next general election after appointment and they may be opposed both in the primary and in the general election. But once elected, the judge may be returned to office every ten years simply by securing the voters' approval on the uncontested retention ballot.

Candidates for the state supreme court in Pennsylvania have usually been the products of partisan politics. Although primaries are the formal means by which candidates are nominated, the party organizations attempt to control the outcome by offering endorsements and campaign support to favored candidates.[9] Only those individuals with years of party service and support are likely to gain the favor of the party leadership. Thus, those individuals recruited to the bench are likely to be dedicated partisans with strongly held political attitudes which may find expression in their decisions.

On the other hand, certain institutional arrangements and political facts of life in Pennsylvania may combine to temper the exercise of partisan voting behavior by judges. First, as noted earlier, the single twenty-one–year term removed the pressure for partisan behavior from the shoulders of the incumbent judge. Judicial decision-making was largely insulated from the political necessity to retain party support for a subsequent re-election bid. The arrangement adopted in 1968 for the uncontested retention of previously elected judges probably functions in much the same way.

Second, intraparty factionalism in both parties has resulted in internal squabbles over the choice of judicial candidates for party endorsement; bitter primary battles are not unknown. As a result, judges sharing the same partisan affiliation on the court may represent different wings of the same party. As the old saying goes, these ostensibly fellow partisans may not always see "eye to eye."[10]

The period from 1972 through 1974 was chosen for study here, a period during which the court's membership was stable and closely divided between four Republicans and three Democrats.[11] Three of the Republicans and one Democrat were originally selected under the previously used system for twenty-one–year terms; these judges had anywhere from six to twelve years remaining on their initial terms in 1972. The remaining Republican and two Democrats were selected under the new election-retention system and each had won a full ten-year term by election.[12]

The results of the scale analysis performed in four major issue areas are presented in Table 22. The mean Democratic score for the defendant in criminal cases, the disadvantaged party in economic cases, the government in regulatory cases, and the liberal position in civil liberties cases exceeds the mean Republican score. But one justice from each party appears not to share the decisional tendencies of his fellow partisans. Among the Democrats, Justice Michael Eagan voted more frequently for the conservative position than did other Democrats in the criminal, economic, and civil liberties cases. Among the Republicans, Samuel Roberts departed significantly from the other Republicans to establish himself as one of the most liberal members on the court.

Bloc analysis of the court's divided decisions in cases involving the rights of the criminal defendant reveals bipartisan bloc formation. Republican Roberts joined with liberal Democrats Louis Manderino and Robert N. C. Nix, Jr., agreeing in a large majority of cases;

**Table 22. Percentage of Liberal Votes in Nonunanimous Cases, Pennsylvania Supreme Court, 1972–1974**

| Criminal Appeals | | Economic Distribution | | Government Regulation | | Civil Liberties | |
|---|---|---|---|---|---|---|---|
| Manderino (D) | 0.89 | Manderino (D) | 0.97 | Roberts (R) | 0.64 | Manderino (D) | 1.00 |
| Roberts (R) | 0.80 | Roberts (R) | 0.86 | Nix (D) | 0.63 | Roberts (R) | 0.70 |
| Nix (D) | 0.68 | Nix (D) | 0.81 | Eagen (D) | 0.62 | Nix (D) | 0.60 |
| O'Brien (R) | 0.51 | Eagen (D) | 0.41 | Jones (R) | 0.46 | Eagen (D) | 0.40 |
| Eagen (D) | 0.41 | O'Brien (R) | 0.39 | Manderino (D) | 0.42 | Jones (R) | 0.40 |
| Pomeroy (R) | 0.33 | Pomeroy (R) | 0.24 | Pomeroy (R) | 0.41 | O'Brien (R) | 0.40 |
| Jones (R) | 0.05 | Jones (R) | 0.09 | O'Brien (R) | 0.37 | Pomeroy (R) | 0.40 |
| | | | | | | | |
| Mean court | 0.52 | | 0.54 | | 0.51 | | 0.56 |
| Mean Democrats | 0.66 | | 0.73 | | 0.56 | | 0.67 |
| Mean Republicans | 0.42 | | 0.40 | | 0.47 | | 0.48 |
| (N = 167) | | (N = 37) | | (N = 35) | | (N = 10) | |

their mean interagreement score is 0.76, significantly above the Willetts criterion of 0.57. Democrat Eagan and Republican Justices Thomas Pomeroy and Benjamin R. Jones were also significantly linked, though to a much weaker extent (mean IA = 0.64). Republican Justice Henry S. O'Brien joined frequently with members of both blocs, voting with the majority in nearly 95% of the non-unanimous criminal decisions. When the bloc analysis is repeated considering only those cases in which more than one justice dissented, the divisions noted above are thereby made more distinct. Moreover, according to the Willetts criteria, the two three-member blocs are significantly different from each other.

In the economic area, Justices Nix, Manderino, and Roberts once again formed a solid liberal voting bloc, agreeing as a group in nearly 70% of the cases in which all three judges participated (Willetts = 0.67). Justices O'Brien and Eagen formed another bipartisan bloc, agreeing in 89% of the nonunanimous decisions. They were joined about two-thirds of the time by Republican Justices Pomeroy and Jones who, as their scale scores indicated, were least supportive of the claims of the economically disadvantaged litigant.

When only those cases with joint dissents are examined, the line of cleavage between the two bipartisan blocs is clarified. In addition, the basic division on the court nearly satisfies the Willetts criterion for significant disagreement in voting behavior. It is probably important to point out that despite the fact that the blocs observed are bipartisan in composition there is fairly strong evidence of the importance of the party variable on the Pennsylvania court. One bloc is composed of two of the three Democrats while the other bloc is composed of three of the four Republicans; most analysts of legislative roll call behavior are satisfied that party-based voting patterns exist when a majority of one party opposes a majority of the other.[13] That criterion is clearly satisfied here.

In cases involving government regulation, the Pennsylvania court divided into three basic subgroups and the lines of cleavage were neither as sharp nor as distinct as those observed in the criminal and economic cases. Justices Nix and Manderino, both Democrats, agreed in 81% of the cases in which they jointly participated. They were joined more often than not by Justice Roberts; the three voted alike in over 65% in which they all participated, registering a mean IA of 0.75, well above the Willetts minimum of 0.67. Justices O'Brien and Pomeroy, both Republicans, also agreed in a significant proportion of the split decisions (74%) as did Republican Justice Jones and Democrat Eagan (68%). An analysis of the cases involving more than one dissenter does not change these basic alignments.

Thus, on matters concerned with the limits of governmental regulatory authority, no basic line of partisan cleavage could be detected on the Pennsylvania court.

In sum, as previous studies have indicated, a moderate amount of partisan voting can be found on the Pennsylvania Supreme Court. On the average, Democratic justices were more liberal in their decisional propensities than the Republican justices. But one judge from each party was found to be more frequently aligned with judges from the opposite party than with his fellow partisans.

The extent of partisanship on the Pennsylvania court is consistent with the formal and informal dimensions of the judicial selection process outlined earlier. The recruitment of partisans to staff the courts is guaranteed by the essentially partisan processes of nomination and election. But intraparty factionalism may bring to the bench individuals who share the same basic party label but not the same general ideological perspective. And the system of merit retention for previously elected judges frees judges from the prospective influences of the partisan constituencies which supported their original bids for office.

### Colorado

Until 1966, when voters approved the adoption of the merit selection plan, partisanship was a central feature of the process of judicial recruitment in Colorado. Candidates for the state supreme court competed on partisan ballots alongside other party nominees for statewide office. Moreover, though candidates for judicial office (and other elective positions) competed in party primaries for nomination, access to the primary ballot was effectively controlled by the parties. In preprimary designating assemblies, each party would qualify for the primary contest any candidate receiving 20% or more of the delegate votes, a procedure which awarded the parties a considerable amount of control over who would be able to compete for, and hence attain, election to the state supreme court.[14]

Thus, as in Indiana, the partisan system of judicial selection can be expected to forge a strong linkage between the party label and the behavior of the judges recruited under that label. However, unlike Indiana, certain other aspects of the processes of nomination and election in Colorado weaken the tie between judges and their party affiliation.

The preprimary convention system is still in use today in Colorado for the selection of nominees to executive and legislative posts. And it remains true today, as it did prior to 1966, that, while the preprimary assemblies may provide the parties with some control over access to the ballot, there is no assurance that all those designated by the parties are birds of the same flock. Intraparty divisions may find expression in the designation of multiple candidates to contest the primary race. And, of course, the voters in the primary and later in the election are under no obligation to pick the candidate most favored by the assembly delegates.

Further, once the general election campaign is underway, the allegiances of nominees to their respective parties are weakened by the fact that "individual candidates for office must in the main conduct their own campaigns. They cannot expect much help from the party organization, and, therefore, have no great sense of responsibility to it."[15] Moreover, the nature of electoral politics in Colorado has demanded, at least in the postwar years, that contestants for public office, be they candidates for executive, legislative, or judicial positions, pursue a "personal" rather than a "partisan" campaign strategy. In addition to an office block ballot form which facilitates if not encourages split-ticket voting, Colorado's voters have been described by one observer as "independent, critical, and unpredictable in their voting habits" and as voters who "ordinarily admire assertions and evidences of 'independence' on the part of their representatives."[16]

Finally, under the elective system, Colorado's high court judges were not frequently required to seek renomination and re-election as they served for ten-year terms (as they do today). Whatever allegiances to the party and to its basic ideology the judges take with them when they assume the bench most certainly wane over a decade's time.

Given this constellation of institutional arrangements and the political environment of Colorado, one would expect some partisan voting by the judges in Colorado but perhaps not as much as observed in either Indiana or Pennsylvania where the parties play a more fundamental role in controlling judicial recruitment and where partisanship during the election campaign is more firmly rooted.

This analysis of partisan voting on the Colorado Supreme Court considers the nonunanimous decisions filed during the years from 1962 through 1968.[17] This span of time has been subdivided into three smaller periods, each defined by a change in membership on the court. During the first two periods (1962–1964 and 1965–1966), the court was composed of five Democrats and two Republicans; in the last period (1967–1968), the court was more closely divided between four Democrats and three Republicans.[18] It is crucial to note here that in the 1966 elections Colorado's voters approved the re-

**Table 23.** *Percentage of Liberal Votes in Nonunanimous Cases, Colorado Supreme Court, 1962–1964*

| Criminal Appeals | | Economic Distribution | | Government Regulation | |
|---|---|---|---|---|---|
| Day (D) | 0.92 | Frantz (D) | 0.71 | McWilliams (R) | 0.82 |
| Sutton (D) | 0.73 | Pringle (D) | 0.60 | Day (D) | 0.65 |
| Frantz (D) | 0.67 | Sutton (D) | 0.53 | Pringle (D) | 0.65 |
| Hall (R) | 0.67 | Moore (D) | 0.50 | Sutton (D) | 0.65 |
| Pringle (D) | 0.58 | McWilliams (R) | 0.47 | Frantz (D) | 0.50 |
| Moore (D) | 0.50 | Day (D) | 0.38 | Moore (D) | 0.50 |
| McWilliams (R) | 0.45 | Hall (R) | 0.31 | Hall (R) | 0.39 |
| Mean court | 0.65 | | 0.50 | | 0.59 |
| Mean Democrats | 0.68 | | 0.54 | | 0.59 |
| Mean Republicans | 0.56 | | 0.39 | | 0.61 |
| (N = 12) | | (N = 17) | | (N = 18) | |

placement of the partisan judicial election system by the merit plan for the selection and retention of all state judges. Yet during the years 1967 and 1968, the last period of the Colorado court examined here, every one of the justices originally had been recruited to the court under the partisan selection system. One might reasonably expect, however, that the merit retention system's virtual guarantee of continued tenure for incumbent judges might result in some diminution in whatever importance party affiliation might be able to claim for the voting divisions which may be observed for the years before 1967.

The results of the scale analysis performed on the decisions of the Colorado court for the first period in three major issue areas are presented in Table 23. These data indicate that the judges of the Colorado Supreme Court were essentially, but not perfectly, distinguishable in their decisional tendencies by partisan affiliation. In those cases concerning the claims of criminal defendants and those of the economically disadvantaged, the average Democratic support for the liberal position exceeded the average Republican support score. But in both issue areas, a Republican justice supported the liberal position more frequently than did one or more of the Democratic justices. In the nonunanimous decisions where the extent of government regulatory authority was at issue, the Republican members of the court occupied opposite polls on the scale, with Justice Robert McWilliams supporting the government's position in 82% of the cases while Frank H. Hall gave his support to the government in only 39% of the decisions. The five Democrats were grouped within

**Table 24. *Percentage of Liberal Votes in Nonunanimous Cases,
Colorado Supreme Court, 1965–1966***

| Criminal Appeals | | Economic Distribution | | Government Regulation | |
|---|---|---|---|---|---|
| Day (D) | 0.93 | Frantz (D) | 1.00 | McWilliams (R) | 0.85 |
| Pringle (D) | 0.69 | Pringle (D) | 0.60 | Schauer (R) | 0.46 |
| Sutton (D) | 0.69 | Sutton (D) | 0.56 | Sutton (D) | 0.33 |
| Frantz (D) | 0.64 | Moore (D) | 0.44 | Day (D) | 0.31 |
| Moore (D) | 0.50 | McWilliams (R) | 0.43 | Frantz (D) | 0.31 |
| McWilliams (R) | 0.36 | Day (D) | 0.40 | Pringle (D) | 0.31 |
| Schauer (R) | 0.17 | Schauer (R) | 0.40 | Moore (D) | 0.23 |
| | | | | | |
| Mean court | 0.57 | | 0.55 | | 0.40 |
| Mean Democrats | 0.69 | | 0.60 | | 0.30 |
| Mean Republicans | 0.27 | | 0.42 | | 0.66 |
| (N = 14) | | (N = 16) | | (N = 13) | |

a narrow range, supporting the government in from 50% to 65% of the cases.

In the 1965–1966 interim, the same basic pattern is apparent. On the average, Colorado's Democratic judges supported the liberal position in criminal appeals and in cases concerned with economic distribution, while Republicans were more likely than Democrats to uphold government regulatory authority (Table 24).

Because of the small number of cases available for analysis, the cases for the first and second periods have been combined for bloc analysis. An inspection of the separate bloc matrices produced for each period confirms that the basic conclusions to be drawn from the data are not fundamentally altered by this aggregation.

In criminal appeals, two overlapping blocs appeared among the Democrats. Justices Leonard V. B. Sutton, Edward Pringle, and Edward Day had a mean interagreement of 0.78, and Justices Sutton, Pringle, and Otto Moore had an average interagreement of 0.77. But this was not a solid four-member bloc inasmuch as Moore and Day agreed in only 58% of the cases, a proportion insufficient to satisfy the Willetts criterion of significant agreement (0.69). Moreover, Republican Justice Robert H. McWilliams did not agree with his fellow Republicans on the court (Frank H. Hall in Period 1, Hilbert Schauer in Period 2) in a significant proportion of cases. In those cases in which two or more dissents were filed, the two Republicans were aligned against at least four of the Democrats only 26.7% of the time; in the large majority of closely decided decisions, therefore, the court did not divide along partisan lines.

**Table 25.** *Percentage of Liberal Votes in Nonunanimous Cases, Colorado Supreme Court, 1967–1968*

| Criminal Appeals | | Economic Distribution | |
|---|---|---|---|
| Day (D) | 1.00 | Pringle (D) | 0.86 |
| Pringle (D) | 1.00 | Day (D) | 0.80 |
| Sutton (D) | 0.71 | Sutton (D) | 0.71 |
| Kelley (R) | 0.57 | Hodges (R) | 0.53 |
| Hodges (R) | 0.43 | Kelley (R) | 0.53 |
| McWilliams (R) | 0.33 | Moore (D) | 0.53 |
| Moore (D) | 0.29 | McWilliams (R) | 0.29 |
| Mean court | 0.62 | | 0.61 |
| Mean Democrats | 0.75 | | 0.73 |
| Mean Republicans | 0.48 | | 0.45 |
| (N = 7) | | (N = 15) | |

Similarly, in the economic distribution cases, the significant voting pairs were just as likely to be bipartisan as partisan in composition. The two Republicans opposed at least four of the court's five Democrats in only 6.3% of the closely decided cases. Partisan voting was more likely in the closely divided government regulation cases, however, as at least four of the Democrats voted in opposition to the two Republicans in 42% of the cases.

The results of the 1966 elections sharpened the partisan division of the court's membership to four Democrats and three Republicans. The analysis of the patterns of voting is hampered somewhat by the small number of nonunanimous cases available, but the results are generally consistent with those observed for the years from 1962 to 1966.

The scales constructed in two major issue areas, presented in Table 25, reveal that, as before, the Democratic judges were on the average more likely than the Republicans to support the criminal defendant and the disadvantaged economic underdog. But in the criminal cases, Democratic Justice Otto Moore supported the claims of the criminal defendant less frequently than did the three Republicans; in the economic area, Moore supported the disadvantaged party in only about half the cases, in identical proportion to the support given the economic underdog by Republican Donald E. Hodges and Paul V. Kelley.

The small number of cases permits only a bloc analysis of all the nonunanimous cases from all the case areas taken together. The results once again reveal no dramatic partisan split on the court.

Democrats Day and Pringle constituted one strong partisan pair (IA = 0.86), joined occasionally by Democrat Sutton (mean IA = 0.73). But Sutton was also a part of a large bipartisan bloc consisting of Republicans Hodges and Kelley and Democrat Moore (mean IA = 0.74). Removing single dissents from the analysis does not substantially alter the results. The data strongly indicate shifting voting alignments in closely divided cases without much regard to the partisan affiliation of the judges.

In general, therefore, the strength of the party variable does not appear as strong as it did in Indiana or even in Pennsylvania. The Democratic judges were, on the whole, more liberal than their Republican colleagues on the bench. But distinct Republican and Democratic voting blocs could not be observed, as was the case in Indiana, nor could stable patterns of alignment essentially partisan in nature be detected, as in Pennsylvania.

## THE NONPARTISAN COURTS: WISCONSIN, UTAH, AND WASHINGTON

### Wisconsin

As the discussion in Chapter 5 indicated, the Wisconsin Supreme Court has been viewed by scholars as the prototype for nonpartisan courts. Candidates for positions on the seven-member court are nominated in nonpartisan primaries and elected on nonpartisan ballots. Both the nomination and the election of justices occur in the spring; in this way, Wisconsin has gone further than any other state to insulate its judicial elections from partisan politics.

The nonpartisan primary system allows individuals not closely identified with either major political party to seek and win judicial office. A candidate may qualify for the ballot merely by gathering the required number of signatures on a nominating petition. The parties, moreover, are not active sub rosa in either the primary or general election campaigns; the candidates must build personal campaign organizations and amass electoral support from among the adherents of both parties.

Individuals more closely identified with the parties and who have been active in partisan politics may reach Wisconsin's high court, however, by securing a gubernatorial appointment to fill a court vacancy. In fact, between 1948 and 1974, two-thirds of the judges selected to the Wisconsin court were originally appointed to their seats. Moreover, each of these judges shared the partisan affiliation of the governor to whom they owed their appointment.

Whatever partisan predispositions are brought to the Wisconsin bench, however, are not reinforced by the judicial election process. The lengthy ten-year terms undoubtedly contribute to the fading importance of partisan attitudes to judicial decision-making as judges are removed from the reinforcing socialization provided by party activism. Moreover, the need to build a bipartisan re-election constituency may actually be a positive incentive for judges to eschew partisan behavior on the bench and adopt more "nonpartisan" postures in their decision-making.

Thus, in his study of the Wisconsin Supreme Court from 1957 to 1966, Adamany was unable to detect partisan patterns of voting behavior whether he used simple support scores, scale analysis, or dissent bloc techniques.[19] Though the judges on the court had been active in partisan politics before reaching the court, party affiliation was wholly unsuccessful in accounting for the patterns of cleavage observed.

The goal here is to replicate Adamany's analysis for the years from 1968 through 1974, a period during which the membership and partisan balance on the Wisconsin court was stable with four Republicans and three Democrats.[20] Three of the four Republican justices (Leo Hanley, Connor T. Hansen, and E. Harold Hallows) originally reached the bench by appointment; Justice Bruce Beilfuss was the only Republican to have obtained his office initially by election. Similarly, Democrats Horace Wilkie and Nathan Heffernan were gubernatorial appointees; Wilkie was appointed in 1962 by Democratic Governor Gaylord Nelson and Heffernan was the appointee of Democrat John Reynolds in 1964. The remaining Democratic justice, Robert Hansen, won election in 1967.

Table 26 presents the results of the Guttman scaling analysis performed on the nonunanimous decisions of the Wisconsin court in the four major case areas. On the average, the Democratic justices were more likely than the Republicans to favor the defendant in criminal cases, the claimant in economic distribution cases, the government in questions of its regulatory authority, and the liberal position in civil liberties decisions. Within each scale, however, it is clear that the Democratic justices were not a unified group. Justices Wilkie and Heffernan consistently occupied the most liberal end of each scale while Robert Hansen was the most conservative justice on the court in every issue area. The division on the criminal appeals cases is most dramatic; in over fifty nonunanimous cases, Heffernan and Wilkie favored the defendant in at least nine of every ten cases, but Hansen did not support the defendant's claim in a single case!

**Table 26. Percentage of Liberal Votes in Nonunanimous Cases, Wisconsin Supreme Court, 1968–1974**

| Criminal Appeals | | Economic Distribution | | Government Regulation | | Civil Liberties | |
|---|---|---|---|---|---|---|---|
| Wilkie (D) | 0.96 | Wilkie (D) | 0.80 | Heffernan (D) | 0.76 | Wilkie (D) | 0.93 |
| Heffernan (D) | 0.90 | Heffernan (D) | 0.76 | Wilkie (D) | 0.71 | Heffernan (D) | 0.80 |
| Hallows (R) | 0.78 | Hallows (R) | 0.63 | Beilfuss (R) | 0.59 | Beilfuss (R) | 0.80 |
| Beilfuss (R) | 0.54 | Beilfuss (R) | 0.51 | Hanley (R) | 0.59 | C. Hansen (R) | 0.67 |
| C. Hansen (R) | 0.31 | C. Hansen (R) | 0.51 | C. Hansen (R) | 0.53 | Hallows (R) | 0.60 |
| Hanley (R) | 0.17 | Hanley (R) | 0.38 | Hallows (R) | 0.47 | Hanley (R) | 0.40 |
| R. Hansen (D) | 0.00 | R. Hansen (D) | 0.37 | R. Hansen (D) | 0.35 | R. Hansen (D) | 0.40 |
| Mean court | 0.52 | | 0.57 | | 0.57 | | 0.66 |
| Mean Democrats | 0.62 | | 0.64 | | 0.61 | | 0.71 |
| Mean Republicans | 0.45 | | 0.51 | | 0.55 | | 0.62 |
| (N = 52) | | (N = 41) | | (N = 17) | | (N = 15) | |

The Republican justices exhibit varying degrees of behavior within the external limits set by the Democratic justices. In the criminal appeals and economic distribution areas, Chief Justice Hallows adopted the liberal position more frequently than any of his colleagues, while in the government regulation and civil liberties cases, Justice Beilfuss seemed most inclined in that direction. The extent to which these Republicans joined forces with the Democratic liberals Heffernan and Wilkie can best be determined by bloc analysis.

The bloc matrix of the interagreement scores of the justices of the Wisconsin court in nonunanimous criminal appeals reveals two well-defined blocs. The Democrats Wilkie and Heffernan were an unmistakable bloc, agreeing in 94% of the nonunanimous cases, well above the minimum Willetts standard of 64%. They were joined in three of every four cases by Republican Hallows. The other bloc was composed of Republicans Connor Hansen and Leo Hanley joined with Democrat Robert Hansen; their average interagreement score is over 0.75. The division between these two major groupings is rather sharp, as no member of either bloc agreed with a member of the other in more than 45% of the cases, though not sufficiently low to satisfy the Willetts criterion of significant disagreement (0.36). Justice Beilfuss appeared to mediate between the opposing blocs, agreeing with every other member of the court (except Robert Hansen) in a substantial majority of the decisions.

Eliminating the single dissents from analysis does not change the basic conclusions reached above, but the results show not only that the members of the two blocs agreed among themselves in a significant proportion of cases, but also that the two blocs were, according to the Willetts criterion, significantly different from each other.

In those cases concerned with the claims of the economically disadvantaged, the Wisconsin court was not so clearly divided. Justices Hanley and Robert Hansen, a Republican and a Democrat, are significantly aligned in the bloc matrix (IA = 0.73, Willetts = 0.65). Similarly, Justices Beilfuss and Connor Hansen, both Republicans, agreed in 80% of the nonunanimous cases as did Justices Heffernan and Wilkie, both Democrats. But the lines separating these various pairs are not clear or sharp. Part of the reason is that in this case area thirteen single dissents were filed, nine of which were authored by Chief Justice Hallows. Considering only those cases in which more than a single dissent was filed, however, the bloc divisions become more distinct. Justices Hallows, Wilkie, and Heffernan formed one bloc (mean IA = 0.74), Connor Hansen and Beilfuss formed a second

(IA = 0.75), and Hanley and Robert Hansen composed a weak third (IA = 0.64, Willetts = 0.68).

In the area of government regulation, the low number of cases makes bloc analysis difficult. But Democrats Heffernan and Wilkie were again solidly in agreement in 94% of the cases. Republicans Beilfuss, C. Hansen, and Hanley voted together in 71% of the cases, registering a mean interagreement of 0.80 and exceeding the Willetts standard of 0.77.

The analysis of civil liberties cases is also hampered by the small number of nonunanimous cases decided. But two strong blocs emerge from the available data. Democratic Justices Wilkie and Heffernan and Republican Beilfuss joined together as a group in thirteen of fifteen (87%) nonunanimous decisions; they were joined in ten of these decisions by Connor Hansen. Least supportive of the civil liberties claims were Justices Hanley and Robert Hansen who agreed in 87% of the cases, supporting the liberal position in only 40% of the split decisions.

These results are sharply at odds with those reported by Adamany in his study of the Wisconsin court. While certainly there is not the kind of sharp party bloc voting as witnessed on the Michigan court, party seems no less important on the Wisconsin Supreme Court than it was found to be on the Pennsylvania court. With but one exception, the Democrats on the Wisconsin court were more liberal in their decisional tendencies than the Republicans; the results of the scale analysis demonstrate that Democrats Heffernan and Wilkie brought to the bench strongly held liberal attitudes and values which found expression in their judicial decision-making.

The patterns of bloc voting are somewhat less conclusive, showing (as the scale scores predicted) that Democrat Robert Hansen agreed only infrequently with his fellow partisans and that on occasion the Democratic liberals were joined by one of the two more liberal Republicans on the court, Beilfuss or Hallows. It is perhaps most notable here that Robert Hansen was the only one of the court's three Democrats originally gaining his seat directly by election. Both Heffernan and Wilkie were, as noted earlier, gubernatorial appointees and regular activists in Democratic party politics in the state prior to their appointments.[21] Hansen had served on the county and circuit courts in Milwaukee County for thirteen years prior to his election to the high court. Compared to the other two Democrats, Hansen's contact with and attachment to the Democratic party was slight. Alternatively, the liberal behavior of Beilfuss and Hallows is perhaps not so surprising when it is considered that before their judicial careers began these two individuals were associated politically with the Progressive wing of the Republican party in Wisconsin.

Why the results here differ so dramatically from those reported by Adamany is not clear. There does not appear to have been any fundamental change in the essentially bipartisan environment of Wisconsin's judicial elections. Nor does there seem to have been an increase in the proportion of individuals with partisan backgrounds who reach the state's high court; indeed, both Wilkie and Heffernan, the most clearly identifiable party activists on the court, were members of the court during some portion of the period covered by Adamany's analysis. It may be simply that Adamany's sample of cases in the areas of workmen's and unemployment compensation was not sufficiently broad to reveal existing patterns of partisan voting, particularly in criminal appeals.

**Utah**

Since 1948, Utah has experimented with three systems of judicial selection. No other state has altered its mode of selecting state supreme court justices in the postwar period more frequently.

From the time of the first state elections in 1895 until 1952, state supreme court justices were elected on the partisan ballot. Until 1938, judicial candidates, like all candidates for public office, were nominated in party conventions. The state experimented with the direct primary for about a decade but in 1947 adopted a mixed convention-primary system similar to the one already in use in its neighboring state of Colorado.

In 1951, however, the legislature adopted a nonpartisan system for the nomination and election of the state's judges. In addition, the primary and general election ballots were separated from the partisan ballot. Incumbent judges were also awarded a number of electoral advantages, including being listed first on the ballot and having the title "Justice" and the label "Incumbent" attached to their names.

Finally, in 1967, the Utah legislature adopted a hybrid of the nonpartisan election and merit systems of judicial selection which remains in use today. The plan provides for all judges to be initially selected by the governor from a list of three candidates suggested by a judicial nominating commission. At the first general election after appointment, the incumbent judge may file for election. If he or she so files, any member of the bar can file in opposition for a contest on a nonpartisan ballot. If more than one opposition candidate enters the race, a primary election reduces the field to two for the general election campaign. The sitting judge is advantaged as before, however, by a favorable ballot position and ballot labels indicating incumbency.

If no candidate files in opposition to the incumbent, the judge faces the electorate on the standard merit retention question of whether or not he or she should be continued in office. In all subsequent re-election bids, the same general rules apply. If the incumbent chooses not to seek re-election, however, no election is held and the governor selects a new judge from the list submitted by the nominating panel, and the process begins anew.

A decade of decisions of the Utah Supreme Court have been examined for this study.[22] From January 1960 to the middle of 1966, the Utah court was composed of three Democrats and two Republicans. All the Democrats (Lester Wade, Roger McDonough, and J. Allen Crockett) originally were elected to the state's high court prior to 1952 under the partisan system. But each had also won re-election at least once on the nonpartisan ballot between 1952 and 1967. The Republicans included Frederic H. Henriod, a private attorney and former bar commissioner, first elected to the court in 1952, the first year of the nonpartisan system, and E. R. Callister, Jr., the state attorney general from 1953 to 1959, appointed by Republican Governor George Dewey Clyde in 1959 and elected to a full term in 1964.

In the second period studied here, from January 1967 to December 1970, two new justices had joined the court to fill the seats left vacant by the deaths of Justices Wade and McDonough in June and November of 1966, respectively. Robert L. Tuckett was appointed by Democratic Governor Calvin Rampton to replace Wade; Albert H. Ellett was elected in an unopposed contest in 1966. Prior to their accessions to the supreme court, both of these Democratic judges had served on city and district courts elected under the partisan system used prior to 1952.

Thus, in both periods, all the justices on the Utah court except one (Henriod)[23] had originally been selected to the judiciary under the partisan system or, in Callister's case, had held a partisan statewide office. Even though the selection system formally became nonpartisan in 1952, most of the judges serving on the Utah court up through 1970 were initially recruited to the judiciary through the partisan political process. These judges most certainly brought strongly held partisan predispositions with them to the bench which could be expected to influence their judicial decisions. Lengthy ten-year terms and the nonpartisan electoral constituency might moderate the influence of party affiliation on the judge's behavior, but, if the results from the analysis of the Wisconsin court are any indication,

**Table 27.** *Percentage of Liberal Votes in Nonunanimous Cases, Utah Supreme Court, 1960–1966*

| Criminal Appeals | | Economic Distribution | | Government Regulation | |
|---|---|---|---|---|---|
| Wade (D) | 0.62 | Wade (D) | 0.80 | McDonough (D) | 0.76 |
| Henriod (R) | 0.55 | Crockett (D) | 0.73 | Crockett (D) | 0.71 |
| Crockett (D) | 0.46 | McDonough (D) | 0.61 | Wade (D) | 0.57 |
| McDonough (D) | 0.46 | Callister (R) | 0.34 | Callister (R) | 0.50 |
| Callister (R) | 0.23 | Henriod (R) | 0.25 | Henriod (R) | 0.35 |
| Mean court | 0.46 | | 0.55 | | 0.58 |
| Mean Democrats | 0.51 | | 0.71 | | 0.68 |
| Mean Republicans | 0.39 | | 0.30 | | 0.43 |
| (N = 13) | | (N = 51) | | (N = 21) | |

partisan attitudes and values are extremely resilient and not easily diluted by institutional arrangements and electoral structures.

The results of the scale analysis for the first period in three issue areas are offered in Table 27. In each area, the average Democratic judge supported the liberal position in a greater proportion of cases than the average Republican judge. In the economic and government regulation cases, all the Democrats supported the position of the economically disadvantaged and the government's claims of regulatory authority more frequently than any of the Republican judges. In the criminal cases, though, Republican Henriod supported the criminal defendant's position in a greater proportion of the cases than two of the Democrats, Crockett and McDonough.

The division between the Democratic and Republican judges on the Utah court is clearest and most pronounced in the economic area. Each of the three Democrats supported the economic underdog in at least 60% of the decisions, whereas the two Republicans, Callister and Henriod, supported the disadvantaged litigant in only 34% and 25%, respectively. The differences by party in the government regulation cases are less dramatic but apparent nonetheless. Republican Henriod voted for the government in only 35% of the cases, and his colleague Callister gave his support to the government position in exactly half the cases in which he participated. Among the Democrats, however, Wade voted with the government in nearly 60% of the cases and Crockett and McDonough supported that position in over 70% of the decisions.

The bloc matrix of the nonunanimous economic decisions of the Utah court for the first period confirms the partisan division on the court. Both the Democratic and Republican blocs satisfy the

**Table 28.** *Percentage of Liberal Votes in Nonunanimous Cases,*
*Utah Supreme Court, 1967–1970*

| Criminal Appeals | | Economic Distribution | | Government Regulation | |
|---|---|---|---|---|---|
| Callister (R) | 0.74 | Crockett (D) | 0.69 | Crockett (D) | 0.65 |
| Tuckett (D) | 0.71 | Tuckett (D) | 0.65 | Ellett (D) | 0.58 |
| Henriod (R) | 0.62 | Ellett (D) | 0.57 | Tuckett (D) | 0.55 |
| Crockett (D) | 0.54 | Callister (R) | 0.33 | Callister (R) | 0.37 |
| Ellett (D) | 0.19 | Henriod (R) | 0.18 | Henriod (R) | 0.31 |
| Mean court | 0.56 | | 0.48 | | 0.49 |
| Mean Democrats | 0.48 | | 0.64 | | 0.59 |
| Mean Republicans | 0.68 | | 0.26 | | 0.34 |
| (N = 28) | | (N = 66) | | (N = 20) | |

Willetts criterion for significant voting agreement. Concealed by the
bloc analysis, however, is the fact that 56.8% of these decisions featured just one dissenting justice. When only those cases with two
dissents are considered, the partisan division on the court is sharpened further. Republicans Henriod and Callister voted alike in 91%
of these closely decided decisions. The three Democrats were not so
solidly linked, voting as a group in about 60% of the cases (mean
IA = 0.73); one of the Democrats would occasionally join the Republicans to form a majority. Nevertheless, according to the Willetts
criteria, not only were the members of the two party blocs significantly linked among themselves, but also the Democrats and Republicans were in significant disagreement over the disposition of
these cases.

Similar results can be observed in the government regulatory
cases. The prevalence of single dissents obscures the basic partisan
division on the court. But in two-thirds of the closely divided decisions, the court was divided along straight party lines.

The results of the analysis of the decisions of the Utah Supreme
Court for the second period are parallel to those reported for the
first. In the scale analysis of the decisions in three major areas (Table
28), Democratic judges were consistently more liberal in their decisional tendencies than the Republicans in those cases concerned
with economic distribution and government regulation. In the criminal decisions, however, Republicans Henriod and Callister were
more supportive of the claims of criminal defendants than both Justices Crockett and Ellett, two of the three Democratic justices. Justice Callister's scale position is particularly noteworthy since he
was the most conservative judge on criminal matters dividing the

court between 1960 and 1966. Among the Democrats, Justice Ellett lagged far behind the rest of the court on the criminal appeals scale, a fact perhaps attributable to conservative attitudes developed during his southern upbringing and education in Alabama and Texas.

Bloc analysis of the criminal cases revealed no sharp division on the court. Callister and Tuckett joined in a significant proportion of cases (IA = 0.74) as did Callister and Henriod (IA = 0.72), but no other pairs of justices were in significant agreement (Willetts = 0.68). When only those cases decided by three-to-two margins are considered, moderate partisan blocs are observable: Democrats Crockett and Ellett agreed in 82% of the cases and Republicans Henriod and Callister voted alike in 73%. However, though the significant voting pairs which did emerge were partisan in composition, they cast votes in the direction opposite to the one expected. Democrat Crockett voted for the criminal defendant in these closely divided decisions only 33% of the time and Democrat Ellett did not cast a single vote for the defendant. On the other hand, Republicans Callister and Henriod supported the defendant in 82% and 58%, respectively, of these cases. Democrat Tuckett voted in the predicted direction, supporting the defendant in 75% of the sharply decided cases.

In economic matters, however, the partisan division is clear and in the expected direction. The prevalence of solo dissents, of course, weakens the appearance of voting blocs. But when only cases with joint dissents are considered, a clear Republican bloc is observed with Justices Henriod and Callister agreeing in 79% of the decisions. The Democratic bloc was slightly weaker, indicating occasional defections (usually by Justice Tuckett) to join with the Republicans. But, importantly, no one of the Democrats agreed with either of the Republicans in more than 30% of the closely split decisions, a proportion sufficiently low according to the Willetts criterion to indicate significant disagreement between the Democrats and Republicans. Of the closely divided cases, 43.8% were decided along straight party lines in favor of the disadvantaged economic litigant, while in 37.5% two of the Democrats were joined by one of the Republicans to form the liberal majority.

The patterns of bloc division in government regulation cases were also somewhat muddled by the patterns of single dissents, but in those few cases decided by three-to-two votes, two-thirds were decided along straight party lines with the Democratic majority holding for the government.

In sum, therefore, in an analysis of a full decade of nonunanimous decisions, the Democratic justices of the Utah Supreme Court were found to be consistently more liberal in their decisional tendencies than the Republican judges, at least with respect to the areas of economic distribution and government regulation. Only in those cases concerned with the claims of criminal defendants were the Democratic judges not consistently more liberal than the Republicans, a fact which upon close inspection may be explained by the importance of other variables, such as religion and regional upbringing, to the judicial decision-making propensities of certain members of the court.[24] Bloc analysis of the voting divisions on the court in the most closely divided cases confirmed that in economic and government regulatory cases, the Utah Supreme Court divided along party lines almost as frequently as the Indiana court did in criminal matters.

The analysis of Utah's supreme court underscores the importance of background characteristics to an understanding of the party variable. Despite a formally nonpartisan system, the court was staffed with individuals with long personal histories of involvement in partisan politics. The reform adopted by the Utah legislature in 1951 may have changed the formal designation of the state's judicial election system from partisan to nonpartisan, but it did not change the fact that even through the decade of the 1960s those individuals serving on the high court either had been recruited to the bench under the partisan system or had previously served at the lower court level during the period of partisan selection. Later recruited to serve on the state supreme court under the nonpartisan system, either by appointment of the governor or by election, these judicial partisans brought their partisan baggage with them. And the data offered here strongly support the inference that the strength of the attitudes and values of these judges, nurtured in partisan politics, was not diminished in any significant measure by the substitution of a nonpartisan or merit system for the partisan one.

### Washington

As in Wisconsin and Utah, the formal process of judicial selection in Washington is nonpartisan. The nine members of the Washington Supreme Court are formally selected for six-year terms in nonpartisan elections held concurrently with the November presidential and mid-term elections. The primary is often the determinative contest, however, for if a candidate gathers a majority of votes in the primary, he or she then is entitled to run unopposed in the general election.

Defeat is rarely visited upon an incumbent judge. As a result, judges in Washington, as elsewhere, serve lengthy careers on the bench. Untimely vacancies in mid-term are common, therefore, and Washington governors since 1948 have been responsible for 76.2% of the initial accessions to the state supreme court. It is at this point that partisanship invades the process of judicial recruitment; Washington governors, like governors elsewhere, have used their powers of judicial appointment to send fellow partisans to the state's high court. Thus, though judges in Washington do not have partisan constituencies upon which they depend for renomination and re-election, they do bring with them to the bench differing partisan allegiances and, therefore, divergent political attitudes and ideologies which can be expected to affect their decision-making on the bench.

The decisions of the Washington Supreme Court for two distinct periods will be considered here.[25] From 1963 to 1967, the court consisted of five Democrats and four Republicans. Consistent with the postwar pattern, two-thirds of the judges serving on the court (three Democrats and three Republicans) were originally appointed to office; each appointee, moreover, shared the party affiliation of the governor who appointed them.

From 1973 through 1974, the court was also closely divided in membership between the parties. The five Democrats serving in the first period continued to serve and were joined by three Republicans, each of whom had been appointed by Republican Daniel Evans, and a self-styled Independent elected to the court in 1970.

The scalogram analysis for the first period is presented in Table 29.[26] The results indicate a surprising amount of difference among the judges along partisan lines. In the three major issue areas, the mean Democratic score for the defendant in criminal cases, the disadvantaged in economic cases, and the government in regulatory decisions exceeded the mean Republican score. The divisions between the parties is clearest on the economic scale; no Democrat supported the economically disadvantaged party in less than 67% of the cases, while no Republican supported the underdog litigant more than 27% of the time. In the government regulation decisions, Democrats supported the government in from 63% to 85% of the split decisions; the Republican judges supported the government position in from only 31% to 52% of the cases. Only in the criminal area did some of the Democrats fail to support the liberal position as frequently as some of their Republican brethren. Democrats Robert T. Hunter and Hugh J. Rosellini lead the court in their support for the criminal defendant (60% and 53%, respectively), but their Democratic colleagues Orris L. Hamilton and Frank Hale voted on behalf of the criminal defendant in only 35% and 28% of the decisions,

**Table 29.** *Percentage of Liberal Votes in Nonunanimous Cases,*
*Washington Supreme Court, 1963–1967*

| Criminal Appeals | | Economic Distribution | | Government Regulation | |
|---|---|---|---|---|---|
| Hunter (D) | 0.60 | Finley (D) | 0.87 | Hale (D) | 0.85 |
| Rosellini (D) | 0.53 | Hunter (D) | 0.85 | Finley (D) | 0.69 |
| Donworth (R) | 0.45 | Rosellini (D) | 0.74 | Hamilton (D) | 0.67 |
| Finley (D) | 0.45 | Hale (D) | 0.71 | Rosellini (D) | 0.67 |
| Weaver (R) | 0.45 | Hamilton (D) | 0.67 | Hunter (D) | 0.63 |
| Hamilton (D) | 0.35 | Donworth (R) | 0.27 | Ott (R) | 0.52 |
| Hale (D) | 0.28 | Ott (R) | 0.24 | Weaver (R) | 0.35 |
| Hill (R) | 0.15 | Weaver (R) | 0.24 | Hill (R) | 0.33 |
| Ott (R) | 0.10 | Hill (R) | 0.13 | Donworth (R) | 0.31 |
| Mean court | 0.37 | | 0.52 | | 0.56 |
| Mean Democrats | 0.44 | | 0.77 | | 0.70 |
| Mean Republicans | 0.29 | | 0.22 | | 0.38 |
| (N = 20) | | (N = 39) | | (N = 27) | |

supporting the defendant less frequently than Republicans Charles T. Donworth and Frank P. Weaver (45%).

Bloc analysis confirms these basic patterns. In the criminal area, bipartisan and often-shifting bloc alignments appear most typical. While a number of significant pairs of justices appear, most of them are bipartisan pairs; moreover, the lowest rate of interagreement among all the justices on the court occurred between Democratic Justices Rosellini and Finley who voted alike on only three of the nineteen cases in which they participated, despite very similar scale scores in support of the criminal defendant. Further, there were no significant blocs consisting of three or more judges, partisan or otherwise. The most consistently linked groups of three judges were bipartisan in membership.

The division on the Washington court in economic cases, however, is more clearly along partisan lines. All the Republicans are joined in a significant proportion of cases (mean IA = 0.72) according to the Willetts criterion (0.65). The Democratic majority is less cohesive and a couple of the interagreement scores (Hamilton, Rosellini, 0.56; Hamilton, Hunter, 0.62) fall below the minimum level of significant agreement (Willetts = 0.65). But Justice Hamilton, the most marginal Democrat in terms of his interagreement scores, appears more closely linked with his fellow Democrats than with the Republican members of the court.

An inspection of the voting patterns of the Washington court in these economic cases reveals that all four Republicans voted alike as a group in exactly half of the cases in which all participated, voting against the claims of the economic underdog in 93.8% of these cases. At least three of the four Republicans joined in 84.4% of the cases, voting against the liberal position 92.6% of the time.

On the Democratic side, the five voted together in slightly more than 40% (40.5%) of the cases in which all five participated, favoring the claims of the economically disadvantaged litigant in every case. At least four Democrats joined in 64.9% of the nonunanimous cases, always in the direction of the liberal position. Exactly one-third (11/33) of the economic cases heard by all nine justices were decided by five-to-four margins; only two of the cases split the court along straight party lines, but a total of eight (72.%) featured at least all but one member of each party voting against each other in the expected directions.

In the government regulation cases, all the significant inter-agreement pairs are partisan, but no major party blocs are apparent. The concentration of significant pairings among the Democrats along the diagonal of the bloc matrix suggests the existence of shifting voting alignments. But an inspection of the voting patterns indicates that four of the five Democrats voted alike in 65.4% of the cases and three of the four Republicans joined in 84.6% of the cases. In those few cases decided by five-to-four margins, none was decided strictly along party lines, but 57.1% (4/7) involved at least all but one member of each party voting against at least all but one member from the other party.

In the second period considered here, from 1973 to 1974, whatever patterns of partisan division which might have existed in the first period were significantly weakened. The results of the scale analysis in Table 30 show that in the criminal and civil liberties cases the mean Republican support score for the liberal position actually exceeded the mean Democratic score. And three Democrats (Hamilton, Hale, Hunter) occupy the most conservative end of both scales while a Republican, Justice Robert F. Utter, had a near perfect record in support of the liberal position in both areas.

In the economic area, the mean Democratic support of the economically disadvantaged did continue to exceed the mean Republican score. But several Republicans supported the liberal position as frequently as or more often than some of the Democrats on the bench. Democrats Hunter and Hale voted to support the economic underdog in 78% and 83% of the split decisions respectively, but Justice Robert Brachtenbach, a Republican, voted in the liberal di-

**Table 30. Percentage of Liberal Votes in Nonunanimous Cases, Washington Supreme Court, 1973–1974**

| Criminal Appeals | | Economic Distribution | | Government Regulation | | Civil Liberties | |
|---|---|---|---|---|---|---|---|
| Utter (R) | 0.95 | Hale (D) | 0.83 | Hale (D) | 0.93 | Utter (R) | 1.00 |
| Rosellini (D) | 0.61 | Hunter (D) | 0.78 | Brachtenbach (R) | 0.73 | Finley (D) | 0.67 |
| Finley (D) | 0.53 | Brachtenbach (R) | 0.65 | Hamilton (D) | 0.73 | Rosellini (D) | 0.67 |
| Stafford (R) | 0.53 | Finley (D) | 0.65 | Rosellini (D) | 0.67 | Brachtenbach (R) | 0.50 |
| Brachtenbach (R) | 0.39 | Utter (R) | 0.56 | Hunter (D) | 0.57 | Stafford (R) | 0.44 |
| Wright (I) | 0.26 | Rosellini (D) | 0.50 | Finley (D) | 0.53 | Wright (I) | 0.44 |
| Hamilton (D) | 0.22 | Wright (I) | 0.50 | Stafford (R) | 0.47 | Hamilton (D) | 0.33 |
| Hunter (D) | 0.22 | Hamilton (D) | 0.47 | Utter (R) | 0.47 | Hale (D) | 0.00 |
| Hale (D) | 0.00 | Stafford (R) | 0.33 | Wright (I) | 0.29 | Hunter (D) | 0.00 |
| (N = 19) | | (N = 18) | | (N = 15) | | (N = 9) | |
| Mean court | 0.41 | | 0.59 | | 0.60 | | 0.45 |
| Mean Democrats | 0.32 | | 0.65 | | 0.69 | | 0.33 |
| Mean Republicans | 0.62 | | 0.51 | | 0.56 | | 0.65 |

rection as frequently (65%) as did Democrat Robert Finley. And Republican Robert Utter voted for the liberal position (56%) slightly more often than Democrats Hugh Rosellini (50%) and Orris Hamilton (47%).

Similarly, in the government regulation area, Democrats were on the average more supportive of the government position than the Republicans. But Republican Brachtenbach did vote to support the government in nearly three of every four split decisions, favoring that position as frequently as four of the five Democrats.

The criminal appeals bloc matrix reveals a number of significantly linked pairs and threesomes, some partisan and some bipartisan in composition. The conservative Democrats, Hunter and Hale, voted alike in 79% of the cases; Hale also joined with Democrat Hamilton in 78% of the cases. A three-member bloc they were not, however, voting as a threesome in only 44.4% of the cases.

A slightly more cohesive voting group consisted of Hale and Hamilton joined by Independent Charles T. Wright; an inspection of the voting patterns indicates the three voted alike in 63.2% of the cases, with a mean interagreement of 0.75 that satisfied the Willetts standard of 0.74. Democrat Hamilton, Independent Wright, and Republican Brachtenbach share a high mean interagreement score (0.74) and they voted alike in nearly 60% of the cases in which all took part (58.8%). Other than these relatively weak groupings, shifting alignments seem more the rule than the exception.

No central line of cleavage divided the court on the economic distribution cases either. The mean interagreement among all pairs of justices is 0.59, reflecting the absence of persistent and sharp divisions. The strongest three-member blocs were bipartisan. Democrat Hamilton was joined by Republicans Utter and Brachtenbach in 80% of the cases; Brachtenbach and Utter were joined by Democrat Finley in 75% of the cases while Democrats Finley and Hunter and Republican Brachtenbach joined as a threesome in 68.8% of the decisions. The overlapping membership of these groupings is indicative of the shifting voting alignments on the Washington court during this period.

Government regulation cases are too few in number and thus the analysis of voting blocs with the Willetts criterion is difficult, but the matrix does reveal one pair of justices, Republicans Utter and Stafford, who agreed in 87% of the split decisions. Other less strongly linked pairs include the bipartisan pairs of Brachtenbach and Finley (IA = 0.73), Brachtenbach and Hamilton (IA = 0.73) and the Democratic pair of Hale and Rosellini (IA = 0.73). But no particularly strong three-person blocs are noticeable. The strongest group on the court, according to an analysis of the bloc matrix and the voting patterns, consisted of Republicans Stafford and Utter and Democrat Finley, who voted alike in about 60% of the decisions.

In summary, then, party affiliation was found to be clearly associated with the decisional differences among the justices of the Washington Supreme Court from 1963 to 1967, especially in those cases involving questions of economic distribution. Party was clearly less impressive, however, in accounting for the lines of cleavage on the court during the period from 1973 to 1974. The explanation(s) for the diminished importance of party from the first period to the second is not immediately clear.

Initially, it is probably safe to assert that the change in the role of party affiliation was not related to the change in Washington's court structure. The creation of a system of intermediate appellate courts in 1970 may have served to change the nature of the case stimuli reaching the high bench. However, scholars generally agree that the creation of an intermediate level of appellate courts serves primarily to "filter out" routine cases and allow more-controversial cases to reach the supreme court for disposition.[27] If the party variable is as important as it is expected to be, then the change in court structure should have precipitated more-frequent occasions for partisan differences to emerge in judicial decision-making, not fewer.

The most likely explanation for the apparent decline in the importance of party affiliation on the Washington court focuses on changes in the court's personnel between the two periods. All the Democratic judges serving in the first period (1963–1967) were also members of the court in the second period (1973–1974). However, none of the Republicans (or the Independent) serving in the latter period had served in the former. All the Republicans reached the bench after 1971 and each owed his appointment to the liberal Republican governor, Daniel Evans.

The liberal behavior of two of Evans' appointees is especially noteworthy. Robert F. Utter was by far the most liberal member of the court in those cases concerning the claims of criminal defendants and in civil liberties decisions; Utter supported the liberal position in 95% of the nonunanimous criminal decisions and in 100% of the split civil liberties cases. Justice Robert P. Brachtenbach was among the more liberal members of the court in both economic distribution and government regulation decisions. The apparent decline in the role of party affiliation in explaining the lines of cleavage on the Washington Supreme Court may in large measure be due, therefore, to the especially liberal behavior of some of the appointees of a liberal Republican governor.

## THE MERIT PLAN COURTS: IOWA AND KANSAS

### Iowa

Prior to 1962, the nine members of the Iowa Supreme Court were nominated by partisan conventions and elected on partisan ballots for six-year terms. But in the fall of that year, the voters ratified a constitutional amendment abandoning their partisan judicial selection system and adopting the merit plan. The change created a fifteen-member State Judicial Nominating Commission, composed equally of seven lay members (appointed by the governor with Senate confirmation) and seven lawyer members (elected by the state bar) and chaired by the most senior associate justice of the supreme court. When a vacancy occurs on the state's high court, the commission provides the governor with a list of three nominees from which the new judge is chosen. After one year, the appointee stands in an uncontested retention election on a separate ballot and every eight years thereafter until the mandatory retirement age is reached.[28]

The nonunanimous decisions of the Iowa Supreme Court from mid-1972 through 1974 have been selected for analysis.[29] During this period the court was composed of five Republicans and four Democrats. The changeover in the Iowa selection system was nearly complete by 1962; all but one of the sitting judges had reached the bench through the merit selection process. Moreover, Republican Edwin Moore, appointed in early 1962 by Republican Governor Norman Erbe, had won his seat on the merit retention ballot in 1964 and was reconfirmed in 1972.

The adoption of the merit selection system did not, however, remove partisan considerations from the process of judicial recruitment. With but one exception, every merit plan appointee sitting on the bench in 1972 shared the partisan affiliation of the governor who appointed them. Only Democrat Mark McCormick, appointed in 1972 by Republican Governor Robert Ray, did not. Moreover, nearly all the judges appointed under the merit plan had been groomed for service on the high court by their prior experiences in partisan political offices as elected county attorneys and/or district court judges (before 1962).[30]

Thus, to the extent that Iowa's governors have been able within the merit selection process to select individuals with partisan predispositions to sit on the state's supreme court, partisan judicial voting patterns might be expected. On the other hand, the impact of past partisan affiliations on judicial behavior might be diminished to the extent that the merit retention ballot has freed judges of the re-

**Table 31.** *Percentage of Liberal Votes in Nonunanimous Cases, Iowa Supreme Court, 1972–1974*

| Criminal Appeals | | Economic Distribution | |
|---|---|---|---|
| Rawlings (D) | 0.89 | McCormick (D) | 0.82 |
| Mason (D) | 0.81 | Reynoldson (R) | 0.78 |
| McCormick (D) | 0.79 | Mason (D) | 0.55 |
| Reynoldson (R) | 0.69 | Rawlings (D) | 0.53 |
| LeGrand (D) | 0.26 | Uhlenhopp (R) | 0.47 |
| Uhlenhopp (R) | 0.26 | Harris (R) | 0.43 |
| Rees (R) | 0.23 | LeGrand (D) | 0.41 |
| Harris (R) | 0.19 | Rees (R) | 0.27 |
| Moore (R) | 0.15 | Moore (R) | 0.25 |
| Mean court | 0.47 | | 0.50 |
| Mean Democrats | 0.69 | | 0.58 |
| Mean Republicans | 0.30 | | 0.44 |
| (N = 27) | | (N = 32) | |

quirement to seek re-election in competitive partisan contests and hence the necessity to return to their partisan constituencies for re-nomination, campaign assistance, and general election support.

The result of the scale analysis applied to the two major areas are presented in Table 31. In both areas, the average Democratic judge supported the liberal position more frequently than the average Republican judge. But among the members from each party, one justice departs significantly from the decisional tendencies of his colleagues on the bench who share his partisan affiliation. Republican Justice W. Ward Reynoldson supported the claims of the criminal defendant in nearly 70% of the nonunanimous decisions and the economically disadvantaged nearly 80% of the time. On the other hand, Democrat Clay LeGrand supported the criminal defendant in barely one-fourth of the cases and adopted the liberal position in divided economic cases only about 40% of the time.

The scale analysis of the nonunanimous criminal appeals suggests the existence of two, essentially partisan blocs on the court. Democrats Maurice E. Rawlings, M. L. Mason, and McCormick, joined by Republican Reynoldson, each supported the claims of the criminal defendant in upward of 70% of the cases. But Republicans Harvey Uhlenhopp, Warren J. Rees, K. David Harris, and C. Edwin Moore, joined by Democrat LeGrand, each supported the defendant in no more than one-quarter of the decisions. A bloc analysis of these nonunanimous criminal decisions confirms this basic alignment but the blocs are not as strong as suspected. Justices Mason and Rawlings, both Democrats, agreed in nearly 80% of the cases. And Republican Reynoldson and Democrat McCormick voted alike in nearly 90% of the split decisions. But as a four-member bloc, they voted alike in only 44% of the cases in which they participated jointly. At the other extreme, Republicans Moore, Harris, and Rees agreed among themselves in a fairly high proportion of cases, voting as a threesome in 65% of the cases in which all participated, registering a mean interagreement of 0.77, comfortably above the Willetts minimum of 0.70. Democrat LeGrand joined this threesome in exactly half the split decisions. Although Republican Harvey Uhlenhopp supported the claims of the criminal defendant in only 26% of the cases, he was not significantly linked with either bloc.

In the economic cases, the blocs on the Iowa court are less clearly defined. Republican Reynoldson and Democrat McCormick are once again in strong agreement, voting alike in over 90% of the split decisions. They were by far the strongest bloc on the court and, based upon the results of the scale analysis, the most supportive of the claims of the economically disadvantaged. The second most cohesive pair on the court included Republicans Rees and Moore, who agreed in 80% of the cases, usually opposing the economic underdog; the scale analysis indicates that Rees and Moore each adopted the liberal position in economic cases in barely one-fourth of the decisions. Between these two extremes, the lines of cleavage are less clearly drawn but they do tend to follow party lines. Democrats Mason, Rawlings, and LeGrand voted as a threesome in 64.5% of the cases (mean IA = 0.73) and Republicans Harris and Uhlenhopp voted similarly in 70% of the cases in which they both participated, in each case satisfying the Willetts criterion (0.67).

These results are perfectly consistent with those previously reported by Beatty.[31] After applying scale and bloc analysis to the decisions of the Iowa Supreme Court from late 1965 to early 1969, Beatty concluded that, though the court rarely divided strictly along party lines, party was the most important factor explaining the lines of cleavage between the judges. Democratic judges were consistently more liberal in criminal appeals and in personal injury cases than Republican judges. Additionally, moderate to strong blocs along party lines were observable in the court's disposition of criminal cases. Insufficient data precluded a full analysis of the underlying bloc structure in the personal injury cases, but the scale scores indicated a greater difference between the opposing partisans in the criminal cases than in the economic.

At the time of Beatty's study, less than half of the court's members had been originally selected through the merit selection process. For this study, nearly the entire court was the product of merit selection. Nevertheless, partisan voting can still be observed, attesting to the continued vitality of partisan attitudes and values held by merit plan appointees even though these judges will not subsequently be held accountable for their judicial decisions by a partisan constituency.

## Kansas

In 1859, Kansas adopted a system of partisan elections for the selection of its state judges. But by the late 1950s, widespread criticism had mounted against the "blatantly partisan political flavor" of the process of judicial selection.[32] As Ashman and Alfini note:

> This process was characterized by many of the "evils" of the political elective system, with judges openly lending support and assistance to political leaders and keeping their "political" contacts alive. Interim appointments to the bench were made strictly on a partisan political basis. Politics was a stepping stone to high judicial office. One supreme court justice was appointed to the court while serving as attorney general. While on the court he ran for governor and won, resigning from the court to become governor. On another occasion the state's lieutenant governor was elected governor, while the governor appointed himself to the supreme court.[33]

As a result of the general discontent with the existing system, the legislature proposed and the voters ratified in 1958 a constitutional amendment providing for the merit selection of the state's supreme court justices.

The eleven-member supreme court nominating commission created by the constitutional change is composed of five lay persons, appointed by the governor, and five lawyers, one elected from each of the state's congressional districts by the lawyers in each district.[34] The chairperson of the commission is also a lawyer, chosen during a statewide balloting of all the attorneys in the state.

When vacancies occur on the supreme court, the nominating commission submits a list of three nominees from which the governor may make the final selection. If the governor does not appoint one of the nominees within sixty days, the power of appointment falls to the chief justice of the court. After serving at least one year in office, the appointed judge faces the Kansas electorate on the uncontested merit retention ballot; a majority of affirmative votes secures a six-year term.

Though the merit plan was originally adopted by the voters in the 1958 election, the transformation from the partisan elective system had not yet been completed by 1972. Two of the court's Republican justices, Harold R. Fatzer (a former attorney general) and Alfred G. Schroeder (a former district judge), were originally recruited to the state's high bench under the partisan system. Each had subsequently sought and twice received confirmation from the electorate on the merit retention ballot, however.

Partisanship, moreover, had already been clearly stamped as a feature of the merit plan in Kansas. Of six judges appointed under the merit plan before 1972, all shared the partisan affiliation of the governor who appointed them. In addition, nearly all the merit plan appointees had personal histories of active involvement in partisan elective politics prior to their accession to the high court, either as elected county attorneys and/or elected district court judges under the old partisan judicial system.

Thus, as in Iowa, the merit plan has not removed partisanship from the judicial selection system and has not resulted in the recruitment of "nonpartisan" judges; those individuals selected to staff the state's highest court have been clearly identifiable by their partisan backgrounds. A certain amount of partisan voting behavior on the bench is, therefore, to be expected. On the other hand, the merit retention system theoretically relieves some of the pressure for partisanship in judicial decision-making by guaranteeing each judge continued tenure without fear of removal by a disappointed or angered partisan constituency.

The period under inspection here spans the years 1972 through 1974.[35] During this time the seven-member court consisted of five Republicans and two Democrats, the closest partisan division of the court's membership in its history. Prior to the appointments of Democrats Perry Owsley and David Prager by Democratic Governor Robert Docking in the final months of 1971, no more than one Democrat at a time had served on the Kansas Supreme Court.

The results of the scale analysis, presented in Table 32, show that the two Democratic justices, Prager and Owsley, occupied the liberal end of the criminal and economic distribution scales, supporting the position of the criminal defendant and the economic underdog in a greater proportion of the cases than any of the Republicans. And although the cases are few and the differences are not sharp, the Democratic justices supported the government in its

**Table 32.** *Percentage of Liberal Votes in Nonunanimous Cases,*
*Kansas Supreme Court, 1972–1974*

| Criminal Appeals | | Economic Distribution | | Government Regulation | |
|---|---|---|---|---|---|
| Prager (D) | 0.91 | Owsley (D) | 0.75 | Owsley (D) | 0.85 |
| Owsley (D) | 0.65 | Prager (D) | 0.67 | Prager (D) | 0.83 |
| Schroeder (R) | 0.57 | Fatzer (R) | 0.55 | Fontron (R) | 0.77 |
| Fontron (R) | 0.55 | Schroeder (R) | 0.53 | Fromme (R) | 0.77 |
| Fatzer (R) | 0.52 | Fontron (R) | 0.51 | Kaul (R) | 0.77 |
| Fromme (R) | 0.39 | Kaul (R) | 0.42 | Fatzer (R) | 0.54 |
| Kaul (R) | 0.39 | Fromme (R) | 0.33 | Schroeder (R) | 0.38 |
| Mean court | 0.57 | | 0.54 | | 0.70 |
| Mean Democrats | 0.78 | | 0.71 | | 0.84 |
| Mean Republicans | 0.48 | | 0.47 | | 0.65 |
| (N = 23) | | (N = 53) | | (N = 13) | |

claims of regulatory authority in a slightly greater proportion of cases than the Republicans.

Bloc analysis of the court's nonunanimous criminal cases does not reveal any sharply drawn partisan blocs, however. The Democrats did agree in three-fourths of the decisions, but Democratic Justice Owsley agreed just as frequently with Republicans Harold R. Fatzer, Alfred G. Schroeder, and Robert H. Kaul.

Overall, one is struck by the high degree of interagreement among all members of the court. The mean interagreement score in the bloc matrix is a very high 0.60, reflecting in large measure an even distribution of single dissents among the members of the court. But even when one removes single-dissent cases from the matrix and considers only those cases more sharply divided, no stable and solid blocs reveal themselves, partisan or otherwise. In seven cases decided by a five-to-two margin, for example, none was decided along party lines and, perhaps more significantly, six different voting alignments can be observed. Interestingly, applying the rigorous Willetts criterion, it is not possible to say that *any* of the pairs of justices in the joint dissent appeals matrix agreed in a significant proportion of cases.

In the nonunanimous economic distribution cases, blocs are more apparent than in the criminal appeals decision, but these groups are by no means sharply defined. Owsley and Prager, the Democrats, agreed in over 80% of the split decisions, forming the most cohesive pair on the court. Various other pairs of judges agreed in a lesser but significant proportion of cases as well, but no stable or consistent groups of judges larger than a pair emerge. Once again, the pattern of the bloc matrix and an inspection of the actual voting patterns indicate that a relatively even distribution of single dissents and shifting voting coalitions are present. Considering only those thirty-one cases in which more than one justice dissented, only two were decided along straight party lines, representing but 3.8% of the total number of nonunanimous decisions. Of the eighteen cases decided by margins of five to two, eleven different pairs of justices joined in dissent. And in thirteen decisions decided by a four-to-three vote, nine different alignments were produced.

In sum, therefore, the divisions observed in the voting patterns of the justices of the Kansas Supreme Court do not appear to have been drawn strictly along partisan lines. Generally speaking, the two Democratic justices remained fairly cohesive in their voting behavior, providing the most consistent support on the court for the claims of criminal defendants and economically disadvantaged litigants. But they were frequently joined by a good share of the Republican judges. In fact, in nearly 85% of the criminal and economic cases which involved more than one dissenter and in which they both voted on the same side of the issue, Democrats Prager and Owsley were joined by at least two, and most often three, of the five Republicans to control the majority decisions. Given the historical dominance of the Republicans in the state and on the court, however, it is perhaps not too unexpected to find the majority party internally divided.

# 7. A Comparative Approach to Party Bloc Voting

ALTHOUGH relatively precise scale and bloc techniques were applied in Chapter 6, the analysis offered heretofore has relied upon rather imprecise estimations and impressions to compare the voting patterns observed on each state court with those of others. This chapter attempts to remedy this problem by applying two measures of party bloc voting to all eight state courts simultaneously. The implications of these findings and those of the preceding chapter for the reform of judicial selection methods can then be explored.

## PARTISAN DISSENT BLOCS ON STATE SUPREME COURTS

One of the techniques available for comparing the extent of party bloc voting on state courts is to examine the nature of those blocs of judges who coalesce in dissent. Unfortunately, as noted in Chapter 5, the analysis of dissent blocs excludes from consideration about half of the important information on partisan voting patterns by ignoring the partisan affiliations of those judges who join together to form a majority. Nevertheless, for comparative purposes, the analysis of dissenting behavior appears to be a useful and reasonable initial approach to the study of partisan voting by state court judges.

A partisan dissenting bloc is defined here as one in which all the members of the court who join together in dissent share the same partisan affiliation. Because the courts vary in size from five to nine members, dissenting blocs also vary in size. On five-judge courts, the only possible dissenting combination other than a single dissent consists of two members. But on seven-member courts, two- and three-judge dissenting combinations may be observed, and dissenting groups as large as four judges can be analyzed on nine-member courts. For each court, the partisanship of the possible dissenting combinations will be reviewed in turn.

Among the courts in this study, only Utah and Indiana contain just five judges each. Although most of the nonunanimous decisions of each court involve lone dissenters, partisan voting blocs were observed in those cases decided by three-to-two margins. On the Indiana court, where criminal cases contribute the bulk of the court's docket, a vast majority of judges who joined together in dissent shared the same party affiliation. In fact, from 1969 to 1972, 97% of the dissenting blocs on the Indiana court in criminal cases were partisan (see Table 33). Similarly, in Utah a high proportion of dissenting judges shared the same party identification. In economic cases, which make up nearly half the nonunanimous decisions of the court, over 85% of the three-to-two decisions from 1960 to 1970 featured partisan dissenting pairs. Although the Indiana court was formally partisan and the Utah court ostensibly nonpartisan, both courts demonstrated very similar amounts of partisan dissenting behavior. Moreover, the extent of partisan dissenting voting did not seem to diminish in either state with the adoption of the merit plan of selection and retention.

Four courts (Pennsylvania, Colorado, Kansas, and Wisconsin) are seven-member courts on which both two- and three-member dissenting judge combinations are possible. An inspection of the partisan composition of the two-member dissenting blocs on these courts in Table 34 reveals that, with but perhaps the exception of Kansas, partisan dissenting pairs are not as frequent as in Indiana and Utah. In Pennsylvania, less than half of the two-member dissenting blocs were composed of fellow partisans. The same is true in Wisconsin where barely over 20% of the two-judge dissents filed in criminal and economic cases (which contribute over 70% of the court's nonunanimous docket) featured dissenting judges sharing the same party affiliation. The analysis of Colorado's dissenting pairs is hindered by the small number of cases, but overall the extent of partisan dissenting behavior does not appear to approach the levels observed on the five-member courts.

The analysis of the three-judge dissent blocs is most appropriately confined to the supreme courts of Pennsylvania and Wisconsin, each of which featured at least three members of each party. In Colorado and Kansas, where the basic partisan division of each court was five to two, any three-member dissenting blocs in which both members of the minor party were joined by another judge would necessarily be bipartisan in composition.

Few of the three-judge dissents on either the Pennsylvania or

**Table 33. *Partisan Dissenting Blocs on Five-Member Courts***

| State<br>Case Area | Frequency<br>of Single<br>Dissents[a] | Two-Member<br>Blocs Percent<br>Partisan[b] |
|---|---|---|
| Indiana (1963–1965) | | |
| Criminal appeals | N = 40/47 | 71.4% (N = 7) |
| Economic distribution | N = 11/12 | — (N = 1) |
| Government regulation | N = 11/14 | — (N = 3) |
| Indiana (1969–1970) | | |
| Criminal appeals | N = 58/98 | 97.5% (N = 40) |
| Economic distribution | N = 6/11 | 80.0% (N = 5) |
| Government regulation | N = 13/14 | — (N = 1) |
| Indiana (1971–1972) | | |
| Criminal appeals | N = 53/73 | 95.0% (N = 20) |
| Economic distribution | N = 5/7 | — (N = 2) |
| Government regulation | N = 11/13 | — (N = 2) |
| Utah (1960–1966) | | |
| Criminal appeals | N = 10/13 | — (N = 3) |
| Economic distribution | N = 29/51 | 90.9% (N = 22) |
| Government regulation | N = 12/21 | 77.8% (N = 9) |
| Utah (1967–1970) | | |
| Criminal appeals | N = 16/28 | 75.0% (N = 12) |
| Economic distribution | N = 32/66 | 79.4% (N = 34) |
| Government regulation | N = 13/20 | 85.7% (N = 7) |

[a] Entries in this column indicate the fraction of cases in each area featuring only one judge in dissent. Thus, in Indiana (1963–1965), 40 of the 47 nonunanimous decisions in the criminal appeals area involved solo dissents.

[b] The percentages in this column represent the proportion of cases involving dissenting blocs of this size in which all the members in dissent shared the same partisan affiliation. The N's listed in parentheses represent the total number of cases in each area featuring dissenting blocs of this size. The percentage of partisan dissenting blocs was not calculated where N < 5.

the Wisconsin courts were partisan. Only in 4% of the criminal cases decided by the Pennsylvania court in four-to-three decisions did all the members in dissent belong to the same party. And partisan dissent blocs formed in less than one-sixth of the economic distribution and government regulation cases. In Wisconsin, not one of the closely divided four-to-three criminal decisions featured dissenters who all shared the same partisan affiliation. And only about one-quarter of the economic decisions of the Wisconsin court sparked partisan blocs in dissent.

Only two nine-member courts, Iowa and Washington, were

**Table 34. *Partisan Dissenting Blocs on Seven-Member Courts***

| State Case Area | Frequency of Single Dissents[a] | Two-Member Blocs Percent Partisan[b] | Three-Member Blocs Percent Partisan[b] |
|---|---|---|---|
| Colorado (1962–1966) | | | |
| Criminal appeals | N = 11/26 | 60.0% (N = 10) | 40.0% (N = 5) |
| Economic distribution | N = 17/33 | 41.7% (N = 12) | — (N = 4) |
| Government regulation | N = 19/31 | 28.6% (N = 7) | 0.0% (N = 5) |
| Colorado (1967–1968) | | | |
| Criminal appeals | N = 1/7 | 50.0% (N = 6) | — (N = 0) |
| Economic distribution | N = 9/15 | 83.3% (N = 6) | — (N = 0) |
| Government regulation | N = 2/6 | — (N = 4) | — (N = 0) |
| Kansas (1972–1974) | | | |
| Criminal appeals | N = 12/23 | 71.4% (N = 7) | — (N = 4) |
| Economic distribution | N = 22/53 | 83.3% (N = 18) | 53.8% (N = 13) |
| Government regulation | N = 6/13 | 80.0% (N = 5) | — (N = 2) |
| Pennsylvania (1972–1974) | | | |
| Criminal appeals | N = 68/167 | 47.9% (N = 48) | 3.9% (N = 51) |
| Economic distribution | N = 10/37 | 35.7% (N = 14) | 15.4% (N = 13) |
| Government regulation | N = 12/35 | 20.0% (N = 15) | 12.5% (N = 8) |
| Wisconsin (1968–1974) | | | |
| Criminal appeals | N = 10/52 | 35.3% (N = 17) | 0.0% (N = 25) |
| Economic distribution | N = 13/41 | 0.0% (N = 17) | 27.3% (N = 11) |
| Government regulation | N = 9/17 | — (N = 4) | — (N = 4) |

a, b The notes accompanying this table are identical to those for Table 33.

studied here. Both courts exhibited partisan dissenting behavior which was more extensive than on the seven-member courts and nearly as impressive as that on the small five-member courts. Table 35 reveals that in those cases decided by seven-to-two margins a large majority of the cases on each court featured dissenters sharing the same party label. Partisan dissent behavior was more frequent on the Iowa court in the criminal area than in Washington, whereas all the two-judge dissents in Washington's economic cases followed party lines while only half of Iowa's did.

Partisan dissents remained relatively frequent among those cases decided by a six-to-three margin on these two courts. But, as before, the frequency of partisan dissents varied by issue area. In Washington, an amazing 92.3% of the economic decisions with three dissenters involved fellow partisans joined in dissent, but none of the criminal cases featured partisan dissenting blocs. In contrast,

**Table 35. Partisan Dissenting Blocs on Nine-Member Courts**

| State<br>Case Area | Frequency<br>of Single<br>Dissents[a] | Two-Member<br>Blocs Percent<br>Partisan[b] | Three-Member<br>Blocs Percent<br>Partisan[b] | Four-Member<br>Blocs Percent<br>Partisan[b] |
|---|---|---|---|---|
| Iowa (1972–1974) | | | | |
| Criminal appeals | N = 3/27 | 83.3% (N = 6) | — (N = 4) | 28.6% (N = 14) |
| Economic distribution | N = 4/32 | 50.0% (N = 8) | 41.7% (N = 12) | 0.0% (N = 8) |
| Government regulation | N = 1/6 | — (N = 2) | — (N = 1) | — (N = 2) |
| Washington (1963–1967)[c] | | | | |
| Criminal appeals | N = 1/20 | 69.2% (N = 13) | 0.0% (N = 5) | — (N = 1) |
| Economic distribution | N = 4/39 | 100.0% (N = 10) | 92.3% (N = 13) | 25.0% (N = 12) |
| Government regulation | N = 3/27 | 83.3% (N = 6) | 54.5% (N = 11) | 14.3% (N = 7) |

[a], [b] The notes accompanying this table are identical to those for Table 33.

[c] The analysis of partisan dissenting blocs was not performed on the Washington Supreme Court for the 1973–1974 period because of the presence of one justice not affiliated with either major party. Similarly, the analysis of intraparty cohesion which follows excludes Washington for this period.

41.7% of Iowa's economic cases sparked partisan dissenting blocs in six-to-three decisions as did 40% of the criminal cases.

The frequency of partisan dissent blocs declines markedly in the cases decided by the close margin of five to four. Well under one-third of these cases decided by the Iowa and Washington courts with four members in dissent involved fellow partisans joined in the minority. Consistent with the pattern observed for smaller-sized dissenting groups of two and three judges, partisan dissents were more likely in economic cases on the Washington court and in criminal cases on the Iowa court.

Though helpful for confirming generally some of the observations drawn from the state-by-state analysis of Chapter 6, dissent bloc analysis may, as noted before, be criticized for ignoring half the available information on judicial voting patterns. While two or more judges of the same party join in dissent, their fellow partisans on the bench might agree with members of the opposition party to form the majority. This problem becomes particularly acute on the larger-sized courts for the study of dissenting blocs of only two or three members.

On the other hand, and just as critically, the dissent bloc technique is also insensitive to those situations in which a large proportion of one party's membership on a court votes in opposition to a large proportion of the other party. Thus, for example, the dissenting bloc analyses of the voting patterns on the high courts in Pennsylvania, Wisconsin, Iowa, and Washington reveal little partisan dissenting behavior in the most closely divided cases. Yet the cluster bloc analysis of each state offered in the last chapter suggested that on each court two essentially partisan voting blocs existed in which all but one member from one party voted consistently in opposition to all but one member of the other party. Though the line of cleavage in such situations is essentially partisan, the dissenting bloc is not considered a "partisan" one under the rigid criterion adopted here because the dissent is not composed exclusively of individuals sharing the same partisan affiliation.

In sum, dissent bloc analysis suffers because it obscures some of the data relevant to measuring the extent of party bloc voting. Further, as a comparative measure, dissenting bloc analysis is not entirely adequate because courts of different sizes feature dissenting bloc combinations of different sizes. Only cross-state comparisons between courts of the same size are possible. It is difficult to hypothesize how the judges on a smaller court would have behaved had they been part of a larger court.

## A NEW MEASURE OF PARTY BLOC VOTING:
## AN ADAPTATION OF THE RICE INDEX

In order to compare the extent of party bloc voting across courts, a truly comparative measure is required of intergroup differences between judges of opposing partisan affiliations on the same court and intragroup cohesion among those judges sharing the same party allegiance. There are, however, a number of inherent methodological problems with which any such measure must cope.

First, the various courts vary in size from five to nine members; the party subgroups also vary in size from two members to five. On a small five-member court, a close partisan division requires only three individuals to join in the majority. But on a closely divided nine-member court, a straight partisan vote requires all five members of one party to vote alike. Intuitively it seems that the maintenance of party lines would be much more difficult on the larger court than on the smaller since the opportunities for a defection from the ranks are more numerous on the larger-sized court.

In a statistical sense, however, the different sized courts lead to a curious paradox. On the one hand, the chance of an individual defecting from fellow partisans *is* greater on a larger court than on a smaller one. On the other hand, though, the probability of any two members voting *alike* is *also* greater on the larger body than on the smaller because on the former "there are proportionally fewer pairs of members who can disagree."[1] The statistical intricacies of this paradox do not concern us here except to the extent that it be realized that a comparative measure of party bloc voting must compensate for the different sized courts and different sized subgroups within those courts.

Second, a comparative measure of partisan voting on state courts must take into account the variation among courts in the intensity of disagreement and division. As Grossman has pointed out, it is a distortion of the concept of bloc voting not to consider the context in which members of the bloc coalesce.[2] It would be misleading to identify as a bloc, for example, five members of the court who join together as part of a larger majority on the court in a case decided by a margin of eight to one. Thus, the analyst wants to be able to distinguish courts on which agreement among some defined subgroup of the court is high while the overall level of cohesion on the court as a whole is low. A party bloc which manages to hang together in closely divided cases is much more impressive than a bloc on a court which is always close to being unanimous.

In 1970 Brams and O'Leary[3] developed what they termed an Agreement Level Index (AL) of intragroup voting cohesion which, based upon the statistical relationships just discussed, can be used for analyzing the behavior of voting groups of different sizes across any number of votes.[4] Ranging in possible values from 0.0 to 1.0, a mean Agreement Level Index can be calculated to measure the cohesion among the members of each party subgroup on each court. High values of this AL Index for each party *could* indicate the existence of party bloc voting. As noted before, however, the levels of intraparty cohesion cannot be considered in isolation and must be compared to the overall level of court cohesion. A cohesive party group is not particularly noteworthy on a court which is generally cohesive and not sharply divided internally.

In order to facilitate the comparison of the levels of intraparty agreement while "controlling" for the overall level of cleavage on state courts, some measure of the overall cohesion of each state court must be introduced. Once a necessary correction is made of the Agreement Level Index for the exclusion of unanimous decisions from the analysis,[5] an overall measure of each court's internal cohesion (hereinafter called the Court Cohesion Index) can be calculated within each court.[6] This comparison is accomplished by a simple ratio in which values of the mean intraparty AL Index are divided by the values of the mean Court Cohesion Index. This Ratio of Relative Party Cohesion produces values, expressed in decimal form, which have no intrinsic meaning or interpretation; their utility is strictly comparative. This ratio gives a party subgroup on a court which was sharply divided in its nonunanimous decisions more "credit" for demonstrating intragroup cohesion than a subgroup with the same level of intragroup agreement observed on a more cohesive court. Thus, a group of judges which exhibits an intraparty Agreement Level Index value of 0.50 on a court with an Index of Court Cohesion of 0.80 produces a Relative Party Cohesion Ratio of 0.63 (0.50/0.80), but the same level of intraparty agreement on a court with a Cohesion Index of 0.40 results in a Relative Party Cohesion value of 1.25 (0.50/0.40).

The Ratio of Relative Party Cohesion reaches its theoretical lower limit of 0.00 when the mean Agreement Level Index is at its minimum value of 0.00 and the mean Court Cohesion Index is at its maximum value of 1.00. When the mean Court Cohesion Index reaches its lower limit of 0.00 and the mean intraparty Agreement Level Index reaches its upper limit of 1.00, the Ratio of Relative Party Cohesion should achieve its theoretical upper limit, but this value is mathematically undefined.[7]

The decimal values of the Relative Party Cohesion Ratio for each of the major case areas are presented in Table 36. Specially marked are those courts on which both of the party subgroups were cohesive relative to the overall level of court cohesion in nonunanimous cases. In concert with the bloc and scale analyses presented earlier, this approach provides some comparative measure of the extent of party bloc voting on state courts.

In the criminal appeals cases, intraparty cohesion for both the Republican and the Democratic subgroups on the court is clearly visible on the Indiana court (1969–1970) and the Iowa Supreme Court. On the remaining courts, the most common pattern observed is a relatively high Relative Cohesion value for one party on the court but not the other. The Democrats in Indiana (1963–1965), Wisconsin, Washington (1963–1967), and Utah (1967–1970) and the Republicans in Kansas were all relatively incohesive compared both to their courts and to their brethren of the opposite party on their courts.

In the cases concerning economic distribution, high amounts of relative cohesion in both parties are apparent on several courts, including Washington (1963–1967), Utah (both periods), Iowa, and Indiana (1969–1970), and to a lesser extent in Pennsylvania. It is by far the strongest on the Washington court for the 1963 to 1967 period for which clear partisan voting had been detected by bloc analysis.

In government regulation decisions, the Washington court is again distinguished by relatively high intraparty agreement in both parties as is the Utah court (1967–1970) and, to a slightly lesser extent, the Iowa and Utah (1960–1966) supreme courts.

Again, it must be stressed that these data are comparative. This reminder is essential, for the extent of partisan voting on some of the courts which nevertheless exhibit low indices of Relative Party Cohesion cannot be gainsaid. In Pennsylvania, for example, the persistent defection of one member of each party from his partisan colleagues on the bench has contributed to the lowered levels of intraparty cohesion. Yet most of the members of each party remained closely allied in opposition to those judges representing the other. Similarly, in Wisconsin, two of the three Democratic judges were nearly always in agreement, but the third, a marginal member of the party at best, proved to be most closely allied with the most conservative of the Republican judges on the court, forcing the Index of Relative Party Cohesion for the Democrats in a downward direction.

Another problem with these data is the inclusion of nonunanimous decisions in which only one dissenting vote was cast. In Indiana, for instance, the concentration of single dissents cast by one

**Table 36. *Index of Relative Party Cohesion***

| State | Criminal Appeals | | Economic Distribution | | Government Regulation | |
|---|---|---|---|---|---|---|
| | Democrats | Republicans | Democrats | Republicans | Democrats | Republicans |
| Colorado (1962–1964) | 0.770 | 1.049 | 0.508 | 0.769 | 0.923 | 0.477 |
| (1965–1966) | 0.980 | 0.857 | 0.460 | 1.095 | 0.838 | 0.622 |
| (1967–1968) | 0.929 | 0.690 | 0.726 | 0.644 | 0.778 | 0.611 |
| Indiana (1963–1965) | 0.153 | 1.047 | 0.185 | 0.815 | 0.785 | 0.633 |
| (1969–1970) | 0.879 | 1.379 | 1.000 | 1.327 | 0.387 | 0.688 |
| (1971–1972) | 0.726 | 0.876 | 0.282 | 1.000 | 0.318 | 0.906 |
| Iowa (1972–1974) | 1.640 | 1.360 | 1.367 | 1.000 | 1.278 | 0.778 |
| Kansas (1972–1974) | 1.194 | 0.468 | 1.547 | 0.491 | 1.431 | 0.310 |
| Pennsylvania (1972–1974) | 0.760 | 0.580 | 1.000 | 0.711 | 0.646 | 0.646 |
| Utah (1960–1966) | 0.896 | 0.351 | 1.035 | 1.123 | 0.667 | 1.150 |
| (1967–1970) | 0.561 | 1.263 | 0.796 | 1.551 | 1.000 | 1.105 |
| Washington (1963–1967) | 0.590 | 1.128 | 1.750 | 2.000 | 1.621 | 1.310 |
| Wisconsin (1968–1974) | 0.133 | 1.300 | 0.739 | 0.630 | 0.393 | 0.934 |

NOTE: $\dfrac{\text{Intraparty Agreement Level (AL)}}{\text{Index of Court Cohesion}}$ = Index of Relative Party Cohesion

(AL Index corrected for exclusion of nonunanimous cases)

judge served to obscure the clear partisan lines of division on the court in the more closely divided cases.

## PARTISANSHIP ON STATE SUPREME COURTS

### The Theoretical Framework

Because of the importance of partisan identification in developing and shaping political attitudes, there are strong reasons to believe that judges' partisan affiliations will be related to their judicial decision-making. Not surprisingly, therefore, previous empirical studies have confirmed that party is the single most important social background characteristic related to the individual decisional propensities of judges. Subsequent case studies of judicial behavior on state supreme courts discovered, however, that the "party variable" did not operate with equal strength and intensity for judges in different states.

The partisanship of the system of judicial selection was hypothesized as the primary factor accounting for the variation observed in the amount of partisan judicial behavior. It may have this impact by two independent, but reinforcing, theoretical linkages. First, partisan judicial systems were hypothesized to be more likely than nonpartisan systems to attract individuals with personal histories of previous activity in party politics and a concomitant allegiance to the general ideological and policy orientations associated with the party. Second, partisan judicial systems were hypothesized to influence judicial decision-making along partisan lines by the prospective influence of a partisan judicial constituency; judges owing their future renomination and re-election bids to party organizations, party workers, and a partisan electoral coalition must anticipate the possible reactions of these partisan "attentive publics" in their judicial decision-making.

Partisanship on state courts was also hypothesized to be related to any one or combination of factors which might mitigate the influence of partisan values in judicial decisions. Long terms of office, political-legal cultural norms discouraging partisanship on the bench, and the consensus-building procedures of collegial court decision-making might temper the occurrence of sharp divisions between judges of opposing partisan affiliation selected through partisan processes of nomination and election.

**Eight Case Studies: The Expectations**

Eight state supreme courts were selected for particular study. Three partisan courts (Indiana, Pennsylvania, Colorado) were expected to exhibit the highest amount of partisan judicial voting behavior. But within the group of partisan states differing degrees of partisan behavior were expected, based upon the configuration of formal systems of judicial selection and informal political arrangements in each state. Indiana, featuring a partisan convention system of nomination, a strong party system, and short terms of office, was expected to produce the highest amount of partisan judicial behavior, similar to that witnessed in several studies of the Michigan Supreme Court. The justices of the Pennsylvania Supreme Court were also expected to exhibit considerable partisan voting owing to the active role of the parties in recruiting and promoting judicial candidates, but not as much interparty cleavage as in Indiana. Occasional intraparty differences within each party have resulted in the selection of judges who share the same party label but not necessarily the same ideological outlook. Moreover, a system of judicial retention for previously elected judges frees Pennsylvania judges from the necessity of fearing the disapproval of a partisan judicial constituency. Finally, judges in Colorado, nominated in preprimary party assemblies, were expected to demonstrate some partisan judicial behavior, but the prospective influence of their partisan constituency was expected to be significantly weakened by lengthy ten-year terms and a style of political campaigning largely independent of the party organizations, requiring essentially personalistic rather than partisan appeals to muster campaign and voter support.

The supreme courts of Wisconsin, Utah, and Washington, each featuring nonpartisan systems for the nomination and election of their justices, were expected to exhibit generally lower levels of partisan cleavage. Nonpartisan primaries and elections allow individuals not closely aligned with either party to gain access to the ballot and, ultimately, a seat on the state supreme court. Moreover, the absence of a partisan constituency produces an environment of decision-making in which partisan values need not find consistent expression; indeed, the need to fashion an electoral coalition from among the ranks of both parties may compel an incumbent to take care not to demonstrate partisan behavior which will estrange part of the constituency.

In each of these states, however, partisan influences have been a significant, though less visible dimension of judicial selection. In Utah, the adoption of the nonpartisan selection system in 1951 followed upon the heels of a partisan judicial selection system. Most of the judges recruited to the Utah Supreme Court since that time either by election or appointment were active in partisan judicial or other elective politics prior to reaching the state supreme court. In both Wisconsin and Washington, the frequency of mid-term deaths and retirements has opened the judicial election process to direct partisan influences through the recruitment by the governor of fellow partisans to fill judicial vacancies.

Finally, the decisions of the supreme courts of Iowa and Kansas were analyzed for evidence of partisan patterns of judicial behavior. Though once utilizing partisan elective systems, each had subsequently adopted the merit system of selection and retention. But eliminating the formal provisions for partisan selection did nothing to eliminate partisanship from the process of merit selection; nearly all the merit plan appointees in these two states shared the partisan affiliation of the governor to whom they owed their appointment. The merit retention system did, however, remove the possibility of a prospective impact upon judicial behavior by eliminating the reliance of an incumbent judge upon a judicial constituency for renomination and re-election. Hence, as in the nonpartisan states, some partisan voting was expected, owing to the partisan backgrounds of those recruited, but less than in the partisan states, in the absence of a partisan judicial constituency.

**The Results**

Scale analysis was applied in the major areas of court decision-making to identify the ideological direction of the voting patterns of supreme court justices in nonunanimous decisions issued by each of the eight state courts. Scale analysis does not allow a very rigorous test for the existence of partisan judicial voting behavior. But it does serve to identify those judges who, on the average over a series of cases, have tended to vote in either a liberal or a conservative direction relative to the other members of the court.

Although other social background and other attitudinal variables which might affect the voting decisions of individual judges were not considered, Democratic judges were found in most instances to be more supportive than Republican judges of the claims of criminal defendants, disadvantaged economic litigants, and (where the number of cases allowed) the claims of individuals alleging deprivations of civil liberties. With respect to the exercise of governmental authority, the Democrats were generally distinguishable as more liberal than the Republicans. In some states, however (as in Indiana during all three of the periods studied), the Republicans registered more liberal votes than their Democratic brethren, a fact which may reflect difficulties discussed earlier concerning the nature of this case category.

In some states, case areas, and time periods, the scale analyses suggested that the relationship between party affiliation and decision-making might be quite dramatic. In several instances, most notably Kansas (all case areas), Indiana (criminal cases in all three periods, economic distribution cases in the second period), Utah (economic distribution and government regulation cases in both periods), Washington (economic and government regulation cases in the first period), and Colorado (criminal cases in the second period), all of the Democratic judges serving on these state courts were more liberal than any of the Republicans with whom they shared the bench. And in most of the other instances, including Pennsylvania (all case areas), Wisconsin (all case areas), Colorado (all cases in the first period, economic cases in the second, and criminal and economic issues in the third), Iowa (criminal and economic distribution cases), Washington (government regulation cases in the second period), and Utah (criminal cases in the first period), this clear distinction between the judges of opposing partisan affiliations was blurred only slightly by the liberal behavior of one Republican judge and/or the conservative tendencies of one Democratic judge. Even in states where the relationship between party and scale position was less consistent, as in Indiana (economic cases in the first period) and Washington (criminal cases in the first period and economic in the second), the average support for the liberal position among each court's Democrats exceeded that recorded for the Republicans on the same bench. In only a small minority of instances did the Republican contingent on a court best the Democratic membership in average support for the liberal result (criminal and civil liberties in Washington in the second period, criminal cases in Utah in the second period, and Colorado's government regulation cases in the first two periods). As noted above, such was also the case in Indiana's government regulation cases in all three of the periods analyzed, but the consistency of the differences between the party groups (though reversed in direction from the expected relationship) suggests that the kinds of regulatory questions posed to that court (and partisan responses to them) differ in some unknown way from those observed on the other state courts.

As the results above suggest, the system of judicial selection appeared not to bear any clear relationship to the decisional propensities of the judges serving on each state court. Democrats serving on nonpartisan or merit plan courts occupied the liberal side of the scale continua as frequently as Democrats serving on partisan courts. Whether the judges were selected and retained under a partisan or a nonpartisan elective system or a merit selection and retention plan, the relationship between party and decisional tendencies was not always perfect but, on the average, Democratic judges were more liberal than their Republican colleagues on the bench.

Bloc analysis was applied to the decisions of each court to clarify the patterns of partisan voting suggested by the relative position of the judges on the issue scales. A more discriminating technique than scaling, bloc analysis allows the inspection of a series of judicial decisions for the frequency with which judges of the same partisan affiliation actually voted alike.

Bloc analysis confirmed that voting blocs drawn along partisan lines were apparent to some degree on all but two of the supreme courts studied (Colorado and Kansas). But, as the scale analysis suggested, the presence of partisan voting blocs was not clearly related to the formal selection system. In Indiana and Utah, a partisan and nonpartisan state, respectively, partisan blocs were clear and unmistakable on those issues most prevalent on each court's docket (criminal cases in Indiana and economic matters in Utah). Partisan voting blocs were also apparent, though not as internally cohesive or exclusive in their membership, on several other courts selected by a variety of arrangements, including Pennsylvania (partisan election/retention), Washington (1963–1967) and Wisconsin (both nonpartisan), and Iowa (merit plan). Only on the Kansas (merit plan) and Colorado (partisan) courts were the voting alignments observed to have been fluid in membership and less clearly drawn along partisan lines. Nevertheless, party was not wholly irrelevant to judicial decision-making on these courts; in both states, voters could be assured that over the long run Democratic judges were more likely to vote in a liberal direction than the Republican judges.

Finally, in an attempt to compare more precisely the extent of partisan voting on the eight state courts, two separate measurement techniques were applied. Dissent bloc analysis compared the frequency with which fellow partisans joined together in dissenting groups of various sizes. A Ratio of Relative Party Cohesion was devised to quantitatively compare the extent of cohesion of each of the two partisan subgroups on each court while controlling for the overall level of court cohesion. Though these relatively precise comparative measures proved to be somewhat insensitive to revealing the full amount of partisanship on state courts exhibiting particular patterns of partisan cleavage (e.g., Wisconsin, Pennsylvania), the results of each exercise confirmed the conclusions of the scale and bloc analyses that some amount of partisan decision-making is a characteristic of most state supreme courts and is not limited to those staffed by any particular method of election or appointment. Of course, in any given state, partisan divisions may be blunted or sharpened, depending upon the constellation of partisan attitudes and values of those sitting as judges, the nature of the issues confronting each court, and other formal and informal aspects of the selection system, including the length of judicial terms, the existence of internal norms of proper judicial behavior, and the use of consensus-building procedures of collegial court decision-making. But all things considered, when disagreement breaks out on state supreme courts, the lines of division will often be partisan in nature.

### Conclusions and Implications

These results suggest several conclusions. First, a certain amount of partisanship appears to be characteristic of the decision-making of most state supreme courts. It is not surprising that this should be so. Inasmuch as partisanship is an important element of either formal judicial selection systems or their informal aspects, it is perhaps inevitable that individuals with prior partisan attitudes and/or loyalties are recruited to serve as supreme court justices. Both as a shaper of past political values and as a continuing influence upon present attitudes, party affiliation serves as one of the most important psychological guides to judicial decision-making in those cases in which disputes between litigants of differing political, economic, and social status and controversial questions of law and public policy are involved.

On the other hand, it is also clear that party does not account for the entire pattern of state court decision-making. On every court at least a certain percentage of the cases are decided by unanimous vote. Among the nonunanimous cases, often just a single judge is found alone in dissent while his party colleagues are part of a bipartisan majority. Further, in some states and in specific issue areas, Democratic judges are not necessarily more liberal than the Republicans occupying the bench. Finally, even where differences in the expected directions between opposing partisans can be identified, the extent of these differences varies by issue area; in some states, economic distribution issues provide the sharpest and most frequent partisan cleavages while in other states criminal appeals or government regulation cases most consistently divide opposing partisans. As outlined earlier, there are any number of reasons why state judges often vote along nonparty lines and why variations exist among the states in the patterns of judicial decision-making. The frequency of nonunanimous decisions and the sharpness of those partisan divisions which do exist will vary depending upon the nature of the issues confronting each court, the constellation of attitudes and values of those sitting as judges, the existence of internal norms of proper judicial behavior, the use of consensus-building procedures of collegial court decision-making, and the like.

It should be noted that it may very well be that, for a variety of reasons, there is more partisan voting occurring on some courts and on some issues than has been revealed here. In the first place, this research has relied upon extremely broad categories of cases in very diverse areas of law. Within these categories, however, there are undoubtedly tremendous differences in the kinds of questions judges are asked to resolve, the state of the existing case law, and the extent to which judges are able to exercise discretion. Further, within these broad categories are cases which differ in the likelihood they pose for eliciting ideological or partisan responses from the judges. Within the economic distribution area, for example, labor-management disputes might be more likely to evoke partisan and ideological divisions among court members than, for example, a consumer suit in a sale of goods case. Finally, this analysis has treated each judicial decision as equal to all others. Though it is a standard convention of judicial behavior research, observers of the courts know that not all cases are equal in their importance for the development of legal principles, in their significance for the formation of public policy, or in their consequences for the citizenry. Had it been feasible to identify those cases involving major issues of public policy, partisan divisions might very well have emerged much sharper than they did here.

Just how important party is for understanding the patterns of state judicial decision-making is therefore difficult to gauge. But viewed in comparative perspective, party appears to be a significant determinant of judicial behavior. In the first place, though social background characteristics do not bear a one-to-one relationship to the possession of specific political attitudes, party has been shown by previous studies to go further than any other single factor in explaining the behavior of the average state appellate judge. Second, though party does not explain all variations in judicial behavior, partisan divisions in judicial voting appear just about as frequently as studies have reported exists in legislative voting. In even the most partisan state legislatures and in Congress, party-based voting is far from perfect.[8] A certain number of legislative decisions are reached by unanimous consent. And "most American legislative parties achieve only modest levels of cohesiveness—and then only fitfully."[9] *Within* the states, that party voting which is observed varies with the issues raised.[10] *Among* the states, the overall relationship of issues to partisan patterns of voting depends upon variations in political circumstances, population and constituency characteristics, state political cultures, and so forth.[11] Thus, though party never explains everything and its importance varies, party appears to explain about as much of judicial behavior as it does of legislative behavior even though judges are almost never subjected as legislators are to direct pressures from party organizational leaders, party caucuses, or the party's elected leader in the executive branch.

To the extent that partisanship does exist on state courts, these results suggest a second conclusion. Of the two theoretical linkages hypothesized between a judicial selection system and judicial behavior, the indirect impact of the system in recruiting individuals with partisan backgrounds is by far the more significant. By comparison, the direct impact of a judicial constituency upon judicial behavior seems not nearly as powerful. Suggestive empirical evidence is provided by the partisan voting observed on the formally nonpartisan courts of Utah, Wisconsin, and Washington (1963–1967). Courts staffed largely by partisan gubernatorial appointees demonstrate considerable partisan judicial behavior despite their "nonpartisan" or "bipartisan" constituencies. Similarly, partisan voting was clearly observable on the Iowa Supreme Court (merit selection and retention), on the Pennsylvania court (partisan selection with merit-type retention), and on the Indiana court (after the partisan system was replaced by the merit plan). In each case, the court was staffed by individuals owing their original accession to partisan politics but who had no continuing prospective incentive to demonstrate their dedication to partisan policy orientations by their on-the-bench behavior. Despite lacking an identifiable partisan constituency, these judges continued to give some expression to intensely held attitudes, values, and orientations which distinguished them along partisan lines.

The results of previous studies also support this conclusion. In her study of the behavior of lower federal and state supreme court judges in Michigan and Ohio in reapportionment disputes, Barber[12] found that 82% "voted consistently with the apparent interest of the party whose label they bore."[13] Significantly, Barber found little difference in the behavior of the elected state judges, who serve fixed terms under the watchful eye of partisan constituencies, and the appointed federal judges serving with the security of life tenure. Though these cases presented issues of a deeply political nature involving the potential distribution of the political power of each party, the state judges were not demonstrably more partisan than the federal judges. Even in the absence of a partisan constituency upon which they depend for continuance in office, the federal judges are the products of a clearly partisan appointment process. And attitudes and values nurtured in partisan politics may find expression in judicial decisions. As Barber notes: "Direct response to the bidding of a political party is probably rare. . . . Indirect response to needs expressed by groups in the political system with which judges have been and may still be identified is more probable. The deepest and possibly unconscious level of response reflects consonance of the values of judges and parties with which they have been affiliated, values which predispose judges both to associate themselves with a given party and to make decisions which favor that party."[14]

In addition, evidence offered in this study and elsewhere supports the view that partisanship on the bench is as much the product of personal attitude and value structures as of the pressures emanating from a judicial constituency either in the party or in the electorate. Partisan judicial behavior is observable to some extent on nearly *all kinds* of issues and not just those "of direct and immediate interest to the state political parties."[15] Thus, judges of opposing political parties differ not just on such highly political issues as reapportionment, but also on issues "on which there is no clear party position or even clear interest."[16]

For those critics concerned that an elective system makes judges dangerously vulnerable to the bidding and direct pressures of partisan political influences, this finding attests to the existence of a relatively "healthy" relationship between party and judicial decision-making. While not denying that judges in specific instances may be "swayed by some subtle [or not so subtle] persuasion of [a] political party"[17] or that political corruption is a disease occasionally infecting the judiciary, the threat to the impartiality of judges posed by an elective system is not a systemic one.[18] Even though freed from the threats and possible sanctions a party organization might impose following an unpopular decision or the rewards it might bestow after a popular one, judges in the nonpartisan and merit plan states continue to bring those partisan values and attitudes nurtured throughout their lifetimes as "important frames of reference" to their decision-making.[19]

A final conclusion which can be drawn from these data concerns the normative implications regarding the choice of judicial selection method. To the extent that it can be judged significant, partisanship appears to be a demonstrable characteristic of judicial decision-making regardless of the formal system of judicial selection. Where formal election arrangements provide for partisan selection, there is an expected and significant amount of partisan judicial voting. That the relationship between party and behavior is far from perfect is attributable to the informal dimensions of judicial selection in each state and the myriad of factors noted earlier which stimulate nonparty judicial behavior. Similarly, even where the judicial selection system is formally nonpartisan elective or the appointive merit plan, a considerable amount of partisan judicial voting occurs, equaling and often exceeding in amount that observed in the formally partisan states. Partisan judicial behavior appears to exist, then, even where there are no formal arrangements providing for partisan selection. The informal dynamics of the nonpartisan elective and merit plan systems allow the placement on the bench of individuals who possess the experiences, perceptions, attitudes, and values of partisans. Not only do these results testify to the strength of party as a background variable and "as a representer of basic attitudes,"[20] they suggest also that there may be some empirical support for a normative preference for partisan elections as instruments of judicial accountability. As things now stand, citizens in the nonpartisan elective and merit plan states witness a considerable amount of partisan behavior by their judges but have virtually no means by which they can control or hold their judicial policy-makers accountable. Partisan judicial elections, in contrast, enable voters to associate judges in a general way with many of the decisions they have made and candidates with those they are likely to make as sitting judges. Since judges appear to behave at least partially in a partisan fashion regardless of the means by which they were originally selected, the partisan ballot would appear to offer citizens the best way to gain control over their judiciary. If voters want to hold judges accountable retrospectively and to exercise some broad prospective influence over the future general course of judicial decisions, partisan elections are a highly desirable alternative to nonpartisan elective and merit plan selection. To the extent that the amount of partisanship in judicial voting approaches that observed in the legislative arena, party seems to be as valuable for helping voters evaluate the behavior of their judges and to predict the behavior of their prospective judges as it is in the selection and retention of legislators.

Of course, some critics will argue that party-based voting is a highly unreliable means for holding policy-makers, whether they be legislative, judicial, or executive, accountable for specific policy decisions. Few modern election theorists, however, place such weighty responsibility upon voters as to require them to be aware of the substance and implications of each and every decision of elected officials. Rather, as noted in Chapter 1, it is much more realistic to evaluate elections by their indirect effects and electorates by less-demanding criteria. Though elections are blunt instruments of accountability, they are effective in maintaining popular control over the outer limits of governmental decision-making. As long as voters can know within such wide limits the general ideological and political orientations of those individuals they put in policy-making positions, they will be able to exercise effective indirect control over their own affairs.

In the context of judicial elections, therefore, since it appears that a certain amount of judicial decision-making will necessarily have a partisan base regardless of the formal selection system, voters can achieve maximum control over the broad outlines of judicial policy through partisan elections (at least as much as they currently seem to have with respect to controlling policy-making in the other two branches of government).

Some critics, of course, may still question the value of party as a mechanism for maintaining even indirect voter control over elected representatives. One does not need to be a disciple of an ideal responsible party model of government to recognize that party discipline in most legislatures is weak on most issues, that the placement of a party in office does not guarantee the enactment of a particular set of programs, that party organizations are weakening, and that popular attachment to and confidence in the established parties is waning.[21] And the fact that these conditions have been observed to be most critical in the legislative setting does not deny their current or eventual application to the judicial branch. On the other hand, given the desire to hold policy-makers accountable and recognizing the value of elections for achieving this purpose, not even the harshest critics of our political parties have suggested a realistic and meaningful alternative basis upon which voters may cast their ballots and still hope to exercise some control over those they elect.

It may yet be argued by some that judges should not be elected but appointed, either through the merit selection process or directly by the governor. By virtue of the partisan nature of judicial appointments under either system, it might be argued that an indirect form of accountability can be obtained.[22] At the same time, the appointive methods are more likely to result in the selection of "higher quality" judges. According to this view, the benefits associated with a higher-quality bench would justify the substitution of indirect for direct accountability. And the federal system of presidential appointments to the Supreme Court provides a good example of how such an appointive system of selection can result in a quality bench and indirect accountability.[23] Even though these appointments are, in essence, for life, the Court has never been for long out of step with the political preferences of the popularly elected branches, as most presidents have been able to appoint a sufficient number of justices to obtain a judiciary with compatible policy views.[24] Under a system where judges serve fixed terms and depend upon gubernatorial reappointment or a merit retention election for continued service in office, there can be an even closer correspondence between the ideological bent of the judges and those whom they serve.

Despite the federal experience, however, none of the reasons supporting appointive selection and the principle of indirect accountability withstands close analysis, particularly when "there ought to be a preference in a representative democracy to allow voters directly to name those who head one of the three independent policymaking departments of government."[25]

In the first place, the capability of the nonelective methods to improve the quality of the bench is problematic. As reviewed in Chapter 1, certainly there has been no dramatic and unequivocal evidence that the nonelective methods have produced better judges.[26] But even conceding for purposes of argument that governors and/or merit nominating commissioners may better be situated than voters to collect and evaluate information concerning those attributes of personality, temperament, judgment, and ability which may make for better judges, it is not clear that either of the appointive methods secures indirect accountability. Although partisan appointments are the norm under the merit plan or straight gubernatorial appointment, the accountability achieved is only partial. As noted in Chapter 1, accountability (whether direct or indirect) must be regular and periodic[27] so that citizens can "revise or reverse disfavored policies by replacing those who promulgated them."[28] Under the merit plan, however, the governor's involvement in judicial selection ends with the initial appointment of each judge; newly elected governors can do nothing to remove those judges appointed by predecessors. And the merit retention election does nothing to secure accountability since it does not allow voters to identify judges with their policy preferences, does not present voters with alternatives, and does not structure voter decisions in directions consistent with their political-ideological preferences. As Chapter 1 indicated, the uncontested merit retention format robs voters of all politically relevant voting cues and works inexorably toward the re-election of incumbents.[29]

Under a system of gubernatorial appointment, the chances for indirect accountability are theoretically greater since newly elected governors can replace judges with incompatible policy views. But the achievement of indirect accountability in fact depends upon the willingness of governors to refuse to reappoint sitting judges who do not share their political or ideological bent. And this is often a difficult task in the face of potential charges from the bench, bar, and the press that a governor is "playing politics" with the state's judiciary, basing appointments on partisanship and patronage instead of quality and ability, and selecting judges for their political views when the tasks of judges are supposed to be nonpolitical. In sum, governors are under almost irresistible pressures to reappoint incumbents regardless of their political views.[30] Except on those occasions when a vacancy on the court is opened by the death or retirement of a sitting judge,[31] governors are not totally "free" to act as the conduit for the expression of the political preferences of the majority which placed them in office.[32] Indirect accountability thus may be thwarted under the system of gubernatorial appointment.

Finally, some of the critics of popular judicial selection will find any arguments and evidence concerning the ability of elections to secure the accountability of judges to be irrelevant at best and totally damning at worst. Those who see securing judicial independence as the function of a judicial selection system will view evidence of partisan judicial voting as either inconsequential (since a position for judicial independence should not depend upon the particular patterns of judicial behavior) or a clear indictment of partisan elections in particular as a clear infringement upon the principle of independence. In any event, without beginning a new debate over which method of selection and retention is best suited to preserving the independence of the judiciary, it is clear that the preservation of accountability is best accomplished through the partisan ballot. Some alternative combination of selection and retention may be better suited to the task of maintaining judicial independence.[33]

# 8. Conclusion: The Continuing Debate over State Judicial Selection

THE DEBATE over the best method of selecting state judges has raged for decades. Partisan and nonpartisan elections, utilized by a majority of states, are supported by those observers who believe elections to be the selection method most appropriate for guaranteeing the popular accountability of state judicial policy-makers. Critics assert that elections are fundamentally inconsistent with the principle of judicial independence, which is vital to the process of neutral and impartial judicial decision-making.

At the heart of the debate over judicial selection, therefore, is a conflict between the values of judicial accountability and judicial independence. Unfortunately, no amount of empirical evidence can be collected which might reconcile this normative clash or establish the rightful pre-eminence of one value over the other. But this debate does not end with a disagreement over the fundamental goals of a judicial selection system. Critics charge that popular elections do not result in the recruitment of the best legal talent to staff the state courts. Additionally, say the critics, even if, for the sake of argument, the principle of judicial accountability is conceded, the nature of judicial election contests and the character of the judicial electorate prevent its realization in practice. Opponents of judicial elections argue, therefore, that the emphasis in judicial selection should be upon "quality" and that a "merit" system of selection and retention is best designed to secure the recruitment of the highest quality legal professionals and to prevent their removal solely for political reasons.

Unfortunately, for both the critics and the supporters of judicial elections, there has been a dearth of factual information on the operation and consequences of the various methods of judicial selection. On the other hand, unlike the conflict between the principles of judicial independence and judicial accountability, the results of empirical research can help inform the debate over whether judicial elections are capable of securing the accountability of judges, whether the elective method unnecessarily sacrifices the quality of the bench, and whether the merit plan improves the overall competence of the judiciary.

The defense of popular elections turns substantially on the issue of accountability. The capacity of elections to hold judges accountable is what commends them over the alternative methods of selection. If elections do not perform this essential function, then the balance of arguments may weigh more heavily on the side of the merit plan if some evidence concerning its ability to raise the quality of the bench can be mustered. The focus of this study, therefore, has been upon the collection of empirical evidence which will contribute to the evaluation of judicial elections as mechanisms of accountability.

For all the statewide judicial elections held in nonsouthern states from 1948 to 1974, empirical data concerning the conduct of partisan and nonpartisan judicial elections and the behavior of judicial electorates have been collected and analyzed. The role of governors in making vacancy appointments to these elective courts and the subsequent electoral fortunes of those appointees were also examined. Finally, a study of the patterns of judicial decision-making on selected state supreme courts was undertaken to test the strength of the linkage between systems of judicial selection and judicial behavior; if elections are to be defended as mechanisms for securing popular control over the direction of judicial policy-making, then some general connection between voters and judicial policy-makers must be demonstrable. The basic findings of this research and their applicability to the objections raised by critics of popular judicial elections may now be reviewed briefly.

## VOTER PARTICIPATION IN JUDICIAL ELECTIONS

The low level of voter turnout in state judicial elections is repeatedly cited by critics as leading evidence that voters are not interested in participating in the selection of their judges. Moreover, their indifference and apathy undoubtedly are accompanied by ignorance of the qualities or issue positions of individual candidates seeking seats on the bench.

An analysis of voter turnout in statewide judicial elections, however, revealed that the level of voter participation is not, as the critics have asserted, merely a reflection of the public's lack of interest in selecting judges. Rather, judicial election turnout is very much determined by the same host of factors which affect turnout in other kinds of elections. Because voters are drawn to the polls by the more salient races for president, governor, and the like, the overall level of participation in state judicial elections is largely a function of the position of judicial contests on the tail of the electoral kite. But apart from election scheduling, the most significant finding was the systematic difference in voter participation between partisan elections, on the one hand, and nonpartisan and merit retention elections, on the other, a variance attributable to two distinctions in the conduct of these kinds of elections. First, partisan judicial elections are more frequently contested than nonpartisan elections or, of course, the uncontested merit retention ballotings. The political parties are able on a permanent basis to provide the organizational incentives, the financial support, and the campaign assistance to encourage individuals to seek judicial office. In states utilizing nonpartisan or merit retention systems, no such permanent organizations or regularized channels of recruitment are present to encourage and promote the candidacy of individuals to challenge incumbent judges. The frequency of uncontested elections in nonpartisan systems and the uncontested merit retention ballots depress voter participation; uncontested races are less likely than contested ones to command voter attention.

The second distinction between partisan and nonpartisan—merit retention ballots which accounts for variations in the levels of voter participation is the presence of a meaningful voter cue on the former and its absence on the latter. In low-salience races, such as those for state supreme court justice, the party label is an invaluable decision-making aid. The party label provides voters with a familiar voting cue which promotes their participation even in the absence of specific information about opposing judicial candidates. In the absence of a party label, voters are forced to rely upon less-meaningful voting cues, such as the familiarity of the names on the ballot. In the absence of a meaningful guide to voting, some bewildered voters may become frustrated and simply withdraw from participating in the selection of a judge from between two candidates who mean nothing to them.

## VOTING BEHAVIOR IN JUDICIAL ELECTIONS

Judicial elections are admittedly, therefore, low-salience electoral events. Voters are not drawn to the polls by the contests between candidates for state supreme court. The low visibility of judicial elections means that the voters know very little about the individual candidates for judicial office. And what opportunities there may be for them to become aware of candidate issue stands are severely limited by the formal and informal norms of proper judicial campaign behavior.

Since voters are not likely and probably not able to make choices in judicial races after a careful assessment of the personal qualifications and issue stands of the opposing candidates, they are forced to look for voting cues which will help them cast their votes. Party labels are the most obvious of the voting cues which voters may utilize. Most voters possess some psychological predisposition which draws them to vote for the candidate of one party or the other, a predisposition which assumes heightened importance in low-salience races about which the voter knows little else except the candidates' partisan attachments. Where partisan labels are not available, voters must rely upon other kinds of short-cut guides to voting, such as the incumbency, name familiarity, or ethnic-religious affiliation of the candidate. And where none of these other nonparty cues are meaningful to the individual voter, votes may be cast on the basis of the sex, nickname, or ballot position of the respective candidates, truly arbitrary decision-making tools.

An analysis of the partisan division of the vote by county in partisan, "mixed," and nonpartisan judicial elections confirmed that the partisan ballot structures voting behavior along partisan lines. A careful inspection of the races conducted in the mixed and nonpartisan states between candidates with opposing partisan affiliations revealed that without party labels voters are not able to identify and vote for judicial candidates on the basis of party but must turn to other kinds of voting guides.

As noted in the conclusion to Chapter 3, these results might be used by the opponents of judicial elections as evidence confirming their worst suspicions about judicial elections. At best, they might say, judicial election voters blindly cast their ballots along partisan lines without sober and rational consideration of the qualifications of individual candidates; at worst, truly arbitrary and irrational voting characterizes the elective method of judicial selection. On the other hand, one might argue that though party labels do not contain specific information concerning individual candidates they do allow voters to cast ballots on the basis of a generalization relevant to their own general approaches to the solution of major public policy issues. Moreover, partisan voting in judicial elections is just as "rational" as it is for the election of officials in other kinds of low-salience races, such as those for congress members, lower state executive positions, and state legislative seats.

## JUDICIAL ELECTIONS AND INITIAL ACCESSION TO THE BENCH

A major complaint against the elective method of judicial selection is that a majority of positions on state courts are not filled by election but by appointment. As a result of the lengthy careers served by judges who are repeatedly re-elected, many judges die in office or are forced by advanced age to leave their posts in the middle of a term. These mid-term vacancies are filled by the appointment of the governor, unchecked either immediately by a confirming body or later by the voters. This malfunctioning of the electoral process, according to critics, leads to "one-man judicial selection" and stands as a major barrier to the achievement of the direct popular accountability of the judiciary.

The analysis of the patterns of initial accessions to state supreme courts in the postwar years revealed that, indeed, slightly over half of the judges initially reached the bench by appointment. And long-term electoral security for incumbents undoubtedly contributes a major explanation for the frequency of mid-term vacancies and the concomitant appointment of successors. Incumbent judges are usually re-elected. This is not, however, a damning indictment of the electoral process as it applies to the selection of judges. If the tendency of the electorate to repeatedly return incumbents to office is evidence of the malfunctioning of judicial elections, then a large shadow must also be cast upon elections for executive and legislative officials at all levels of government.

Additionally, significant variation among the states in the proportion of initially appointed judges was detected, ranging from about 25% in some states to over 80% in others. Though precise testing was not possible, the extent to which elective state courts are staffed by gubernatorial appointees appears to be a function not just of the security of tenure for incumbents, but also of the fixed length of judicial terms and, perhaps, the provisions of state retirement laws and pension plans.

Most importantly, the proportion of initially appointed judges was found to be related to the type of judicial selection system. In partisan and "mixed" states, only about 40% of the judges were gubernatorial appointees, but in the states with nonpartisan elections two of every three judges reached the bench by appointment. A large part of the differences between systems was found to be attributable to differences in the extent of electoral competition. As noted earlier, nearly all the elections held in the partisan and mixed states were contested while less than half of those in the nonpartisan states were contested; incumbents were, accordingly, much more vulnerable to electoral defeat in the former than in the latter, less likely to serve lengthy terms on the bench, and less likely to leave the bench in mid-term and necessitate the appointment of a replacement.

## JUDICIAL ELECTIONS AND THE CONTROL OF GUBERNATORIAL APPOINTMENTS

Though gubernatorial appointments are a major aspect of initial selection in both partisan and nonpartisan elective systems, partisan elections allow the electorate the maximum opportunity to maintain control over the process. In making judicial appointments, whether in partisan, mixed, or nonpartisan states, governors usually select individuals who share their partisan affiliation. This selection is made independent of any immediate check which might be imposed by a body charged with confirming gubernatorial appointments. But under certain conditions and circumstances, the electorate has proven itself capable of exercising its power to reject gubernatorial appointees seeking election for the first time.

Where partisan ballots are used, the appointees of "minority party" governors or the rare cross-party appointees of "majority party" governors are nearly always rejected by the voters. Even where nonpartisan ballots are used in the general election, but partisan nominations and accompanying partisan cues are emitted during the campaign, enough voters have been able to cast ballots in ways which result in the rejection of gubernatorial appointees who do not share the long-term partisan affiliation of a majority. In states utilizing nonpartisan systems of nomination and election, however, governors may appoint their fellow partisans with impunity. The electorate is likely neither to remove an appointee who does not share their partisan outlook nor to punish the governor making such an appointment. Indeed, because gubernatorial appointees so often seek election unopposed in the nonpartisan systems, the electorate is only infrequently offered the opportunity to exercise its checking power. When appointees are opposed, the voters have no way of knowing the partisan affiliation of the incumbent or the challenger;

the only voting cue the voters may have is the name familiarity of the incumbent or a ballot label which indicates incumbency. The result is that voters usually stamp their approval upon individuals whom they had no role in naming in the first place and whose general political outlooks remain unknown to them.

## JUDICIAL ELECTIONS AND JUDICIAL BEHAVIOR

Partisan judicial elections, therefore, may have several things to commend them over nonpartisan elections. Partisan elections maximize voter participation in the selection of judges, structure the voting decisions of the electorate in directions relevant to the resolution of political issues, reduce the proportion of gubernatorial vacancy appointments, and enable voters to exercise some control over gubernatorial appointments. Additionally, partisan elections are superior to both nonpartisan elections and nonelective methods of judicial selection as instruments of judicial accountability. Voters could not, of course, hope to influence the direction of judicial policy by casting partisan ballots if the judges selected did not exhibit distinctive decision-making differences along partisan lines. But the results of scalogram and bloc techniques applied to the decisions of state supreme courts, supplemented by evidence produced in previous studies, confirm basic decision-making differences between Democratic and Republican judges on courts selected under partisan nomination and election procedures. Further, however, comparative measures of the extent of partisan voting on nonpartisan and merit plan courts revealed that there is as much partisan decision-making on these courts though there is no formal provision for partisan selection or retention. In the nonpartisan states, governors place fellow partisans in mid-term judicial vacancies. In merit plan systems, the partisan nature of the process by which judicial nominating commissions are staffed, the political dynamics of intracommission deliberations, and the partisan role of the governor in making final selections combine to result in the placement of partisans on the bench. The result of these informal aspects of nonpartisan election and merit selection is as much partisanship on the bench as one observes in the formally partisan selection systems.

The party affiliations of judges do not, as noted repeatedly, explain all the judicial behavior on a state court. But neither does party explain all aspects of the voting behavior of the electorate or all the variations in political behavior generally. If popular control is the objective served by electing public officials, it safely can be said that, in light of previous studies of legislative behavior, partisan elections are about as effective in assisting voters to retrospectively evaluate and prospectively predict the behavior of judges as they are with respect to the selection of legislators and executives. To abandon judicial elections as ineffective instruments of democratic control would logically also require the abandonment of elections for the selection of most nonjudicial officials. Voters may not be able to exercise strict control over governmental policy-making, but in their choice of officials they express their preferences on the direction they wish policy to take. By accepting or rejecting officeholders or candidates associated in general ways with policies, voters can exercise very substantial indirect control upon the exercise of governmental power, whether the governmental arena is executive, legislative, or judicial.

## THE QUESTION OF JUDICIAL QUALITY REVISITED

Even critics willing to concede that partisan elections secure judicial accountability may raise the nagging question of whether the quality of the bench is unduly compromised by popular judicial selection. Of course, not everyone would agree that this crisis of quality is any greater with respect to the judiciary than for the other elected branches or that alternative judicial selection methods are superior to partisan elections in this respect. But even if as a general proposition it is admitted that judicial service requires special technical skills and intellectual abilities, and that partisan elections may not optimize the chances of selecting individuals with these qualities, it may just be a sacrifice that must be offered in exchange for the achievement of institutional accountability.

As discussed in Chapter 3, there has been no shortage of efforts to increase the awareness and knowledge of voters concerning the professional qualifications of those seeking to be elected to judgeships. Though it is by no means clear that they are in fact the result of an objective and detached assessment of professional abilities, bar polls and bar association rankings and endorsements of judicial candidates have been designed ostensibly to help voters choose "more qualified" judges. Voter information materials distributed in pre-election packets are designed for the same purpose. Unfortunately, the low salience of judicial elections makes it most doubtful that these educative efforts have had the intended effects.

One recent reform proposal which combines the bar's concern for professional competence with the elective format calls for prospective judicial candidates to be screened by a panel of lawyers and lay persons before being allowed on the ballot.[1] Versions of this plan vary depending upon the election system in use, but obviously it is designed to merge the merit judicial nominating commission with popular elections. Presumably, those elected would be well qualified for the bench regardless of the voters' eventual choice. Unfortunately, pre-election screening of judicial candidates may present some federal constitutional problems, including possible infringement upon an individual's right to run for elective office and abridgement of the fundamental right to vote by restriction of the range of choice of candidates available to the electorate.[2] Perhaps equally as important, such pre-election screening allows unrepresentative and unaccountable political influences at a critical stage in the selection of public officials.

Perhaps the way to improve voters' attention to the qualifications of those they are voting for is to increase the saliency of judicial elections. And the key to raising the saliency of judicial elections is to stimulate voter perceptions that the outcome of judicial elections will make a difference to their lives. As Grossman has noted, "since judicial candidates rarely attempt an intelligent discussion of issues, the voters are asked to make an impossible choice, to perform a relatively meaningless act,"[3] and thus their lack of interest in and knowledge about judicial elections is hardly surprising.

One possible reform to spur the voters' interest in judicial campaigns and, presumably, their desire to inform themselves about the choices presented, is to allow candidates to present and debate their views on judicial policy questions and their general political and judicial philosophies. Unfortunately, most critics would not advocate such a "politicization" of judicial campaigns even if one of its benefits would be an electorate more interested in informing itself concerning the qualifications of those seeking judgeships. Indeed, in its drive for the adoption of the merit plan, the reform segment of the legal profession has attempted to reduce the debate over judicial selection to the issue of which system is best suited to recruiting individuals who meet the highest standards of professional competence. The political and policy-making dimensions of appellate judicial service have been minimized.

Critics warn that by speaking to specific issues in judicial campaigns candidates would compromise the impartiality of the judiciary or at least the appearance of impartiality upon which public support for the courts ultimately depends. However, as Grossman suggests, a candidate could "endeavor to inform the electorate . . . about his general views on important and controversial social and political issues without announcing or promising how he would decide any particular case that might come before him."[4] Moreover, it is just as likely that a careful debate of judicial policy issues would significantly increase public confidence in the judiciary by exposing "the workings of the [electoral] process and the values of the aspirants" to public view.[5] Programmatic judicial campaigns might invite candidates to pronounce issue positions unrelated to judicial performance,[6] but the questionable relevance of electoral appeals also characterizes nonjudicial elections. With experience, voters would learn to sort out the meaningful from the irrelevant. Indeed, occasional excursions off the campaign platform of relevance may be a price worth paying in order to heighten the attention of voters in the selection of their judges. "If voters are able to perceive that they have a stake in the outcome they are more likely to participate and, at least arguably, choose better judges."[7]

Inasmuch as most attempts to educate a disinterested electorate will be insufficient, considering the pitfalls of giving the legal profession a strategic screening function in the elective process and given the likely resistance of the profession to the politicization of judicial campaigns, judicial elections might just as well be left alone. And though the party label may not help voters to pick the "most qualified" candidate, it nevertheless performs a critical function in structuring voter choice along party lines. Party affiliation serves as the means by which the electorate can maintain control over the third policy-making branch of state government.

## A FINAL NOTE: ON TRIAL AND APPELLATE COURTS

The conclusions of this research necessarily must be limited in their application to the debate over the selection of state appellate judges. Because appellate judges, especially those serving on state courts of last resort, are clearly policy-making officials, the study of the role of elections in maintaining popular accountability is especially appropriate. But the limits imposed by this study do not render unnecessary the need for detailed study of the selection of state trial judges and continued discussion over whether the standards of accountability appropriate for appellate judges apply with equal force to the trial level.

Some commentators have argued that essential differences between trial and appellate courts might justify different selection methods for the judges sitting at different levels. As Barber notes, "the trial judge and the appellate judge differ in role, tasks, working procedures, and prestige," differences which might justify the election of higher court judges but some other method of selection, such as the merit plan, for trial judges who require greater insulation from improper political influences.[8]

Not only do appellate courts engage in more-frequent and explicit instances of policy-making than trial judges, but judges at the higher level "are subject to fewer pressures for political favors, in fact have fewer favors to dispense, make collegial decisions so that one judge cannot control the outcome of a case, and tend to be insulated from politics by the 'aura of power, dignity, and remoteness' of the appellate environment."[9] At the trial level, however, individual judges are engaged primarily in the disposition of particular controversies where "the potential for partiality and personality is greater" than at the appellate court level.[10] Trial judges also possess more patronage at their disposal which they may use to reward campaign supporters and to secure political allies.[11] At this level, therefore, elections bring into play what some have called the "extractive" aspects of politics based on a "concern for jobs, contracts, power, and patronage, characteristics unrelated to the making of policy."[12] Indeed, it was precisely these kinds of abuses connected with the elective trial courts in the nation's major metropolitan areas that initially sparked the ultimately widespread dissatisfaction with popular elections. It has been argued, therefore, that the merit system is best suited for the selection of trial judges, providing them with the security of tenure necessary to resist the political pressures that test their impartiality.[13]

Although strong reasons might exist to support the popular election of appellate judges and the merit selection of trial judges, the trend in state judicial selection reform has been in the opposite direction. The merit plan has been most frequently adopted at the appellate level, while popular elections have remained predominant for the selection of trial judges. The reasons for this are many and not crucial here.[14] What is important is the fact that the merit plan is most prevalent and continues to make its greatest inroads upon popular elections in the selection of judges to sit on state supreme courts.[15] Thus, although limited to the analysis of supreme court elections, this study assumes particular importance in the continuing debate over state judicial selection.

# Appendixes

**Appendix I. Percentage Distribution of Nonunanimous Cases in Selected States, by Issue Area**

| States | Total No. of Cases | Criminal Appeals | Domestic Cases | Economic Distribution | Government Regulation | Civil Liberties | Residual Category |
|---|---|---|---|---|---|---|---|
| Colorado (1962–1964) | 68 | 17.6% | 7.4% | 25.0% | 26.5% | 0.0% | 23.5% |
| (1965–1966) | 49 | 28.6% | 6.1% | 32.7% | 26.6% | 0.0% | 6.1% |
| (1967–1968) | 31 | 22.6% | 6.5% | 48.4% | 19.4% | 0.0% | 3.2% |
| Indiana (1963–1965) | 98 | 48.0% | 12.2% | 12.2% | 14.3% | 1.0% | 12.2% |
| (1969–1970) | 138 | 71.0% | 6.5% | 8.0% | 10.1% | 2.2% | 2.2% |
| (1971–1972) | 105 | 69.5% | 1.9% | 8.6% | 12.4% | 4.8% | 2.9% |
| Iowa (1972–1974) | 80 | 33.7% | 11.2% | 40.0% | 7.6% | 2.5% | 5.0% |
| Kansas (1972–1974) | 108 | 21.3% | 8.3% | 49.1% | 12.0% | 3.7% | 5.6% |
| Pennsylvania (1972–1974) | 318 | 52.5% | 9.7% | 11.6% | 11.0% | 3.1% | 11.9% |
| Utah (1960–1966) | 124 | 10.5% | 20.2% | 41.1% | 16.9% | 0.0% | 11.3% |
| (1967–1970) | 148 | 18.9% | 11.5% | 44.6% | 13.5% | 1.4% | 10.1% |
| Washington (1963–1967) | 115 | 17.4% | 6.9% | 33.9% | 23.5% | 0.0% | 18.3% |
| (1973–1974) | 74 | 25.7% | 2.7% | 24.3% | 20.3% | 12.2% | 14.9% |
| Wisconsin (1968–1974) | 133 | 39.1% | 3.0% | 30.8% | 12.8% | 11.3% | 3.0% |

## Appendix II. Scale Coefficients

Below are listed the values of the Coefficient of Reproducibility (CR) and the Coefficient of Scalability (S) achieved when Guttman scaling analysis was applied to the decisions of eight state supreme courts in four major areas of law. These scales form the basis for the discussion of judicial voting behavior on these courts presented in Chapter 6.

In each case area below, the value of CR is presented first, followed by the value of S. Generally, analysts consider values of 0.900 for CR or 0.600 for S to be the minimum acceptable levels for the identification of a valid scale.

| State | Criminal Appeals | Economic Distribution | Government Regulation | Civil Liberties |
|---|---|---|---|---|
| Colorado (1962–1964) | 0.866/0.607 | 0.851/0.630 | 0.843/0.587 | — |
| (1965–1966) | 0.894/0.643 | 0.906/0.730 | 0.922/0.741 | — |
| (1967–1968) | 0.917/0.667 | 0.863/0.588 | 0.846/0.538 | — |
| Indiana (1963–1965) | 0.987/0.750 | 0.881/0.720 | 0.838/0.450 | — |
| (1969–1970) | 0.967/0.797 | 0.889/0.684 | 0.843/0.522 | — |
| (1971–1972) | 0.931/0.709 | 0.844/0.650 | 0.857/0.591 | — |
| Iowa (1972–1974) | 0.844/0.533 | 0.806/0.449 | 0.870/0.588 | — |
| Kansas (1972–1974) | 0.856/0.610 | 0.813/0.511 | 0.856/0.458 | — |
| Pennsylvania (1972–1974) | 0.923/0.719 | 0.933/0.685 | 0.797/0.489 | 0.841/0.522 |
| Utah (1960–1966) | 0.841/0.615 | 0.862/0.527 | 0.845/0.568 | — |
| (1967–1970) | 0.838/0.488 | 0.835/0.486 | 0.809/0.500 | — |
| Washington (1963–1967) | 0.801/0.426 | 0.874/0.449 | 0.800/0.392 | — |
| (1973–1974) | 0.893/0.609 | 0.834/0.522 | 0.798/0.409 | 0.945/0.778 |
| Wisconsin (1968–1974) | 0.967/0.824 | 0.867/0.631 | 0.866/0.644 | 0.914/0.679 |

# Notes

## 1. Judicial Elections and the Debate over State Judicial Selection

1. For more-detailed and specific historical accounts, see Evan Haynes, *The Selection and Tenure of Judges*; and Glenn R. Winters, "The Merit Plan for Judicial Selection and Tenure: Its Historical Development," in *Judicial Selection and Tenure*, ed. Glenn R. Winters, pp. 29–44.
2. Burton M. Atkins, "Judicial Elections: What the Evidence Shows," *Florida Bar Journal* 50, no. 3 (March 1976): 152.
3. For a comparison of merit plans currently in use, see Burton M. Atkins, "Merit Selection of State Judges," *Florida Bar Journal* 50, no. 4 (April 1976): 203–207.
4. This is true in every state except Illinois, where judges must obtain an extraordinary majority of 60% of the votes cast to retain office. A court challenge to this provision on federal equal protection grounds was rejected in *Lefkovits* v. *State Board of Elections*, 400 F. Supp. 1005 (N.D. Ill., 1975), affirmed 424 U.S. 901 (1976).
5. The experience of the merit plan in Missouri has been exhaustively studied by Richard A. Watson and Rondal G. Downing, *The Politics of the Bench and the Bar*.
6. In 1976, twelve states were using partisan elections and thirteen states were using nonpartisan elections for the initial selection of their supreme court justices. Seven states staffed their high courts by gubernatorial appointment and five by legislative election. Many states use different methods for the initial selection and subsequent retention of their judges. Moreover, many states use different selection methods to fill judgeships at the various levels of their court systems. The details of specific selection plans used in each state can be found in Sari S. Escovitz (compiler), *Judicial Selection and Tenure*, a pamphlet published by the American Judicature Society, 1975. The compilation reported here is based on the results of a recent unpublished survey made available to me by the American Judicature Society.
7. R. Stanley Lowe, "Voluntary Merit Selection Plans," *Judicature* 55, no. 4 (November 1971): 161–168.

8. This calculation is based upon the unpublished survey by the American Judicature Society (see n. 6).

9. The repeated reference here to "the critics" is not meant to pejoratively label those who have opposed popular judicial selection. Nor is it meant to portray a singularly united and monolithic corps dedicated to abolishing judicial elections. What follows is a composite of the various arguments which have been leveled against judicial elections, one which fully recognizes that few of the opponents make such a comprehensive attack. By the ordering of the arguments presented, I have attempted to give appropriate emphasis to those points considered by "the critics" to be the most fundamental and serious and to distinguish their more secondary or casual concerns about elective judicial selection. Since most of the opponents of judicial elections raise many of the same arguments, it would be quite impossible to assign credit to any one author for a specific point. A representative sample of the criticisms of judicial elections can be found in Winters (ed.), *Judicial Selection and Tenure*. The references noted hereafter draw, for illustrative purposes, from the judicial selection literature produced since 1948, but the basic arguments were offered originally much earlier. Some of the most persuasive postwar writing in opposition to judicial elections has been offered by a former associate justice of the Texas Supreme Court. See W. St. John Garwood, "Judicial Revision: An Argument for the Merit Plan for Judicial Selection and Tenure," *Texas Tech Law Review* 5 (1973–74): 1–19; idem, "Popular Election of Judges Is Not Sacrosanct," *Florida Bar Journal* 38 (June 1964): 349–355; idem, "Democracy and the Popular Election of Judges: An Argument," *Southwestern Law Journal* 16 (1962): 216–243.

10. Garwood, "Democracy and the Popular Election of Judges," p. 234.

11. Dorothy W. Nelson, "Variations on a Theme: Selection and Tenure of Judges," *Southern California Law Review* 36 (1962–63): 31.

12. This statement is attributed to Fred L. Williams, a former judge of the Missouri Supreme Court, by Jack Peltason, "Merits and Demerits of the Missouri Court Plan," in *Judicial Selection and Tenure*, ed. Winters, pp. 96–97.

13. Watson and Downing, *The Politics of the Bench and the Bar*, p. 331.

14. Ibid., p. 352.

15. Ibid., pp. 43–48.

16. These restrictions are outlined by Allan Ashman and James J. Alfini, *The Key to Judicial Merit Selection*, pp. 72–74.

17. The following discussion is based upon the analysis by Watson and Downing, *The Politics of the Bench and the Bar*, pp. 19–43.

18. Ibid., p. 43.

19. Ibid., p. 33.

20. Ibid., p. 43.

21. Ashman and Alfini, *The Key to Judicial Merit Selection*, pp. 75–76.

22. The political relationship between the nominating commission and the governor is discussed by Watson and Downing, *The Politics of the*

*Bench and the Bar*, pp. 101–109. Other evidence I have collected appears to suggest that, at least at the supreme court level, governors are usually able to appoint individuals sharing their partisan affiliation and do so a large percentage of the time. For the states of Kansas, Iowa, and Colorado, the appointees under the merit plan through 1974 shared the appointing governor's party affiliation in 100%, 90.9%, and 100%, respectively, of the cases. In Alaska and Missouri, the governor and his appointee have been of the same party in 72.7% and 75.0% of the appointments.

23. Warren Burnett, "Observations on the Direct Election Method of Judicial Selection," *Texas Law Review* 44, no. 6 (June 1966): 1100–1101.
24. James H. Guterman and Errol E. Meidinger, *In the Opinion of the Bar*, p. 11.
25. Watson and Downing, *The Politics of the Bench and the Bar*, p. 293.
26. *A.B.A. Code of Professional Responsibility*, Canon 8, EC 8–6.
27. Maurice Rosenberg, "The Qualities of Justice—Are They Strainable?" *Texas Law Review* 44 (June 1966): 1063–1080.
28. Ashman and Alfini, *The Key to Judicial Merit Selection*, pp. 61–63.
29. Ibid., pp. 64–65.
30. Ibid., pp. 66–68.
31. Ibid., p. 193.
32. Otto B. Mullinax, "Judicial Revision: An Argument against the Merit Plan for Judicial Selection and Tenure," *Texas Tech Law Review* 5 (1973–74): 29.
33. Watson and Downing, *The Politics of the Bench and the Bar*, pp. 272–308, especially pp. 282–289.
34. Herbert Jacob, "The Effect of Institutional Differences in the Recruitment Process: The Case of State Judges," *Journal of Public Law* 13, no. 1 (1964): 104–114.
35. Bradley C. Canon, "The Impact of Formal Selection Processes on the Characteristics of Judges—Reconsidered," *Law and Society Review* 6 (May 1972): 579–593. See also Walter A. Borowiec, "Pathways to the Top: The Political Careers of State Supreme Court Justices," *North Carolina Central Law Journal* 7 (Spring 1976): 280–285; and Larry L. Berg et al., "The Consequences of Judicial Reform: A Comparative Analysis of the California and Iowa Appellate Systems," *Western Political Quarterly* 28 (June 1975): 263–280.
36. Canon, "The Impact of Formal Selection Processes," p. 588.
37. Watson and Downing, *The Politics of the Bench and the Bar*, pp. 302–304.
38. Ibid., p. 225.
39. American Judicature Society, "Merit Retention Elections in 1972," *Judicature* 58 (January 1973): 252.
40. William Jenkins, Jr., "Retention Elections: Who Wins When No One Loses?" *Judicature* 61 (August 1977): 80.
41. Mullinax, "Judicial Revision," pp. 32–33.
42. Burnett, "Observations on the Direct Election Method," p. 1099. Bur-

nett attributes these quotations to Judge Tom Stovall, "Judicial Babies and Constitutional Storks," *Texas Bar Journal* 26 (1963):256.

43. Jenkins, "Retention Elections," p. 84, quotes an Arizona political journalist as saying that incumbent judges are virtually assured re-election on the merit retention ballot "short of committing incest at high noon at Central and Van Buren."

44. Watson and Downing, *The Politics of the Bench and the Bar*, p. 225.

45. Both the results in Missouri reported by Watson and Downing, ibid., p. 225, and those by Jenkins, "Retention Elections," p. 86, support this contention.

46. Watson and Downing, *The Politics of the Bench and the Bar*, p. 223.

47. Jenkins, "Retention Elections," pp. 83–86.

48. Watson and Downing, *The Politics of the Bench and the Bar*, p. 225.

49. Jenkins, "Retention Elections," p. 86.

50. "Note: Judicial Selection in North Dakota: Is Constitutional Revision Necessary?" *North Dakota Law Review* 48 (1971–72):334.

51. See Glenn R. Winters (ed.), *Judicial Discipline and Removal*.

52. Lewis Mayers, *The American Legal System*, p. 386.

53. American Bar Association, Section of Judicial Administration, *The Improvement of the Administration of Justice*, p. 45.

54. See the American Bar Association's *Code of Judicial Conduct*, Canon 7 (B) (2), governing the solicitation of judicial campaign funds. On means of financing judicial election campaigns, see Robert A. White, "New Approach to Financing Judicial Campaigns," *American Bar Association Journal* 59 (December 1973):1429–1430.

55. Mayers, *The American Legal System*, p. 387.

56. Rosenberg, "The Qualities of Justice," p. 1069.

57. Garwood, "Democracy and the Popular Election of Judges," p. 229.

58. Richard A. Watson, "Judging the Judges," *Judicature* 53 (February 1970): 283–285.

59. Kathleen L. Barber, "Selection of Ohio Appellate Judges: A Case Study in Invisible Politics," in *Political Behavior and Public Issues in Ohio*, ed. John J. Gargan and James G. Coke, p. 182.

60. Jack Peltason, *Federal Courts in the Political Process*, p. 3.

61. Donald Horowitz, "The Courts as Guardians of the Public Interest," *Public Administration Review* 37, no. 2 (1977):151–154.

62. Reapportionment cases, for example, present issues of clear partisan conflict and interest. See the study by Kathleen L. Barber, "Partisan Values in the Lower Courts: Reapportionment in Ohio and Michigan," *Case Western Reserve Law Review* 20 (February 1969):401–421.

63. Nelson, "Variations on a Theme," p. 6.

64. An excellent collection of writings on the subject is Leonard Levy (ed.), *Judicial Review and the Supreme Court*. The debate over judicial review is superbly analyzed by Levy in the opening essay, "Judicial Review, History, and Democracy: An Introduction," pp. 1–42.

65. Ibid., p. 15.

66. Ibid., p. 1.

67. Francis D. Wormuth and S. Grover Rich, Jr., "Politics, the Bar, and the Selection of Judges," *Utah Law Review* 3 (Fall 1953):465.
68. Ibid., p. 462.
69. Eugene Rostow, "The Democratic Character of Judicial Review," in *Judicial Review and the Supreme Court*, ed. Levy, p. 91.
70. This expression is suggested by Levy, ibid., p. 24.
71. Ibid., p. 38.
72. See Robert A. Dahl, "Decision-Making in a Democracy: The Supreme Court as a National Policy-Maker," *Journal of Public Law* 6 (Fall 1957): 279–295.
73. Henry Steele Commager, "Judicial Review and Democracy," in *Judicial Review and the Supreme Court*, ed. Levy, p. 68.
74. Burton M. Atkins and Henry R. Glick, "Environmental and Structural Variables as Determinants of Issues in State Courts of Last Resort," *American Journal of Political Science* 20 (February 1976):97–115. For 1966, civil liberties cases consumed an average of only 1.7% of state court dockets, ranging from a low of 0% in several states to a high of 5.7% in Delaware.
75. James Willard Hurst, *The Growth of American Law*, pp. 134–138.
76. Robert F. Drinan, "Judicial Appointments for Life by the Executive Branch of Government: Reflections on the Massachusetts Experience," *Texas Law Review* 44 (June 1966):1103.
77. Less than a handful of states provide for their state supreme court judges to serve life terms or the equivalent. Judges in Massachusetts and Rhode Island serve life terms, judges in New Hampshire serve a term expiring when age seventy is reached, and New Jersey's judges are appointed for an initial seven-year term and then reappointed to life terms.
78. In 1974, the mean length of term for judges serving on state supreme courts was nearly eight years, ranging from a low of six years to a high of fifteen years.
79. Gerald M. Pomper, *Elections in America*.
80. See Richard W. Boyd, "Popular Control of Public Policy: A Normal Vote Analysis of the 1968 Election," *American Political Science Review* 66 (June 1972):443–444.
81. Pomper, *Elections in America*, p. 38.
82. Angus Campbell et al., *The American Voter*, pp. 169–187.
83. See the discussion and accompanying citations in Gerald M. Pomper, *Voters' Choice*, p. 8.
84. Bernard R. Berelson et al., *Voting*, pp. 305–323.
85. Pomper, *Elections in America*, especially in Chap. 2, pp. 32–40.
86. E. E. Schattschneider, *The Semi-Sovereign People*, p. 139.
87. See Pomper's discussion of the problem of electoral results serving as mandates for the implementation of specific policies in *Elections in America*, pp. 246–252.
88. Ibid., pp. 25–32.
89. Ibid., p. 67.
90. Ibid., p. 96.

91. Ibid., pp. 68–98, especially pp. 92–98.
92. Campbell et al., *The American Voter*, pp. 216–265.
93. Pomper, *Elections in America*, p. 96.
94. Ibid., pp. 257–263.
95. Norman H. Nie et al., *The Changing American Voter*, p. 347.
96. The scholarly literature supporting the importance of party affiliation in subpresidential elections is discussed in Chap. 3.
97. John L. Sullivan and Robert E. O'Connor, "Electoral Choice and Popular Control of Public Policy: The Case of the 1966 House Elections," *American Political Science Review* 66 (December 1972): 1257.
98. Herbert Jacob, "Judicial Insulation: Elections, Direct Participation, and Public Attention to the Courts in Wisconsin," *Wisconsin Law Review*, no. 3 (1976), p. 808.

## 2. Turnout in State Judicial Elections

1. See, for example, Stephen E. Lee, "Judicial Selection and Tenure in Arizona," *Law and the Social Order* (1973), p. 59, n. 22; and Kathleen L. Barber, "Ohio Judicial Elections: Nonpartisan Premises with Partisan Results," *Ohio State Law Journal* 32 (Fall 1971): 770–774.
2. Richard A. Watson and Rondal G. Downing, *The Politics of the Bench and the Bar*, p. 226, n. 39.
3. Allen T. Klots, "The Selection of Judges and the Short Ballot," in *Judicial Selection and Tenure*, ed. Winters, pp. 80–81.
4. The most recent published surveys are Charles A. Johnson et al., "Salience of Judicial Candidates and Elections," *Social Science Quarterly* 59 (September 1978): 371–378; and Cynthia Owen Philip et al., *Where Do Judges Come From?* pp. 90–106. The level of voter knowledge about judicial elections is given more detailed attention in Chap. 3.
5. Jack Ladinsky and Allan Silver, "Popular Democracy and Judicial Independence: Electorate and Elite Reactions to Two Wisconsin Supreme Court Elections," *Wisconsin Law Review*, no. 1 (1967), p. 132.
6. The only published study is David Adamany and Philip Dubois, "Electing State Judges," *Wisconsin Law Review*, no. 3 (1976), pp. 731–779. Among the unpublished works are Susan Blackmore Hannah, "An Evaluation of Judicial Elections in Michigan, 1948–1968," Ph.D. dissertation, Michigan State University (1972); and Burton Atkins and Michael McDonald, "Electoral Rule Changes and Voter Participation in Judicial Elections: A Longitudinal Analysis of the Florida Supreme Court," paper prepared for delivery at the 1977 meeting of the Florida Political Science Association.
7. Adamany and Dubois, "Electing State Judges."
8. Atkins and McDonald, "Electoral Rule Changes," pp. 17–18.
9. The leading work of this voluminous literature is, of course, Campbell et al., *The American Voter*, especially pp. 89–115.
10. See Lester Milbrath, "Individuals and Government," in *Politics in the American States*, ed. Herbert Jacob and Kenneth N. Vines, pp. 42–43.

11. For a critical discussion of this approach, see Jae-On Kim et al., "Voter Turnout among the American States: Systemic and Individual Components," *American Political Science Review* 69 (March 1975): 107–109.

12. Several studies have examined the impact of registration requirements upon the level of voting turnout in national and local elections. The leading one is Stanley Kelley, Jr., et al, "Registration and Voting: Putting First Things First," *American Political Science Review* 61 (June 1967): 359–377.

13. Robert H. Blank, "State Electoral Structure," *Journal of Politics* 35 (November 1973): 988–994.

14. The literature linking electoral competition to voting turnout is discussed later in this chapter.

15. Lester W. Milbrath, *Political Participation*, p. 96.

16. Ibid., pp. 101–102.

17. Milbrath, "Individuals and Government," p. 35, Table 2.

18. Ibid., pp. 35–36. Milbrath reports, for example, that from 1948 to 1968, turnout in state elections for the U.S. House of Representatives held concurrently with the presidential election trailed the turnout in the presidential races by from 2.4% to 6.2% (computed from Table 2, p. 35).

19. Ibid., pp. 36–37. Turnout in mid-term gubernatorial and U.S. Senate races averages about 15–20% below presidential election turnout.

20. Studies of voter turnout in primary elections include V. O. Key, Jr., *American State Politics*, pp. 134–136; Malcolm E. Jewell, "Voting Turnout in State Gubernatorial Primaries," *Western Political Quarterly* 30 (June 1977): 236–254; and Austin Ranney, "Turnout and Representation in Presidential Primary Elections," *American Political Science Review* 66 (March 1972): 21–24.

21. There is no systematic evidence to support this point, but examples from specific states are consistent with it. In California, for instance, see John R. Owens et al., *California Politics and Parties*, p. 58 (Table 3–1), pp. 72–74, p. 95 (Table 3–4), p. 98 (Table 4–1).

22. Austin Ranney and Leon D. Epstein, "The Two Electorates: Voters and Nonvoters in a Wisconsin Primary," *Journal of Politics* 28 (August 1966): 601–602; Austin Ranney, "The Representativeness of Primary Electorates," *Midwest Journal of Political Science* 12 (May 1968): 237.

23. Austin Ranney, "Parties in State Politics," in *Politics in the American States*, ed. Jacob and Vines, p. 97.

24. Albert K. Karnig and B. Oliver Walter, "Municipal Elections: Registration, Incumbent Success, and Voter Participation," in *The Municipal Yearbook* (1977), pp. 68–71.

25. Robert R. Alford and Eugene C. Lee, "Voting Turnout in American Cities," *American Political Science Review* 62 (September 1968): 796–813.

26. Eugene C. Lee, "City Elections: A Statistical Profile," in *The Municipal Yearbook* (1963), p. 83. See also idem, *The Politics of Nonpartisanship*, pp. 134–136; and Howard D. Hamilton, "The Municipal Voter: Voting and Nonvoting in City Elections," *American Political Science Review* 65 (December 1971): 1135–1140.

27. Lee, "City Elections," p. 83; Karnig and Walter, "Municipal Elections," p. 70.
28. V. O. Key, Jr., *Politics, Parties, and Pressure Groups*, p. 646.
29. The effects of the different ballot forms upon the ability of voters to complete their ballots are discussed later in this chapter. The leading study is Jack L. Walker, "Ballot Forms and Voter Fatigue: An Analysis of the Office Block and Party Column Ballots," *Midwest Journal of Political Science* 10 (November 1966): 448–463.
30. Hannah, "An Evaluation of Judicial Elections in Michigan," Chap. 2.
31. Ibid., p. 62, Fig. 2.3. In contrast, from 92% to 98% of those participating in the top statewide election voted in the race for Congress and 94% to 97% cast ballots in the state legislative races (pp. 62–63).
32. Ibid., p. 130. The rank-order correlation between turnout in supreme court elections and competitiveness was −0.316 indicating, contrary to the usual hypothesis, that as competition increased, turnout decreased, a phenomenon inconsistent with the major propositions of voting behavior.
33. Adamany and Dubois, "Electing State Judges," pp. 742–746. The states studied were New York, Pennsylvania, Michigan, Ohio, and Wisconsin.
34. Ibid., pp. 744–745, especially Table 2.
35. Ibid., p. 745.
36. Ibid., p. 742. Mean turnout in Wisconsin's judicial elections was usually about 26%, but those held concurrently with the presidential primary witnessed mean turnout of 38%.
37. Ibid., p. 742. In only five of the supreme court elections held in nonpresidential years from 1946 to 1973 did the turnout rise above 30%. In every case, highly controversial referenda coincided with the supreme court balloting. "Such issues as tax-supported transportation of parochial school students, reapportionment, the length of sheriff's terms, the elimination of a two-term limit for sheriffs, and a state lottery were all apparently more interesting to voters than supreme court contests, and these issues drew voters to the polls who incidentally voted for supreme court justice."
38. Ibid., p. 743. In competitive races held in nonpresidential years, the mean turnout was 26%; in noncompetitive races where the winning judicial candidate captured more than 60% of the vote or was unopposed, mean turnout was 25%, a difference of only 1%. Highly contested presidential primaries, however, jumped the judicial election turnout over the 40% mark.
39. As previous studies have done, the estimates of turnout used here are based upon the number of individuals casting valid ballots in each election as a proportion of the population in each state of voting age. Election returns by county were gathered for the years 1948 to 1974 for the offices of president, U.S. senator, governor, and state supreme court justice. In many instances, state election returns were reprinted in published state manuals or election pamphlets on file in the Wisconsin Historical Society Library. In other cases, election returns were secured

directly from the office in each state with the primary responsibility for the conduct of statewide elections, usually that of the secretary of state. Estimates of the voting-age population for each state are published periodically by the Bureau of the Census in the biennial editions of the *Statistical Abstract of the United States*. Readers interested in the specific estimates used and special data manipulations required in the calculation of turnout in some states should see Philip L. Dubois, "Judicial Elections in the States: Patterns and Consequences," Ph.D. dissertation, University of Wisconsin (1978), pp. 480–481, n. 56.

40. Initially, the eleven southern states of the Confederacy were excluded because of the unique characteristics of the politics and population of that region during most of the period of this study (see V. O. Key, *Southern Politics*, pp. 491–508). Since most of the southern states employ partisan judicial elections, this exclusion is somewhat serious. But a sufficient number of nonsouthern states have utilized partisan judicial elections in the postwar period to allow an analysis of voter participation under this ballot form. Moreover, the exclusion of the southern states prevents spurious inferences due to the coincidence of region and judicial election system.

    Every nonsouthern state employing *statewide* judicial elections during some or all of the 1948–1974 period was included. A full listing of these states by election system can be found in Tables 6, 7, and 8. States switching their judicial election systems during the period are listed more than once.

    Three states (Maryland, Nebraska, Oklahoma) were excluded because their elections for state supreme court justice are (or were) conducted by district. Additionally, merit retention elections first held in 1974 in Wyoming and Montana (following a 1972 change in each state from nonpartisan elections to the merit plan) were excluded, considered too few in number for meaningful analysis.

    One final caveat concerns the election returns of South Dakota. In 1960, the state legislature provided that county election officials need count only one ballot in uncontested elections. Some counties took advantage of this time- and money-saving provision while others counted all the votes cast. An inspection of the returns after 1960 reveals that the *reported* turnout was cut by half by the new vote-counting procedure. Thus, only those elections held from 1948 to 1958 are included here.

41. Kim et al., "Voter Turnout among the American States," pp. 107–123; and Robert H. Blank, "Socio-Economic Determinism of Voting Turnout: A Challenge," *Journal of Politics* 36 (August 1974): 732–752.

42. Compare the range of voter turnout in the 1968 presidential election in nonsouthern states—from 76.9% in Utah to 43.6% in Arizona. The average turnout for gubernatorial and senatorial races in nonpresidential years from 1952 to 1960 ranged from 64.6% in Idaho to 43.5% in Arizona. See Milbrath, "Individuals and Government," pp. 38–39 (Table 4) and p. 36 (Table 3).

43. The labels "core" and "peripheral" voters were developed by Angus Campbell as part of his "surge and decline" theory to explain short-term fluctuations in turnout and the partisan direction of the vote. See his "Surge and Decline: A Study of Electoral Change," in *Elections and the Political Order*, ed. Angus Campbell et al., pp. 40–62.
44. Ibid., p. 42.
45. Ibid., p. 43.
46. The exception is Nevada where mean turnout in the mid-term years exceeded the mean presidential year turnout by 1.7%. When the dampening effects of uncontested races upon turnout are removed, however (see the discussion later in this chapter), presidential-year judicial election turnout in Nevada does exceed the mid-term level of participation as expected.
47. The "major partisan office" is defined as the presidential, gubernatorial, or U.S. senatorial contest which attracted the most voters in each election year.
48. Campbell et al., *The American Voter*, pp. 85–115.
49. Andrew T. Cowart, "Electoral Choice in the American States: Incumbency Effects, Partisan Forces, and Divergent Partisan Majorities," *American Political Science Review* 67 (September 1973): 835.
50. Barber, "Ohio Judicial Elections," p. 776.
51. As a rule, the difference in participation caused by an uncontested balloting is greater in the partisan than in the nonpartisan states. Though uncontested ballotings are of little importance theoretically, ballot forms probably explain much of this difference. In both Iowa and New Mexico, the partisan ballot is equipped with a device to allow a straight ticket vote in a single motion. When a judicial race on the ballot goes uncontested (i.e., when only one party column has a candidate for the supreme court), voters who pull the party lever on the voting machine or mark the party circle on the paper ballot in the column of the party *not* offering a judicial candidate have their ballots in the supreme court race go unrecorded; there is simply no candidate in the column for which their vote can be registered. In the nonpartisan states, the judicial balloting is entirely separate from the partisan ballot; voters are usually warned specifically on the ballot that the nonpartisan ballot has no connection with the party ballot used for the selection of partisan officials or with the straight party circles or levers and that individual voting choices must be made separately. When voters do not cast a vote in an uncontested race on the nonpartisan judicial ballot, it is not an artifact of "unrecorded" votes.
52. Among the partisan states studied here, Indiana, Iowa, and New York (until 1967) used party conventions to nominate judicial candidates. Colorado, Utah, and New York (after 1967) used preprimary nominating conventions to select or endorse candidates to compete in party primaries. The remaining states used partisan primaries only.

The high proportion of uncontested races in Table 3 for the New York

Court of Appeals deserves some attention. These races were not "uncontested" in the usual sense of the word. Rather, these elections involved single candidates who received the nomination of both major parties in the state. Listed on the ballot as the nominee of each party, a candidate actually runs against himself for election. This is due to an informal tradition observed by the parties to give joint support to any previously elected incumbent seeking re-election. In any event, only those elections actually contested between two or more different candidates were included in the analysis of judicial election participation in New York.

53. It is recognized, of course, that the strength of parties in recruiting candidates and in influencing the conduct of the direct primary varies across states and within states with the level of the office being contested. On the incentives and rewards at the disposal of party organizations to secure party workers and to recruit candidates for political office, see Frank Sorauf, *Party Politics in America*, pp. 86–98; on the party's role in the direct primary, see pp. 217–223.

54. All but three of the nonpartisan states studied here nominate the supreme court candidates by nonpartisan primaries. In Michigan, judicial candidates run on nonpartisan general election ballots following nomination by partisan conventions. In Ohio and Arizona (until the merit plan was adopted in 1974), party primaries are used. The party convention system used in Michigan has, as Table 3 indicates, guaranteed that each election will be contested. Similarly, in Ohio, nearly 90% of the general elections have been contested. In contrast, nearly 60% of Arizona's judicial elections from 1948 to 1974 went uncontested. According to one observer of Arizona judicial politics, the central reason is, as one might suspect, that the parties played only a minor role in recruiting and endorsing candidates for the primary. "Apparently, the parties [did] not [believe] it necessary to fill their slates by offering candidates for judicial posts, and in many primaries, one party or the other offer[ed] no candidates for available judicial positions" (see Lee, "Judicial Selection and Tenure in Arizona," pp. 54–56, 68).

55. These hypotheses about the effects of ballot form upon voter fatigue were originally explored by Walker, "Ballot Forms and Voter Fatigue," pp. 448–463.

56. See Angus Campbell and Warren E. Miller, "The Motivational Basis of Straight and Split Ticket Voting," *American Political Science Review* 51 (June 1957): 299–300.

57. It seems most likely that it is the device which allows a straight party vote and not the party column format per se which contributes to the reduction of roll-off from the top of the ballot. Walker demonstrates that in Montana a switch from the party column ballot to an office block format actually resulted in a *reduction* of voter fatigue. But Montana's party column ballot did not include a device for straight party voting; voters who wanted to vote a party line still had to make a number of

separate marks all along the party column. And the office block format which was adopted contained clearly stated voting instructions to guide the voter through the ballot, thus reducing voter confusion and fatigue.

58. As Walker noted, it is important to realize that there are a number of variations of the basic ballot forms which may facilitate or impede the completion of the ballot, including the relative clarity of instructions to the voters (see n. 57). This observation is equally applicable to this analysis.

59. Walker, "Ballot Forms and Voter Fatigue."

60. Ibid., pp. 456–457, especially Table 4.

61. Ibid., pp. 460–461.

62. Campbell, "Surge and Decline," pp. 52–53.

63. Ibid., pp. 58–59, especially Table 3–5. A recalculation of Campbell's tabular data shows that 10% of the peripheral voters reported failing to vote a complete ticket, compared to only 2% of the core voters.

64. See Walker, "Ballot Forms and Voter Fatigue," p. 451, nn. 9–10; Sorauf, *Party Politics in America*, pp. 195, 241. See also Norman C. Thomas, "Voting Machines and Voter Participation in Four Michigan Constitutional Revision Referenda," *Western Political Quarterly* 21 (September 1968):409–419.

65. Again, the extent to which voting machines are used might affect the amount of roll-off from the top of the partisan ballot to the nonpartisan judicial contests. See n. 64.

66. It cannot go without mention that, apart from whether or not the nonpartisan judicial ballot is physically separated from the partisan general election ballot, the states vary significantly with respect to other details of the judicial ballot, most particularly the clarity of the printed instructions designed to help voters complete the ballot. For examples of some of these variations, see Dubois, "State Judicial Elections," pp. 489–490, n. 94.

67. Explaining the variations among the states in the amount of increased roll-off in presidential years over mid-term years is not such an easy task. Part of the variation may be accounted for by the scheduling of the other statewide elections. In Montana, Utah, and Washington, all the statewide officers are elected in the presidential election years only. Thus, the ballot is much longer and more formidable than in the mid-term years when only U.S. Senate, House, and some state legislative posts are contested. Accordingly, the differences in roll-off between the presidential and mid-term years are greatest in these three states: 5.0% in Utah, 5.9% in Montana, and a whopping 16.5% in Washington. In the remaining states, the mean differences range from 2.9% in Minnesota to 4.5% in Ohio.

68. The exceptionally large difference in Missouri between mean mid-term and presidential-year roll-off (13.2%) is perhaps explained by the thesis advanced in n. 67. Missouri is the only one of the merit retention states electing *all* its statewide officers (except supreme court justices) in the presidential years only.

69. In addition to the four states in Table 9, Wyoming and Montana switched from nonpartisan elections to merit plans in 1972; their first retention elections in 1974 were too recent for meaningful comparative analysis to be performed. The selection system in Utah changed from partisan to nonpartisan elections in 1951 and, in 1967, to a variant of the merit plan which allows incumbents to be challenged in nonpartisan elections; unchallenged incumbents run on the retention ballot. For ease of comparison, Utah is not included in Table 9, but the effect of the ballot changes is equally clear. When the partisan ballot was in use, mean roll-off in contested races was only 1.3%. Under the nonpartisan ballot, mean roll-off was 11.8% in contested elections. And in the uncontested merit retention ballotings held since 1967, the mean roll-off was 24.9%.

70. The relationship between the perceived closeness of an election and the likelihood of an individual going to the polls was demonstrated empirically by Campbell et al., *The American Voter*, pp. 99–100.

71. This term has been coined by Virginia Gray in her "A Note on Competition and Turnout in the American States," *Journal of Politics* 38 (February 1976): 154. The theory was originally advanced by Key in his *Southern Politics*, pp. 507–508, 523–526.

72. Thomas R. Dye, *Politics, Economics, and the Public*, p. 70; James A. Robinson and William H. Standing, "Some Correlates of Voter Participation: The Case of Indiana," *Journal of Politics* 22 (February 1960): 96–99; and C. Richard Hofstetter, "Inter-Party Competition and Electoral Turnout: The Case of Indiana," *American Journal of Political Science* 17 (May 1973): 351–366.

73. Blank, "Socio-Economic Determinism," pp. 742–743; Gray, "A Note on Competition and Turnout," pp. 154–156.

74. See n. 32 and the accompanying text for a discussion of Hannah's unpublished results in Michigan.

75. See n. 38 and the accompanying text.

76. Where more than one judicial race was decided in any election year, the most competitive one (i.e., where the division of the vote between the two major candidates was closest to 50%–50%) and its corresponding level of participation were used. This data manipulation was based upon the assumption that if voters were drawn to a particularly closely contested supreme court contest they would also be likely to cast votes in the other judicial races on the ballot.

77. The use of election results is a post hoc measure designed to approximate the extent to which a particular election was perceived by voters to be a closely contested one in which their individual votes might make an important difference. Though there are some obvious dangers with such a technique, absent survey data to enlighten us about voter perceptions of each election, the actual closeness of the election results must serve as an acceptable surrogate indicator.

78. Milbrath, "Individuals and Government," p. 41, reports a rank-order correlation of 0.807 between state rankings of turnout in gubernatorial and

U.S. senatorial contests held in nonpresidential years from 1952 to 1960 and a measure of interparty competition.

79. Atkins and McDonald, "Electoral Rule Changes," p. 17.

## 3. Voting Behavior in State Judicial Elections

1. The poll was conducted by the Elmer Roper organization in three New York locations (New York City, Buffalo, and Cayuga County). The results vary by place but the New York City results are typical. Of those voters going to the polls, 75% voted in the judicial election but only 39% had paid attention to the judicial candidates before the election and only 19% could name any one of the judicial candidates for whom they had voted (Allen T. Klots, "The Selection of Judges and the Short Ballot," in *Judicial Selection and Tenure*, ed. Winters, pp. 78–80).

2. These results of this Roper poll are reported in Philip et al., *Where Do Judges Come From?* p. 97.

3. Ladinsky and Silver, "Popular Democracy and Judicial Independence," p. 161. It should be noted that the Wisconsin results are based upon a survey of the entire voting-age population in the state whereas the New York results are based upon a survey of voters attending the polls on election day.

4. Philip et al., *Where Do Judges Come From?* report the results of this 1973 survey of New York voters by the Daniel Yankelovich polling organization commissioned by the Institute of Judicial Administration.

5. Ibid., p. 95.

6. The survey data indicate that 73% of those going to the polls said they voted in the chief judge contest. But official election statistics indicate that 83% of the voters attending the polls in 1973 cast a ballot in the judicial race, indicating an unusual survey "underreport" of 10%. This result suggests that the races for judicial office are of such low salience that voters who may have voted forget that they cast a ballot in the judicial election. This possibility is given more detailed attention by David Adamany and Philip Dubois, "The 'Forgetful' Voter and an Underreported Vote," *Public Opinion Quarterly* 39 (Summer 1975): 227–231.

7. Philip et al., *Where Do Judges Come From?* p. 103. But only 18% of those polled said that they did not vote for chief judge because they "didn't care that much" about the election.

8. Ladinsky and Silver, "Popular Democracy and Judicial Independence," p. 161.

9. Jacob, "Judicial Insulation," p. 814, Table 6.

10. Philip et al., *Where Do Judges Come From?* pp. 102, 104–105.

11. American Bar Association, *Code of Judicial Conduct*, Canon 7(B) (1)(c).

12. Ibid., Canon 7(A)(2) and 7(A)(4).

13. For an illuminating case history of such a judicial election campaign, see Ladinsky and Silver, "Popular Democracy," pp. 147–151. An excellent case study of the highly spirited contest for the position of chief judge of the New York Court of Appeals in 1973 also reveals the

strength of these norms upon the conduct of judicial campaigns even in a partisan political setting. See Philip et al., *Where Do Judges Come From?* especially pp. 20–89.

14. Wallace S. Sayre and Herbert Kaufman, *Governing New York City*, p. 554.
15. See Guterman and Meidinger, *In the Opinion of the Bar*.
16. Philip et al., *Where Do Judges Come From?* pp. 99–102.
17. Lee, "Judicial Selection and Tenure in Arizona," p. 61.
18. In Arizona, only about 60% of the bar respond to the statewide poll. See ibid., p. 61. Participation in the judicial polls taken by the Cleveland Bar Association during the decade 1960–1970 averaged 41.8% of the eligible lawyers, declining to 35.4% in 1970. See Barber, "Ohio Judicial Elections," p. 786, Table 12.
19. See Guterman and Meidinger, *In the Opinion of the Bar*, pp. 31–34.
20. Watson and Downing, *The Politics of the Bench and the Bar*, p. 223.
21. In Ohio from 1960 to 1970 the Cleveland Bar Association and the Cuyahoga County Bar Association each endorsed well over 80% of the incumbents seeking re-election to the appellate bench (Barber, "Ohio Judicial Elections," p. 787). Henderson and Sinclair report that state bar polls taken to solicit member opinions on the candidates for the Texas appellate courts resulted in the endorsement of incumbents in all but two of thirty-three contested elections from 1952 to 1966 (Bancroft C. Henderson and T. C. Sinclair, "The Selection of Judges in Texas," *Judicial Selection and Tenure*, ed. Winters, p. 159). In Arizona bar polls, over 90% of the judges seeking trial and appellate posts from 1958 to 1972 won bar endorsements (Lee, "Judicial Selection and Tenure in Arizona," pp. 61–62). Finally, in Missouri, all the appellate and trial judges seeking retention from 1948 to 1974 received the approval of a majority of the state bar; over 90% of the judges received affirmative votes from better than 70% of the lawyers (Watson and Downing, *The Politics of the Bench and the Bar*, p. 223).
22. A survey of American lawyers revealed that "trial experience" and "judicial experience" were the qualifications deemed most important for judicial office (Jack Ladinsky and Joel B. Grossman, "Organizational Consequences of Professional Consensus," *Administrative Science Quarterly* 11 [June 1966]:91).
23. Henderson and Sinclair, "The Selection of Judges in Texas," p. 158. Watson and Downing, *The Politics of the Bench and the Bar*, p. 233, also suggest that another reason incumbents are overwhelmingly favored in bar polls is that a sentiment exists among lawyers "that once a lawyer gives up his practice to go on the bench, it is sort of 'dirty pool' to turn him out of office and force him to build up a clientele again after most of his clients have taken their legal business elsewhere. Therefore, all doubts about a judge's capabilities are generally resolved in his favor."
24. The divergent results of bar polls taken by rival bar associations in the major metropolitan areas in Missouri under both the partisan elective system and the merit plan are noted by Watson and Downing, *The Poli-*

*tics of the Bench and the Bar*, pp. 20–43, 222–223. In New York City, the Democrats are said to dominate the Bronx and Kings County Bar Associations while the Republicans control the New York County Lawyers Association (see Philip et al., *Where Do Judges Come From?* pp. 31–34, 82–84, 116–118). Bar groups in Ohio also appear to be controlled by particular political-legal interests (see Kathleen L. Barber, "Selection of Ohio Appellate Judges," in *Political Behavior and Public Issues in Ohio*, ed. Gargan and Coke, p. 221).

25. Watson and Downing, *The Politics of the Bench and the Bar*, pp. 37–43.
26. Paul D. Beechen, "Can Judicial Elections Express the People's Choice," *Judicature* 57 (January 1974):242–246.
27. David W. Adamany and George W. Agree, *Political Money*, p. 120.
28. The results reported here rely upon the discussion of studies by Adamany and Agree, n. 27, at p. 121 and p. 122 (Table 7–1), drawn from Donald G. Balmer's, *State Election Services in Oregon*, pp. 58–60.
29. Beechen, "Can Judicial Elections Express the People's Choice," pp. 244–245.
30. Philip E. Converse, "The Concept of a Normal Vote," in *Elections and the Political Order*, ed. Campbell et al., pp. 9–39.
31. Warren E. Miller and Teresa E. Levitin, *Leadership and Change*, pp. 37, 33–49.
32. Ibid., p. 34.
33. The literature examining the extent of issue voting in presidential elections is now reaching staggering proportions. A fine summary of these works and some of the better examples are contained in Richard G. Niemi and Herbert F. Weisberg, *Controversies in American Voting Behavior*. See also Nie et al., *The Changing American Voter*.
34. Cowart, "Electoral Choice in the American States," p. 835.
35. See, most particularly, ibid. and Miller and Levitin, *Leadership and Change*, pp. 39–41 and the accompanying citations.
36. Cowart, "Electoral Choice in the American States," pp. 839–850. See also Alan I. Abramowitz, "Name Familiarity, Reputation, and the Incumbency Effect in a Congressional Election," *Western Political Quarterly* 28 (December 1975):668–684; and Albert D. Cover, "One Good Term Deserves Another: The Advantage of Incumbency in Congressional Elections," *American Journal of Political Science* 21 (August 1977): 523–541.
37. Recent research on voting in senatorial and congressional elections suggests that incumbency may be of increasing importance in structuring voter behavior. In addition to those works cited in n. 36, see Warren Lee Kostroski, "Party and Incumbency in Postwar Senate Elections," *American Political Science Review* 67 (December 1973):1213–1234. Other research has focused upon congressional voting behavior as affected by the state of popular satisfaction with the president's performance in office and the administration's ability to manage the economy. Recent examples include Francisco Arcelus and Allan H. Meltzer, "The Effect

of Aggregate Economic Variables on Congressional Elections," *American Political Science Review* 69 (December 1975): 1232–1239; Samuel Kernell, "Presidential Popularity and Negative Voting: An Alternative Explanation of the Midterm Congressional Decline of the President's Party," *American Political Science Review* 71 (March 1977): 44–66.

38. At least in Ohio, party workers stationed at the polls distribute lists of the party candidates, including those for the judiciary, to the voters ("Note: Judicial Selection and Tenure: The Merit Plan in Ohio," *University of Cincinnati Law Review* 42 [1973]: 268). This was not the case in Arizona, however (see Lee, "Judicial Selection and Tenure in Arizona," pp. 54–56, 68, and n. 54 accompanying Chap. 2).

39. S. Sidney Ulmer, "The Political Party Variable in the Michigan Supreme Court," *Journal of Public Law* 11 (1962): 354.

40. The nonpartisan ballot alone, of course, does not necessarily eliminate sub rosa activity by political parties or functionally equivalent groups in endorsing, promoting, and campaigning on behalf of judicial candidates. In Minnesota, for example, the Farmer-Labor party's role in endorsing particular candidates for judgeships is well documented. See Malcolm C. Moos, "Judicial Elections and Partisan Endorsement of Judicial Candidates in Minnesota," *American Political Science Review* 35 (February 1941): 69–75. See also Charles R. Adrian, "Some General Characteristics of Nonpartisan Elections," *American Political Science Review* 46 (September 1952): 766–776; and Charles Mayo, "The 1961 Mayoral Election in Los Angeles: The Political Party in a Nonpartisan Election," *Western Political Quarterly* 17 (June 1964): 325–337.

This is not to say that all such activity is successful. In Minnesota, for example, incumbents discovered that the most promising election strategy was to campaign as an incumbent and with other incumbents seeking re-election, regardless of their party affiliation. The Farmer-Labor party, which typically endorsed liberal candidates, was unable to persuade those judges from campaigning with the conservative officeholders seeking re-election. Moos was led to conclude that this "incumbent strategy" was so successful that "the effects ... of partisan endorsements for candidates for election to the supreme court ... have ... been negligible" (pp. 71–72).

41. Barber, "Ohio Judicial Elections," p. 778.

42. The correlation statistic used was Pearson's product-moment correlation coefficient. Whenever possible, state supreme court elections were correlated with a concurrent gubernatorial race. In those states using four-year gubernatorial terms, supreme court races occurring *between* gubernatorial races were paired in the correlational analysis with the election for governor occurring two years previously. In Michigan (until 1963) and Wisconsin, judicial elections held in the spring had to be paired with nonconcurrent gubernatorial races. Off-season judicial races held in odd-numbered years were paired with the November election immediately preceding the spring contest. Judicial elections held in

even-numbered years were correlated with the fall elections held later in the same years. Because both Michigan (prior to 1963) and Wisconsin (until 1970) used two-year gubernatorial terms, these ground rules for the pairing of spring judicial elections with the fall gubernatorial balloting resulted in the correlation of races no more than a few months apart. Only the 1973 race in Wisconsin, correlated with the 1970 governor's race, did not satisfy this generalization.

As a rule, the correlational analysis was a relatively straightforward procedure. But in a number of states (most notably Colorado, Michigan, and Iowa, but also at one time or another in a number of others), judicial candidates have run for office in "at large" or "multiwinner" balloting arrangements. Where more than one full-term position is being filled in a given year, twice as many candidates as there are positions to be elected compete against one another. Each voter is entitled to cast as many votes as there are positions being filled. This arrangement required a slight manipulation of the data in order for the analysis of the party division of the vote by county to be performed. For four-person races, the Republican judicial candidate receiving the most votes was paired with the Democratic candidate receiving the fewest votes. And the top vote collector from between the Democrats was paired with the low vote getter from between the Republicans. Where six candidates competed for three slots, the same pairing of high and low finishers from each party was used but, in addition, the "middle" vote collectors from each party were paired. The proportion of the two-party vote gathered by the Democratic candidate in each pairing was then calculated by county and each race correlated with the appropriate gubernatorial contest.

43. The dangers of making inferences about individual voting behavior from the results of aggregate data analysis are discussed by Austin Ranney, "The Utility and Limitation of Aggregate Data in the Study of Electoral Politics," in *Essays on the Behavioral Study of Politics*, ed. Ranney, pp. 91–102.

44. A relaxed set of criteria was used to identify the partisan affiliations of candidates in nonpartisan judicial elections. First, self-identification in a published biographical source demonstrated partisan attachment. Second, previous service in a partisan elective office, unsuccessful attempts for nomination or election to partisan office, and prior service as a partisan appointee to a public office helped identify candidates by party. Finally, service in any political party organization office, acting as a party representative to a state constitutional convention, or being a delegate to a national nominating convention were accepted as indices of partisan affiliation.

The major biographical sources used included state manuals, the regional and national editions of *Who's Who*, and *The Directory of American Judges, 1955*. Supplemental biographical information was provided by legislative research bureaus, supreme court librarians, and major metropolitan newspaper libraries.

45. "Temporally contiguous" elections refers to those elections held adjacent in time. An important caveat, however, is that only those contiguous gubernatorial elections which were paired in contested judicial races in the correlational analysis were included in the calculation of intercorrelations. In nonpartisan states, where contested judicial races did not necessarily occur every biennial election year, the gubernatorial and judicial races intercorrelated may not have been held in successive biennial or even quadrennial election years. Additionally, where more than one judicial race in a given year was available for intercorrelation, the "most partisan" one (based upon the magnitude of the correlation coefficient for the partisan division of the vote) was selected for intercorrelation.

46. See n. 43.

47. Jack E. Holmes, *Politics in New Mexico*, p. 115.

48. Ibid., p. 138.

49. Ibid., especially Chap. 4.

50. The standard deviation is a statistical measure which indicates the spread or variation of a series of data values from the mean of those values. The greater the spread of values around the mean, the larger the standard deviation. For these data, high standard deviations indicate that the correlations of the party division of the vote for governor and justice in a state are, on the average, more variable than in a state in which the standard deviations are low (see Herbert Blalock, *Social Statistics*, pp. 80–81).

51. Individual case studies of voting behavior in these states are included in Frank Jonas (ed.), *Western Politics*.

52. These differences and their effects on voting in congressional elections are considered by Abramowitz, "Name Familiarity, Reputation, and the Incumbency Effect," pp. 668–671, 676–680.

53. See David R. Mayhew, *Congress: The Electoral Connection*, pp. 49–77.

54. Key, *Southern Politics*, p. 41.

55. Stuart Nagel, *Comparing Elected and Appointed Judicial Systems*, pp. 20–21, 23.

56. Gary C. Byrne and J. Kristian Pueschel, "But Who Should I Vote For for County Coroner?" *Journal of Politics* 36 (August 1974):778–784.

57. Henry M. Bain, Jr., and Donald S. Hecock, *Ballot Position and Voter's Choice*.

58. A similar analysis is offered by Barber, "Ohio Judicial Elections," pp. 778–781.

59. Celebrezze is a famous Democratic name in Ohio. Anthony D. Celebrezze served as mayor of Cleveland from 1952 until his 1962 appointment by President Kennedy as secretary of the Department of Health, Education, and Welfare. Celebrezze was subsequently appointed to the federal court of appeals by President Johnson.

   In his initial successful election bid for the Ohio Supreme Court in 1972, Frank D. Celebrezze defeated his Republican opponent, Robert

Leach, in the most partisan race of the postwar years ($r = 0.81$). His 1974 re-election race against Sheldon Taft was the fourth most partisan of the thirty-six postwar contests. And the intercorrelation of the two races involving Celebrezze was 0.77, confirming the clear and consistent partisan response of the voters to a readily identifiable partisan.

60. See n. 42.

61. The 1966 race in which Republican and Irish Catholic challenger Thomas E. Brennan defeated incumbent Otis M. Smith (a Black and a Catholic) had a correlation of only 0.12 for the party division of the vote. In 1974, John W. Fitzgerald was involved in a four-person race for two slots; Fitzgerald, a Republican, and Thomas M. Kavanaugh, a Democrat, were both elected in races clearly decided along nonparty lines ($r = 0.08$, 0.16). Both candidates undoubtedly were helped by name familiarity: Kavanaugh was the well-known incumbent and Fitzgerald, a judge of the state court of appeals, was the son of former attorney general and governor, Frank D. Fitzgerald. But the appeal of their Irish Catholic names (though Fitzgerald is a Congregationalist) cannot be dismissed as a factor entirely. This point is given additional attention in the discussions of Michigan elections in Chap. 4.

62. The rise of Republicanism in Arizona is given detailed attention in Chap. 4.

63. The 1952 contest in which Democrat Levi S. Udall was elected was a moderately partisan one, with a correlation for the partisan division of the vote of 0.59.

64. See the discussion and citations in n. 40.

65. This race sparked some interesting litigation over ballot labels which were to accompany the name of the junior Gallagher. Under Minnesota law, each candidate should have been designated on the ballot as a candidate "for the office of Associate Justice of the Supreme Court to which Thomas Gallagher was elected for the regular term." Several of the junior Gallagher's opponents brought legal action to compel further identification on the ballot so that the voters would not mistake the son for his father, the incumbent. The supreme court agreed, noting that candidates for the judiciary "run on a nonpartisan ticket without benefit of party, platform, or issues. They have little time for campaigning. They are known mainly by their names, and the opportunity for confusion where the names are identical or even similar is rife." The court, in *Foley* v. *Donavan* (144 N.W. 2d 600, 1966), ordered the younger Gallagher to be distinguished from his father by the insertion of their middle names in the appropriate places on the ballot. Although Gallagher won a runaway primary victory against five opponents, he was defeated in the general election by Republican Peterson. "The public controversy and a strong, politically well-known opponent prevented the incumbent's mantle from being passed from father to son" (Robert A. Heiberg, "Social Backgrounds of the Minnesota Supreme Court Justices, 1858–1968," *Minnesota Law Review* 53 [1969]:908).

66. However, the intercorrelation of the two races involving Batjer was

quite high ($r$ = 0.85), indicating the stability of his partisan and personal support in the electorate.

67. In 1962, Republican John F. Raper squared off against Democrat Norman Gray. Because the attorney general in Wyoming is appointed by the governor with the advice and consent of the state senate, the office (and thus the partisan affiliation of its occupant) may not be as visible to the public as in those states where the position is elective.

68. Adamany and Dubois, "Electing State Judges," p. 760.

69. Jacob, "Judicial Insulation," p. 808.

70. V. O. Key, Jr., *The Responsible Electorate*.

71. Ibid., pp. 52–59, 91.

72. Ibid., p. 44.

73. This literature is too voluminous to cite in detail. For an extensive bibliography of studies conducted prior to 1972, see John H. Kessel, "The Issues in Issue Voting," *American Political Science Review* 66 (June 1972):459, n. 1. The most recent book-length works are Nie et al., *The Changing American Voter*, and Pomper, *Voters' Choice*.

74. Walter Dean Burnham, *Critical Elections and the Mainsprings of American Politics*, pp. 7–13.

75. This possibility is explored by Miller and Levitin, *Leadership and Change*, pp. 191–199; Nie et al., *The Changing American Voter*, pp. 350–352; Pomper, *Voters' Choice*, pp. 90–118, 203–204.

76. Studies have not generally confirmed this hypothesized relationship, however. See Pomper, *Voters' Choice*, pp. 204–225; and Nie et al., *The Changing American Voter*, Chap. 11.

77. See, in particular, Miller and Levitin, *Leadership and Change*, Chaps. 3–7.

78. Pomper, *Voters' Choice*, pp. 36–37, 166–182, 194–203.

79. Nie et al., Chaps. 11 and 19. And see Pomper, *Voters' Choice*, pp. 205–208.

80. Pomper, *Voters' Choice*, pp. 170–178. See also David E. RePass, "Issue Salience and Party Choice," *American Political Science Review* 65 (June 1971):389–400. But see Michael Margolis, "From Confusion to Confusion: Issues and the American Voter (1956–1972)," *American Political Science Review* 71 (March 1977):31–43.

81. David E. RePass, "Levels of Rationality among the American Electorate," paper delivered at the Annual Meeting of the American Political Science Association, 1974.

82. RePass, "Issue Salience," p. 395. See also Pomper, *Voters' Choice*, pp. 155–157.

83. Pomper, *Voters' Choice*, pp. 167–170.

84. Ibid., p. 180, and the studies discussed therein at pp. 178–182.

85. The quotation is from ibid., p. 148; on the distinctive images presented to the voters by parties and their candidates, see pp. 145–151.

86. Ibid., p. 173; on voter perceptions of party positions, see pp. 170–173. See also RePass, "Issue Salience."

87. These studies are discussed in Chap. 5 in the section entitled "Party as a Social Background Characteristic."

88. The case analyses are reviewed in Chap. 5 in the section entitled "Partisanship on State Supreme Courts."

### 4. Appointment and Election: Patterns of Accession to Elective Courts

1. Glenn R. Winters, "One-Man Judicial Selection," in *Judicial Selection and Tenure*, ed. Winters, p. 86.

2. James Herndon, "Appointment as a Means of Initial Accession to Elective State Courts of Last Resort," *North Dakota Law Review* 38 (January 1962): 64–65.

3. For example, Heiberg, "Social Backgrounds of the Minnesota Supreme Court Justices," p. 903. From 1930 to 1968, 77.3% of Minnesota's Supreme Court justices reached the bench by appointment. In Texas, two of every three judges serving on all courts during the 1940–1962 period were appointed to office (Bancroft C. Henderson and T. C. Sinclair, "The Selection of Judges in Texas," in *Judicial Selection and Tenure*, ed. Winters, p. 153).

4. Winters, "One-Man Judicial Selection," pp. 86–87.

5. Ibid., p. 86.

6. Herndon, "Appointment as a Means of Initial Accession," pp. 64–65.

7. Barber, "Ohio Judicial Elections," p. 769.

8. Kenneth N. Vines, "The Selection of Judges in Louisiana," in *Studies in Judicial Politics*, ed. Kenneth N. Vines and Herbert Jacob, p. 114.

9. Herndon, "Appointment as a Means of Initial Accession," p. 67.

10. Ibid., p. 68.

11. Ibid., p. 69. Herndon considered a state's electoral system to be "stable" if no shifts in the partisan control of the governorship occurred. A "proximate" shift was one in which one party displaced the other in control of the governor's office and received from 50.1% to 54.9% of the statewide two-party vote. A displacement occurring with the winning party capturing more than 55.0% of the two-party vote was considered a "gross" shift.

12. Ibid., pp. 69–71.

13. According to Herndon's data, among the states with partisan judicial elections, the difference in the proportion of judges reaching the bench by appointment between states experiencing "gross" electoral shifts and states classified as "stable" is only 4.7%. But for the states utilizing semipartisan and nonpartisan selection, this difference is 16.2% (see ibid., Table VIII, p. 71).

14. Barber, "Ohio Judicial Elections," p. 770.

15. Indeed, the very length of judicial terms in all states would dictate that a large number of mid-term vacancies would occur. The most common judicial terms for judges of state courts of last resort are 6, 8, and 10 years, from 1½ to 2½ times the customary 4-year terms awarded major public officials. In 1974, the fixed terms of judges serving on elective

state supreme courts ranged from a low of 6 years to a high of 15 years, averaging 7.9 years.

16. The twenty-two states in this analysis are listed in Table 13. The elective states excluded and the reasons for their exclusion are discussed in n. 40 accompanying Chap. 2. The names of judges in each state, their tenures, and the means by which they reached their state high courts were collected, when available, from state manuals and bluebooks. Additional information from some states was supplied by the legislative reference bureaus or the supreme court librarians. Finally, where necessary, state and regional court reporters were consulted to obtain court membership listings. Appointments made by governors to fill newly created positions on the state supreme court or appointments made on an explicitly temporary basis were not included.

17. Herndon's study encompassed all thirty-six of the state supreme courts using elective judicial selection from 1948 to 1957.

18. Information concerning the constitutional and statutory provisions in the states regarding the filling of judicial vacancies has been compiled from various sources, including state manuals and state statutes and constitutions.

19. This is true in Minnesota, New York, Ohio, and Wisconsin (since 1963). During the years prior to 1970 when partisan elections were used, this was also the case in Indiana.

20. The American Judicature Society has devoted an entire issue to the subject of judicial compensation and retirement. See *Judicature* 58 (November 1974): 197–202 for a useful comparative summary of state retirement provisions. This survey provides a useful state-by-state summary of retirement provisions and an excellent comparative summary.

21. Herndon, "Appointment as a Means of Initial Accession," pp. 67–68.

22. Note in Table 13 that in no state is the proportion of initially appointed judges less than 25%. Thus, at the very least, fully one-fourth of the judges on elective state courts of last resort typically are initially appointed and not elected to office. Although no data have been collected on this point, judicial positions are certainly one of the elective public offices most frequently filled by appointment. The lengthy terms make it almost impossible to be otherwise.

23. Although the data are not complete, it is known that judges in some states have lost in primary elections and never reached the general election contest. For Idaho, Oregon, and Washington, these figures (where known) are included in Table 13 because the primary in these states is, in effect, the election. In Idaho, a judicial candidate receiving a majority of the votes cast in the nonpartisan primary is declared elected to the office and is not required to stand for the November election. In Oregon and Washington, a candidate receiving a majority of primary votes runs unopposed in the general election.

24. Republican Morris Schillinglaw, appointed in 1958 by Republican Governor Edwin L. Mechem, was defeated in the 1958 election. While Dem-

ocrat John Burroughs narrowly defeated Mechem in the gubernatorial race by collecting 50.5% of the vote, Schillinglaw was being beaten by Democrat David Carmody, who attracted 62.6%. In 1970, three Republican judges, all appointees of Republican Governor David Cargo, were defeated while seeking election to the bench. Three Democratic judicial candidates won their seats on the supreme court by outpolling their party's gubernatorial candidate, Bruce King, by anywhere from 0.3% to 3.9% of the statewide vote.

25. Augustus Seymour, a Republican, was appointed by Democratic Governor Thomas J. Mabry in 1950 but lost his 1954 bid for the bench to Democrat Henry A. Kiker, who collected 58.5% of the vote. At the same time, Democrat John F. Simms, Jr., was winning the governorship back from the Republicans by attracting 57% of the vote.

26. The tie of New Mexico gubernatorial politics to presidential politics is more dramatically clear when it is noted that since statehood was conferred at the end of the first decade of this century New Mexico's voters have returned a governor of the president's party in every presidential election year except 1924 and 1960. See Holmes, *Politics in New Mexico*, pp. 2–3.

27. Ibid., p. 3.

28. Thomas J. Mabry, a Democrat, also served two consecutive terms beginning in 1946.

29. Holmes, *Politics in New Mexico*, pp. 3, 119–144.

30. Ibid., pp. 3–4.

31. It is not entirely possible, of course, to estimate the ultimate impact upon the state's initial accession patterns caused by the appointment and subsequent election defeat of five Republican judges. But if the five Democrats elected in defeating the Republican appointees are removed from the analysis, then 58.8% of New Mexico's high court judges have been initially appointed. This high percentage of initial accessions by appointment inferentially supports the proposition that Democratic judges, secure from effective electoral challenge, serve long tenures on the bench and then die or retire in mid-term necessitating the appointment of a successor to fill the vacancy.

32. The historical dominance of Republicans in Iowa is traced by Harlan Hahn, *Urban-Rural Conflict*, pp. 33–69, 133–134, 167.

33. Ibid., pp. 80–81. The reasons behind the 1956 and 1958 Democratic gubernatorial victories are discussed at pp. 80–83.

34. Justice Thornton did not face the electorate again until 1964 after the completion of his first term. By that time, however, the merit retention system was in effect and Thornton was easily re-elected with 90.9% of the vote.

35. A further check on this relationship for 1962 is not possible since no supreme court races were held in that year; and in 1962 Iowa voters adopted a constitutional amendment eliminating the partisan election system and providing for the merit selection and retention of their judges.

36. Herndon, "Appointment as a Means of Initial Accession," p. 67.
37. James W. Drury, *The Government of Kansas*, pp. 28–33.
38. Ibid., p. 32.
39. The states of New York and Pennsylvania have not been included in this analysis. In New York, the frequency with which incumbents seeking re-election have been endorsed by both the major parties has reduced the number of contested elections available for analysis (see Chap. 2, n. 52). In Pennsylvania, the twenty-one–year term used prior to 1968 caused judicial elections to be relatively infrequent events.
40. "Note: Judicial Selection and Tenure in Indiana: A Critical Analysis and Suggested Reform," *Indiana Law Journal* 39 (Winter 1964): 370, n. 32.
41. Ibid., Appendix, p. 386.
42. Democratic fortunes in Indiana were limited to the elections of 1948, 1958, 1964, and 1970. Indiana adopted the merit system in 1970, and the first retention elections were held in 1972.
43. Curtis Martin, "Colorado: The Highest State," in *Western Politics*, ed. Jonas, pp. 123, 121–122.
44. In 1952, 1958, and 1966, the party winning the governor's office captured four of the five other statewide offices. But in 1950, 1954, and 1962, the party losing the gubernatorial race won two of the statewide posts. In 1956, the parties split the six statewide offices, with the Democrats winning the offices of governor, secretary of state, and treasurer, while Republicans were elected lieutenant governor, auditor, and attorney general.
45. Curtis Martin and Rudolph Gomez, *Colorado Government and Politics*, pp. 125–126. In the postwar period, the Colorado senate and house were controlled by different parties after the 1948 and 1964 elections.
46. Ibid., p. 119.
47. The results of the two polls were originally reported by John Fenton (citing a 1958 Louis Harris poll) and Thomas Flinn. Both surveys are discussed by John J. Gargan and James G. Coke, "The Study of Ohio Government and Politics," in *Political Behavior and Public Issues in Ohio*, ed. Gargan and Coke, p. 18.
48. Ibid., p. 19.
49. Ibid.
50. Ibid., p. 20, quoting John Fenton, *Midwest Politics*, p. 145.
51. Gargan and Coke, "The Study of Ohio Government and Politics," p. 20.
52. In the most complete previous analysis of Ohio judicial elections, Professor Kathleen Barber asserts that the Republican dominance of the supreme and appellate courts is not explained simply by the notion that "Ohio is a Republican state." Rather, noting frequent Democratic victories in the major executive and legislative contests, Barber argues that the nonpartisan judicial ballot gives an added advantage to Republican candidates. Voters of higher socioeconomic status who tend to vote Republican are those who pay more attention to politics, are able "to cope with the directionless nonpartisan judicial ballot," and thus are more likely to vote, casting their ballots for Republican candidates in the

minor statewide and legislative offices conducted on the partisan ballot and in the judicial contests on the nonpartisan ballot. In my view, however, the overall partisan preference of Ohio voters for Republicans is a much more powerful explanation of Republican dominance of the judiciary than Barber realized. As Chapter 3 demonstrated, idiosyncratic, nonparty voting cues determine most voter behavior on the nonpartisan ballot. And name familiarity and incumbency have worked most to the advantage of Democratic candidates. Given the electoral record, it might be argued that if Ohio judges were elected on a partisan ballot the judiciary would be more Republican than it has been under the nonpartisan format. See Barber, "Ohio Judicial Elections," pp. 774–781. For a detailed analysis of the "partisan bias" of nonpartisan elections, see Willis D. Hawley, *Nonpartisan Elections and the Case for Party Politics*, pp. 22–106.

53. Rhodes won his second gubernatorial term in 1966 with a 62.2% share of the vote. Nixon narrowly won the 1968 presidential balloting with 51.3% of the votes.

54. William Brown beat Schneider comfortably (55.1%), but fellow Democrat Celebrezze won only a narrow victory (51.2%) over Republican Leach.

55. Rhodes' share of the gubernatorial vote was only 50.2%. But Chief Justice O'Neill, also a Republican, received 65.5% of the votes cast. Democrat Celebrezze also won easily with 57.4%.

56. The results of the statewide elections in Arizona from 1911–1962 are summarized by Bruce B. Mason and Heinz R. Hink, *Constitutional Government in Arizona*, p. 66.

57. Ross R. Rice, "Amazing Arizona: Politics in Transition," in *Western Politics*, ed. Jonas, pp. 48–49.

58. Ibid., p. 48.

59. Mason and Hink, *Constitutional Government in Arizona*, p. 65; and John S. Goff, *Arizona Civilization*, p. 112.

60. Rice, "Amazing Arizona," p. 50.

61. Ibid., p. 68.

62. Goff, *Arizona Civilization*, p. 58. The split in the Arizona Democratic party is also noted by Mason and Hink, *Constitutional Government in Arizona*, p. 65.

63. Mason and Hink, *Constitutional Government in Arizona*, p. 65.

64. In 1963, a constitutional revision removed the governor's power to fill mid-term vacancies on the judiciary and gave the supreme court the power to assign a retired judge to temporarily fill a court vacancy until a special election could be held. But no vacancies occurred on the court during the next few years, and in 1968 the power to fill vacancies was returned to the governor. See Albert L. Sturm and Margaret Whitaker, *Implementing a New Constitution*, pp. 147–148.

65. This calculation does not include the results of the very unusual 1972 judicial election in which two positions were contested to fill vacancies

being caused by the retirements of Justices Paul G. Adams and Eugene Black. Besides the two nominees from each of the two major parties, five other political parties, each formed solely to contest the judicial races, each nominated a candidate of their own. The nine-person race was won by Mary Coleman, one of the Republican nominees, and Charles Levin, the nominee of the Nonpartisan Judiciary party. Many voters may have associated Levin with the Democratic party, however, since he is the cousin of Sander M. Levin, the Democratic nominee for governor in both 1970 and 1974, and Carl Levin, a Detroit city councilman. See the *Detroit News*, 5 and 8 September 1972.

66. It is interesting to note that several justices of the Michigan Supreme Court since 1948 have been Irish Catholics, including Harry F. Kelly, Thomas M. Kavanaugh, Michael D. O'Hara, Thomas Giles Kavanaugh, Thomas E. Brennan, and John W. Fitzgerald (who is Irish but not Catholic). If the proof is in the pudding, then perhaps Michigan's judicial pudding is eighty-six proof, spiked with Irish Whiskey!

67. Hannah, "An Evaluation of Judicial Elections in Michigan," pp. 117–122, 204–205.

68. Three supreme court justices in Washington have been defeated since 1948, but because Washington's court is the largest of the nonpartisan state supreme courts (with nine members), the three incumbents defeated represent only one-tenth of the court's total membership since 1948.

69. Another Democrat, J. Philip Johnson, was appointed in June 1974 by Governor Link but was defeated in the 1974 primary. These data were not available for analysis.

70. The correlation of the race involving Freebourn with the 1948 gubernatorial race was 0.54; the contest involving Bottomly correlated at 0.48 with the governor's race.

71. Actually, recent reforms in several states have placed some restrictions upon the governor's power to fill judicial vacancies. In Arizona (prior to the total switch to the merit plan), Florida, Idaho, and Tennessee, governors are legally limited in filling vacancies to a list of nominees provided by a merit nominating commission. Other states, like Maryland and Pennsylvania, have instituted such limitations by nonconstitutional means, usually by executive order of the governor. These so-called voluntary merit plans are reviewed by Lowe, "Voluntary Merit Selection Plans," pp. 161–168.

In Illinois and Pennsylvania, an odd combination of the partisan election and merit plan systems limits gubernatorial vacancy appointments. When vacancies occur, the supreme court in Illinois and the governor in Pennsylvania make an appointment until the next general election. In Pennsylvania, where a voluntary merit plan is used, appointments occurring when the senate is in session require the approval of two-thirds of that body. In both states, a judge appointed to the bench must run on the partisan ballot to retain office for the first full term.

Once elected, however, judges seek re-election on an uncontested retention ballot. The current means by which judicial vacancies are filled are
surveyed by Escovitz (comp.), *Judicial Selection and Tenure.*

72. Well over 90% of the appointments to the federal bench go to individuals who share the president's partisan affiliation. See Harold Chase,
*Federal Judges,* Chap. 1.

## 5. Partisanship and Judicial Accountability

1.  The functions of elections for both the political system and the individual voters are reviewed by Richard Rose and Harve Mossawir, "Voting
and Elections: A Functional Analysis," *Political Studies* 15 (1967): 173–
179.
2.  This view of the function of party affiliation has been the accepted gos-
pel in political science since publication of *The American Voter.* See
Campbell et al., *The American Voter,* pp. 120–145.
3.  See the discussion and accompanying citations in the final pages of
Chap. 3.
4.  Campbell et al., *The American Voter,* pp. 123–126.
5.  Ibid., pp. 128–136.
6.  Sidney Verba and Norman H. Nie, *Participation in America,* pp. 209–
228.
7.  Herbert McCloskey et al., "Issue Conflict and Consensus among Party
Leaders and Followers," *American Political Science Review* 54 (June
1960): 406–427; Verba and Nie, *Participation in America,* pp. 267–285.
8.  Rodney Mott et al., "Judicial Personnel," in *Judicial Behavior,* ed.
Schubert, pp. 197, 200. See also Canon, "The Impact of Formal Selection Processes," pp. 583–585.
9.  Walter F. Murphy and Joseph Tanenhaus, *The Study of Public Law,*
p. 107.
10. The notion of a judicial election constituency was first suggested by
David W. Adamany, "The Party Variable in Judges' Voting: Conceptual
Notes and a Case Study," *American Political Science Review* 63 (March
1969): 69–72.
11. The role of party organizations in the processes of nominating and electing candidates to office is discussed by Sorauf, *Party Politics in America,* pp. 216–223.
12. Ibid., p. 229.
13. Ibid., pp. 216–223, 343–347.
14. Adamany, "The Party Variable in Judges' Voting," pp. 69–72.
15. Adamany and Dubois, "Electing State Judges," p. 766.
16. Bradley C. Canon and Dean Jaros, "External Variables, Institutional
Structure, and Dissent on State Supreme Courts," *Polity* 3 (Winter
1970): 184.
17. Adamany and Dubois, "Electing State Judges," p. 767. Empirical support
for the assertion that long terms diminish partisanship in judicial voting

behavior is provided by John S. Prochera, "Selection, Tenure, and Judicial Behavior: Institutional Characteristics and Partisan Voting in State Courts of Last Appeal," paper delivered at the Annual Meeting of the Southern Political Science Association, 1975.

18. Adamany, "The Party Variable in Judges' Voting," p. 60.
19. Henry Robert Glick, *Supreme Courts in State Politics*, pp. 69–87.
20. Ibid., pp. 55–68, 88–120.
21. This point was made first by Adamany, "The Party Variable in Judges' Voting," p. 72. A resident court is one in which the justices live in one geographical location and spend their working hours in adjacent offices at the court. In contrast, members of a nonresident court live and work in various locations throughout the state, meeting in person only infrequently for conferences, to hear oral arguments, or to issue opinions. Some of the internal procedures of state supreme courts have been surveyed by Stanford S. McConkie, "Decision-Making in State Supreme Courts," *Judicature* 59 (February 1976): 337–343.
22. This basic schema has been suggested by others in attempts to understand the nature of the relationship between judicial selection systems and patterns of state court decision-making. See Burton M. Atkins and Henry R. Glick, "Formal Judicial Recruitment and State Supreme Court Decisions," *American Politics Quarterly* 2 (October 1974): 432–433. A conceptually similar model in a different empirical setting is offered by Dean Jaros and Bradley C. Canon, "Dissent on State Supreme Courts: The Differential Significance of Characteristics of Judges," *Midwest Journal of Political Science* 15 (February 1971): 326–329.
23. The best discussions of social background analysis, its assumptions, and inherent theoretical problems are Joel B. Grossman, "Social Backgrounds and Judicial Decisions: Notes for a Theory," *Journal of Politics* 29 (1967): 334–351; and Sheldon Goldman, "Backgrounds, Attitudes, and the Voting Behavior of Judges: A Comment on Joel Grossman's 'Social Backgrounds and Judicial Decisions,'" *Journal of Politics* 31 (1969): 214–222.
24. Goldman, "Backgrounds, Attitudes, and Voting Behavior," p. 216.
25. Stuart S. Nagel, "Political Party Affiliation and Judges' Decisions," *American Political Science Review* 55 (December 1961): 843–850.
26. Ibid., pp. 846–847.
27. Sorauf, *Party Politics in America*, pp. 347–356.
28. See McCloskey et al., "Issue Conflict and Consensus."
29. Don R. Bowen, "The Explanation of Judicial Voting Behavior from Sociological Characteristics of Judges," Ph.D. dissertation, Yale University (1965).
30. Stuart S. Nagel, "Multiple Correlation of Judicial Backgrounds and Decisions," *Florida State University Law Review* 2 (Spring 1974): 258–280.
31. The most recent effort in this field is Sheldon Goldman, "Voting Behavior on the U.S. Court of Appeals Revisited," *American Political Science*

*Review* 69 (June 1975):491–506. For an early analysis of the social background literature, see Joel B. Grossman, "Social Backgrounds and Judicial Decision-Making," *Harvard Law Review* (1966), pp. 1151–1164.

32. Bowen, "The Explanation of Judicial Voting Behavior," p. 197.

33. Kathleen L. Barber, "Ohio Judicial Elections," p. 765.

34. Glendon Schubert, *Quantitative Analysis of Judicial Behavior*, pp. 129–142.

35. Ulmer, "The Political Party Variable in the Michigan Supreme Court," pp. 352–362.

36. Ibid., p. 361.

37. Malcolm M. Feeley, "A Comparative Analysis of State Supreme Court Behavior," Ph.D. dissertation, University of Minnesota (1969), pp. 181–224; and idem, "Another Look at the 'Party Variable' in Judicial Decision-Making: An Analysis of the Michigan Supreme Court," *Polity* 4 (Fall 1971):91–104.

38. Feeley, "Another Look at the 'Party Variable,'" p. 104.

39. Adamany, "The Party Variable in Judges' Voting."

40. Ibid., p. 71.

41. Ibid., p. 72.

42. Ibid., p. 73.

43. See Daryl R. Fair, "An Experimental Application of Scalogram Analysis to State Supreme Court Decisions," *Wisconsin Law Review* (Spring 1967), pp. 449–467; Feeley, "A Comparative Analysis of State Supreme Court Behavior," pp. 134–180.

44. Edward N. Beiser and Jonathan J. Silberman, "The Political Party Variable: Workmen's Compensation Cases in the New York Court of Appeals," *Polity* 3 (Summer 1971):521–531; and Feeley, "A Comparative Analysis of State Supreme Court Behavior," pp. 94–134.

45. Adamany and Dubois, "Electing State Judges," p. 767.

46. Glick, *Supreme Courts in State Politics*, p. 136.

47. Ibid., p. 109.

48. See Sayre and Kaufman, *Governing New York City*, pp. 546–547.

49. Philip et al., *Where Do Judges Come From?* p. 1. In 1967, New York adopted the hybrid system of preprimary nomination used in a number of other states, including Colorado, Massachusetts, Connecticut, Utah, and Rhode Island. A majority of the state committee of each party designate their preferred candidate for the primary, but any candidate receiving at least 25% of the committee vote is also placed on the ballot. Other candidates may qualify for the primary by fulfilling the requirements for the circulation of nominating petitions among party members.

50. Jerry K. Beatty, "Decision-Making on the Iowa Supreme Court—1965–1969." *Drake Law Review* 19 (May 1970):342–367.

51. Feeley, "A Comparative Analysis of State Supreme Court Behavior," pp. 225–268.

52. Watson and Downing, *The Politics of the Bench and the Bar*, p. 324.

53. These include the exclusion of memorandum opinions, the concentration on votes and not the content of concurring opinions, and the assumption that all the justices were responding to the same issues in each case. In addition, courts relying heavily upon court commissioners were not included in this analysis.

54. As Schubert has done, the unit of analysis used here is the case and not the opinion. The underlying assumptions of this convention are that "each justice makes a separate decision in each case" and that "when several cases are grouped for common disposition, the Court is making simultaneous, multiple decisions" (Schubert, *Quantitative Analysis*, p. 79).

55. Kenneth N. Vines and Herbert Jacob, "State Courts," in *Politics in the American States*, ed. Jacob and Vines, p. 300, Table 9. In 1966, state court dissent rates ranged from 1.2% to 46.5%.

56. The leading published works investigating the determinants of state court dissent rates are Jaros and Canon, "Dissent on State Supreme Courts," pp. 322–346; Canon and Jaros, "External Variables, Institutional Structure, and Dissent on State Supreme Courts," pp. 175–200; and John W. Patterson and Gregory T. Rathjen, "Background Diversity and State Supreme Court Dissent Behavior," *Polity* 9 (Summer 1976): 610–622.

57. For calculating the rate of nonunanimous cases, *per curiam* opinions were excluded unless they exceed one page in length in the regional reporter. This is a modification of a similar convention used by Canon and Jaros, "External Variables, Institutional Structure, and Dissent on State Supreme Courts," p. 185, n. 34.

58. The distribution of nonunanimous cases among the five major case areas and the residual category are displayed in Appendix I.

59. This is essentially the approach taken by Nagel, "Political Party Affiliation and Judges' Decisions."

60. Beiser and Silberman, "The Political Party Variable," p. 527.

61. The mechanics and assumptions of scale analysis are discussed by Murphy and Tanenhaus, *The Study of Public Law*, pp. 126–140.

62. This definition of the liberal-conservative dichotomy was formulated by Nagel, "Political Party Affiliation and Judges' Decisions," and has been adopted by nearly every other student of judicial behavior.

63. Harold Spaeth, "Warren Court Attitudes toward Business: The 'B' Scale," in *Judicial Decision-Making*, ed. Glendon Schubert, p. 88.

64. Another problem associated with the analysis of government regulatory cases may be raised by an alteration in the axis of liberal-conservative differences over the issue which has occurred in the last decade or so. A significant proportion of the political left has become increasingly suspicious of, if not hostile toward, government agencies and officials. In some cases decided by younger liberal judges in recent years, an anti-government vote may reflect this particular attitude and not an "inconsistent" tendency toward conservatism. It is impossible to know for cer-

tain, however, which judges and how many cases might be affected by this factor. For some suggestive evidence, see Nie et al., *The Changing American Voter*, pp. 125–128.

65. The computation of these statistics is explained by Murphy and Tanenhaus, *The Study of Public Law*, p. 135.

66. See Appendix II.

67. Because "scalability" was not achieved in all instances, liberal support scores rather than scale positions will be reported here in decimal form.

68. Adamany, "The Party Variable in Judges' Voting," p. 61.

69. The application of bloc analysis to the study of judicial voting behavior is discussed by Murphy and Tanenhaus, *The Study of Public Law*, pp. 159–176.

70. See the discussion of Joel B. Grossman, "Dissenting Blocs on the Warren Court: A Study in Judicial Role Behavior," *Journal of Politics* 30, no. 4 (1968): 1076–1081.

71. This technique of bloc analysis was used by Feeley, "A Comparative Analysis of State Supreme Court Behavior." See also his "Another Look at the 'Party Variable,'" and John Sprague's, *Voting Patterns of the United States Supreme Court*.

72. The measure is described by Lee F. Anderson et al., *Legislative Roll-Call Analysis*, pp. 40, 63.

73. The problems involved in constructing bloc matrices are given extended treatment by Sprague, *Voting Patterns of the United States Supreme Court*, pp. 21–31.

74. Murphy and Tanenhaus, *The Study of Public Law*, p. 163.

75. David B. Truman, *The Congressional Party*, pp. 48–50. The major steps of matrix construction are easily summarized. First, enter the highest interagreement score in the upper left-hand cell of the matrix. Second, search the list of pairs of judges for the next highest agreement score between a pair that includes one of the judges already placed in the matrix. Third, continue in the same manner to search the list of pairs for judges linked to one or more of the judges already in the matrix until all pairs are exhausted.

76. Peter Willetts, "Cluster-Bloc Analysis and Statistical Inference," *American Political Science Review* 66 (June 1972): 569–582, especially pp. 570–574.

77. Ibid., p. 574, Table 2. As Willetts suggests (p. 573), upper cutoff points were used when the number of roll-calls or cases was above thirty.

78. Grossman, "Dissenting Blocs on the Warren Court," p. 1077.

79. Murphy and Tanenhaus, *The Study of Public Law*, pp. 164–165.

80. Ibid., p. 163.

81. Adamany, "The Party Variable in Judges' Voting," p. 61.

### 6. Partisan Voting on State Courts: Eight Case Studies

1. See n. 56, accompanying Chap. 5.

2. Atkins and Glick, "Environmental and Structural Variables as Determi-

nants of Issues," pp. 97–115. The distribution of nonunanimous cases in each state by issue area can be found in Appendix I.

3. Glick, *Supreme Courts in State Politics*, pp. 69–87.

4. See, for example, Bowen, "The Explanation of Judicial Voting Behavior from Sociological Characteristics of Judges"; Nagel, "Multiple Correlation of Judicial Backgrounds and Decisions," pp. 258–280.

5. On state court decision-making procedures, see McConkie, "Decision-Making in State Supreme Courts," pp. 337–343.

6. See Sheldon Goldman and Thomas P. Jahnige, *The Federal Courts as a Political System*, pp. 185–190, for an analysis of the relevant literature on intracourt influences on judicial decision-making. On the role of the chief justice, see Craig R. Ducat and Victor E. Flango, *Leadership in State Supreme Courts*.

7. The first period includes all the nonunanimous decisions issued from January 1963 through December 1965, included in West's Regional Reporters from 187 N.E.2d through 211 N.E.2d. Period 2 includes cases decided between January 1969 and December 1970, reported in volumes 243 N.E.2d through 265 N.E.2d of the regional reporter. The third period includes cases decided from January 1971 through December 1972, reported in volumes 265 N.E.2d through 291 N.E.2d. Because the court's membership was highly variable from 1966 to 1968, this period was not analyzed here.

8. See the discussion by Allan Ashman, "Philadelphia's Judges: How They Are Selected and Retained," in *Judicial Selection and Tenure*, ed. Winters, pp. 164–166.

9. Glick, *Supreme Courts in State Politics*, pp. 135–136.

10. See the earlier discussion of the Pennsylvania Supreme Court in Chap. 5.

11. The cases decided during the period from January 1972 through December 1974 are reported in volumes 287 A.2d through 330 A.2d of the Atlantic Regional Reporter.

12. The Republicans included Justices Roberts, O'Brien, and Jones; the holdover Democrat was Justice Eagen. The justices selected under the new system were Republican Thomas Pomeroy and Democrats Nix and Manderino.

13. See Sorauf, *Party Politics in America*, pp. 348–351.

14. Martin, "Colorado: The Highest State," pp. 117–120.

15. Ibid., p. 124.

16. Ibid., pp. 114, 123.

17. The Colorado Supreme Court considered nearly half its cases in departments, deciding only 54.3% *en banc*. Fortunately, all the dissents registered during the 1962–1968 period were filed in *en banc* decisions.

18. The first period covers decisions made between 1 January 1962 and 4 December 1964, reported in volumes 368 P.2d to 396 P.2d, the Pacific Regional Reporter. The second period includes decisions made from 29 January 1965 to 9 January 1967, reported in volumes 399 P.2d through 423 P.2d. The third period, from 10 January 1967 to 1 April 1968, in-

cludes decisions reported in volumes 422 P.2d to 439 P.2d.

19. Adamany, "The Party Variable in Judges' Voting," pp. 57–73. See the discussion of the Wisconsin Supreme Court in Chap. 5.

20. The cases analyzed here were decided between 2 January 1968 and 1 August 1974, reported in volumes 155 N.W.2d through 219 N.W.2d, the Northwest Regional Reporter.

21. Justice Heffernan was a former U.S. attorney in Wisconsin's western district and a former deputy state attorney general under Attorney General John Reynolds, who was later elected governor and appointed Heffernan to the court. Wilkie was a Democratic state senator at the time of his appointment.

22. This decade of decisions has been divided into two periods. The first includes cases decided between January 1960 and June 1966, reported in 348 P.2d to 415 P.2d. The decisions for the second period, from January 1967 through December 1970, are found in 422 P.2d to 479 P.2d.

23. There is, however, no doubt as to Justice Henriod's partisan allegiance as he identified himself as a Republican in all the published biographical sources.

24. There are indications that religion might be an important background variable which confounds the analysis of criminal cases on the Utah Supreme Court. During Period 1, the court included three Mormons (Wade, Crockett, and Henriod) and one Catholic (McDonough), religious backgrounds usually thought to foster more-conservative attitudes on matters of crime and punishment. During Period 2, Crockett and Henriod were joined by Ellett, neither a Mormon nor a Catholic but a judge whose conservative record on criminal cases may reflect conservative attitudes spawned during his upbringing and education in the southern states of Alabama and Texas.

25. Period 1 covers decisions issued beginning on 1 February 1963 and ending with the last day of 1966, reported in 378 P.2d through 422 P.2d. Period 2 begins in January 1973 and ends with decisions issued in December 1974, reported in 505 P.2d through 529 P.2d.

26. During the first period, 80% of the cases were decided by two five-member divisions. Dissents were filed in 11.5% of all cases, but 87.8% of the dissents were filed in cases heard *en banc*. In the second period, all the court's decisions were made *en banc*. The analysis here, as in Colorado, rests upon *en banc* decisions only.

27. See Canon and Jaros, "External Variables, Institutional Structure, and Dissent on State Supreme Courts," pp. 184–185, 192–193. See also Atkins and Glick, "Environmental and Structural Variables as Determinants of Issues."

28. The mandatory retirement age in Iowa is 72 years, but judges selected prior to July 1, 1965, may serve until the age of 75.

29. The decisions from mid-1972 through calendar 1974, reported in 199 N.W.2d to 225 N.W.2d, are analyzed here. Over three-fourths of Iowa's cases were decided by two rotating panels of five justices, each of which

included the chief justice. Dissents were filed in 26.5% of the cases handled by division, but they comprised only 16.7% of the court's non-unanimous decisions. The vast majority of nonunanimous decisions (83.7%) occurred in cases heard *en banc*. And of the cases heard by the full court, 46.5% provoked dissent.

30. Only Democratic Justice McCormick seems not to have had prior experience in partisan politics before ascending to the state's highest court.

31. Beatty, "Decision-Making on the Iowa Supreme Court, 1965–1969," pp. 349–367. See the discussion of the Iowa court in Chap. 5.

32. Ashman and Alfini, *The Key to Judicial Merit Selection*, p. 209.

33. Ibid.

34. The nominating commission originally was composed of thirteen members. The 1962 reapportionment resulted in the loss of one congressional seat, however, and thus the removal of one lay person and one lawyer from the commission.

35. The cases analyzed may be found in volumes 492 P.2d through 530 P.2d, covering decisions issued during the years 1972–1974.

## 7. A Comparative Approach to Party Bloc Voting

1. Stephen J. Brams and Michael K. O'Leary, "An Axiomatic Model of Voting Bodies," *American Political Science Review* 64 (June 1970):458.

2. Grossman, "Dissenting Blocs on the Warren Court," pp. 1080–1085.

3. Brams and O'Leary, "An Axiomatic Model of Voting Bodies," especially pp. 458–460.

4. In a critique of the Agreement Level Index developed by Brams and O'Leary, Richard Born and Christopher Nevison discovered that the AL Index is merely the square of the well-known Rice Index of Cohesion when applied to roll-call votes having two voting options. For simplicity's sake, calculations of the AL Index are best understood in terms of the Born-Nevison reformulation:

$$\text{Agreement Level (AL)} = (\text{Rice Index})^2 + \frac{(\text{Rice Index})^2 - 1}{\left[\dfrac{(k-1)}{(k-r)r}\right]N^2 - 1}$$

where $k$ is the number of voting options ($k = 2$ in judicial voting analysis) and $r$ is the remainder when $N$ (the number of members in the voting body) is divided by $k$.

The Rice Index of Cohesion is calculated by the formula:

$$\frac{m_1 - m_2}{N}$$

where $m_1$ is the number of judges voting in the majority, $m_2$ is the number of dissenting votes, and $N$ is the total number of voting members ($m_1 + m_2$). See Richard Born and Christopher Nevison, "The 'Agreement Level' Measure and the Rice Index of Cohesion Revisited," *Ameri-*

*can Journal of Political Science* 18 (August 1974): 617–624. The Rice Index and its applications are discussed by Anderson et al., *Legislative Roll-Call Analysis*, pp. 32–35.

5.  This adjustment is necessary because the Rice Index, which forms the basis for the AL Index, only attains the value of 1.0 when all members of a voting body have voted on the same side of an issue, i.e., unanimously. But the exclusion of unanimous cases in judicial behavior research gives the Rice Index an effective upper limit less than 1.0, depending upon the size of the court. The AL Index can be adjusted, however, to take into account the exclusion of unanimous cases; the effect of this adjustment is to scale the AL Index from 0.0 to 1.0, where 1.0 represents the most cohesive court possible given the exclusion of unanimously decided cases. That is, the AL Index achieves the value of 1.0 *whenever the court is as cohesive as it can be* given that in each case at least one dissent will be found. This correlation takes two mathematical forms, depending upon whether the number of justices participating in a decision is odd or even. For even-sized groups, the corrected AL Index (or the Court Cohesion Index) is calculated by:

$$\frac{N^2 \, (\text{Rice Index})^2}{N^2 - 4N + 4} \; .$$

For odd-sized groups, the corrected AL, or Court Cohesion Index, is equal to:

$$\frac{N^2 \, (\text{Rice Index})^2 - 1}{N^2 - 4N + 3} \; ,$$

where $N$ is the size of the participating group on each roll call or vote.

The mathematical derivation of this adjustment to the AL Index and a table of corrected values for the possible divisions on different-sized courts can be found in Philip L. Dubois and Paul F. Dubois, "Measuring Dissent Behavior on State Courts: An Application and an Adaptation of Known Measurement Techniques," *Polity*, forthcoming (1980).

6.  The Court Cohesion Index is simply the AL Index applied to the whole court and corrected for the exclusion of unanimous cases.

7.  In practice, however, since the Court Cohesion Index never assumes a value less than 0.25 for any of the courts in any of the issue areas of this study, the Ratio of Relative Party Cohesion would not exceed 4.0, even if the mean intraparty Agreement Level Index registered a perfect 1.0.

8.  See Sorauf, *Party Politics in America*, pp. 350–351, Tables 1 and 2.

9.  Ibid., p. 357.

10.  Ibid., pp. 349–353.

11.  Ibid., pp. 353–356.

12.  Kathleen L. Barber, "Partisan Values in the Lower Courts: Reapportionment in Ohio and Michigan," *Case Western Reserve Law Review* 20 (February 1969): 401–421.

13.  Ibid., p. 406.

14.  Ibid., p. 403. But see also Thomas G. Walker, "A Note Concerning Par-

tisan Influences on Trial Judge Decision-Making," *Law and Society Review* 6 (May 1972): 645–649. Studying the behavior of federal district court judges in civil liberties cases from 1963 to 1968, Walker found only a weak relationship between the decisional tendencies of judges and their party affiliations. But it is not clear whether his findings are attributable to the kind of judges involved (federal judges with secure tenure) or the nature of the issues studied.

15. Feeley, "Another Look at the 'Party Variable' in Judicial Decision-Making," p. 104. This conclusion, of course, does not apply to the "domestic" case area where neither partisan nor ideological differences were expected.

16. This point, among others, is addressed by ibid., pp. 99–104. See also Martin A. Levin, "Urban Politics and Judicial Behavior," *Journal of Legal Studies* 1 (January 1972): 193–221. The results of Levin's study of the sentencing decisions of criminal court judges in Minneapolis and Pittsburgh support the view that the indirect influence of a judicial selection system in recruiting individuals with particular attitudes and values which affect judicial decisions is more powerful than the direct influence of a partisan or nonpartisan judicial constituency.

17. Sorauf, *Party Politics in America*, p. 376.

18. Recall that there is a major difference between "impartiality" and "independence." See the discussion in Chap. 1 at the section entitled "Judicial Independence."

19. Sorauf, *Party Politics in America*, p. 379.

20. Ibid., p. 377.

21. See Everett Carll Ladd, Jr., with Charles D. Hadley, *Transformations of the American Party System*, pp. 291–304.

22. Readers should not confuse the concept of *direct accountability* with the *indirect effects* of elections in securing *direct* accountability. In the context used here, accountability may be achieved indirectly through the appointment of judges by governors who are periodically subject to voter approval. By appointing judges from his or her own party, a governor staffs the judiciary with individuals who maintain political values that the voters endorsed when they elected the governor; accountability is thus indirectly obtained. For a thorough discussion of the achievement of direct accountability through the indirect effects of elections, see the section "Judicial Accountability: Do Elections Guarantee Popular Control?" in Chap. 1.

23. Obviously, with the provision for life tenure and other constitutional protections for judges, the framers were not concerned so much with securing accountability as they were with preserving judicial independence. Nevertheless, the federal system has often been cited as a model for the design of state judicial selection systems by the devotees of independence and of accountability. "If the bar and the public are alert to the importance of good judges, the appointing power is necessarily inclined to attempt to secure competent personnel within party limits, since he

will be identified with the appointments and as an agent of the people is subject to popular control. The respect accorded the federal bench and its prestige generally lends support to those who favor the appointive system" (Arthur T. Vanderbilt, "Judges and Jurors: Their Functions, Qualifications, and Selection," *Boston University Law Review* 36, no. 1, [1956]:49).

24. See Dahl, "Decision-Making in Democracy," pp. 279–295. But see David Adamany, "Legitimacy, Realigning Elections and the Supreme Court," *Wisconsin Law Review* (1973):790–846; and Jonathan D. Casper, "The Supreme Court and National Policy Making," *American Political Science Review* 70 (March 1976): 50–63.

25. Adamany and Dubois, "Electing State Judges," p. 773.

26. See the discussion in "The Question of Judicial Quality," in Chap. 1.

27. On the elements of accountability generally, see the discussion in "Judicial Accountability: Do Elections Guarantee Popular Control?" in Chap. 1.

28. Adamany and Dubois, "Electing State Judges," p. 768.

29. Admittedly, in the minds of those committed to the principle of judicial independence and those concerned with the recruitment of high-quality individuals to serve on the bench, the security of incumbents is one of the virtues of the merit plan and not one of its vices. The argument here responds to those who might argue that the merit selection and retention system successfully combines a quality bench with indirect judicial accountability. To my knowledge, no one has yet advanced this argument, but it is certainly a plausible one given the evidence on partisanship in merit selection appointments (see Chap. 1, n. 22). This argument with respect to gubernatorial appointment and reappointment is much more common.

30. Though no studies of appointment practices in those states using gubernatorial selection and reappointment have been done, it does appear that in many such states informal traditions of bipartisan judicial appointments have existed for many years. Such informal traditions relieve the partisan pressures upon the appointing official to sacrifice quality for partisanship in making judicial appointments. Indeed, in some states for local trial courts, bipartisan judicial selections are required by constitutional provisions (see Vanderbilt, "Judges and Jurors," p. 40, n. 45).

31. Alternatively, on a rare number of occasions, an incumbent judge may be charged with unethical behavior on or off the bench or his or her performance in office may be so widely regarded as inadequate that there is clear support for removal. A governor must always weigh the political risks which attend the removal of a sitting judge, however.

32. Note that presidents never are faced with the dilemma of having to remove one judge and appoint a replacement. By virtue of the constitutional provision for judges to serve "during good behavior," openings on the federal bench occur only through the death, retirement, or resigna-

tion of sitting judges; all of a president's appointments, therefore, are to "open" slots.

At this point some might argue that the electorate cannot have it both ways—they cannot, on the one hand, want the governor to replace incumbents with individuals holding more-compatible ideologies and, on the other hand, blame the governor for sacrificing quality for partisanship when doing so. In actuality, of course, citizen attitudes toward this question are probably not well developed and are largely ambivalent. Few voters, indeed, are likely to punish a governor for judicial appointments one way or the other. But many governors obviously perceive political liabilities in removing incumbents for partisan or ideological reasons. Undoubtedly, the widely held myth within the society that judges are not engaged in political activity supports these perceptions. In any event, the pressure upon governors to make "nonpartisan" or "bipartisan" judicial appointments may stand in the way of the achievement of indirect accountability as defined here. See n. 30.

33. Neither accountability nor independence, of course, is obtained by the system of initial selection or the method of retention alone. Rather, most selection systems combine with the length of judicial terms (ranging from six years to life for state courts of last resort) to produce a delicate balance between accountability and independence. Longer terms reflect a desire to provide protection for the value of independence; shorter terms reflect significant concern about maintaining judicial accountability. See Adamany and Dubois, "Electing State Judges," pp. 768–772, for a detailed discussion of whether state judges should be accountable or independent.

## 8. Conclusion: The Continuing Debate over State Judicial Selection

1. See W. David Curtiss, "Screening Judicial Candidates for Election," *Judicature* 59 (February 1976): 320–323; and Martin Kaminsky, "A Proposal for Mandatory Preselection Screening of State Court Judges," *St. Johns Law Review* 51 (1977): 516–563.

2. See Curtiss, "Screening Judicial Candidates," pp. 322–323, and the citations therein at nn. 8–9; and Kaminsky, "A Proposal for Mandatory Preselection Screening," pp. 553–557.

3. Joel B. Grossman, "A Political View of Judicial Ethics," *San Diego Law Review* 9 (June 1972): 809–810.

4. Grossman, "A Political View of Judicial Ethics," p. 815.

5. Ibid., p. 810.

6. Ibid., p. 815.

7. Ibid., p. 810.

8. Kathleen L. Barber, "Selection of Ohio Appellate Judges: A Case Study in Invisible Politics," in *Political Behavior and Public Issues in Ohio*, ed. Gargan and Coke, p. 184.

9. Ibid., p. 185, quoting Mayers, *The American Legal System*, p. 395.

10. Ibid.
11. See Mayers, *The American Legal System*, p. 387. See also Sayre and Kaufman, *Governing New York City*, pp. 530–531, 538–543.
12. Barber, "Selection of Ohio Appellate Judges," p. 186.
13. Others have argued, however, that the merit plan is best applied to the selection of appellate judges. In this view, trial judges should be "closer to the people" and base their decisions more closely upon community sentiments; elections are, accordingly, perfectly proper for the selection of trial judges. Moreover, because the public has more direct contact with trial than with appellate courts, voters are said to be in a much better position to evaluate the work of trial judges and to participate intelligently in their selection. See Watson and Downing, *The Politics of the Bench and the Bar*, pp. 254–257.
14. The reform movement for the merit plan has been most successful where the political parties (or other relevant political groups with a stake in judicial selection) have had the least to lose by a change in selection method. At the appellate level, there are relatively few judgeships (and associated personnel) involved compared to the trial court level. Merit plan supporters openly acknowledge that once the merit plan has been used for awhile at the appellate level and has gained public acceptance and legitimacy attempts can then be made to extend it to cover the selection of the more numerous trial court positions. See Garwood, "Judicial Revision," p. 3.
15. By my count, only eight states had adopted the merit plan formally for the selection of trial court judges by 1976. In contrast, thirty-one states used some form of partisan (14 states) or nonpartisan (17) elections, while seven states featured gubernatorial appointment, three used election by the legislature, and one featured appointment by the judiciary.

# Bibliography

## Books

Adamany, David W., and Agree, George E. *Political Money: A Strategy for Campaign Financing in America.* Baltimore: Johns Hopkins Press, 1975.

American Bar Association, Section of Judicial Administration. *The Improvement of the Administration of Justice.* 5th ed. Chicago: American Bar Association, 1971.

Anderson, Lee F.; Watts, Meredith W., Jr.; and Wilcox, Allen R. *Legislative Roll-Call Analysis.* Evanston: Northwestern University Press, 1966.

Ashman, Allan, and Alfini, James J. *The Key to Judicial Merit Selection: The Nominating Process.* Chicago: American Judicature Society, 1974.

Bain, Henry M., Jr., and Hecock, Donald S. *Ballot Position and Voter's Choice: The Arrangement of Names on the Ballot and Its Effect on the Voter.* Westport, Conn.: Greenwood Press, 1957.

Balmer, Donald G. *State Election Services in Oregon.* Princeton: Citizens' Research Foundation, 1972.

Berelson, Bernard R.; Lazarsfeld, Paul F.; and McPhee, William N. *Voting.* Chicago: University of Chicago Press, 1954.

Blalock, Herbert. *Social Statistics.* New York: McGraw-Hill, 1960.

Burnham, Walter Dean. *Critical Elections and the Mainsprings of American Politics.* New York: W. W. Norton and Company, 1970.

Campbell, Angus; Converse, Philip E.; Miller, Warren E.; and Stokes, Donald E. *The American Voter.* New York: John Wiley and Sons, 1960.

——; ——; ——; and ——, eds. *Elections and the Political Order.* New York: John Wiley and Sons, 1966.

Chase, Harold. *Federal Judges: The Appointing Process.* Minneapolis: University of Minnesota Press, 1972.

Drury, James W. *The Government of Kansas.* Rev. ed. Lawrence: University Press of Kansas, 1970.

Ducat, Craig R., and Flango, Victor E. *Leadership in State Supreme Courts: Roles of the Chief Justice.* Beverly Hills: Sage Publications, 1976.

Dye, Thomas R. *Politics, Economics, and the Public.* Chicago: Rand McNally and Company, 1966.

Escovitz, Sari S. (comp.). *Judicial Selection and Tenure*. Chicago: American Judicature Society, 1975.

Fenton, John. *Midwest Politics*. New York: Holt, Rinehart, and Winston, 1966.

Gargan, John J., and Coke, James G., eds. *Political Behavior and Public Issues in Ohio*. Kent: Kent State University Press, 1972.

Glick, Henry Robert. *Supreme Courts in State Politics: An Investigation of the Judicial Role*. New York: Basic Books, 1971.

Goff, John S. *Arizona Civilization*. Cave Creek, Ariz.: Black Mountain Press, 1970.

Goldman, Sheldon, and Jahnige, Thomas P. *The Federal Courts as a Political System*. 2d ed. New York: Harper and Row, 1976.

Guterman, James H., and Meidinger, Errol E. *In the Opinion of the Bar: A National Survey of Bar Polling Practices*. Chicago: American Judicature Society, 1977.

Hahn, Harlan. *Urban-Rural Conflict: The Politics of Change*. Beverly Hills: Sage Publications, 1971.

Hawley, Willis D. *Nonpartisan Elections and the Case for Party Politics*. New York: John Wiley and Sons, 1973.

Haynes, Evan. *The Selection and Tenure of Judges*. New York: National Conference of Judicial Councils, 1944.

Holmes, Jack E. *Politics in New Mexico*. Albuquerque: University of New Mexico Press, 1967.

Hurst, James Willard. *The Growth of American Law: The Lawmakers*. Boston: Little, Brown and Company, 1950.

Jacob, Herbert, and Vines, Kenneth N., eds. *Politics in the American States: A Comparative Analysis*. 2d ed. Boston: Little, Brown and Company, 1971.

Jonas, Frank, ed. *Western Politics*. Salt Lake City: University of Utah Press, 1961.

Key, V. O., Jr. *American State Politics: An Introduction*. New York: Alfred A. Knopf, 1956, 1972.

———. *Politics, Parties, and Pressure Groups*. 5th ed. New York: Thomas Y. Crowell Company, 1964.

———. *Southern Politics*. New York: Vintage Books, Alfred A. Knopf, 1949.

———, with the assistance of Milton C. Cummings, Jr. *The Responsible Electorate: Rationality in Presidential Voting, 1936–1960*. New York: Vintage Books, 1966, 1968.

Ladd, Everett Carll, Jr., with Hadley, Charles D. *Transformations of the American Party System: Political Coalitions from the New Deal to the 1970s*. New York: W. W. Norton and Company, 1975.

Lee, Eugene C. *The Politics of Nonpartisanship*. Berkeley: University of California Press, 1960.

Levy, Leonard, ed. *Judicial Review and the Supreme Court: Selected Essays*. New York: Harper and Row, 1967.

Liebman, Charles, ed. *Directory of American Judges*. Chicago: American Directories, 1955.

Martin, Curtis, and Gomez, Rudolph. *Colorado Government and Politics.* Boulder: Pruett Press, 1964.

Mason, Bruce B., and Hink, Heinz R. *Constitutional Government in Arizona.* Tempe: Arizona State University, Bureau of Government Research, 1963.

Mayers, Lewis. *The American Legal System.* Rev. ed. New York: Harper and Row, 1964.

Mayhew, David R. *Congress: The Electoral Connection.* New Haven: Yale University Press, 1974.

Milbrath, Lester W. *Political Participation: How and Why Do People Get Involved in Politics.* Chicago: Rand McNally and Company, 1965.

Miller, Warren E., and Levitin, Teresa E. *Leadership and Change: The New Politics and the American Electorate.* Cambridge, Mass.: Winthrop Publishers, 1976.

Murphy, Walter F., and Tanenhaus, Joseph. *The Study of Public Law.* New York: Random House, 1972.

Nagel, Stuart. *Comparing Elected and Appointed Judicial Systems.* Beverly Hills: Sage Professional Papers in American Politics, 1973.

Nie, Norman H.; Verba, Sidney; and Petrocik, John R. *The Changing American Voter.* Cambridge, Mass.: Harvard University Press, 1976.

Niemi, Richard G., and Weisberg, Herbert F., eds. *Controversies in American Voting Behavior.* San Francisco: W. H. Freeman and Company, 1976.

Owens, John R.; Costantini, Edmond; and Wechsler, Louis F. *California Politics and Parties.* New York: Macmillan Company, 1970.

Peltason, Jack. *Federal Courts in the Political Process.* New York: Doubleday, 1955.

Philip, Cynthia Owen; Nejelski, Paul; and Press, Aric. *Where Do Judges Come From?* New York: Institute of Judicial Administration, 1976.

Pomper, Gerald M. *Elections in America: Control and Influence in Democratic Politics.* New York: Dodd, Mead, and Company, 1968, 1973.

———. *Voters' Choice: Varieties of American Electoral Behavior.* New York: Dodd, Mead, and Company, 1975.

Ranney, Austin, ed. *Essays on the Behavioral Studies of Politics.* Urbana: University of Illinois Press, 1962.

Sayre, Wallace S., and Kaufman, Herbert. *Governing New York City: Politics in the Metropolis.* New York: Russell Sage Foundation, 1960.

Schattschneider, E. E. *The Semi-Sovereign People: A Realistic View of Democracy in America.* New York: Holt, Rinehart, and Winston, 1960.

Schubert, Glendon. *Quantitative Analysis of Judicial Behavior.* Glencoe, Ill.: Free Press; and East Lansing: Michigan State University Bureau of Social and Political Research, 1959.

———, ed. *Judicial Behavior in Theory and Research.* Chicago: Rand McNally and Company, 1964.

———, ed. *Judicial Decision-Making.* London: Free Press of Glencoe, 1963.

Sorauf, Frank. *Party Politics in America.* 2d ed. Boston: Little, Brown and Company, 1972.

Sprague, John. *Voting Patterns of the United States Supreme Court: Cases in Federalism, 1889–1959*. Indianapolis: Bobbs-Merrill Company, 1968.

Sturm, Albert L., and Whitaker, Margaret. *Implementing a New Constitution: The Michigan Experience*. University of Michigan Governmental Studies, no. 50. Ann Arbor: University of Michigan Institute of Public Administration, 1968.

Truman, David B. *The Congressional Party: A Case Study*. New York: John Wiley and Sons, 1959.

Verba, Sidney, and Nie, Norman H. *Participation in America: Political Democracy and Social Equality*. New York: Harper and Row, 1972.

Vines, Kenneth N., and Jacob, Herbert, eds. *Studies in Judicial Politics*. Tulane Studies in Political Science, vol. VIII. New Orleans: Tulane University Press, 1962.

Watson, Richard A., and Downing, Rondal G. *The Politics of the Bench and the Bar: Judicial Selection under the Missouri Non-partisan Court Plan*. New York: John Wiley and Sons, 1969.

Winters, Glenn R., ed. *Judicial Discipline and Removal: Selected Readings*. Chicago: American Judicature Society, 1973.

———, ed. *Judicial Selection and Tenure: Selected Readings*. Rev. ed. Chicago: American Judicature Society, 1973.

## Articles

Abramowitz, Alan I. "Name Familiarity, Reputation, and the Incumbency Effect in a Congressional Election." *Western Political Quarterly* 28 (December 1975): 668–684.

Adamany, David. "Legitimacy, Realigning Elections and the Supreme Court." *Wisconsin Law Review* (1973), pp. 790–846.

———. "The Party Variable in Judges' Voting: Conceptual Notes and a Case Study." *American Political Science Review* 63 (March 1969): 57–73.

———, and Dubois, Philip. "Electing State Judges." *Wisconsin Law Review*, no. 3 (1976), pp. 731–779.

———, and ———. "The 'Forgetful' Voter and an Underreported Vote." *Public Opinion Quarterly* 39 (Summer 1975): 227–231.

Adrian, Charles R. "Some General Characteristics of Nonpartisan Elections." *American Political Science Review* 46 (September 1952): 766–776.

Alford, Robert R., and Lee, Eugene C. "Voting Turnout in American Cities." *American Political Science Review* 62 (September 1968): 796–813.

———. "Merit Retention Elections in 1972." *Judicature* 56 (January 1973): 252–254.

American Judicature Society. "Judicial Retirement Plans." *Judicature* 58 (November 1974): 197–202.

Arcelus, Francisco, and Meltzner, Allan H. "The Effect of Aggregate Economic Variables on Congressional Elections." *American Political Science Review* 69 (December 1975): 1232–1239.

Atkins, Burton M. "Judicial Elections: What the Evidence Shows." *Florida Bar Journal* 50, no. 3 (March 1976): 152–157.

———. "Merit Selection of State Judges." *Florida Bar Journal* 50, no. 4 (April 1976): 203–211.

———, and Glick, Henry R. "Environmental and Structural Variables as Determinants of Issues in State Courts of Last Resort." *American Journal of Political Science* 20 (February 1976): 97–115.

———, and ———. "Formal Judicial Recruitment and State Supreme Court Decisions." *American Politics Quarterly* 2 (October 1974): 427–449.

Barber, Kathleen L. "Ohio Judicial Elections: Nonpartisan Premises with Partisan Results." *Ohio State Law Journal* 32 (Fall 1971): 762–789.

———. "Partisan Values in the Lower Courts: Reapportionment in Ohio and Michigan." *Case Western Reserve Law Review* 20 (February 1969): 401–421.

Beatty, Jerry K. "Decision-Making on the Iowa Supreme Court—1965–1969." *Drake Law Review* 19 (May 1970): 342–367.

Beechen, Paul D. "Can Judicial Elections Express the People's Choice?" *Judicature* 57 (January 1974): 242–246.

Beiser, Edward N., and Silberman, Jonathan J. "The Political Party Variable: Workmen's Compensation Cases in the New York Court of Appeals." *Polity* 3 (Summer 1971): 521–531.

Berg, Larry L.; Green, Justin J.; Schmidhauser, John R.; and Schneider, Ronald S. "The Consequences of Judicial Reform: A Comparative Analysis of the California and Iowa Appellate Systems." *Western Political Quarterly* 28 (June 1975): 263–280.

Blank, Robert H. "Socio-Economic Determinism of Voting Turnout: A Challenge." *Journal of Politics* 36 (August 1974): 732–752.

———. "State Electoral Structure." *Journal of Politics* 35 (November 1973): 988–994.

Born, Richard, and Nevison, Christopher. "The 'Agreement Level' Measure and the Rice Index of Cohesion Revisited." *American Journal of Political Science* 18 (August 1974): 617–624.

Borowiec, Walter A. "Pathways to the Top: The Political Careers of State Supreme Court Justices." *North Carolina Central Law Journal* 7 (Spring 1976): 280–285.

Boyd, Richard W. "Popular Control of Public Policy: A Normal Vote Analysis of the 1968 Election." *American Political Science Review* 66 (June 1972): 429–449.

Brams, Steven J., and O'Leary, Michael K. "An Axiomatic Model of Voting Bodies." *American Political Science Review* 64 (June 1970): 449–470.

Burnett, Warren. "Observations on the Direct Election Method of Judicial Selection." *Texas Law Review* 44 (June 1966): 1098–1102.

Byrne, Gary C., and Pueschel, J. Kristian. "But Who Should I Vote For for County Coroner?" *Journal of Politics* 36 (August 1974): 778–784.

Campbell, Angus, and Miller, Warren E. "The Motivational Basis of Straight and Split Ticket Voting." *American Political Science Review* 51 (June 1957): 293–312.

Canon, Bradley C. "The Impact of Formal Selection Processes on the Characteristics of Judges—Reconsidered." *Law and Society Review* 6 (May 1972): 579–593.

———, and Jaros, Dean. "External Variables, Institutional Structure, and Dissent on State Supreme Courts." *Polity* 3 (Winter 1970): 175–200.

Casper, Jonathan D. "The Supreme Court and National Policy Making." *American Political Science Review* 70 (March 1976): 50–63.

Cover, Albert D. "One Good Term Deserves Another: The Advantage of Incumbency in Congressional Elections." *American Journal of Political Science* 21 (August 1977): 523–541.

Cowart, Andrew T. "Electoral Choice in the American States: Incumbency Effects, Partisan Forces, and Divergent Partisan Majorities." *American Political Science Review* 67 (September 1973): 835–853.

Curtiss, W. David. "Screening Judicial Candidates for Election." *Judicature* 59 (February 1976): 320–323.

Dahl, Robert A. "Decision-Making in a Democracy: The Supreme Court as a National Policy-Maker." *Journal of Public Law* 6 (Fall 1957): 279–295.

Drinan, Robert F. "Judicial Appointments for Life by the Executive Branch of Government: Reflections on the Massachusetts Experience." *Texas Law Review* 44 (June 1966): 1103–1116.

Dubois, Philip L., and Dubois, Paul F. "Measuring Dissent Behavior on State Courts: An Application and an Adaptation of Known Measurement Techniques." *Polity* (Forthcoming 1980).

Fair, Daryl R. "An Experimental Application of Scalogram Analysis to State Supreme Court Decisions." *Wisconsin Law Review* (Spring 1967), pp. 449–467.

Feeley, Malcolm M. "Another Look at the 'Party Variable' in Judicial Decision-Making: An Analysis of the Michigan Supreme Court." *Polity* 4 (Fall 1971): 91–104.

Garwood, W. St. John. "Democracy and the Popular Election of Judges: An Argument." *Southwestern Law Journal* 16 (1962): 216–243.

———. "Judicial Revision—An Argument for the Merit Plan for Judicial Selection and Tenure." *Texas Tech Law Review* 5 (1973–74): 1–19.

———. "Popular Election of Judges Is Not Sacrosanct." *Florida Bar Journal* 38 (June 1964): 349–355.

Goldman, Sheldon. "Backgrounds, Attitudes, and the Voting Behavior of Judges: A Comment on Joel Grossman's 'Social Backgrounds and Judicial Decisions.'" *Journal of Politics* 31 (1969): 214–222.

———. "Voting Behavior on the U.S. Court of Appeals Revisited." *American Political Science Review* 69 (June 1975): 491–506.

Gray, Virginia. "A Note on Competition and Turnout in the American States." *Journal of Politics* 38 (February 1976): 153–158.

Grossman, Joel B. "Dissenting Blocs on the Warren Court: A Study in Judicial Role Behavior." *Journal of Politics* 30, no. 4 (1968): 1068–1090.

———. "A Political View of Judicial Ethics." *San Diego Law Review* 9 (June 1972): 803–815.

————. "Social Backgrounds and Judicial Decision-Making." *Harvard Law Review* (1966): 1551–1564.

————. "Social Backgrounds and Judicial Decisions: Notes for a Theory." *Journal of Politics* 29 (1967): 334–351.

Hamilton, Howard D. "The Municipal Voter: Voting and Nonvoting in City Elections." *American Political Science Review* 65 (December 1971): 1135–1140.

Heiberg, Robert A. "Social Backgrounds of the Minnesota Supreme Court Justices: 1858–1968." *Minnesota Law Review* 53 (1969): 901–937.

Heller, Francis H. "The Justices of the Kansas Supreme Court 1861–1975: A Collective Portrait." *University of Kansas Law Review* 24 (1975–76): 521–535.

Herndon, James. "Appointment as a Means of Initial Accession to Elective State Courts of Last Resort." *North Dakota Law Review* 38 (January 1962): 60–73.

Hofstetter, C. Richard. "Inter-Party Competition and Electoral Turnout: The Case of Indiana." *American Journal of Political Science* 17 (May 1973): 351–366.

Horowitz, Donald. "The Courts as Guardians of the Public Interest." *Public Administration Review* 37, no. 2 (1977): 148–154.

Jacob, Herbert. "The Effect of Institutional Differences in the Recruitment Process: The Case of State Judges." *Journal of Public Law* 13, no. 1 (1964): 104–119.

————. "Judicial Insulation—Elections, Direct Participation, and Public Attention to the Courts in Wisconsin." *Wisconsin Law Review*, no. 3 (1966), pp. 801–819.

Jaros, Dean, and Canon, Bradley C. "Dissent on State Supreme Courts: The Differential Significance of Characteristics of Judges." *Midwest Journal of Political Science* 15 (February 1971): 322–346.

Jenkins, William, Jr. "Retention Elections: Who Wins When No One Loses?" *Judicature* 61 (August 1977): 79–86.

Jewell, Malcolm E. "Voting Turnout in State Gubernatorial Primaries." *Western Political Quarterly* 30 (June 1977): 236–254.

Johnson, Charles A.; Shaefer, Roger C.; and McKnight, R. Neal. "Salience of Judicial Candidates and Elections." *Social Science Quarterly* 59 (September 1978): 371–378.

Kaminsky, Martin. "A Proposal for Mandatory Preselection Screening of State Court Judges." *St. John's Law Review* 51 (1977): 516–563.

Karnig, Albert K., and Walter, B. Oliver. "Municipal Elections: Registration, Incumbent Success, and Voter Participation." *Municipal Yearbook* (1977), pp. 65–72.

Kelley, Stanley, Jr.; Ayres, Richard E.; and Bowen, William G. "Registration and Voting: Putting First Things First." *American Political Science Review* 61 (June 1967): 359–377.

Kernell, Samuel. "Presidential Popularity and Negative Voting: An Alternative Explanation of the Midterm Congressional Decline of the President's Party." *American Political Science Review* 71 (March 1977): 44–66.

Kessel, John H. "The Issues in Issue Voting." *American Political Science Review* 66 (June 1972): 459–465.

Kim, Jae-On; Petrocik, John R.; and Enokson, Stephen N. "Voter Turnout among the American States: Systematic and Individual Components." *American Political Science Review* 69 (March 1975): 107–123.

Kostroski, Warren Lee. "Party and Incumbency in Postwar Senate Elections." *American Political Science Review* 67 (December 1973): 1213–1234.

Ladinsky, Jack, and Grossman, Joel B. "Organizational Consequences of Professional Consensus." *Administrative Science Quarterly* 11 (June 1966): 79–106.

———, and Silver, Allan. "Popular Democracy and Judicial Independence: Electorate and Elite Reactions to Two Wisconsin Supreme Court Elections." *Wisconsin Law Review*, no. 1 (1967), pp. 128–169.

Lee, Eugene C. "City Elections: A Statistical Profile." *Municipal Yearbook* (1963), pp. 74–84.

Lee, Stephen E. "Judicial Selection and Tenure in Arizona." *Law and the Social Order* (1973), pp. 51–80.

Levin, Martin A. "Urban Politics and Judicial Behavior." *Journal of Legal Studies* 1 (January 1972): 193–221.

Lowe, R. Stanley. "Voluntary Merit Selection Plans." *Judicature* 55 (November 1971): 161–168.

McCloskey, Herbert; Hoffman, Paul J.; and O'Hara, Rosemary. "Issue Conflict and Consensus among Party Leaders and Followers." *American Political Science Review* 54 (June 1960): 406–427.

McConkie, Stanford S. "Decision-Making in State Supreme Courts." *Judicature* 59 (February 1976): 337–343.

Margolis, Michael. "From Confusion to Confusion: Issues and the American Voter (1956–1972)." *American Political Science Review* 71 (March 1977): 31–43.

Mayo, Charles. "The 1961 Mayoral Election in Los Angeles: The Political Party in a Nonpartisan Election." *Western Political Quarterly* 17 (June 1964): 325–337.

Moos, Malcolm C. "Judicial Elections and Partisan Endorsement of Judicial Candidates in Minnesota." *American Political Science Review* 35 (February 1941): 69–75.

Mullinax, Otto B. "Judicial Revision—An Argument against the Merit Plan for Judicial Selection and Tenure." *Texas Tech Law Review* 5 (1973–74): 21–34.

Nagel, Stuart S. "Multiple Correlation of Judicial Backgrounds and Decisions." *Florida State University Law Review* 2 (Spring 1974): 258–280.

———. "Political Party Affiliation and Judges' Decisions." *American Political Science Review* 55 (December 1961): 843–850.

Nelson, Dorothy W. "Variations on a Theme—Selection and Tenure of Judges." *Southern California Law Review* 36 (1962–63): 4–54.

Note: "Judicial Selection and Tenure in Indiana: A Critical Analysis and Suggested Reform." *Indiana Law Journal* 39 (Winter 1964): 364–386.

————: "Judicial Selection and Tenure: The Merit Plan in Ohio." *University of Cincinnati Law Review* 42 (1973): 255–349.

————: "Judicial Selection in North Dakota: Is Constitutional Revision Necessary." *North Dakota Law Review* 48 (1971–72): 327–340.

Patterson, John W., and Rathjen, Gregory T. "Background Diversity and State Supreme Court Dissent Behavior." *Polity* 9 (Summer 1976): 610–622.

Ranney, Austin. "The Representativeness of Primary Electorates." *Midwest Journal of Political Science* 12 (May 1968): 224–238.

————. "Turnout and Representation in Presidential Primary Elections." *American Political Science Review* 66 (March 1972): 21–37.

————, and Epstein, Leon D. "The Two Electorates: Voters and Non-Voters in a Wisconsin Primary." *Journal of Politics* 28 (August 1966): 598–616.

RePass, David E. "Issue Salience and Party Choice." *American Political Science Review* 65 (June 1971): 389–400.

Robinson, James A., and Standing, William H. "Some Correlates of Voter Participation: The Case of Indiana." *Journal of Politics* 22 (February 1960): 96–111.

Rose, Richard, and Mossawir, Harve. "Voting and Elections: A Functional Analysis." *Political Studies* 15 (1967): 173–179.

Rosenberg, Maurice. "The Qualities of Justices: Are They Strainable?" *Texas Law Review* 44 (June 1966): 1063–1080.

Stovall, Thomas F., Jr. "Judicial Babies and Constitutional Storks." *Texas Bar Journal* 26 (March 1963): 201–202, 255–258.

Sullivan, John L., and O'Connor, Robert E. "Electoral Choice and Popular Control of Public Policy: The Case of the 1966 House Elections." *American Political Science Review* 66 (December 1972): 1256–1268.

Thomas, Norman C. "Voting Machines and Voter Participation in Four Michigan Constitutional Revision Referenda." *Western Political Quarterly* 21 (September 1968): 409–419.

Vanderbilt, Arthur T. "Judges and Jurors: Their Functions, Qualifications, and Selection." *Boston University Law Review* 36, no. 1 (1956): 1–76.

Walker, Jack L. "Ballot Forms and Voter Fatigue: An Analysis of the Office Block and Party Column Ballots." *Midwest Journal of Political Science* 10 (November 1966): 448–463.

Walker, Thomas G. "A Note Concerning Partisan Influences on Trial Judge Decision-Making." *Law and Society Review* 6 (May 1972): 645–649.

Watson, Richard A. "Judging the Judges." *Judicature* 53 (February 1970): 283–290.

White, Robert A. "New Approach to Financing Judicial Campaigns." *American Bar Association Journal* 59 (December 1973): 1429–1430.

Willetts, Peter. "Cluster-Bloc Analysis and Statistical Inference." *American Political Science Review* 66 (June 1972): 569–582.

Wormuth, Francis D., and Rich, S. Grover, Jr. "Politics, the Bar, and the Selection of Judges." *Utah Law Review* 3 (Fall 1953): 459–466.

## Unpublished Works

Atkins, Burton, and McDonald, Michael. "Electoral Rule Changes and Voter Participation in Judicial Elections: A Longitudinal Analysis of the Florida Supreme Court." Paper delivered at the 1977 meeting of the Florida Political Science Association.

Bowen, Don R. "The Explanation of Judicial Voting Behavior from Sociological Characteristics of Judges." Ph.D. dissertation, Yale University, 1965.

Dubois, Philip L. "Judicial Elections in the States: Patterns and Consequences." Ph.D. dissertation, University of Wisconsin, 1978.

Feeley, Malcolm M. "A Comparative Analysis of State Supreme Court Behavior." Ph.D. dissertation, University of Minnesota, 1969.

Hannah, Susan Blackmore. "An Evaluation of Judicial Elections in Michigan, 1948–1968." Ph.D. dissertation, Michigan State University, 1972.

Prochera, John S. "Selection, Tenure, and Judicial Behavior: Institutional Characteristics and Partisan Voting in State Courts of Last Appeal." Paper delivered at the 1975 annual meeting of the Southern Political Science Association, Nashville.

RePass, David E. "Levels of Rationality among the American Electorate." Paper delivered at the 1974 annual meeting of the American Political Science Association, Chicago.

# Index